THE FEUDALISM DEBATE

The Feudalism Debate

Edited by

HARBANS MUKHIA

MANOHAR

2026

First published 1999
Reprinted 2026

ISBN 978-81-7304-284-3

Published by
Ajay Kumar Jain *for*
Manohar Publishers & Distributors
4753/23 Ansari Road, Daryaganj
New Delhi 110 002

Printed and bound in India

Contents

Acknowledgements 7

Contributors 8

Prologue: The Feudalism Debate and After
HARBANS MUKHIA 9

Modes of Production and Non-European Pre-Colonial Societies: The Nature and Significance of the Debate
T.J. BYRES 13

Was There Feudalism in Indian History?
HARBANS MUKHIA 34

How Feudal was Indian Feudalism?
R.S. SHARMA 82

The Uniqueness of the East
CHRIS WICKHAM 112

The Universalization of a Concept: 'feudalism' to 'Feudalism' in Chinese Marxist Historiography
ARIF DIRLIK 149

Classifying Pre-Colonial India
IRFAN HABIB 186

Politics, Peasants and the Deconstruction of Feudalism in Medieval India
BURTON STEIN 198

Peasant Production and Medieval Indian Society
HARBANS MUKHIA 237

The Feudalism Debate: The Turkish End—'Is Tax-*vs.*-Rent' Necessarily the Product and Sign of a Modal Difference?
HALIL BERKTAY 266

Pre-Capitalist Modes of Production in Non-European Societies
ASHOK RUDRA 318

Acknowledgements

Manohar Publishers wish to thank Frank Cass & Co. Ltd., London, for permission to reprint the special issue of *The Journal of Peasant Studies* on 'Feudalism and Non-European Societies', 1985 (also released as a book), and two subsequent articles and publish these in India as *The Feudalism Debate.*

The editor recalls with pleasure and gratitude the collaboration with T.J. Byres in editing the special issue.

Frank Perlin first suggested the idea of a volume on this comparative problematic and the editor considers it a privilege to acknowledge this debt.

HARBANS MUKHIA

Contributors

HALIL BERKTAY is Professor at Ataturk Arastirmalari Enstitusu, Bogazici Universitesi, Bebek, Istanbul, Turkey.

T.J. BYRES is Professor of Economics at the School of Oriental and African Studies, London University and Editor, *The Journal of Peasant Studies.*

ARIF DIRLIK is Professor of History at Duke University, U.S.A.

IRFAN HABIB was Professor of History, Aligarh Muslim University, Aligarh, India, now retired.

HARBANS MUKHIA is Professor of Medieval History, Jawaharlal Nehru University, New Delhi and Editor, *The Medieval History Journal.*

LATE ASHOK RUDRA was Professor of Economics at Viswa Bharati, Santiniketan, India.

R.S. SHARMA has retired as Professor of History at the University of Delhi.

LATE BURTON STEIN was last located at the School of Oriental and African Studies, London University.

CHRIS WICKHAM is Professor of History at the University of Birmingham and Editor, *Past and Present.*

Prologue
The Feudalism Debate and After

Harbans Mukhia

Sometime during the 1970s and 1980s discussion and debates were initiated on the problematic of feudalism in three widely distant regions, all falling within the English-speaking world, i.e. Britain, India and Australia. They culminated in the simultaneous appearance of three volumes. Two of these started off as debates in the pages of journals on individual essays published in them earlier; these later materialized as books, one being published both as a special issue of the journal as well as a book.

In 1976 *Past and Present* published the University of California, Los Angeles's Professor Robert Brenner's essay 'Agrarian Class Structure and Economic Development in Pre-Industrial Europe' which essentially re-iterated the superiority of the classical Marxian methodology of looking at history through the prism of class struggle for optimal explanatory results. This he did in the context of the different paths that England and France had followed into the modern world of capitalism, itself a classic Marxist problematic. The agreements and disagreements registered with this methodology, particularly in its application by Brenner, transcended the Marxist/anti-Marxist divide in the essays that came in response. In 1985 all ten essays were put together in a book with the somewhat queer title, *The Brenner Debate*, edited by T.H. Aston and C.H.E. Philpin; the book also carried a brief introduction by R.H. Hilton.

In 1981 Harbans Mukhia's article, 'Was There Feudalism in Indian History?', first read as Presidential Address to the Medieval History Section of the Indian History Congress at its fortieth session in 1979, was published in *The Journal of Peasant Studies*. The article, also written in a strongly assertive Marxist mould, sought to examine both the concept of feudalism and its historicity in the comparative context of medieval Western Europe and medieval India. Its focus, besides the conceptual concerns, was on looking at the ecology, technology and social forms of labour use in two of the regions where the term 'feudalism' is freely used.

It also implicitly sought to redefine class struggle not merely as observed in its overt violent manifestation, but also in its silent, quotidian form embedded in the daily toil in the very process of production in agriculture.

In 1985 the journal published a special double issue, which debated Mukhia's article, with six contributions, a reply by Mukhia and a long discussion of the nature and significance of the debate by T.J. Byres, the journal's editor and the special issue's co-editor along with Mukhia. Since the debate had traversed into several regions of the non-European world—China, Turkey, Iran and Arabia, besides India—it got the title 'Feudalism and Non-European Societies' which was also the title of the book published the same year by the journal's publishers, Frank Cass of London. The debate, however, spilled over the special issue into three other papers which subsequently appeared in that journal, the last in January 1993.

Also in 1985 an anthology of twelve essays, entitled *Feudalism: Comparative Studies*, edited by Edmund Leach, S.N. Mukherjee and John Ward covering several European and non-European regions, but not part of any debate, was published in Sydney.

The single date for the appearance of all three volumes is clearly a coincidence, but the issue of feudalism seems to have acquired significant enough dimensions around that time to have engendered discussion, and considerably heated debates at least in the two internationally respected journals. What could explain the surge of the problematic to the forefront?

Marxism still exercised hegemonic presence within the academia, especially in the discipline of history in large chunks of the English-speaking world during the decade between the mid-1970s and the mid-1980s. That it should therefore set the terms of debates in the discussion of feudalism, as of several other social science debates was, therefore, quite unsurprising. But why feudalism?

I believe the appearance of Karl Marx's *Grundrisse* in English translation in 1973 perhaps made a substantial difference. Until then, while Marx-Engels' works relating to capitalism had received detailed attention, their views on pre-capitalist society were gathered unsystematically in the form of scattered remarks. *Grundrisse*, however, filled that large gap of knowledge about the construction of pre-capitalist social and economic typology within the Marxist frame. Parts of *Grundrisse* had earlier appeared in Eric Hobsbawm's edited work, *Pre-Capitalist Economic Formations* in 1964; but the 1973 edition was the complete thing and it stimulated interest in the study of feudalism as a mode of production in different regions of the world within the Marxist discourse. It also began to give rise to some doubts about the feudalism typology, primarily the problem of reconciling the Marxist conceptual construction of capitalism as the first universal system and the notion of the universality of feudalism, which was anterior to capitalism. Indeed, as it came to be argued later, the concept of feudalism as a Marxist construct in particular came about only as its adversary, capitalism, had established its hegemony and had defined itself in terms of purely economic coercion of the primary producer, i.e. the worker. Non- or extra-economic coercion as the defining element of pre-capitalist forms of production could not possibly have been conceptualized before the notion of economic coercion had been articulated. In other words, feudalism, as a form of extra-economic coercion, arose only as an anti-thesis of capitalism; or, in still other words, feudalism cannot be defined in its own terms but only in terms laid down by its negation, i.e. capitalism.

This does put some strain on the attempt to construct a typology of feudalism, a typology moreover that is credited with universal validity. There is besides the problem of perception which any retroactive constitution of a typology tends to overlook. Can one, for example, seek to reconstruct a medieval observer's perception of what the observer did not even know was feudalism, for it came to be so characterized only with the advent of capitalism? And can one confidently state that medieval observers in all societies evolved a uniform view of their social and economic milieus which were long afterwards to be put under the single heading of feudalism?

In Indian historiography the notion of feudalism had entrenched itself firmly between 1956 and 1965, between the appearance of D.D. Kosambi's *An Introduction to the Study of Indian History* and R.S. Sharma's *Indian Feudalism*. Primarily, however, Indian feudalism was envisioned as the state's creation through land grants; it was not seen as a mode of production even when its protagonists were avowedly Marxist.

Harbans Mukhia's essay 'Was There Feudalism in Indian History?' sought to question the relevance of the concept of feudalism to India on theoretical as well as empirical grounds, even as it attempted to extend the field of the debate to questions that go beyond the administrative fiat which had hitherto constituted the agency of the formation of feudal society in India; in lieu of feudalism, the notion of a free peasant economy was formulated, which distinguished medieval Indian from medieval West European economy and society. The questioning of some of the received wisdom understandably led to both fierce defence on its behalf as well as further questions in what often came to be referred to as 'The Feudalism

Debate'. It was this extensive questioning of all firmly held views, including Mukhia's, that turned the debate into a most satisfying experience, for it emphasized exploration rather than agreement.

Unfortunately, Frank Perlin's contribution to the debate has had to be dropped because of extreme linguistic complexity and inordinate length; however, references to his article by other contributors have been retained. Two of the other three articles published after the appearance of *Feudalism and Non-European Societies* have been included here. References to articles in *The Journal of Peasant Studies* have been replaced by page numbers in this volume thus: (Dirlik, 151) or, Sharma (87).

Modes of Production and Non-European Pre-Colonial Societies: The Nature and Significance of the Debate

T.J. Byres

MARX AND NON-CAPITALIST SOCIETIES

Marx's great *quaesitum* was 'to reveal the economic law of motion of modern society' (Marx, 1976: 92)—the law of motion of capitalism. This, his life's work, he achieved with immense power. Modern Marxists may dispute the nature of latter-day capitalism—or, indeed, that of capitalism in its earlier phases—and may question certain of Marx's formulations. But they do so in relation to a formidable body of work, which stands on deep and solid foundations.

Marx's basic quest led him to explore the logic of pre-capitalist societies, as part of his concern with the transition to capitalism. This exploration provides a thread which runs through his writing, from the earliest texts to those of his later years. It may be seen, for example, in *The Economic and Philosophical Manuscripts, The German Ideology, The Communist Manifesto, A Contribution to the Critique of Political Economy* (in the celebrated Preface), the journalism of the early 1850s, the *Grundrisse, Capital, Theories of Surplus Value,* and throughout his voluminous correspondence. These parts of Marx's writings, frequently no more than *obiter dicta* and sometimes (as in the *Grundrisse*) obscure, are often brilliantly original and illuminating. They are, however, tantalizingly brief, fragmented and incomplete. They derived, indeed, from 'a seriously defective knowledge of the Oriental world (though based on the best sources available in his day)' (Ste. Croix, 1981: 155).[1] Marx, towards the end of his life, was also led to speculate on post-capitalist societies, that is, on socialism [as in the *Critique of the Gotha Programme*]; and even on the possibility of achieving socialism without an intervening epoch of capitalism—with respect to Russia, in his correspondence with Vera Zasulich [an issue exhaustively treated in Shanin (ed.) (1983)]. Here, too, and to an even greater extent, the writing is insubstantial and speculative, though again rich in insight.

Marx's writing on both pre-capitalist societies and socialism has been much examined and invoked in relation to contemporary Third World countries and the complex problems which their analysis confronts. It is the former which concerns us here. One of the great issues facing Marxist historians is the categorizing or placing of pre-colonial, non-European societies (or social formations). That is an intellectual problem of immense significance, with respect to the past, in its own right. It also, however, bears crucially upon our understanding of the present. That understanding—of the character of contemporary social formations, of the nature of the dominant mode of production and of any transitions which may be under way—can only be woefully defective in the absence of an adequate treatment of the past.

Central questions here, as yet unresolved, are whether all the modes of production identified by Marx—most clearly and succinctly in the Preface—need necessarily be accepted, on a basis of our present knowledge; whether those which have been part of the European historical experience should be expected to be replicated, either in close similarity or in deviant form, in non-European societies; whether the modes of production defined by Marx exhaust the relevant possibilities. Perhaps most prominent in relation to the first question is the acceptability of the notion of an Asiatic mode of production. The second question is the essential one addressed in this volume, with respect to the applicability of feudalism in the context of pre-colonial, non-European societies. The third question possibly becomes, if not the Asiatic mode and if not feudalism, then, within a Marxist analysis, what? This last question is one which has hardly begun to be posed. Yet, if some of the arguments which follow are valid, it may well have to figure prominently on the Marxist agenda. It is, perhaps, a weakness of Harbans Mukhia, whose paper gave rise to the present collection, that he does not address it at all. To that we will return.

THE PRESENT DEBATE

The articles in this volume by Dirlik, Habib, Sharma, Stein and Wickham represent a direct response to an article by Mukhia published in an earlier issue of the *Journal of Peasant Studies* (Mukhia, 1981). That article was entitled 'Was There Feudalism in Indian History?'. Taking West European feudalism, as revealed by the work of relevant economic and social historians and seen in Marxist terms, as the model for reference, Mukhia subjects pre-colonial India to searching scrutiny. He concludes that one cannot categorise pre-colonial India as feudal. He does so on the grounds, essentially, that while medieval Europe had as its *differentia specifica* the structured dependence of the whole peasantry upon the lords, pre-colonial Indian society was characterized by self-dependent or free peasant production. The various responses to his article, whether or not they agree with his judgement, are critical in one way or another of the way he poses the problem and the manner of his treatment. His notion of feudalism, his reading of the West European evidence, his rendering of Indian history, and, especially, his positing of free peasant production in India, all come under attack. The responses also range beyond the confines of India, among non-European societies. In his second article in the volume Mukhia responds to that body of criticism. A debate has been joined. That it is an important debate, in the problem it addresses, seems obvious. It is a debate which is likely to continue. It is a debate, moreover, which promises to be lively, controversial, and fruitful.

All of the aforementioned writers are professional historians. They are also either Marxists or sympathetic to the Marxist approach and the questions it raises, and concerned to consider most seriously the application of Marxist historical analysis. The issue considered is essentially one that lies within the Marxist discourse (though, of course, it has great relevance for non-Marxists, too, just as Marxist historians must take due cognizance of non-Marxist historical scholarship). It is, basically: how does one categorize, in Marxist terms, pre-colonial, non-European societies? It is a *general* question of fundamental importance. Mukhia's original article, as we have seen, related to India, and denied that Indian society could be seen as a variant of feudalism. Habib, Sharma and Stein confine themselves to India: the first two being concerned mainly with northern India, while Stein performs a most valuable service by bringing south India to the centre of the historical stage. Habib and Stein, from very different viewpoints, would deny the feudalism categorization for India: the former in explicitly Marxist terms, the latter from a less obviously Marxist position. Sharma, who has been the major exponent of the feudalism thesis for India, contrariwise, enters a spirited and eloquent defence of the feudalism notion, in orthodox Marxist terms.

India, of course, is a non-European country of exceptional importance. But the argument extends far beyond India, to *all* non-European countries. Dirlik, indeed, relates it specifically to China, another non-European country of exceptional significance: providing us with a critical account of the views of Chinese Marxist historians on the question. Wickham, from a background as a Europeanist, examines specific periods of the histories of China, Iran and Turkey, in this respect. Other parts of Asia, manifestly, deserve detailed treatment, and so, too, do Africa and Latin America. We have not managed to supply that in this collection. But, of course, a growing body of historical writing exists to make it possible. It is hoped that we may be able to consider it in contributions to future issues of the *Journal of Peasant Studies*. Of non-European countries, Japan has, perhaps, attracted most attention in these terms and appears to command the greatest agreement. There is a near consensus, among Marxists and non-Marxists alike, that Japan, from the fourteenth and fifteenth centuries until the demise of the Tokugawa state in 1867 and its replacement by the unitary Meiji state, represented an archetypal example of a developed feudalism, with strong resemblance to European feudalism (see, for example, Anderson (1974b: 411-28, passim, and 435-61) for a judicious account of the evidence; and see Marx (1976: 878), Bloch (1965, I: 211, 213, 228; II: 382, 446-7, 452), Boutrouche (1959: 281-91), and Jouen des Longrais (1958)). Even Japan, however, is not uncontroversial in this respect [as Mukhia pointed out in his original article (n. 5)—see, for example, Moulder (1977)].

It is not my purpose to summarize here the arguments of the various contributors; nor to pass critical judgement on them. Readers can do that for themselves. Harbans Mukhia has given a provisional response to his critics, and readers will make their own decision as to its adequacy. The debate, moreover, will not stop in these pages. It will surely continue, both on the theoretical terrain and in terms of the concrete analysis of individual non-European societies of the pre-colonial era. What I shall do, rather, at the risk of being banal, is to remind the reader of the relevant Marxist categories in such a debate; to highlight some of the major issues at stake (which may, indeed, be connected with one's reading of what these categories are); and to suggest why the debate is of considerable significance, both in relation to our understanding of the *past* and with respect to our treatment of the *present* (why past and present commingle in such a way that the present cannot be comprehended without serious reference to the past).

THE RELEVANT MARXIST CATEGORIES AND SOME BASIC ISSUES

Let us recall, firstly, that when we consider the relevance or irrelevance of the category feudalism, we are examining the nature of the *dominant mode of production* in a particular society, or, to use the Marxist notion, in a particular *social formation*. I would insist upon the central importance of the mode of production concept, despite, for example, Cohen's recent attempt (in an excellent book) to persuade us to discard it in favour of his preferred usage, *economic structure* (Cohen, 1978: 79-84). Marx himself consistently used this category. While it is true that he used it, in his voluminous writings, with quite different, although related meanings (Banaji, 1977: 4-5; Cohen, 1978: 79-84), his particular meaning is always obvious from the context. Moreover, in the epochal and general sense in which it is employed here, and in which Marx used it at various key junctures (as, for example, in the Preface to *A Contribution to the Critique of Political Economy*), it is perfectly clear. It is established practice among Marxist historians to use the notion, and, given its clarity and its analytical power, there is no good reason to abandon it. Among our contributors, Perlin seems dissatisfied with it, although not quite ready to throw it overboard; and Stein does not work with it very obviously. For the others it remains central.

We now turn to the relevant definitions of the categories in question. That done, we may proceed to indicate the general importance of pursuing a mode of production analysis.

By mode of production we mean, following Hindess and Hirst in their *Pre-Capitalist Modes of Production* (and to accept their definition—or, more accurately, this part of it—is neither to condone the view of history expressed in that book, a view which, in essence, is absurd, nor to follow its authors' tergiversations in subsequent works), 'an articulated combination of relations and forces of production' (1975: 9). It is essential to note that no treatment within a general mode of production analysis, such as the theme of this volume demands, can be deemed adequate without careful treatment of *both* relations and forces of production. That, certainly, was Marx's own practice. To the question of whether one or other might be regarded as 'dominant' in the ensemble I will come presently. Here I am making the more limited point that, quite independently of the question of dominance, there is no warrant for privileging one or other. It is a weakness of some of the contributions to this volume that they do not meet this requirement. Stein, for example, has little to say about the forces of production.

Moreover, the proposition that these two primary elements in a mode of production must be seen to be articulated is important. That is to say, an analysis which consists of no more than a 'sample juxtaposition of a set of relations and a set of forces' (Hindess and Hirst, 1975: 11) must be seen as seriously defective. There must be demonstrated and determinate *correspondence* (to use a notion which appears in the Preface to *A Contribution to the Critique of Political Economy*[2]) between the two. Here we must tread carefully, if we are to avoid misunderstanding. We do not propose a reading of 'articulated combination' which implies rigidity, mechanical correspondence, or an absence of that rich diversity which is to be found in different instances of the same mode of production. To argue that forces and relations of production constitute an articulated combination is not to insist, as Hindess and Hirst do, that in a particular mode of production coherence requires that a *single* set of productive forces articulates with a *single* set of relations of production (a point to which one of our contributors, Wickham, draws our attention). That, indeed, is an unacceptably restrictive interpretation, which actual historical analysis—the concrete analysis of different concrete situations—simply could not sustain.[3] What I do suggest as essential, however, to an adequate treatment of the issues at stake in the present discussion is clear and careful specifying of the precise relationship between forces and relations of production. From such a specifying, the underlying logic of the articulation—of the relevant correspondence—should emerge. It is this which helps define the mode of production's 'law of motion'. If it does not emerge, then the analysis must be deemed incomplete, and the questions addressed by our contributors incapable of satisfactory answer. My own view is that while Mukhia touches upon the manner of articulation, and while others of the contributors (Habib, Sharma, Wickham) approach it, the debate suffers, as yet, from its incomplete examination. It remains shadowy, impressionistic and problematic.

Those familiar with Hindess and Hirst will have noted that from the above definition of mode of production I have omitted the critical element that it is an 'articulated combination' which is 'structured by the dominance of the relations of production'. It is not at all clear precisely what meaning one is to ascribe to such a proposition. What does seem necessary, however, is to leave open whether it is relations of production or forces of production that are dominant within a mode of production. It is not obvious that one can, within a Marxist treatment, make categorical statements of a general kind on this matter. There seems to be no binding reason, in theory, why one should posit relations of production or forces of production as dominant. Marx himself can be shown to have argued for *each*.[4] Among the most cogent of recent Marxist writing, we find powerful statements of either position: with Brenner, for example, arguing for the primacy of relations of production [in the context of European feudalism (Brenner, 1976)]; and Cohen arguing a detailed case for the forces of production (Cohen, 1978). We should, I think, leave the issue open in a general sense. That does not, however, preclude a position being established in a particular instance. Indeed, it is essential that it be investigated in as many instances as possible. Certainly, here is an issue to which all of our contributors should be sensitive. It is not at all clear that they are.

We proceed to articulation and dominance in another crucial sense, in the present context. Above, I have posited that our concern is with the nature of the dominant mode of production in a particular social formation. That we should recognize the existence of more than one mode of production is most important. To proceed in terms of a single mode of production can only be unrewarding and stultifying. We need the notion of a *social formation*. A social formation, we may say, following Anderson, is a 'concrete combination of different modes of production, organized under the *dominance* of one of them (Anderson, 1974a: 22). Anderson reminds us that 'the purport of the concept of social formation is precisely to underline the plurality and heterogeneity of possible modes of production within any given historical and social totality' (1974a: 22). It is a timely reminder, which may find greater response in future contributions to the present debate. Among the writers here assembled, Perlin, for example, wishes to abandon the social formation concept altogether, although he would not, one supposes, quarrel with the need to capture 'plurality and heterogeneity'. How one might do that, within a Marxist framework, without recourse to the notion of a social formation is not obvious. Wickham, by contrast, makes overt use of the social formation idea, and shows that it can give rise to fruitful hypotheses. Stein, with his 'three sets of peasant ecotypes', seems to be acknowledging the need for a social formation analysis, and, indeed, he does actually use the term, 'social formation' (or, alternatively, 'socio-economic formation'). But his usage seems to me to depart somewhat from a recognizably Marxist position. Habib and Sharma both make explicit use of the social formation formulation, and then proceed, essentially, to the delineation of the *dominant* mode of production, in India: for Sharma, feudalism; and for Habib a mode of production which he identifies as the 'medieval Indian system' ('for such is the name I would give it until a better one is offered'). It is worth noting that explicit use of the social formation idea has the considerable merit of alerting one to, or of allowing one to encompass in one's analysis, that most important aspect of concrete historical situations: substantive, regional diversity. To proceed in terms of a single mode of production is to increase the risk of being blind to such diversity. Diversity exists in both large and small geographical areas. It may assume particular significance, however, where, as with, say, India and China, the geographical spread is vast. Among our contributors, Dirlik and Stein, especially, stress the need to recognize regional diversity.

Let us note, with respect to analysis in terms of a social formation, that the concept's structuring ideas of 'articulation' and 'dominance' are by no means unproblematic. Precisely what 'articulation' might entail, either in strict theoretical terms or in the treatment of concrete situations, is not immediately self-evident. Those who have operated with the idea—as, most prominently, in the case of the so-called theory of articulation of modes of production—have failed, for the most part, to rise above simple assertion: the assertion that articulation is of central significance. As Wolpe has pointed out, in this writing no more than 'the first steps have been taken towards the formulation of a more rigorous concept of articulation' (Wolpe, 1980; 42) (Wolpe in an heroic attempt to survey the relevant literature, and identify the major lacunae). Similarly, the criteria whereby one might identify dominance remain unspecified. Marx himself uses the idea [in, for example, the *Grundrisse* (Marx, 1973: 106-7) and in *Theories of Surplus Value* (Marx, 1971a: 419-21)], in passages which are suggestive but incompletely developed.[5] A modern Marxist historian of distinction, Anderson (whose definition of social formation I have quoted above), *asserts* dominance: as with the slave mode of production in classical Greece, 'which governed the complex articulation of each local economy and gave its imprint to the whole civilization of the city-state' (Anderson, 1974a: 22). The idea is an attractive one, with considerable intuitive appeal. It remains a metaphor, however, with all of the attendant dangers of reductionism, or of resort to residuary hypothesis. 'Dominance' needs to be demonstrated rather than merely asserted. Moreover, it cries out for rigorous statement in formal terms. And so one could go on. But the recognition of difficulty here suggests not that we need throw up our hands in despair and reach for other categories (which is what Perlin appears to be doing); it indicates, rather, that we have been alerted to the complexity of our task and to the need for further elaboration of the Marxian categories.

THE SIGNIFICANCE OF CORRECTLY IDENTIFYING THE NATURE OF THE DOMINANT MODE OF PRODUCTION

We may now proceed to a statement of the sense in which the capturing of the nature of the dominant mode of production is important. We may start with an observation by Dobb, the initiator of the most distinguished of Marxist debates, that on the transition from feudalism to capitalism (Dobb, 1963; Hilton (ed.), 1976). Dobb noted:

> . . . save for comparatively brief intervals of transition, each historical period is moulded under the preponderating influence of a single, more or less homogenous economic form, and is to be characterized according to the predominant type of socio-economic relationship. . . . Our chief interest will not lie in the first appearance of some new economic form. Nor will the mere appearance of it justify a description of the succeeding period by a new name. Of much greater significance will be the stage when the new form has grown to proportions which enable it to place its imprint on the whole society and to exert a major influence in moulding the trend of development. (Dobb, 1963: 11)

From this most cogent statement certain important issues may be identified.

Contained in Dobb's statement, obviously, are the social formation idea and its crucial component, dominance. I have already noted the difficulties associated with giving rigorous, operational meaning to the notion of dominance. That I will not pursue. What I stress here is that locating the dominant mode of production in any social formation is crucially important precisely because that mode of production does 'place its imprint on the whole of society' and does 'mould the trend of development'. We cannot grasp the structure and dynamic of a particular society, unless we understand the nature of its dominant mode of production and identify that mode of production's 'law of motion'. Marx makes the point in a passage in the *Grundrisse*, which is worth citing at length. Marx starts with a general statement of why the dominant mode of production is so critical:

> In all forms of society there is one specific kind of production which predominates over the rest, whose relations thus assign rank and influence to the others. It is a general illumination which bathes all the other colours and modifies their particularity. It is a particular ether which determines the specific gravity of every being which has materialized within it. (1973: 106-7)

Marx proceeds to illustrate this argument with specific instances, which are, assuredly, germane to the present debate:

> For example, with pastoral peoples (mere hunting and fishing peoples lie outside the point where real development begins). Certain forms of tillage occur among them, sporadic ones. Landed property is determined by this. It is held in common, and retains this form to a greater or lesser degree according to the greater or lesser degree of attachment displayed by these peoples to their tradition, e.g. the communal property of the Slavs. Among peoples with a settled agriculture—this settling already a great step—where this predominates, as in antiquity and in the feudal order, even industry, together with its organization and the forms of

property corresponding to it, has a more or less landed-proprietary character; is either completely dependent on it, as among the earlier Romans, or, as in the Middle Ages, imitates, within the city and its relations, the organization of the land. In the Middle Ages, capital itself—apart from pure money-capital—in the form of the traditional artisan's tools etc., has this landed-proprietary character. In bourgeois society it is the opposite. Agriculture more and more becomes merely a branch of industry, and is entirely dominated by capital. Ground rent likewise. In all forms where landed property rules, the natural relation still predominant. In those where capital rules, the social, historically created element. Ground rent cannot be understood without capital. But capital can certainly be understood without ground rent. Capital is the all dominating economic power of bourgeois society. It must form the starting-point as well as the finishing-point, and must be dealt with before landed property. After both have been examined in particular, their interrelation must be examined. (1973: 107)

Here, then, we have a helpful statement of the sense in which, within an analysis rooted in historical materialism, the dominant mode of production exercises its influence. It is in this logic that the present debate finds its *raison d'être*. It is of quite fundamental importance whether pre-colonial, non-European societies can be shown to be dominated by a variant of feudalism, by an Asiatic mode of production, or by some other mode of production. The essential premise of the debate that follows is that this remains an open question. The modes of production identified by Marx do not necessarily exhaust the relevant possibilities.

Our contributors are all sensitive to the importance of a mode of production analysis. It is not, of course, necessary that they all enter a defence of such an approach. That would, indeed, be tedious. Among them, however, Wickham and Dirlik do, and it is most interesting to see such a defence from practising historians. Dirlik also provides, in his treatment of Chinese Marxist historiography, a striking illustration of the great political significance that a concern for correctly identifying the dominant mode of production in a specific social formation has had, for more than half a century, in China. Readers can peruse this for themselves. But I would note aspects of what each of these historians has to say.

Wickham reminds us of what, after all, lies behind such analysis. We attempt to categorize world history in Marxist terms, let us remember, not for the gratuitous acquisition of knowledge, and not, one hopes, in blind obedience to 'the devotional element in such categorisations', but, as Marx himself did, because 'we understand the world better by so doing, so that we can change it'. That, surely, is the bedrock upon which our analysis must rest. In other words, we start from our desire to change the present or the future (we cannot, after all, change the past: we can only reinterpret it), a desire which, if it is to be pursued realistically, requires an understanding of the past. Past and present interpenetrate and commingle. That is an axiom of Marxist history. It gives *contemporary* meaning to the present debate.

Dirlik, for his part, is at pains to defend the mode of production approach, but only if it is pursued in a manner appropriate to genuine historical analysis. The Marxist historian's central, working concept, mode of production, is, indeed, pivotal, inasmuch as it 'is, ultimately, a mode of producing that not only transforms the world, but embodies in its process all the material and spiritual constituents of its social context'. If this is so, its investigation cannot but be of fundamental importance. But our notions of mode of production, social formation (and class) must not derive from that 'scientistic idealism' which is a feature of certain forms of modern Marxism, and which 'feeds upon itself by creating ever novel abstractions': abstractions which 'are so far removed from concrete existence that they serve no purpose either in understanding the world or in changing it'. It is a salutary warning, which we do well to bear in mind. Theory, and its concomitant, abstraction are of course essential—as Dirlik insists—but not as ends in themselves. One is reminded, here, of Lenin's frequent warnings against 'over-abstract formulation', 'empty abstraction' and 'abstract generalities',[6] which, in an evocative formulation, he contrasted with 'what is most important, that which constitutes the very gist, the living soul of Marxism—a concrete analysis of a concrete situation'.[7] In the present debate, what is obviously called for is, again to quote Lenin, 'concrete analysis of precise and definite historical situations'.[8] It is this which, in the end, will establish the nature of the dominant mode of production in pre-colonial non-European societies.

Dirlik draws to our attention how, in a very real and immediate sense, the question of the dominant mode of production has proved a most critical issue: in the context of both pre-1949 and post-Liberation China. Chinese Marxist historiography, in both periods, has been informed by the principle that 'how one stage (of history) is conceived must shape how the remainder of history is conceived'. That conceptualization allows us to understand the present and its contradictions, and to delimit the future and its possibilities. In both the pre- and post-Liberation periods, the issue of categorization has been 'not an abstract intellectual question' but one with profound political implications. In the former era, it related to the nature of the revolutionary strategy best suited to the liberation of China. That, it was held, could only be determined in relation to the nature of pre-capitalist society. The diagnosing of whether China was or had been bourgeois, feudal, or Asiatic was held to be of fundamental importance for a revolutionary strategy. Only with an accurate diagnosis could the prospects for revolution and the correct way of achieving it, within the matrix of world capitalism, be assessed. Then, after 1949, within the context of the attempt to build socialism, it has been held that the nature of society at the moment of revolution determines the nature of any socialism that may be achieved. Socialism is unlikely to assume to same form in all places. The development strategy necessary to achieve socialism must be informed by an accurate knowledge of the dominant tendencies in pre-socialist society. Clearly, if this is so, the nature of the dominant mode of production at the moment of revolution is crucial. That, it is further held, can only be grasped via an understanding of its antecedents.

If the Chinese view is correct, then, manifestly, the present debate has important implications for contemporary Third World countries: including in that category both those countries in which a capitalist path is being attempted and those in which socialism, in the sense which attaches to post-1949 China, is the goal. For the former group of countries—even in those where one might argue that capitalism has become the dominant mode of production—the precise nature of the major contradictions (that is, of the kind of capitalism likely to be secured), and, therefore, of the appropriate revolutionary strategy, might be held to derive from the identity of previous dominant modes and the manner of their demise. For the latter, the quality of socialism that might be attempted will be similarly influenced.

I would stress that one must here distinguish most sharply the *principles* which underlie the Chinese position and the *manner* in which the Chinese have sought to apply them. One might accept the former (as I would) and reject the latter. Dirlik, certainly, provides a strong case for having serious reservations with respect to Chinese practice in this regard. The tenacity with which the feudalism position has been argued by Chinese Marxist historians may, perhaps, owe more to a dogmatism born of prior political necessity than it does to due recognition of 'concrete analysis of precise and definite historical situations'. What emerges is the need for adequate awareness of the dangers which may lie in the pursuit of valid principles.

Before turning to the final set of concerns to which I shall draw attention, I would comment on the relevance of the present debate to the contemporary political economy of the country whose distant past was the subject of the initial salvo by Mukhia: India. The most sophisticated, extensively argued and passionate debate among Indian Marxists in the past two decades has related to the nature of the mode of production in contemporary Indian agriculture. The contributions to that debate are now numerous, and the debate continues. I cannot possibly do justice here to the debate in general or to any of its individual contributions [for a most useful, recent, summary of the debate see Thorner (1982)]. What does emerge from it is its need for secure historical mooring. Such mooring is attempted by some of the contributors, but nowhere back beyond the colonial era. The absence of a strong corpus of Marxist historical work on colonial India raises serious difficulties. The result, with reference to the mode of production in agriculture debate, has been, quite often, a kind of do-it-yourself history, and sometimes, even, what can only be described as historical fiction (written with little awareness of the historical work that has been done). A view of contemporary India which portrays it as dominated by semi-feudalism [see, for example, Bhaduri (1973), Prasad (1973; 1974)] cries out for firm historical location, in both the colonial and the pre-colonial eras. Yet it is almost completely innocent of such location, and in its absence must be deemed to be defective. The location, if it is to be satisfactory, must surely start in pre-colonial India. Even those formulations which are explicitly historical in their orientation, such as Banaji's notion of a colonial mode of production (argued impressively in Banaji, 1972)—a notion later taken up by Alavi [see, for example, Alavi (1975; 1981)]—are hardly adequate in their rendering of colonial history. They are totally inadequate in their pre-colonial mooring. The relevance, for present-day India, of the debate set in motion by Mukhia cannot, I think, be gainsaid.

ALTERNATIVE MODES OF PRODUCTION?

We may now address the issue touched upon at the end of the first section of this article. This relates to the possible need to identify, explicitly and rigorously, modes of production other than those discussed by Marx. Do we need such alternative modes of production, in order to encompass the structural characteristics—the particular articulated combinations of forces and relations of production—of pre-colonial non-European societies? I cannot offer a firm answer to that question. All that I can hope to do is to draw attention to some of the relevant considerations raised by the debate that takes place in the following pages.

If we start with out initial concern, feudalism, and *if* we reject it as an accurate categorization—or even if, less surely, we have serious doubts about it—then what? Marx himself, of course, did reject it for countries such as India and China (although not for Japan), and having done so favoured the notion of an Asiatic mode of production. Here we have a possible alternative contender to feudalism as the relevant mode of production dominant in pre-colonial, non-European social formations. With the exception of Stein, our contributors are of one voice in dismissing it as a realistic possibility—dismissing it, more or less, with contempt: and Stein's version is so far removed from anything that Marx said, and so manifestly not a serious attempt to define a mode of production in a Marxist sense (stressing, merely, the 'importance' of irrigation in south India), as hardly to constitute a serious effort at rehabilitation. Others, too, have dismissed the Asiatic mode, on a variety of grounds: ranging from its theoretical incoherence to its inaccuracy in representing the observed empirical characteristics of the societies in question [see, for example, Thorner (1966, reprinted in Thorner, 1980), Anderson (1974b: 462-549), Hindess and Hirst (1975: 178-220)]. But it is by no means the case that the concept has been totally abandoned in current Marxist discourse [a recent collection of arguments in its favour may be seen in Bailey and Llobera (eds.) (1981)]. It has, for example, been suggested as appropriate as a categorization of the Ottoman Empire [see Islamoglu and Keyder (1981); Keyder (1976)]. It has also attracted the attention of certain Marxist anthropologists: for example, Godelier [see his piece in Bailey and Llobera (eds.) (1981)]. One should, perhaps, leave it as a possibility, which may cover some non-European social formations: a possibility, pending further investigations.

Let us suppose, however, that serious doubt, at least, has been cast upon both feudalism and the Asiatic mode as adequate categorizations of the dominant mode of production in non-European social formations (and, as far as the Asiatic mode is concerned, we must, of course, pay serious attention when a group of historians such as those represented in this volume, with mastery of modern knowledge of the societies in question, find no support for it). If not feudalism, or the Asiatic mode, then what? It is a frontier to which some of our contributors lead us inexorably, and of which all are aware. Yet it is a frontier which none of them passes beyond satisfactorily. Ahead is a *terra incognita* which, surely, those who reject both feudalism and the Asiatic mode, and who wish to retain a Marxist political economy view, must enter more boldly. We may briefly illustrate the nature of the impasse.

Mukhia, in his original article, after a swingeing attack upon the possibility of considering pre-colonial India to have been a variant of feudalism, concludes:

To argue against the notion of an Indian feudalism need not lead one to the acceptance of the Asiatic mode of production. Indeed, the concept of the Asiatic

> mode of production is based on the absence of private property in land, which is far from the generally accepted view among Indian historians today. It is evident that a wide range of social formations have existed in the world prior to their subjection to the universality of capitalism, and this range cannot be exhausted with the concepts of feudalism and the Asiatic mode of production. (Mukhia, 58-9)

What lies beyond the frontier remains a mystery. Dirlik is hardly more helpful. He responds to the predominant Chinese assertion of a feudal past, which he sees as unacceptable, with the suggestion: 'The multiplication of available modes of production (other than feudalism, the Asiatic mode, and capitalism) in order to account for the complexity of historical development would seem to be a possible answer to this problem.' That may be so. But he does not himself proceed in that direction.

It would be quite unjustified to carry this criticism of Mukhia and Dirlik too far. They cannot be held to have been remiss in failing to do—in what was, inevitably, short compass—that which lies beyond their chosen task: a task admirably pursued in each case. But it does need to be stressed that the next crucial step remains to be taken.

Two of our contributors do proceed into the unknown terrain: Habib and Wickham. Habib does so hesitantly (as the quotation from him given above suggests), with his notion of 'a medieval Indian system'. That is surely little more than a negative, descriptive category: it serves to draw attention to the unacceptability of either feudalism or the Asiatic mode, but without capturing the dynamic of a whole complex epoch (whose features Habib has explored brilliantly and seminally in his previous written work—references to which may be found in the article by Habib in this volume). Wickham suggests that this is a variant of 'nothing more than claims in traditional historical fashion for the historical uniqueness of specific areas'. That is an excessively harsh judgement on a historian who has contributed massively to the Marxist analysis of pre-colonial India, and more than any other to our understanding of Mughal India. It remains true, nevertheless, that Habib does hesitate too much, when boldness is called for.

Wickham himself argues the existence of social formations in pre-colonial Asia that can best be understood in terms of the articulation of a 'tributary' mode (the inverted commas are his own—indicating, perhaps, some unease?) and a feudal mode. But what is this 'tributary mode of production'? It is a notion borrowed from Samir Amin (Amin, 1976). Wickham uses it to distinguish a mode of production in which exploitation of the peasantry is achieved by tax-raising (the defining characteristic of the tributary mode), from one in which exploitation of the peasantry proceeds via coercive rent-taking (which, for him, defines feudalism). Despite Wickham's assertions to the contrary, and despite his robust dismissal of the Asiatic mode, this tributary mode bears more than a passing resemblance to that much-maligned notion. He says: 'the Asiatic mode *as it has always been formulated* cannot be regarded as having any analytical validity' (emphasis mine). What he seems to have done (following Amin) is to re-formulate it—without village autarky and communality, and with classes—and present it in a watered-down version. Are we not witnessing the Asiatic mode being sneaked in through the back door? If not an example of 'defeatism' (which is his charge against Habib—and others such as Mukhia and Perry Anderson), it may represent his own inability to escape from that 'straitjacket' into which others (he says—those who have persisted, dogmatically, with feudalism and the Asiatic mode) have forced Asian history. Even so, we should not be prevented from giving close attention to the reasoned case that Wickham makes for the articulation of his tributary mode and feudalism: in varying relationships of dominance/subordination, but with the former retaining dominance in such a way as to frustrate the emergence of a hegemonic feudalism.

We may say, then, borrowing a distinction made by Marx in relation to the impact of colonialism [in his article, 'The Future Results of the British Rule in India' (Marx and Engels, 1975, 12: 217-18)], that while some of our contributors, according to their own lights, may have fulfilled a 'destructive' mission, in calling into doubt the relevance of feudalism or the Asiatic mode, their 'regenerative' mission awaits fulfilment. But need we be so insistent upon this analytical obligation? Need one seek a rigorous statement of alternative modes of production? It is, I think, an important question. It is an appropriate one upon which to conclude this essay and hand the reader over to the true participants in the debate.

We do have the example of one distinguished Marxist historian—Maxime Rodinson, in what he had to say of medieval Islam—who steadfastly refuses to classify [having rejected for the Muslim world the feudalism or Asiatic mode categorization (Rodinson, 1977: 58-68)]. Rodinson insists, of 'pre-capitalist' or 'primitive modes of production' generally (and not only with respect to the Muslim world), that: 'If one were to try to classify the modes of production thus observed, the result would be an infinite variety' (1977: 74). His chosen solution is as follows:

> If labels are needed, I would suggest the following terms: 'modes of production in which there is exploitation', adding as appropriate, the adjective 'communal' or 'individual'. The corresponding economic systems could be called in general 'pre-capitalist systems of exploitation', and categories could be distinguished among

them, if need be, by means of expressions such as: predominantly communal (or individual), predominantly agrarian (or pastoral), etc. (1977: 66)

Is this an acceptable solution?

Rodinson's solution is not, I think, satisfactory. His treatment of *diversity* in the medieval Muslim world (for example, see pp. 66-7) is, to be sure, salutary and enlightening. Similar, and even greater diversity, quite certainly, could be shown in, say, India or China or the Ottoman Empire, and needs to be explored with care and integrated into any serious Marxist analysis (as I have already suggested). But to postulate an *infinite* variety of modes of production—which, somehow, precludes the need for rigorous statement—is to use the concept in a casual way. It is a way, let us stress, quite at variance with Marx's own practice: the practice noted earlier, which sought to identify modes of production in the epochal sense (the sense in which they are discussed by Dobb and by Marx in the *Grundrisse*—both as already cited—and by Marx in the Preface). Rodinson insists at one point: 'I would not hesitate to abandon Marx's views if they seemed ill-founded' (1977: 60). That is a desirable working principle. But here, I would submit, Marx's practice is not ill-founded. To contemplate an infinite variety of modes of production—for, let us say, India or China, or indeed the mediaval Muslim world—is to empty the concept of mode of production of its analytical content. Social formations of the kind we are discussing are likely to be *dominated* (difficulties in giving concrete shape to that notion notwithstanding) by a *single* mode of production over long stretches of time. They are likely to be of 'long duration'.[9] It is these single modes of production, of epochal significance, which are not exhausted by Marx's listing, if the arguments of such as Mukhia, Habib and Dirlik (in their different ways) are valid. It is at that level that alternative modes of production must be sought; and at that level they can only be finite and relatively few in number. At that level, moreover, they assuredly require rigorous and full statement, theoretical coherence, and an exploration of their essential 'laws of motion'. It is a formidable task. It is, however, an analytical obligation which those who reject the applicability of feudalism or the Asiatic mode of non-European societies cannot escape. They may, of course, be wrong in their rejection.

NOTES

1. A selection may be seen in Marx and Engels (1979). See also Marx (1964).
2. Thus: 'In the social production of their life, men enter into definite, necessary relations which are independent of their will, relations of production which

correspond to a definite stage of development of their material productive forces' (Marx and Engels, 1971: 5, emphasis mine). That translation was by Brian Trench. In the Dobb edition of the *Contribution*, instead of 'which correspond to' we have 'appropriate to' (Marx, 1971b: 20). The essential idea is the same.

3. Ironically, Hindess and Hirst, in the aforementioned book, make the following observation:

   > The concept of mode of production as an articulated combination of relations and forces does not preclude the possibility of variation at the level of the relations or of the forces of production. On the contrary the structure of a determinate mode of production specifies a complex space of variation and the variant forms that are possible within that space. Variant forms are not contingent empirical deviations from the purity of the general concept of the mode of production. The concept of a determinate mode of production defines the specific variant forms that are possible as a necessary effect of its structure. (1975: 12)

   And so on. But they do not abide by this important principle in their own subsequent analysis (as Wickham, in this collection, points out, with respect to their treatment of the Asiatic mode of production).

4. Primacy of the forces of production is suggested in a famous passage in the Preface to *A Contribution to the Critique of Political Economy*:

   > At a certain stage of their development, the material productive forces of society come into conflict with the existing relations of production, or (and this is simply the legal expression of the same thing), with the property relations within which they have operated up to that time. These relations change from forms of development of the productive forces into their fetters. There then begins an epoch of social revolution. (Marx, 1971b: 21)

In the second, celebrated passage (from Volume 3 of *Capital*), Marx states his view of the significance of the relations of production, and their quintessential embodiment, the mode of extracting surplus labour, in terms which may be construed very differently from those implied in the first quotation. The second passage reads:

> The specific economic form, in which unpaid surplus labour is pumped out of direct producers, determines the relationship of rulers and ruled, as it grows directly out of production itself and, in turn, reacts upon it as a *determining element*. Upon this, however, is founded the entire formation of the economic community which grows up out of the production relations themselves, thereby simultaneously its specific political form. It is always the direct relationship of the owners of the conditions of production to the direct producers—a relationship always naturally *corresponding* to a definite stage in the development of the methods of labour and thereby its social productivity—which reveals the *innermost secret, the hidden basis of the entire*

> *social structure,* and with it the political form of the relation of sovereignty and dependence, in short the corresponding specific form of the state. (Marx, 1962: 772, emphasis mine)

Here the position appears clearly to be that within a given mode of production relations of production hold primacy, reacting upon production 'as a determining element'. One notes, again, the idea of 'correspondence'.

5. As pointed out by Cohen (1978: 78). The passage from the *Grundrisse* I quote below. Cohen notes: 'The concept of dominance deserves more clarification than I am able to supply here' (1978: 78). It is a great pity that Cohen did not attempt such clarification. His characteristically lucid and precise exposition might have shed light upon what remains an unsatisfactorily worked out notion.
6. See Lenin (1960–80, 1: 445; 5: 487; 7: 369). The first warning occurs in Lenin's *Economic Content of Narodism,* and is directed against the Narodniks; the second is in *What Is To Be Done?*, and is said of certain 'revolutionary' writers; and the third is in *One Step Forward, Two Steps Back,* and is said of Plekhanov. Here is a preoccupation which recurs in Lenin's thought, and appears from the very earliest writing through to the end of his life. He raised it, almost, to a binding epistemological principle: viz., 'There is no such thing as abstract truth. Truth is always concrete' (9: 86–i.e. *Two Tactics of Social Democracy in the Democratic Revolution*). Marxists and non-Marxists alike were taken to task for failing to abide by it.
7. Lenin (1960–80, 31: 166). This was written in 1920, in a piece for the journal *Kommunismus.*
8. See Lenin (1960–80, 31: 165).
9. Banaji provides an excellent definition of 'long duration', as follows: 'The long duration is the least perceptible, and in a sense, the slowest of all forms of historical time. Its effectivity is staggered across centuries, and its reality only measured on that scale' (Banaji, 1977: 27). Banaji proceeds, appositely in this context: 'Insofar as Marx conceived of modes of production in a broader, more truly historical sense as "epochs of production" of "epochs in the economic development of society", he implied they were objects of this magnitude'.

REFERENCES

Alavi, Hamza, 1975, 'India and the Colonial Mode of Production', *Economic and Political Weekly,* Vol. X, Nos. 33, 34, 35 (Special Number, August).

———, 1981, 'Structure of Colonial Formations', *Economic and Political Weekly,* Vol. XVI, Nos. 10, 11, 12 (Annual Number, March).

Amin, Samir, 1976, *Unequal Development,* Hasocks.

Anderson, Perry, 1974a, *Passages from Antiquity to Feudalism,* London.

———, 1974b, *Lineages of the Absolutist State,* London.

Bailey, Anne M. and Joseph R. Llobera, eds., 1981, *The Asiatic Mode of Production. Science and Politics,* London.

Banaji, Jairus, 1972, 'For a Theory of Colonial Modes of Production', *Economic and Political Weekly,* Vol. VII, No. 52 (23 December).

———, 1977, 'Modes of Production in a Materialist Conception of History', *Capital and Class,* Vol. 3 (Autumn).

Bhaduri, Amit, 1973, 'Agricultural Backwardness under Semi-Feudalism', *Economic Journal,* Vol. 83, No. 329 (March).

Bloch, Marc, 1965, *Feudal Society,* 2 volumes, London.

Boutrouche, R., 1959, *Seigneurie et feodalite, I: Le Premier age des liens d'homme a homme,* Paris.

Brenner, Robert, 1976, 'Agrarian Class Structure and Economic Development in Pre-Industrial Europe', *Past and Present,* No. 70 (February).

Cohen, G.A., 1978, *Karl Marx's Theory of History. A Defence,* Oxford.

Dobb, Maurice, 1963, *Studies in the Development of Capitalism,* revd. edn., London.

Godelier, Maurice, 1981, 'The Asiatic Mode of Production', in Bailey and Llobera, eds., *The Asiatic Mode of Production. Science and Politics,* London.

Hilton, Rodney (ed.), 1976, *The Transition from Feudalism to Capitalism,* London.

Hindess, Barry and Paul Q. Hirst, 1975, *Pre-Capitalist Modes of Production,* London.

Islamoglu, Huri and Caglar Keyder, 1981, 'The Ottoman Social Formation', in Bailey and Llobera, eds., *The Asiatic Mode of Production. Science and Politics,* London.

Joen des Longrais, FF., 1958, *L'Est et l'ouest,* Paris.

Kahn, Joel S. and Joseph R. Llobera, eds., 1981, *The Anthropology of Pre-Capitalist Societies,* London.

Keyder, Caglar, 1976, 'The Dissolution of the Asiatic Mode of Production', *Economy and Society,* Vol. 5, No. 2 (May).

Lenin, V.I., 1960-80, *Collected Works,* Moscow.

Marx, Karl, 1962, *Capital,* Vol. III, Moscow.

———, 1964, *Pre-Capitalist Economic Formations,* with an Introduction by Eric Hobsbawm, London.

———, 1971a, *Theories of Surplus Value,* Part 3, London.

———, 1971b, *A Contribution to the Critique of Political Economy,* edited with an Introduction by Maurice Dobb.

———, 1973, *Grundrisse,* Harmondswoth, Middlesex.

———, 1976, *Capital,* Vol. I, Harmondsworth, Middlesex.

Marx, Karl and Friedrich Engels, 1971, *Historical Materialism,* London.

———, 1975, *Collected Works,* London.

———, 1979, *Pre-Capitalist Socio-Economic Formations,* London.

Moulder, Francis V., 1977, *Japan, China and the Modern World Economy: Towards a Reinterpretation of East Asian Development, c. 1600 to 1918,* Cambridge.

Mukhia, Harbans, 1981, 'Was There Feudalism in Indian History?', *Journal of Peasant Studies,* Vol. 8, No. 3 (April).

Prasad, Pradhan, 1973, 'Production Relations: Achilles Heel of Indian Planning', *Economic and Political Weekly,* Vol. VIII, No. 19 (12 May).

———, 1974, 'Reactionary Role of Usurers' Capital in India', *Economic and Political Weekly,* Vol. IX, Nos. 32-4 (Special Number, August).

Rodinson, Maxime, 1977, *Islam and Capitalism,* Harmondsworth, Middlesex.

Ste. Croix, G.E.M. de, 1981, *The Class Struggle in the Ancient Greek World,* London.

Shanin, Teodor, ed., 1983, *Late Marx and the Russian Road. Marx and the 'Peripheries of Capitalism',* London.

Thorner, Alice, 1982, 'Semi-Feudalism or Capitalism? Contemporary Debate on Classes and Modes of Production in India', *Economic and Political Weekly,* Vol. XVII, Nos. 49, 50, 51 (4, 11 and 18 December).

Thorner, Daniel, 1966, 'Marx on India and the Asiatic Mode of Production', *Contributions to Indian Sociology,* Vol. IX (December).

———, 1980, *The Shaping of Modern India,* New Delhi.

Wolpe, Harold, ed., 1980, *The Articulation of Modes of Production,* London.

Was There Feudalism in Indian History?

Harbans Mukhia

To discuss a problem such as 'Was There Feudalism in Indian History?' one should, in fairness, begin by defining one's terms. What, in other words, is feudalism? Unfortunately the answer to this simple question varies with the historian who makes the attempt.[1] If there is no universally applicable definition of feudalism, there is an objective reason for it, which has critical significance for our argument: feudalism was not a world-system; capitalism was the first world-system.[2] It follows therefore that there is no universally applicable abstraction of feudalism as there is of capitalism. When we speak of capitalism in its abstract form, as generalized commodity production where labour itself is a commodity,[3] we do so because of our awareness that all of humanity was, during the nineteenth and twentieth centuries, subjected to the force of this production system through different stages of antecedent developments. Feudalism, on the other hand, was, throughout its history, a non-universal, specific form of socio-economic organization—specific to time and region, where specific methods and organization of production obtained.[4]

It is necessary to lay stress on this point here, for it is lost sight of when feudalism is defined as a system based on 'non-economic compulsion' or as a 'redistributive world system' or in even more general terms as an agrarian economy with a fairly cohesive ruling class siphoning off the agrarian surplus through the use of overt or covert force.[5] These definitions seek to identify an entire social and economic structure in terms of the political or juridical basis of the exploitation of the primary producer, the peasant; they do not take into account the totality of the production system. They seek to identify a mode of production by merely referring to the relations of exploitation. Secondly, these definitions are so broad as to cover all pre-capitalist systems in one sweep, for all pre-capitalist societies were characterized by primarily agricultural production, unequal division of property and non-economic coercion by the ruling class which appropriated the peasants' surplus in a variety of forms—rent (in labour, cash or kind) or revenue or in the form of servile or bonded labour. The use of the term 'feudal' in such a broad sense fails to demarcate the specifics of the feudal social and economic organization from the pre-feudal ones in Europe and from other, non-European, medieval, social and economic systems.[6] It therefore does not explain much.

I shall, in the following pages, try to establish these demarcating lines by suggesting the specificity of feudalism to Western Europe between the fifth or the sixth century and the fifteenth. Feudalism also developed in its classic form in eastern Europe between the sixteenth and the eighteenth century and possibly in Japan during the Tokugawa regime in particular. I am, however, constrained to leave these regions out of the discussion in this paper, hopefully without causing much harm to my argument. Since Western Europe always provides the reference-point for any discussion of feudalism in India, or, for that matter, elsewhere, I shall also attempt a comparison between medieval Western Europe and medieval India. The focus of this comparison will be on the respective conditions of labour which are determined by interaction between nature and social organization and which, in turn, determine the dominant characteristics of a social formation.

I

Feudalism, like other social formations before or after it, was a transitional system. As such it stood mid-way in the transition of the West European economy from a primarily slave-based system of agricultural production[7] to one dominated by the complementary classes of the capitalist farmer and the landless agricultural wage-earner, but in which the free peasantry also formed a significant element. It is necessary to suggest here that the term 'free peasant' as used in this paper is not concerned with the legal freedom of the peasant to alienate his proprietary rights in land or implements or the usufruct of his land; it is even less concerned with the absence of legal restriction on the peasant's mobility. Legal restrictions on the alienation of land acquire social significance only in the context of a fairly developed land market, just as legal restrictions on a peasant's mobility become important only if there is a developed labour-market so that the peasant, by being made immobile, is deprived of a competitive price for his labour. In the absence of these features of developed land and labour markets—which, indeed, characterized the era of the rise of capitalism and were thus bound to be absent earlier—not all the legal freedoms would make much difference to the fate of the peasant. The economic, rather than the legal, significance of the term 'free peasant' therefore denotes a peasant who, quite independently of his social or juridical status, earns his and his family's subsistence off his own (including his family's) material resources and labour. In other words, he (or his family) does not render labour to any one else either in performance of labour service (for purposes of production) or for wages. This does not, of course, exempt him from the obligation to part with his surplus produce in the form of taxes to the State, or, on its behalf, to its officials. None the less, he retains complete control over the process of production on his land through his (and his family's) labour[8] and is assured of a relatively more certain, though perhaps no higher level of, subsistence[9] than peasants who are 'unfree'.

As slavery became an increasingly uneconomic element in the production process of late Graeco-Roman Antiquity,[10] the European slaves, freedmen and, for reasons of growing insecurity, allodialists with varying resources were transformed into different strata of dependent peasantry.[11] This transformation never succeeded in eradicating social and economic differences within the class of peasants;[12] nor were the allodialists completely eliminated from any region in any period.[13]

With slavery becoming increasingly unproductive and the capitalist farmer, along with the landless agricultural worker co-existing with free peasant economy still to develop a long way in the future, the feudal economy came to be characterized by an intermediate and transitional feature which formed the core of the feudal mode of production in its early phase: in the early feudal economy the peasant, irrespective of his social or juridical condition, came to acquire certain hereditary rights for the use of land and other resources even when they belonged to the lord; on the other hand, his and his family's labour potential was always in excess of the resources on which it could be fully expended. In general, as Georges Duby has put it, with the exception of a stratum of the class of allodialists, the area of arable land cultivated by the tenanted manses, varying greatly in size, 'was always less than the amount of land which in theory corresponded to the physical capacity of a peasant family'.[14] One could perhaps add that this would be equally true of small peasant families, legally free but economically dependent on the sale of their labour to supplement their income from the land and that the limitation of resources would include agricultural implements and draught animals, in addition to land.

This hiatus between the labour potential of a peasant family and its resources (used for production) appears to have constituted the distinctive characteristic of the feudal mode of production in its formative stages; it enables us to distinguish the feudal mode of production from the salve and the capitalist modes in Europe[15] and from other medieval economies in different regions of the world.[16] The agrarian economy of the ancient Graeco-Roman region depended largely on the separation of the producer from the means of production under conditions of slavery facilitating the appropriation of his entire labour by the owners of the latifundia. Capitalist agriculture, on the other hand, is characterized by the separation of the producer from the means of production under the conditions of a wage labour-market, so that surplus value is appropriated by kulaks through the sale of the produce. Co-existing with it, though far from being its rival, is free peasant production with regional and temporal variations. In the feudal system in its classic form, the producer is neither completely separated from the means of production, nor is he an independent economic being. Indeed, it is via this intermediate feature that the Western European economy effected its transition from slavery to capitalism. This feature formed the objective basis of the appropriation of the peasants' surplus labour by the feudal lords primarily for purposes of agricultural production.

Non-economic coercion by the feudal lords, then, consisted of a system of exploitation of the structured labour surplus, or excess of the labour potential of the peasant family over its resources. This hiatus formed the basis of the availability of labour for the cultivation of the lord's demesne through forced labour or, marginally, hired labour. This form of coercion became part of the conditions of labour and subsistence, and hence far more effective than any amount of overt force. The dependence of the entire peasantry (including the serfs, but barring a stratum of allodialists) on the lords was thus structured in the production-process, for the lord controlled, even if only partly, the use of labour-time for production on the peasant's manse.

This view of feudalism based on *the structured dependence of the entire peasantry on the lords* (with the only exception of the crust of independent allodialists) enables us to take into account the dynamism of feudal society and to understand its development during the eleventh, twelfth and thirteenth centuries and its decline in the fourteenth as the culmination of peasant resistance generated in the course of the daily toil in the field during the preceding centuries. For this dynamism was also structured in the hiatus between the peasant family's labour power and its productive resources.

For the surfeit of labour power of the peasant family and the lord's demand for it were not quite symmetrical. In a system of agricultural production based on an intensive use of labour (including the wastage of labour in traversing vast fields), where the returns on labour were abysmal and where the period available for agricultural operations was brief, the input or withdrawal of even small amounts of labour made considerable difference to output, whether on the lord's demesne or the peasant's own manse. Hence a silent struggle between the lord and the peasant to push the limits of the surfeit labour in the one's or the other's direction. This silent class struggle occurred in the actual process of tilling the soil.[17] If the lord imposed rigorous supervision over the peasant's toil, the peasant had on his side inertia and deception and, of course, the merciful incompetence and corruptibility of the supervisory staff. If the lord endeavoured to exact labour beyond the time that the peasant could spare from the cultivation of his own land, the peasant was also constantly on the watch for opportunities to steal from the lord's time and devote it to his own manse. Such opportunities were not rare, particularly at the peripheries of the manor where supervision was less rigorous, or wherever the peasant manse might lie adjacent to the demesne.[18]

The labour-intensive nature of agricultural production was conditioned by a number of factors. The chief constraint upon medieval European agriculture was the lack of manure.[19] The implements used were relatively primitive,[20] and even the draught power of the animals was under-used owing to defective methods of harnessing them;[21] this limited the period for which land was under the plough. All these factors necessitated extensive cultivation, and the seeds had to be spread out on the field, the deeper fertility of which remained unutilized. Extensive cultivation in turn meant wastage of labour in traversing long distances on the field itself and from the nucleated village settlements to the outlying fields.[22]

Thus in the few weeks available for actual cultivation there was great demand for manual labour on which agricultural practices were so heavily dependent.[23] This might perhaps explain the relative stability of village settlements in Western Europe during the eighth, ninth and tenth centuries,[24] for agricultural operations at every level, from the lord to the humble peasant, required a stable supply of labour.

This great demand for manual labour in turn conditioned some other aspects of early feudal society; labour services were so organized as to place the heaviest burden on those with least resources—those who had nothing else to give except labour with bare hands.[25] It is in this context that the question of population also assumes a peculiar complexity. For medieval Europe, in what Marc Bloch has called the 'first feudal age', was both over and under-populated at the same time. It was over-populated during the larger part of the year when peasants had little to do and had to subsist off the forest products such as wild fruits, honey and wild animals and were periodically wiped out by famines;[26] but during the brief period when agricultural operations were to be carried out there was an acute scarcity of labour.[27]

If this scarcity were to be overcome, it would be necessary to make a more intensive use of soil-fertility and to forge some labour-saving devices. West European society as a whole was thus poised for technological development with a direct bearing on agriculture.[28]

The centuries after AD 1000 witnessed technical development which related primarily to implements and agricultural practices; manuring remained almost as meagre as earlier. Most of the tools and techniques that spread widely in Western Europe during the first three centuries of the second millennium AD had been known to Europe in theory or practice for varying lengths of time, though their application had been very limited. Only in this period did conditions evolve for their wide social acceptance.[29] On the whole this era was marked by a 'technical dynamism'.[30]

The agricultural progress of these centuries, particularly of the twelfth and thirteenth, following the use of better implements and practices and a more effective use of human and animal labour, led to a phenomenal rise in the productivity of land and labour. The seed: yield ratio which stood at 1:1.6 or at best at 1:2.5 during the ninth and tenth centuries came to stand at 1:4 during the thirteenth.[31] The magnitude of this advance can be assessed from the fact that a rise in the ratio from 1:2 to 1:3 would double the amount of food available for consumption. This continued to be the average ratio until the sixteenth century in many regions of Western Europe and in some of them even up to the nineteenth.[32]

Indirectly, following a rise in the productivity of land, the size of holding necessary to maintain a peasant family declined sharply from about a hundred acres a manse on an average in the ninth century to anywhere between twenty and thirty in the thirteenth.[33] While the ninth century was characterized by the existence of full manses, in the twelfth century the quarter manse had become the standard unit of a tenure.[34]

Reduction in the size of the holding minimized the wastage of labour in agricultural production; the rise in productivity on the other hand stimulated the growth of population. The availability of greater amounts of food (and particularly vegetable proteins) made possible by agricultural progress should have allowed population to grow at the lower end of society where scarcity of foodgrains and proteins was a constraint on reproduction. The relative decline in the frequency and intensity of famines during the first three centuries after 1000 assisted in population growth at the peasants' level; later on, during the fourteenth century, when food again became scarce and famines resumed their dismal visitations with customary ferocity, it was at the peasants' level that death took its largest toll.[35] Life expectancy also appears to have risen from about 25 years in the Roman Empire to 35 in England of the thirteenth century.[36] However, the problem of the growth or decline of population is not related merely to the productivity of land; the uncertainty of production, and, even more important, the unequal distribution of produce (and resources in general) played a more decisive role.[37]

At any rate, even though the benefits of the rise in productivity were differentially distributed, the rural poor also shared in it and were assured of a certain amount of secure nutrition; this was not a negligible impetus to human multiplication. Duby has noted that the influx of men to the towns during the centuries of agricultural progress originated in villages with more generous harvests.[38] There is a consensus among historians that between 1000 and 1300 there was considerable growth of population.[39]

Many of these developments—diminution in the amount of land necessary to provide subsistence to a peasant family, the more effective use of soil-fertility through better tools and techniques, the rise in population—caused extensive land-reclamation in Europe, starting hesitantly in the late tenth or early eleventh century and reaching its peak in the second half of the twelfth. In the thirteenth century it began to taper off and was gradually replaced by increased pastoral activity.[40] Initially it was the peasants who reclaimed land in search of lessening their encumbrances.[41] Group-migration from old villages notwithstanding, the consequence of the land-reclamation movement was individualization—both of the holdings and cultivation.[42] Individualization was also reflected in the break-up of the large kinship groups into nuclear family units.[43]

The movement for land-reclamation was soon taken over by the lords and it became far more organized.[44] There was, however, a distinction in the condition of peasants on the two types of land reclaimed. On the piece cleared by himself, the peasant had a greater autonomy and therefore lighter burdens; on the lord's reclaimed land, on the other hand, the peasant's dependence and burdens were greater, though in comparison to peasants in the old villages they were substantially lighter.[45]

The conditions of labour in West European countryside had changed. As the productivity of land rose with the introduction of relatively capital-intensive technology, the price of land and implements also rose; on the other hand, the demand for manual labour declined. Consequently, the burden of forced labour now shifted from bare manual work to work with a plough-team;[46] it shifted, in other words, from the lowest rung of society to a rung or two above it. The peasant also, seized by the legitimate desire to raise more produce from his own land, became increasingly reluctant to render labour service.[47] Thus unpaid labour was once again becoming an uneconomic proposition in West European history, as it had earlier become under slavery. On the other hand, the growing peasant population made labour available in the expanding labour-market. It was thus that the process of 'commutation' of forced labour into payments in cash and kind started. There was, besides, the process of 'enfranchisement' whereby the dependent peasant purchased his freedom ('the franchise') off the lord. Indeed, the lords encouraged commutation and enfranchisement, for these brought them ready incomes, whereas they could hire in the expanding labour-market such labour as they required for the cultivation of their estates. The peasant, for his part, also welcomed commutation or enfranchisement.[48] Payment of a fixed amount of cash or kind in rent, wherever it was so fixed, would enable him to devote more attention to his own manse and he would be the exclusive beneficiary of increased production or higher prices. Franchise would permit him to become independent once and for all, so that he could look after his land or migrate to places where he would obtain the highest price for his labour. However, some caution is called for in assessing the progress of commutation and enfranchisement. These did not proceed in a linear progression; there was many a reversal on the way.[49] None the less there was definitive lightening of the peasant's many burdens.

Commutation and enfranchisement made a differential impact on the different strata of feudal lords. Whereas the seigneurs[50] still had various sources of their income intact—the right to mint coins, the administration of justice[51] which was being increasingly used to collect fines, the establishment of 'monopolies',[52]—the smaller lords with no seigneurial authority had increasingly to shift to new forms of subsistence. They took to cultivating the demesne with their own, and hired, labour and selling the produce in the market[53] which was increasingly influencing the patterns of agricultural production. The agricultural progress of the eleventh, twelfth and thirteenth centuries had considerably increased the marketable surplus in the countryside and this in turn led to a noticeable growth of trade and urbanization in this period. On the other hand, trade and urban centres began, to an extent, to determine the patterns of production in the countryside. Of course, the demand for agricultural produce was growing in rural areas as well wherever the landless agricultural worker, being paid his wages in cash, had to buy his subsistence. Rural artisans were similarly placed.

The problem of the role of trade and towns in the decline of feudalism in Europe has been examined by many historians and it is not necessary to go into the highly controversial theme here.[54] It does, however, appear on balance that the main direction of peasant migration in Western Europe in the first five centuries after AD 1000 had been within the countryside itself. By and large, it was land with lesser encumbrances that beckoned the peasants to uproot themselves from their old villages and resettle at long distances; the town played at best a marginal role in this movement. Indeed, when the West European peasantry broke into rebellions of literally continental dimensions during the fourteenth century, one of their chief demands was the right to free mobility, whereas most cities on the continent looked on passively whenever they did not help the lords suppress these uprisings.[55]

The changes in the West European countryside then, which had resulted from the interaction of the developing social structure and the given means of production in the first feudal age, undermined the very basis of feudal society. These changes had, above all, led to a process of differentiation in the countryside and the emergence of the complementary classes of the kulak and the landless agricultural worker together with—as a subordinate element and with great regional variations—the free peasant.[56]

With the increased marketable surplus in the countryside, trade began to assume increasing importance in the West European economy from the eleventh century,[57] though it had never been absent earlier.[58] The use of the horsehoe-nail in this period greatly improved transport which in turn assisted in the promotion of trade.[59] There were, of course, considerable regional and local price variations and local price fluctuations. The short-term price fluctuations, however, occurred in the background of a long-term average price-rise. The twelfth and thirteenth centuries were marked by a rise in production followed by a rise in prices.[60] Clearly, demand was growing faster than the supply.

Conditions were thus very favourable for production for the market. Both productivity and prices were rising. Labour could be hired. Wages would decline as the demand for foodgrains rose—both resulting from growing population. It was also possible, of course, on some manors to combine production for the market with the use of the serf's unpaid labour.[61] These conditions began increasingly to drive agricultural production into the patterns of commerce and this in turn lent strength to the process of differentiation.

There were many sources of the rise of the class of kulaks, the most important amongst them being the bigger lords' agents or bailiffs, etc.[62] These agents, often originating at the lowest rungs of society,[63] were familiar with agricultural practices at first hand; they did not, however, consider touching the plough as beneath their dignity; nor did they scruple to grab money at every opportunity whether from the peasants, the lords, the merchants or from God's own house, the Church.[64] Their power over the peasants corresponded to the lord's power.[65] But there was an incipient conflict between them and their masters. For as commercialization of agriculture proceeded, the agents took the lord's demesne on 'farm' or gradually purchased land. On this they employed their own and family labour supplemented by hired labour, with a view to selling its produce. They were thus emerging as alternative bases of economic power within feudal society. This class of much-maligned *nouveaux riches,* of low social origins and moderate cultural tastes, the butt of the aristocracy's ridicule,[66] driven by the desire for profit—this class formed one of the chief dynamic elements in the late medieval economy of Western Europe.

Besides the agents, the small lords, pushed by the need to sell in the market but constrained by the limits of their resources found themselves alongside the bailiffs.[67] There were also the merchants, urban and rural, who entered the arena in search of profit.[68] They 'farmed' fragments of large estates which the lords were willing to hand over to them when feudal rents were declining.[69] They gradually purchased land on which they employed hired labour, the produce being sent to the market. They tried to expand the scale of production by reinvesting the returns.[70]

Some peasants were also able to rise. The number of such peasants was rather small and at any rate they were, in most cases, better off at the starting point than those from whose ranks they had risen. Some cases of peasants taking the lord's demesne on 'farm' have also been noted.[71]

The small and marginal peasants, on the other hand, by and large, became landless agricultural workers. To use the new, capital-intensive technology, the small (and marginal) peasant had to depend upon loans. He had also to borrow money if he desired his franchise, or if he migrated elsewhere where he would need sustenance for the initial breathing period. He was thus subject to stiff borrowing conditions, either by the merchant-moneylender or the lord. The former would buy off a part or whole of the peasant's surplus produce in advance repayment of the loan or the interest and thus deprive him of the advantage of price-rise. The lord, on the other hand, would impose stiff conditions, including, at times, labour services.[72] Real freedom came only to those peasants who had their own resources to buy it.[73] The lord also adjusted to the economic benefits of the age by replacing hereditary tenancies with fixed-time tenures and gradually even the latter with tenancies-at-will so that at each renewal of a tenure the advantage of any rise in productivity or prices could accrue to him.[74]

The small and the marginal peasants were thus subject to the pressure of many forces. Deprived of the protection of the lord, the village community or even his own group of kinsmen, the slightest vagary of production or prices would compel this peasant to sell or forfeit his mortgaged land and implements and he would immediately go reeling into the ranks of the landless looking for work in the labour market. It is perhaps true that socially the small peasant suffered a depression in his status on losing his bit of land but economically, even as a landless agricultural wage-earner, he was better off than he was as a small peasant.[75] But his situation could last only so long as the society as a whole registered economic progress. With the slightest setback in the economy, those who were at its lower end had to pay the heaviest price. Famine would make its terrible appearance and wipe out large numbers of resourceless peasants.[76]

It was thus that feudal society was growing and, in the process, giving birth to two inter-related classes, and reviving an older one in greater strength, which were to destroy the parent structure through various stages and forms of struggle. The initial thrust for capitalist development originated in the countryside.

The agricultural progress of the twelfth and thirteenth centuries consisted primarily of extension of the arable into the forest and the pasture; and it had also reduced the period of the fallow thereby utilizing the existing soil-fertility more intensively. This could, however, go on only up to a point for a shrinking pasture would reduce the animal population which in turn would diminish the quantity of manure, scarce as it already was. The forest on the other hand, also maintained a delicate ecological balance which would be disturbed by cutting down trees in large numbers. Besides, apart from wood, the demand for which was on the increase,[77] they provided supplementary food to both men and animals.

Historians are generally agreed that agricultural progress had begun to recede from the beginning of the fourteenth century all over Western Europe, though the intensity of the recession varied regionally, for the land reclamation movement during the preceding two centuries had over-reached itself.[78] Given the unequal distribution of resources, the declining yields from the more marginal of the reclaimed lands, were beginning to weaken and sweep off numbers from the poorer strata.[79] The availability of labour was itself, perhaps, inhibiting any further technical development.

The fourteenth century witnessed great social upheavals. There was also considerable ecological disturbance which was reflected in an appreciable fall in the temperature and continuous rainfall for long periods such as in 1315–17. Famines resumed their dismal visitations and there was a series of epidemics. The famine of 1315–17 deprived Western Europe of a tenth of its population.[80] The Black Death of 1348–50 was only one in a series of disasters, though the most catastrophic of them;[81] it wiped out anywhere between a quarter and a half of the population. Nor did the epidemics cease after this terrible toll. Thus, even assuming a lower death rate of 25 per cent in 1350, the West European population had lost 40 per cent of its strength during the course of the fourteenth century,[82] even if we assume that those who suffered acute malnutrition but still survived could be counted as full members of the work-force.[83]

The immediate consequence of these disasters was a price-scissors effect: the prices of foodgrains fell owning to a fall in demand, but wages and the prices of industrial goods were on the rise.[84] This was a direct challenge to the lords' standards of living, for their incomes from the land were declining but the cost of agricultural production and prices of luxury goods were rising. This should have reinforced the process of differentiation within the class of landlords, for the smaller ones, with no other source of income than land, were ruined more easily than the bigger ones who could still rely upon court-fines, monopolies, etc.[85] Land was also available more freely now and in this way the free peasantry re-emerged in strength.[86]

The aristocracy, on the other hand, took resort to war and plunder. Everywhere in Western Europe this was a period of extensive wars—the Hundred Years' War in France, the Wars of the Roses in England, in Germany and Italy; in Spain and Flanders. Even the resurgence of the state during this period added its weight to the crisis by raising the level of its demand for taxes.[87]

But then it was not these developments which created the 'general crisis' of feudalism. Feudal society had, in the past, been familiar with over-population, wars, famines and deaths. The general crisis was, on the other hand, the result of the determination of men to get over the impasse according to their situation in society.[88] The class of feudal lords, faced with declining incomes and rising expenditures, still commanded the power of the state and took resort to an overt use of it. The State, which was reviving all over Western Europe at this time, intervened on behalf of the lords by fixing wages at the pre-Black Death level, and by legally restricting peasant mobility—unlike in the first feudal age when peasant immobility was part of the production system. This was a challenge to the landless wage-earner, the small and marginal peasant who earned their living in part by selling their labour and the emerging class of kulaks who hired labour and therefore required a mobile peasantry. The 'feudal reaction' assumed similar forms everywhere.

The peasantry, on the other hand, was so situated as to be able to defend its gain much more forcefully than ever before, for demand for labour was much greater than the available supply. The desolate lands also provided the opportunity to those peasants who had the other necessary means to emerge as free peasants. The peasantry thus responded to the 'feudal reaction' by bursting out in a string of rebellions everywhere in Western Europe.[89]

The fourteenth century saw a series of minor peasant uprisings and some really massive rebellions, spread all over the hundred years. A remarkable feature of these great rebellions was that most of them occurred in the most prosperous rural regions of Western Europe and were led by the most prosperous sections of the peasantry: the Flanders rebellion of 1323-7, the Grand Jacquerie of 1358, north of Paris; the Tuchin movement in central France from the 1360s to the end of the century, and, of course, the great peasant uprising of 1381 in the East Anglia region of England. The fifteenth century witnessed the massive outburst of the *remensas* of Catalonia.[90] Germany also had a series of peasant uprisings in the fourteenth and fifteenth centuries.[91]

It is also remarkable that in regions where poverty prevailed, the peasantry remained passive. In central Italy, rent-racking of the peasantry led to a decline in the rate of growth of population, but, sadly, engendered no rebellion.[92] When the Grand Jacquerie was up in arms in the region north of Paris, one of the most prosperous regions in European countryside, the area to the south-west of Paris, where poverty reigned, remained inert.[93]

The peasantry was thus rising to defend the gains it had made thanks to the emergence of a new mode of production in the countryside;[94] for rebellions occurred by and large in those areas where the emergence of the new mode of production was more pronounced, and peasants were acquiring self-confidence, so essential to the act of rebellion, which, after all, is an act of great humanism.

By the end of the fourteenth century the failure of the feudal reaction had become apparent.[95] From the beginning of the fifteenth century Western Europe began to recover its bases of strength. The ground for this recovery had been prepared by the preceding 'crisis' that had undermined much of the economic and social system which had become outmoded by its own tremendous onward movement. The attainment of the abstraction of capitalism was yet a long way off.[96] But the movement had been set firmly in its direction.

II

Expression of grave regret over the lack of adequate information on almost all crucial points of the social history of ancient and medieval India is perhaps the inevitable starting point of all historical research on these periods. The poverty of information gets even more hurtful when it stands face-to-face with the almost embarrassing riches of evidence on medieval Europe. If, therefore, what follows in the pages below appears to be a string of conjectures and speculations, at least part of it could, perhaps, be blamed on the collective misfortune of historians that so little of the evidence from India's ancient and medieval centuries has survived.

If the meaning of the term 'feudalism' differs from one historian to another, as we noted earlier, it follows that the period of the history of a country—in this case India—characterized as feudal would also vary widely according to each historian's understanding of feudalism. Thus while some Soviet historians of India have found traces of feudalism in the *Arthasastra* of Kautilya,[97] for R.S. Sharma Indian feudalism originated in the fourth century AD, reaching its peak during the eleventh and twelfth centuries.[98] With the establishment of the Delhi Sultanate, for political and economic reasons, feudalism, in B.N.S. Yadava's view, began to decline.[99] The distinguished Russian historian of the nineteenth century, M.M. Kovalevski, on the other hand, believed that the process of 'feudalization' in India started precisely with the 'Muslim conquests'.[100] For D.D. Kosambi, whose writings on Indian history justly enjoy a privileged status, the feudal system broke down around the middle of the seventeenth century, under Aurangzeb;[101] Col. James Tod, on the other hand, was witness to the functioning of what he believed was the classic form of feudalism in Rajasthan in the early nineteenth century.[102]

The point of comparison in the works of the historians mentioned above, and of many others who have considered the problem of Indian feudalism, invariably rests in medieval Western Europe. This is understandable, for so long as we remain concerned with the question, 'Was there feudalism in India?', we must seek to answer it in the light of the most developed form of feudal social organisation, which was West European. This comparison is quite independent of the answer to the question raised here. It is thus that Tod compared early nineteenth-century Rajasthan with the West European feudal system as described in Hallam's *Middle Ages* (published 1824),[103] and found that four of the six elements which comprised feudalism were prevalent in Rajasthan.[104] D.D. Kosambi also drew upon Marion Gibb's *Feudal Order* and Maurice Dobb's *Studies.*[105] R.S. Sharma and B.N.S. Yadava have repeatedly referred to Western Europe by way of comparison.[106] It is in relation to medieval Europe that Satish Chandra finds, 'in many respects' a similarity in the Indian concept of landownership.[107]

D.D. Kosambi provided a fresh outline for the study of Indian feudalism—his famous concept of feudalism from above and feudalism from below[108]—an outline that was unfortunately found inadequate by some other historians.[109] It was R.S. Sharma who first made a systematic study of Indian feudalism in his book and in various articles.[110] B.N.S. Yadava has added a great many details to Sharma's work by studying northern India in the early medieval period, particularly during the twelfth century.[111]

The main theme in the works of Sharma and Yadava is woven around the assumed antagonism between trade and urban life on the one hand and feudalism on the other,[112] and, particularly, the rise in importance of landed intermediaries owing to an increasing number of grants of land by the state to its officials and to the Brahmans in charity; this resulted in the subjection of the peasantry to the intermediaries and in the peasants' dependence on them. R.S. Sharma visualizes the development in India of almost all components of West European feudalism—serfdom,[113] manor,[114] self-sufficient economic units,[115] the process of feudalization of crafts and commerce,[116] apart, of course, from declining trade and urbanization. The elements which had allegedly undermined the European feudal structure, namely, the revival of trade and towns, the flight of the peasants to the towns to escape excessive impoverishment at the hands of the lord and the process of commutation of forced labour into monetary payments—all these, in Sharma's view, developed in India also and similarly undermined Indian feudalism.[117] Indeed, the only important determinant of European feudalism which Professor Sharma could not trace in India was foreign invasions[118]—and B.N.S. Yadava has made up even this deficiency by drawing attention to the barbarian, particularly the Hun, invasion of India which shattered the lame Gupta empire and contributed to the rise of feudalism. 'The Gurjara-pratihara empire', says Yadava, 'arose in Northern India like the feudal Frankish Carolingian Empire.'[119] Of all these, the most critical element of Indian feudalism, in Professor Sharma's and and Professor Yadava's view, consisted of the growing dependence of the peasantry on the landed intermediaries following the grant of more and more rights to them by the state. The dependence was manifested in terms of increasing restrictions on the peasant's mobility and his subjection to forced labour, which in turn was becoming increasingly intensive.[120]

It is not possible here to go into all the points made by Sharma and Yadava in establishing the similarity between Indian and European feudalism; at any rate, it is hard to have to disagree with the work of such eminent historians. I would confine my comments to some of the important arguments advanced in support of an Indian feudalism.

The alleged antagonism between feudalism and the trade-urbanization complex has been a matter of great dispute between historians ever since Henri Pirenne's days; increasingly, however, the two are being seen as less incompatible than was the case in the 1930s and the 1940s—a mere point that we have noted earlier. At any rate, even in terms of historical evidence, D.C. Sircar and, more effectively, B.D. Chattopadhyaya have questioned the extent of the decline of trade and urbanization in the period concerned.[121]

More important, however, is the fact that while R.S. Sharma and B.N.S. Yadava have established considerable similarity in the features of Indian and European feudalism, the one basic difference appears to have been overlooked by them: in Europe feudalism arose as a result of a crisis of the production relations based on slavery on the one hand and changes resulting from growing stratification among the Germanic tribes on the other, the two coming into what Perry Anderson calls a 'catastrophic collision of two dissolving anterior modes of production—primitive and ancient'.[122] In other words, European feudalism developed essentially as changes at the base of society took place; in India, on the other hand, the establishment of feudalism is attributed by its protagonists primarily to state action in granting land in lieu of salary or in charity, and the action of the grantees in subjecting the peasantry by means of legal rights assigned to them by the State. It is, indeed, a moot point whether such complex social structures can be established through administrative and legal procedures.

Above all, however, it is the concept of the peasantry's 'dependence' that appears to be of uncertain value in the context in which it has been used. The evidence marshalled by Sharma and Yadava at best establishes the increasing *exploitation* of the peasantry; dependence, on the other hand, should consist of an extraneous control over the peasant's process of production, and this has yet to be proved in the Indian context. If one speaks of European peasants' 'dependence' on the lord, it is primarily because such dependence had become rooted in his very conditions of labour, as we have seen in section I above. The critical element in such dependence was the diversion of at least a part of peasant's labour from his own process of production to that of the lord. It is doubtful whether this could be said of India. The nature of forced labour in India—of which there is considerable evidence throughout her history—is in its very essence different from that in Europe, for in India it is very rarely used for purposes of production.[123] There is, indeed, an objective reason for the absence of serfdom in Indian history, for conditions of production in India did not require serf-labour, as I shall try to argue below. Thus forced labour in India remained, by and large, an incidental manifestation of the ruling class' political and administrative power rather than a part of the process of production.

Certain specif features of Indian agrarian history could, perhaps, be clearly enough established, even though only a small segment of it has been studied. The fertility of Indian soil in general appears to have been far higher than that of Europe until as late as the nineteenth century.[124] Nature, on the other hand, permitted the Indian peasant to subsist at a much lower level of resources than his European counterpart. Secondly, and in part conditioned by the factors just mentioned, Indian agrarian history has been characterized predominantly by a free peasantry (in the economic rather than in the legal sense).

A number of indicators point to the high fertility of land in India, though, of course, there was considerable regional variation.[125] The cultivation of two crops, of one crop in each field, every year, which even the spread of the three-field rotation in Europe from the tenth or the eleventh century onwards could not ensure, was a feature of Indian agriculture from at least the Vedic period onwards.[126] Indeed, three crops are also mentioned in our sources which do not appear to treat the phenomenon as exceptional. It is quite difficult to establish whether every field yielded two or three crops a year; some of the references do clearly suggest that such indeed was the case, though it may be rash to accept their suggestion for all soils. Obviously, some lands did bear crops twice or thrice a year.[127]

But even if we were to ignore this evidence, the outstanding fact still remains that no field remained uncultivated for more than a part of the year, something that even the three-field rotation was unable to achieve in late medieval Europe. Indeed, the negligible incidence, if not the complete absence, of the system of fallow in ancient and medieval India is a remarkable testimony to the high fertility of the Indian soil. Historians, while using the term 'fallow', have almost invariably referred in fact to either virgin or abandoned lands, or, at best, lands withdrawn from cultivation for brief periods, which corresponds to permitting the land a lea.[128] Fallow land, unlike the virgin or the abandoned land, is an integral part of the cycle of cultivation. Indeed, it has to be ploughed more often than the land sown, for its soil must be repeatedly pulverized and weeds ploughed back or burnt down to be turned into green manure or potash. The practice of the fallow obviously suggests a soil that is quickly exhausted; the lea, or a brief withdrawal of the plough from the field, on the other hand, would be adequate for a soil relatively less prone to exhaustion. William Tennant, writing at the end of the eighteenth century, noted that '. . . the Indian allows it (his field) a lea, but never a fallow', though he ascribes this to the general backwardness of Indian agricultural techniques.[129] Some other evidence also suggests the practice of the lea, but rarely of the fallow. The *Ain-i-Akbari* describes the second of its four categories of land as one that '(the peasants) do not cultivate for a time and thereby increase its strength'.[130] The *Risala-i-Ziraat* also mentions the prevailing practice, in the second half of the eighteenth century in Bengal, of the cultivation of fields in alternate years.[131] It is quite possible, of course, that instead of following the practice of the fallow, it would be simpler to abandon the exhausted fields and reclaim new ones, for, after all, there was no scarcity of land.[132] But there is very little evidence to suggest that it was widespread. Indeed, the reclamation of land is, after all, a costly process and would hardly be resorted to unless the cost of the restoration of soil-fertility through the use of manure outweighed the cost of reclamation. And manure, as Irfan Habib reasonably argues, should have been available in far greater quantity in the centuries before the beginning of the twentieth than after it.[133]

The system of manuring appears to have developed into a fine art if we go by the minute details of the methods and ingredients of preparing manures for different plants. It is far from certain whether Vedic Indians practised manuring.[134] But the *Arthasastra*,[135] the *Brhatsamhita*, the *Agni Purana*,[136] the *Krsi-Parasara*[137] and the *Upavana-Vinoda*,[138] among others, describe in very great detail the elements of which manures were made. The elements varied from cow-dung and goat's and sheep's droppings to the fat of the pigs[139] and the flesh of the cows;[140] green manure and a mixture of honey and clarified butter with some other elements have also been recommended. Some of these preparations were meant for treatment of seeds before they were sown to ensure better germination.

Nor were the agricultural implements and practices too primitive for their age. Almost definitive evidence of the use of the plough has been uncovered at a pre-Harappan site, Kalibangan in Rajasthan, belonging broadly to the first half of the third millennium BC.[141] The Vedic age, of course, used the plough,[142] and it has naturally continued in use ever since. The size and weight of the plough varied from region to region and, perhaps, from one stratum of the class of agriculturists to another.[143] It is true, as Elliot so derisively states, that the Indian plough—'simple . . . and wretched in construction'—merely scratched the topsoil,[144] but this appears to have been primarily due to the fact that the fertility of most soils in India lies at the surface.[145] Elliot himself noted that 'when anything like a mould-board is required, the people have sufficient ingenuity to frame one'.[146] Construction of a deep-penetrating plough should not have been beyond their capability, if it were required.

The literature of successive periods refers to many other implements used for agricultural production, besides the plough. The Vedic literature mentions the sickle and the sieve;[147] the *Ramayana* of Valmiki refers to the spade.[148] The *Amarkosa* speaks of the hoe and the harrow, besides mortar and pestle for separating the grain from the chaff, and the winnowing fan, etc.[149] The *Krsi-Parasara* gives, with many details, the names and the dimensions of various parts of the plough.[150] From about 600 BC the use of iron in making agricultural implements appears to have been on the increase.[151] It is, on the other hand, difficult to establish the origin of the seed-drill, but this important device which, in Elliot's words, 'has only within the last century been introduced into English field husbandry . . . has been in use in India from time immemorial'.[152]

Experts in agriculture recommended the ploughing of the field more than once, sometimes as many as five times.[153] It is not easy to say how far the recommendations were actually heeded, but Grierson did notice the ploughing of the field five times in modern Bihar;[154] although, of course, it might be a phenomenon of recent origin. Weeding was to take place twice.[155] Given the two or three crops in the year, crop rotation was 'practically a gift of nature and to know the combination which best suited particular soils would have been a matter of experience'.[156] The system of transplantation was also known;[157] and so was the treatment of diseased plants.[158]

It is in irrigation that the most important technological advance has been registered in ancient and medieval Indian agriculture. The *Rgveda* mentions some devices for water-lift (probably from a tank), but the technical details of these are as yet unknown.[159] The *Arthasastra* also refers to several methods of obtaining irrigation water from rivers, lakes, tanks and wells;[160] the Mauryan state apparently imposed a heavy irrigation cess—ranging from one-fifth to one-third of the produce[161]—even when the source of water was privately owned.[162]

It was the spread of the noria from about the seventh century and of the Persian wheel from around the time the Delhi Sultanate was established in north India, that appear to have made a critical difference to the extension of agriculture at least in the Panjab,[163] the fertility of whose soil Abul Fazl considered unrivalled.[164] The canals, on the whole, appear to have been marginal to agricultural production. Firuz Shah Tughlaq[165] and Shah Jahan[166] did order the construction of canals, but for all practical purposes canal irrigation appears to be a more recent phenomenon.

If, owing to the natural richness of the soil and the relatively efficient tools and techniques, agricultural productivity in India was high, the subsistence level of the peasant was very low—thanks to climatic conditions, and, as we shall argue later, social organization. Consequently, the amount of land considered necessary for the subsistence of a peasant family in India was estimated at anywhere between nine and fourteen acres in the fifth century BC.[167] Unfortunately, there is little evidence to go by for the later periods of our history on this point, but unless we assume a significant decline in soil-fertility or rise in the subsistence level, this size of landholding was hardly likely to have changed drastically. Indeed, such a landholding, with traditional implements and practices, but with a reasonably assured supply of irrigation water, should even today earn the peasant family the pittance that it needs to survive and reproduce itself.

The relatively small size of holdings in India had the principal effect of averting the wastage of labour in the process of production which occurred in Europe; consequently far less labour was required for agricultural operations here. Moreover, these operations could be spread over a much longer period in the course of the year than in Western Europe. Thus there does not appear to have been a highly concentrated demand for large amounts of labour during short periods. It is thus that the absence of serfdom in Indian history, except for some marginal incidence,[168] becomes intelligible. Indeed, even Sharma and Yadava are led by their evidence to conclude that serfdom was far from being the dominant feature in India.[169] For the process of production in India did not create an acute scarcity of labour; enserfment of the peasant therefore was hardly necessary. It is not as if the ruling class or the state in India was more compassionate to the primary producer than the feudal lords or the medieval state in Europe; it resorted even to enslavement of the peasants and the artisans[170] whenever it felt the need. But such need arose rarely and for short periods of time.

When historians, therefore, describe the Indian peasant as a serf[171] or a 'near-serf', they do so primarily on the basis of legal restrictions imposed on his mobility, the absence of the right to free alienation of land, and, of course, his subjection to the rendering of forced labour.[172]

It is true that the state in India, concerned as it primarily was with the collection of revenue from land, made it obligatory on the part of the cultivator to keep his field constantly under the plough. The *Arthasastra* recommends that the 'lands may be confiscated from those who do not cultivate them and given to others; or they may be cultivated by village labourers and traders, lest those who do not properly cultivate them might pay less (to the government)'.[173] The *Arthasastra* also places restrictions on the free alientation of land or the free mobility of peasants, once again with a view to preventing the loss of revenue: 'Tax-payers shall sell or mortgage their fields to taxpayers alone; Brahmans shall sell or mortgage their *Brahmdeya* or gifted lands only to those who are endowed with such lands; otherwise they shall be punished with the first amercement. The same punishment shall be meted out to a tax-payer who settles in a village not inhabited by tax-payers.'[174] The state was advised even to compel the peasants to grow an additional crop on their fields if the king found himself financially straitened.[175] Manu prescribes the imposition of a fine on a cultivator who does not cultivate his field in proper time nor guard the crop against animals.[176] All this, however, did not violate the owner's title to the land even if it had been cultivate by another.[177] Indeed, the period for which the title remained legally valid went on increasing from 10 years at the time of Manu (*c.* second century AD) to 105 years in the thirteenth century, with limits fixed at 20 years, 60 years and 100 years between these dates.[178]

Thus, when Aurangzeb's *firman* to Muhammad Hashim[179] on the one hand recognized the peasant's ownership of land[180] (including the right to sell or mortgage it[181]) and on the other advised the use of persuasion and, if necessary, compulsion, to have the peasant till his land, it was really reiterating a very ancient Indian position.[182] If the state asserted its right to ensure uninterrupted cultivation of land, or to collect the revenue due to it even when the peasant neglected to cultivate his field,[183] or else to have the land tilled by another in case the owner had fled, the extent of its actual enforcement would vary from one situation to another. In the seventeenth century when the incidence of desertion of land had assumed serious dimensions, the state's insistence on its right became more emphatic.[184]

However, one aspect needs to be kept in view while discussing the problem of peasant immobility: we can hardly speak of a developed labour—or land—market in ancient and medieval India, though hired agricultural labour and instances of sale or mortgage of land have been mentioned in our sources.[185] Thus, it is primarily the economic, more than the legal, limitations on mobility which confined the peasant to his village,[186] though, of course, we must not visualize the ancient and medieval Indian peasant as completely immobile. Even if we were to accept state intervention in uniformly enforcing restriction on the peasant's movement or on his right freely to alienate his land, his mastery over the means and the process of production still remained intact, provided, of course, that he cultivated his field (in such manner as he chose) and paid the revenue to the state or its assignees.[187] It is true, as many historians have pointed out, that the pre-modern Indian peasant did not enjoy modern or bourgeois proprietary rights in land, for he could not freely alienate, abandon or abuse his land;[188] obviously no historian expects the peasant to have enjoyed such a right. But then is it merely a legal problem? If, by some stretch of the imagination, these legal rights could be granted to the peasant of the ancient and medieval past, would they have made a material difference to his situation, other things remaining the same—when he could rarely find a buyer for his land or labour or when he could not easily give up cultivation for some other occupation? At any rate, the absence of these rights did not deprive him of control over his field or the plough or—above all—his labour.

And it is in this sense that we have earlier defined a free peasant, following Marx's insight. The question of the legal ownership of land, which has been discussed by a very large number of historians of ancient and medieval India,[189] and the other legal rights carries, at best, a moderate significance in the actual socio-economic context.

In this sense, free peasant production appears to have been consolidated in post-Maurya times. In the Buddhist literature large farms are met with, sometimes with as many as five hundred ploughs, tilled by a gang of hired labourers.[190] The *Arthasastra* also speaks of state farms worked by 'slaves, labourers and prisoners'.[191] But in Gupta and post-Gupta times these large farms, whether owned by individuals or by the state, are no longer referred to; instead, there is the transformation of the *sudras* into petty producers. By the first half of the seventh century most, if not all, *sudras* had become peasants.[192] In part, at least, the spread of peasant production appears to have been due to the state policy of extending cultivation. The Maurya state undertook to settle new villages, or resettle deserted ones, 'either by inducing foreigners to immigrate' or by transferring excess population from the densely populated regions of the kingdom.[193] But individual reclamation of land may have become more common in post-Maurya times—a phenomenon reflected in the formulation of the *bhumicchidranyaya*: the field belongs to him who first removes the weed, as the deer to him who first shoots it.[194] It is reasonable to assume that with the spread of the noria and the Persian wheel, to which reference has been made earlier, considerable reclamation should have taken place at the hands of those who could afford the price of the apparatus.[195] The medieval Indian state gives the impression of extreme keenness to extend cultivation if only because more evidence has survived from this period. Thus the grants made by the state in charity comprised two equal halves of cultivated and waste lands.[196] Among the duties of the revenue-collector of the Mughal state enumerated in the *Ain* is reclamation of wasteland for cultivation and prevention of arable land from falling waste.[197] Various other officials and semi-officials were similarly charged; the Karoris,[198] the Zamindars,[199] even the Jagirdars.[200] Thus when Aurangzeb's *firman* to Muhammad Hashim unambiguously recognizes the peasant's title to land reclaimed by him,[201] it merely establishes the continuity of a very old Indian practice of encouraging the extension of cultivation by individual peasants.

The primarily free peasant form of agricultural production gradually evolving from post-Maurya times, thus characterized the agrarian economy of ancient and medieval India. This need not, however, blind us either to the existence of other classes in the countryside or to the extreme poverty of the peasants, or to the considerable changes within the agricultural economy of pre-modern times.

It is no longer necessary to try to prove the existence of stratification in the ancient and medieval Indian countryside, for there is now hardly any dispute about it. The Caste-system in particular appears to have maintained economic and social disparities, especially in making landless agricultural labour available for the cultivation of the lands of big land-owners.[202] When, therefore, we speak of free peasant production, it is by and large in terms of its primacy in the production system.[203]

If the Indian peasant's control over the process of production demarcated him from his medieval European counterpart, there is little reason to believe that he also enjoyed a higher standard of living. We have noted earlier that nature in India allowed the peasant to subsist off very meagre resources; what nature permitted as the minimum level was made the maximum by social organization. There are continual references in our sources to the heavy demand of revenue and other taxes from the peasants and the consequent miserable level of their existence. The Pali texts draw a pitiful picture of peasants' poverty.[204] Kautilya prescribes between one-fifth and one-third as irrigation cess, even when the source of irrigation is privately owned as we have noted earlier.[205] As R.P. Kangle argues, with the *bhaga* or land revenue being fixed at one-sixth, the total would amount to one-half of the produce for peasants paying one-third as irrigation cess.[206] The law-books had 'unalterably' laid down the rate of land revenue demand in the range of one-twelfth to one-sixth depending on the nature of the soil and its yields. Yet the actual collection varied between one-tenth and one-third according to the status of the ruler. Indeed, a specimen document in the *Lekhapaddhati* reveals that at times, up to two-thirds of the produce was being collected in the eleventh and twelfth centuries.[207] In the *Sukranitisara*, different portions of which belong to centuries after the eleventh, the recommended land revenue rates vary between one-sixth and one-half of the produce.[208] King Lalitaditya of Kashmir (eighth century) gave advice to his heirs which Sultan Balban was to repeat in turn to his own heirs, five centuries later: Do not allow the villagers to accumulate more than they need for bare subsistence lest they revolt.[209] D.C. Sircar and B.N.S. Yadava have enumerated the formidable number of taxes and cesses collected from peasants and artisans[210] and if Yadava reaches the conclusion that 'mostly the peasants appear to have been left with a bare margin for subsistence'[211] in the twelfth century, he is by no means overstating the case. It is in continuation of this tradition that the Sultans of Delhi and the Mughal Emperors collected anywhere between a quarter and a half of the produce as revenue from land.[212] It is possible, of course, that with technical progress such as the introduction of the noria and the Persian wheel and with great diversification of crops,[213] the value of produce from the land increased and the state raised its demand for revenue, but this is an aspect that needs to be carefully examined before a statement can be made with confidence.[214]

The characteristics of agrarian history discussed earlier—high fertility of land, low subsistence level and free peasant production—also explain the relative stability in India's social and economic history. It is, after all, true that there has hardly been any concentrated social effort caused by acute tensions to change completely the means, the methods and the relations of production. Indeed, barring the *arghatta* (noria) and the Persian wheel, one can hardly speak of a major break in the means of agricultural production. It appears that the features we have already discussed have some relationship with the absence of these major breaks. In India, unlike Europe, there appears to have been no prolonged and acute scarcity either of labour or production; the routine increase in demand could perhaps have been met by the routine extension of agriculture.

Thus with a high quantum of agrarian surplus available in the form of land-revenue and cesses, etc., to the state—which formed the chief instrument of exploitation[215]—because of high fertility of land and the low subsistence level of the peasant,[216] a kind of equilibrium existed which facilitated the state's appropriation of the peasants' surplus in conditions of relative stability. Whenever the state tried from time to time to trespass upon the limits of the equilibrium, the peasantry reacted by either abandoning cultivation or even resorting to violence.[217] But it needs perhaps to be admitted that such cases of active resistance were rather rare, and, except for the peasant rebellions of Aurangzeb's reign, remained largely localized. For once the state's intrusion had been resisted, balance was again restored.

In combination with this factor, the peasant's independent control over his process of production eliminated the possibility of acute social tensions which might have necessitated significant changes in the entire system of production. The conflicts that characterized the economic history of pre-British India were conflicts over the distribution and redistribution of the surplus rather than over a redistribution of the means of production, which had changed the face of the medieval European economy.[218] The conflicts over the redistribution of the surplus were resolved by and large within the existing social framework. It is thus that even when the Mughal empire was collapsing, one gets the impression that the class of zamindars at various levels was turning out to be the main beneficiary of this collapse. It was, in other words, an older form of property that was re-emerging in strength.[219] Medieval Indian society did not have enough tension in it to lead it to the bourgeois system of production.[220]

To argue against the notion of an Indian feudalism need not lead one to the acceptance of the Asiatic mode of production.[221] Indeed, the concept of the Asiatic mode of production is based on the absence of private property in land,[222] which is far from the generally accepted view among Indian historians today. It is evident that a wide range of social formations have existed in the world prior to their subjection to the universality of capitalism, and this range cannot be exhausted with the concepts of feudalism and the Asiatic mode of production. Irfan Habib has questioned the validity of the concepts of feudalism and the Asiatic mode of production for Indian history[223] and has suggested a neutral term, namely, the Indian medieval economy.[224] I have perhaps been quite rash in emphasizing free peasant production as the characteristics feature of the Indian medieval economy. But a critique of the existing straitjackets of feudalism and the Asiatic mode of production may have this much to recommend it: it might clear the path in search of a typology more specific to pre-British India. Additionally, it might draw us away from Euro-centrism in the study of history.[225]

NOTES

An earlier version of this paper was first read as the Presidential Address, Medieval India Section, Indian History Congress, 40th Session, 1979. It was later discussed in three seminars respectively organized by the School of Social Sciences; Jawaharlal Nehru University, New Delhi; Department of History, Erasmus University, Rotterdam; and Society for the Study of Feudalism, Sorbonne, Paris. I was fortunate to receive written or oral comments from Maurice Aymard, Guy Bois, Barun De, Irfan Habib, R.H. Hilton, Iqtidar Alam Khan, Frank Perlin, Burton Stein and Immannuel Wallerstein; it is a privilege to acknowledge my debt of gratitude to them all.

1. Marc Bloch's classic description of the fundamental features of European feudalism is well-known everywhere: 'a subject peasantry; widespread use of service tenement (i.e. the fief) instead of a salary, which was out of the question; the supremacy of a class of specialized warriors; ties of obedience and protection which bind man to man and, within the warrior class, assume the distinctive form called vassalage; fragmentation of authority—leading inevitably to disorder; and, in the midst of all this, the survival of other forms of association, family and state, of which the latter, during the second feudal age, was to acquire renewed strength', *Feudal Society*, tr. L.A. Manyon, Chicago, 1964, p. 446. To Joseph R. Strayer and Rushton Coulborn 'Feudalism is primarily a method of government, not an economic or a social system, though it obviously modifies and is modified by the social and economic environment', 'The Idea of Feudalism', in R. Coulborn, ed., *Feudalism in History*, Princeton, 1956, p. 4. For Henri Pirenne feudalism was a 'closed estate economy' where production was largely for consumption and trade was practically absent, *Economic and Social History of Medieval Europe*, tr. I.E. Clegg, London, 1958 (first published 1936), pp. 7-12. Even historians sharing a common analytical methodology, namely Marxism, have understood feudalism in a very wide range of meanings. Thus, whereas Paul Sweezy's conception

of feudalism is virtually akin to that of Henri Pirenne, in R.H. Hilton, ed., *The Transition from Feudalism to Capitalism,* London, 1976, pp. 33-56 and 102-8, Maurice Dobb equates it with serfdom, *Studies in the Development of Capitalism,* revd. edn., London, 1963, rpt. 1972 (first published 1946), pp. 35-7; for Perry Anderson it was 'the specific organization in a vertically articulated system of parcellized sovereignty and scalar property that distinguished the feudal mode of production in Europe', *Lineages of the Absolutist State,* London, 1977 (first published 1974), p. 408.

In the Indian context R.S. Sharma characterises the period between AD 300 and 1200 as feudal when he finds most features of West European feudalism having developed here, *Indian Feudalism c. 300-1200,* Calcutta, 1965, pp. 1-2, 7, 16, 52-3, 63-4, 154, 158, 271, etc. S. Nurul Hasan, on the other hand, calls medieval India feudal even though she 'did not have *any* of the characteristics of Western European feudalism', *Thoughts on Agrarian Relations in Mughal India,* New Delhi, 1973, p. 2 (emphasis added).

2. Clearly other pre-capitalist universal categories such as 'stone age', 'bronze age', etc., do not stand in the same class as a highly organized mode of production with an advanced social organization.
3. Karl Marx and F. Engels, *Selected Works,* Vol. I, Moscow, 1969, pp. 160-2.
4. Cf. the perceptive remark of Jean Suret-Canale: '*By its very nature,* capitalism, as well as being one of the great stages of human progress, also assumes a universal value, destroying or reducing to the status of residual survivals, the previous modes of production. *A fortiori,* such universality appertains to socialism. But one cannot project this universality of the last two stages of social development on to the history which precedes them', cited in Marian Sawer, *Marxism and the Question of the Asiatic Mode of Production,* The Hague, 1977, p. 208 (emphasis original).
5. Thus Maurice Dobb, equating feudalism with serfdom, explains the latter term as a type of exploitation that is enforced and perpetuated through 'so-called "extra economic compulsion" in some form', *Capitalism, Development and Planning,* New York, rpt. 1970, pp. 2-3. R.H. Hilton also accepts the equation of serfdom with 'non-economic compulsion', though he does not define feudalism as the equivalent of serfdom, Hilton, ed., *Peasants, Knights and Heretics,* Cambridge, 1976, p. 4. 'Redistributive world system' is Immannuel Wallerstein's term. This world system is 'based on a mode of production wherein a surplus is extracted from agricultural producers normally in the form of tribute to sustain an imperial (or state) bureaucracy at a given level of consumption', 'From Feudalism to Capitalism—Transition or Transitions?' *Social Forces,* Vol. 55, No. 2, December 1976, p. 281, n. 2. This term is as general as 'non-economic compulsion' or 'pre-capitalist society', and is therefore hardly superior to it.

   S. Nurul Hasan understands feudalism to mean a primarily agrarian economy where the surplus is appropriated by a 'fairly closed' ruling class through both non-economic coercion and the role played by it in agricultural as well as the subsidiary handicrafts production, *Thoughts,* pp. 1-2.

Perry Anderson has sharply criticized universalist definitions of feudalism, which, with suitable modifications, would equally appertain to different regions of the medieval world, *Lineages*, pp. 401-12. His criticism arises from the assumed similarity of the 'infrastructure' of economies in different parts of the pre-capitalist world, economies that are imprecisely defined by and large in terms of 'large landownership with small peasant production, where the exploiting class extracts the surplus from the immediate producer by customary forms of extra-economic coercion—labour services, deliveries in kind, or rents in cash—and where commodity exchange and labour mobility are correspondingly restricted', ibid., p. 401. He suggests that since '*all* modes of production in class societies prior to capitalism extract surplus labour from the immediate producers by means of extra-economic coercion . . . pre-capitalist modes cannot be defined *except* via their political, legal and ideological superstructures, since these are what determine the type of extra-economic coercion that specifies them. The precise forms of juridical dependence, property and sovereignty that characterize a pre-capitalist social formation, far from being merely accessory or contingent epiphenomena, compose on the contrary the central indices of the determinate mode of production dominant within it', ibid., p. 404 (emphasis original). Anderson himself defines feudalism, as we have noted earlier, as the specific organization of the seigneurial and serf classes 'in a vertically articulated system of parcellized sovereignty and scalar property that distinguished the feudal mode of production in Europe', ibid., p. 408. Quite apart from the problem with defining a mode of production (even a pre-capitalist one) in terms of the politico-legal specifics, into which we need not go here, Anderson has unnecessarily accepted the notion of similarity between the 'economic infrastructures' of different medieval regions. The similarity exists only when the definitions are wide, and therefore futile, enough to cover all of these economies (definitions such as 'non-economic coercion'); in fact the histories of these medieval regional economies have followed quite divergent paths even when they were all primarily agrarian economies and even when surplus was extracted through non-economic compulsion in all of them. Japan's feudalism is the only one outside Europe the genuineness of which is accepted by most analysts from Karl Marx to Marc Bloch to Anderson himself, although even there divergent opinions have not gone unrecorded. See Karl Marx, *Capital*, Vol. I, Moscow, 1954, p. 718 n.; Marc Bloch, *Feudal Society*, pp. 446-7, 452; Perry Anderson, *Lineages*, pp. 413-17, 435-61. Frances V. Moulder on the other hand suggests that certain similarities in the political structure between Tokugawa Japan and European feudalism notwithstanding, Japan's history was closer to China's than Europe's, *Japan, China and the Modern World Economy: Towards a Reinterpretation of East Asian Development c. 1600 to 1918*, Cambridge, 1977, pp. 25, 71-90.

In India the chief protagonists of an 'Indian feudalism' seek to establish the system's kinship with its European counterpart not so much in terms of the 'economic infrastructure' as in politico-juridical and ideological terms in consonance with unequal social distribution of property, though they make do with a simple, rather than a fanciful, language. See R.S. Sharma, *Indian Feudalism* and 'Problem of Transition from Ancient to Medieval in Indian History', *The Indian Historical Review*, Vol. I, No. 1, March 1974, pp. 1-9; B.N.S. Yadava, *Society and Culture in Northern India in the Twelfth Century*, Allahabad, 1973. R.S. Sharma's persuasive scholarship has indeed inspired a large body of literature on Indian 'feudalism' written along the lines suggested by him.

6. Thus is S. Nurul Hasan able to use the terms 'feudal' and 'pre-capitalist' as synonyms: 'the Mughal system was feudal and pre-capitalist in character', *Thoughts*, p. 3.
7. There are, of course, divergent opinions regarding the primacy of slavery in the economy of Graeco-Roman Antiquity. A.H.M. Jones and R.H. Hilton believe that the ancient economy was dependent on the majority of small independent peasants rather than large latifundia cultivated by slaves. See Jones, 'The Economic Basis of Athenian Democracy', *Past and Present*, No. 1, Feb. 1952, pp. 13-31, and Hilton, *Bond Men Made Free: Medieval Peasant Movements and the English Rebellion of 1381*, London, 1973, p. 10. M.I. Finley, on the other hand, suggests the ratio of slaves to free citizenry at around 3 or 4:1 in the fifth or fourth centuries BC, precisely the period Jones is concerned with, 'Was Greek Civilisation Based on Slave Labour?', *Historia*, VIII, 1959, pp. 58-9 cited in Perry Anderson, *Passages from Antiquity to Feudalism*, London, 1974, pp. 22-3, n. Anderson himself suggests a ratio of 3:2 after considering various other estimates, ibid.
8. This is essentially how Marx had understood the term, *Capital*, Vol. III, Moscow, 1971, pp. 804, 807.
9. 'Subsistence' as a Marxian concept includes 'the maintenance and reproduction of the producer', Marx, *Capital*, Vol. I, p. 512. Clearly subsistence needs would vary from region to region according to the climate and from class to class according to custom. They would also vary with time as nature's productive capacity is utilized more fully. But in any pre-socialist society, given the class division, they are likely to approximate more closely to 'the natural wants imperatively calling for satisfaction' (ibid) at the lowest rungs of society than at the middle and higher rungs.
10. M.I. Finley, *The Ancient Economy*, London, 1973, pp. 85-7; Marc Bloch, *French Rural History*, tr. by Janet Sondheimer, London, 1976, p. 68; Bloch, 'The Rise of Dependent Cultivation', M.M. Postan, ed., *Cambridge Economic History of Europe*, Vol. I, 2nd edn., Cambridge, 1966, p. 248; Georges Duby, *Early Growth of European Economy: Warriors and Peasants from the Seventh to Twelfth Century*, tr. by Howard B. Clarke, New York, 1974, p. 40 (hereafter *Warriors and Peasants*); Perry Anderson, *Passages*, pp. 18, 25-8, 79, 82.
11. Marc Bloch, *Feudal Society*, pp. 171-3; Bloch, 'The Rise of Dependent Cultivation', pp. 255-6; Bloch, *French Rural History*, pp. 72-4, 76-7, 85-90; Georges Duby, *Rural Economy and Country Life in the Medieval West*, tr. Cynthia Postan, London, 1968, pp. 33-5; Duby, *Warriors and Peasants*, pp. 88-

9; R.H. Hilton, *Bond Men Made Free*, pp. 33-5; Perry Anderson, *Passages*, p. 149.

12. Marc Bloch, *Feudal Society*, p. 180; G. Duby, *Warriors and Peasants*, pp. 40, 87-8, 90-1; Perry Anderson, *Passages*, p. 148; R.H. Hilton, *Bond Men Made Free*, pp. 42-4.
13. Marc Bloch had once argued that in England, where feudalism was much more thoroughgoing because of being imposed from above after the Norman Conquest, the spread of the manor completely wiped out all traces of allodial property, *Feudal Society*, pp. 187-9, 244, 248. More recently it has been suggested that feudal land tenures, along with other feudal institutions, had developed in England before the Conquest which only accentuated their further development, while features of the pre-feudal past continued to exist as subsidiary elements; see J.O. Preswich, 'Anglo-Norman Feudalism and the Problem of Continuity', *Past and Present*, No. 26, Nov. 1963, pp. 39-57.
14. G. Duby, *Rural Economy*, pp. 33-5, 40.
15. Maurice Dobb did make this distinction in terms of unfreedom of the serf as the reflection of a property relation which asserted itself as a direct relationship between rulers and servants, *Studies*, p. 35. This distinction hinges on the juridical basis of unfreedom rather than on the economic basis, though it does have economic 'content' as Dobb asserted. More important, while the equation of feudalism with serfdom may faithfully describe the numerical preponderance of serfs in the production system, the bi-polar division between lords and serfs excludes from its purview the vital multi-polar tensions which were leading the feudal society on to hectic growth, and, ultimately, to its decline. Dobb's bi-polar division of feudal society explains feudalism's decline in terms of impoverishment of the peasantry owing to the lord's demand for more revenue; this explanation assumes a static level of production. In fact, feudalism declined owing to its tremendous onward march. For a detailed review of Maurice Dobb's argument, see Harbans Mukhia, 'Maurice Dobb's explanation of the Decline of Feudalism in Western Europe—a Critique', *Indian Historical Review*, Vol. VI, Nos. 1-2, July 1979-Jan. 1980, pp. 154-84.

    We have already commented on Perry Anderson's delimitation of West European feudalism's specificities, which, indeed, are such that pre-thirteenth century early medieval India, at least, can find herself comfortably placed there much against Anderson's will.
16. China is another major region of the world which is said to have had its feudalism, beginning with the Chou dynasty in about 1050 BC. The distinguished Chinese historian, Wu Ta-k'un has, however questioned the validity of the concept of Chinese 'feudalism', 'An Interpretation of Chinese Economic History', *Past and Present*, No. 1, Feb. 1952, pp. 1-13.
17. F.L. Ganshof and A. Verhurlst, 'France, the Low Countries and Western Germany', *Cambridge Economic History*, pp. 314-15.
18. G. Duby, *Warriors and Peasants*, pp. 89-90, 94-5.
19. Charles Parain, 'The Evolution of Agricultural Technique', *Cambridge*

Economic History, pp. 133-4, 145-6; Marc Bloch, *French Rural History*, p. 25; G. Duby, *Rural Economy*, pp. 24-5; Duby, *Warriors and Peasants*, p. 169.

20. Charles Parain, op. cit., pp. 128-9, 148-57; G. Duby, *Rural Economy*, pp. 17-21; Lynn White Jr., *Medieval Technology and Social Change*, London, 1973 (first published 1962), pp. 41-3, 53.
21. Charles Parain, op. cit., pp. 144-5; Lynn White, op. cit., pp. 59-60.
22. Marc Bloch, *Feudal Society*, pp. 60-1; G. Duby, *Rural Economy*, pp. 6, 14.
23. G. Duby, *Rural Economy*, p. 18; Charles Parain, op. cit., pp. 129-31, 152-3, 157-9.
24. G. Duby, *Rural Economy*, pp. 6-7, 14-15.
25. Marc Bloch, *French Rural History*, pp. 72-4; G. Duby, *Rural Economy*, pp. 40-2; R.H. Hilton, *Bond Men Made Free*, pp. 61, 85-6.
26. G. Duby, *Rural Economy*, pp. 12-15; G. Duby, *Warriors and Peasants*, pp. 78-83.
27. G. Duby, *Rural Economy*, pp. 38-9, 48-9.
28. Marc Bloch and G. Duby have argued that the incentive for technological development came from the lord's estates. See Bloch, 'Medieval Inventions' in his *Land and Work in Medieval Europe*, tr. J.E. Anderson, 1967, p. 182, and Duby, *Warriors and Peasants*, pp. 95-6, 177, 229-30. For the suggestion that the society as a whole created this development see Harbans Mukhia, 'Maurice Dobb's Explanation' pp. 20-5.
29. Perry Anderson, *Passages*, p. 183.
30. Lynn White, op. cit., p. 88.
31. G. Duby, *Rural Economy*, pp. 25-7; 103; C. Parain, op. cit., p. 125; Lord Beveridge, 'The Yield and Price of Corn in the Middle Ages', in E.M. Carus-Wilson, ed., *Essays in Economic History*, Vol. I, London, 1966 (first published 1954) pp. 15-16.
32. G. Duby, *Rural Economy*, p. 102.
33. R.H. Hilton, *Bond Men Made Free*, p. 28. The manse comprised the amount of land necessary to maintain one household at subsistence level; it therefore differed from region to region according to soil-fertility and customary subsistence needs of the peasant family unit. See Robert Latouche, *The Birth of Western Economy*, tr. E.M. Wilkinson, London, 1961, p. 82 and A. Gurevich, 'Representations of Property during the High Middle Ages', *Economy and Society*, Vol. VI, No. 1, Feb. 1977, p. 8.
34. G. Fourquin, *Lordship and Feudalism in the Middle Ages*, tr. Iris and Lyton Sells, London, 1976, p. 168.
35. G. Duby, *Rural Economy*, pp. 294-5.
36. R.S. Lopez, *The Birth of Europe*, London, 1967, p. 398, cited in Perry Anderson, *Passages*, p. 190.
37. E.A. Kosminsky suggests, in passing, the significance of unequal distribution of property in feudal society in this context, 'The Evolution of Feudal Rent in England', *Past and Present*, No. 7, April 1955, p. 22.
38. G. Duby, *Warriors and Peasants*, pp. 198-9.
39. J.C. Rusell, *Late Ancient and Medieval Populations*, Philadelphia, 1958, pp. 102-

13; Russell, 'Population in Europe', in Carlo M. Cipolla, ed., *The Fontana Economic History of Europe*, Vol. I, London, 1972, pp. 39-40; M.M. Postan, *The Medieval Economy and Society*, London, 1975 (first published 1972), pp. 35-6, J.Z. Titow, 'Some Differences Between Manors and their Effects on the Condition of the Peasant in the Thirteenth Century', *Agricultural History Review*, Vol. X, No. 1, 1962, pp. 1-2; Maurice Dobb, *Studies*, p. 47; Marc Bloch, *French Rural History*, p. 16; Duby, *Rural Economy*, pp. 119-22.

40. G. Duby, *Rural Economy*, pp. 81-7; Duby, *Warrior and Peasants*, pp. 199-210.
41. Hermann Aubin, 'The Land east of the Elbe and German colonization eastwards', *Cambridge Economic History*, pp. 455-6; E. Miller, 'The English Economy in the Thirteenth Century: Implications of Recent Research', *Past and Present*, No. 28, July 1964, p. 33; Patricia Croot and David Parker, 'Agrarian Class Structure and Economic Development', *Past and Present*, No. 78, February 1978, p. 39; G. Duby, *Warriors and Peasants*, pp. 201, 208.
42. B.K. Roberts, 'A Study of Medieval Colonisation in the Forest of Arden, Warwickshire', *Agricultural History Review*, Vol. XVI, 1968, p. 102; Leopold Genicot, 'Crisis: from the Middle Ages to Modern Times', *Cambridge Economic History*, pp. 733-4; Ganshof and Verhurlst, op. cit., pp. 297-8; G. Duby, *Warriors and Peasants*, p. 205.
43. Marc Bloch, *Feudal Society*, pp. 137-41; Joan Thirsk, 'The Family', *Past and Present*, No. 27, April 1964, pp. 117-22. Laslett, however, is reluctant to accept the notion that changes in family structures correspond to social transformations, *The World We Have Lost*, cited in Hans Medick, 'The proto-industrial family economy: the structural function of household and family during the transition from peasant society to industrial capitalism', *Social History*, Vol. I, No. 3, October 1976, pp. 292-3.
44. G. Duby, *Warriors and Peasants*, pp. 205-8.
45. G. Duby, *Rural Economy*, p. 77.
46. Ibid., pp. 115-16, 207-8.
47. Ibid., pp. 207-8, 263-4; Lynn White, op. cit., p. 65. Andrew Jones argues that labourers' perquisites had to be created in England during the thirteenth and fourteenth centuries to obtain speedy and efficient use of customary labour, 'Harvest Customs and Labourers' Perquisites in Southern England, 1150-1350; the Corn Harvest', *Agricultural History Review*, Vol. XXV, 1977 p. 14.
48. Marc Bloch, *French Rural History*, pp. 106-12; G. Duby, *Rural Economy*, p. 208; Duby, *Warriors and Peasants*, pp. 91-2.
49. M.M. Postan, 'The Rise of a Money Economy', in Carus-Wilson, ed., op. cit.; Vol. I, p. 7; R.H. Hilton, 'Freedom and Villeinage in England' in Hilton, ed., *Peasants, Knights and Heretics*, p. 181; P.D.A. Harvey, 'The English Inflation of 1180-1220', in ibid., pp. 74-5; G. Duby, *Warriors and Peasants*, p. 222; E.A. Kosminsky, 'Services and Money Rents in the Thirteenth Century', in Carus-Wilson, ed., *Essays in Economic History*, Vol. II, 1966 (first published 1962), pp. 39-42 where he suggests that villeinage remained a more important part of labour-supply on the larger estates while the smaller ones depended more on hired labour.

50. Among the lords were the seigneurs, or the banal lords, whose authority was derived from their exercise of the *ban*, theoretically the king's power to give orders, but actually usurped by lords from the eighth century onwards. Since it was by nature an arbitrary power, its flexibility as a source of income and authority was much prized by the seigneurs who had both land and men within their jurisdiction. Then there were the landlords whose control extended to the land. Besides, there were the non-territorial lords who derived their income from the right to collect taxes, tithes, etc., a right they had either earned or had simply usurped. See Marc Bloch, *Feudal Society*, p. 251; J.S. Critchley, *Feudalism*, London, 1978, p. 67; G. Duby, *Warriors and Peasants*, pp. 174-7; Guy Forquin, op. cit., pp. 133-6.
51. The power to administer justice was as stratified as the class of lords; see Critchley, op. cit., p. 57; also Marc Bloch, *French Rural History*, pp. 78-80; Guy Fourquin, op. cit., pp. 185-6; G. Duby, *Warriors and Peasants*, pp. 211-13, 227, 249-51.
52. The 'monopolies' comprised the mills for grinding corn, the oven for baking bread, the winepress for the grapes, and the bull and boar for replenishing the livestock of the village, etc. These monopolies were fiercely contested by the peasants; see Marc Bloch, *Land and Work in Mediaeval Europe*, pp. 135-68; Bloch, *Feudal Society*, p. 251; G. Duby, *Warriors and Peasants*, pp. 222-3, 227-9.
53. E.A. Kosminsky, 'Services and Money Rent', op. cit., pp. 46-8.
54. However, the paper on 'Maurice Dobb's Explanation' referred to earlier discusses this question in some detail on pp. 34-8.
55. R.H. Hilton, *Bond Men Made Free*, pp. 128-9, 130, 132 and 206-7 where Hilton discusses the attitude of the urban bourgeoisie towards the Grand Jacquerie, the Catalan *remensas*, the Tuchin rebellion and other peasant movements respectively.
56. L. Genicot and G. Duby have discussed this process of differentiation in considerable detail and with impressive clarity. See L. Genicot, op. cit. and Duby, *Rural Economy*, *passim*.
57. G. Duby, *Rural Economy*, pp. 126-65.
58. See for the existence of money and exchange in classical feudalism of earlier centuries Marc Bloch, 'Natural economy or money economy: a pseudo dilemma', in his *Land and Work in Mediaval Europe*, pp. 230-44. Witold Kula, constructing a 'model' of feudal economy, suggests the existence of 'monetary' and 'natural' sectors within every feudal 'enterprise' big or small, *An Economic Theory of the Feudal System*, tr. Lawrence Garner, London, 1976, p. 133.
59. R.S. Lopez, 'The Evolution of Land Transport in the Middle Ages', *Past and Present*, No. 9, April 1956, p. 24. Marc Bloch notes the construction of a large number of bridges all over Europe during the twelfth century, *Feudal Society*, pp. 69-70.
60. G. Duby, *Rural Economy*, pp. 302-5; Perry Anderson, *Passages*, p. 191. The rise

in agricultural prices was especially sharp in England between 1180 and 1220; see P.D.A. Harvey, 'The English Inflation of 1180-1220', in *Peasants, Knights and Heretics*, pp. 57-8.

61. G. Duby, *Rural Economy*, pp. 263-4; M.M. Postan, 'The Rise of a Money Economy', op. cit., p. 7.
62. The large size of the noble or clerical domains within the range of 2,000 to 4,000 acres necessitated the recruitment of bailiffs to supervise production, storage, consumption sale, etc. For the size of the estate, Perry Anderson, *Passages*, p. 140. See also Guy Fourquin, op. cit., p. 172; G. Duby, *Warriors and Peasants*, pp. 46-7, 229; G. Duby, *Rural Economy*, pp. 228-31 and *passim*. In Duby's *Rural Economy*, scattered at many places, is perhaps the best account of the transformation of the class of agents into rich farmers or kulaks.
63. Marc Bloch, *French Rural History*, pp. 191-2; G. Duby, *Warriors and Peasants*, p. 47; Henri Pirenne, op. cit., pp. 60-1.
64. G. Duby, *Warriors and Peasants*, p. 229; Duby, *Rural Economy*, pp. 219, 245.
65. G. Duby, *Rural Economy*, pp. 244-5.
66. G. Duby, *Warriors and Peasants*, pp. 257-8.
67. E.A. Kosminsky, 'Services and Money Rent', op. cit., pp. 46-8; Kosminsky, 'The Evolution of Feudal Rent', op. cit., p. 35n.; G. Duby, *Rural Economy*, p. 247; Duby, *Warriors and Peasants*, pp. 176-7.
68. Guy Fourquin, op. cit., pp. 80-2; G. Duby, *Rural Economy*, p. 129.
69. L. Genicot, op. cit., pp. 715-16.
70. Marc Bloch, *French Rural History*, p. 124.
71. G. Duby, *Rural Economy*, p. 236.
72. Ibid., pp. 252-9, 285. The intensification of labour services on the English estates towards the end of the thirteenth century has been sufficiently highlighted by Kosminsky, 'Services and Money Rents', op. cit., pp. 46-7, and Hilton, 'Freedom and Villeinage in England', op. cit., pp. 181, 184.
73. G. Duby, *Rural Economy*, pp. 256-7.
74. Ibid., pp. 257-8.
75. L. Genicot suggests that during the fourteenth and the fifteenth centuries the small landowners suffered a depression and the landless agricultural workers and marginal farmers registered an improvement in their economic conditions, so that 'at the end of the Middle Ages not the whole but the greater part of the rural population shared approximately the same economic standard of life', op. cit., pp. 728-31. See also G. Duby, *Rural Economy*, pp. 152, 280, 305.
76. G. Duby, *Rural Economy*, p. 286.
77. Ibid., pp. 141-5.
78. Ibid., pp. 317ff.; Perry Anderson, *Passages*, pp. 197-9; Marc Bloch, *French Rural History*, pp. 17, 112; M.M. Postan, *The Medieval Economy and Society*, pp. 63-79; R.H. Hilton, *Bond Men Made Free*, p. 16; E. Miller, 'The English Economy of the Thirteenth century', op. cit., p. 38. Guy Bois makes the point in the classic Marxist idiom: 'Above all, the system had exhausted its possibilities for expansion in a virtually complete conquest of the cultivable

area', 'The Transition from Feudalism to Capitalism' (mimeo), presented to the Indo-French Seminar on the same theme at the University of Delhi, Jan. 1979, p. 21.

79. G. Duby, *Rural Economy*, pp. 294-5.
80. For disturbed ecological balance, etc., Perry Anderson, *Passages*, pp. 198-9; for famines and epidemics, G. Duby, *Rural Economy*, p. 295. Also Ian Kershaw, 'The Great Famine and Agrarian Crisis in England 1315-22', in Hilton, ed., *Peasants, Knights and Heretics*, pp. 85-132.
81. Philip Ziegler, *The Black Death*, London, 1970 (first published 1969); Perry Anderson, *Passages*, p. 201.
82. J.C. Russell, *Late Ancient and Medieval Populations*, p. 131.
83. Duby suggests that the middle-aged resisted epidemics with greater strength, *Rural Economy*, p. 308. This should reflect the decreasing resistance of the younger generation perhaps because of diminishing nourishment owing to the declining returns from the land. Slicher van Bath very sensitively discusses the physical and mental consequences of prolonged malnutrition, *Agrarian History of Western Europe, 500-1850,* tr. O. Ordish, London 1963, pp. 11, 84.
84. Thus, for example, while between the thirteenth and the mid-fifteenth century agricultural prices fell by 10 per cent, wages rose by 250 per cent, R.H. Hilton, *Bond Men Made Free*, p. 154; Genicot, op. cit., pp. 684, 692, 694; G. Duby, *Rural Economy*, pp. 307-8, 320; Guy Bois, 'Note on the movement of prices in feudal economic systems' (mimeo), p. 2.
85. G. Duby, *Rural Economy*, p. 316.
86. Cristobal Kay, 'Comparative Development of the European Manorial System and the Latin American Hacienda System', *Journal of Peasant Studies*, Vol. II, No. 1, October 1974, p. 72.
87. L. Genicot, op. cit., pp. 699-700; Guy Fourquin, op. cit., p. 210.
88. Guy Bois, 'Transition' op. cit., pp. 21-6; R.H. Hilton, 'A Crisis of Feudalism', *Past and Present*, No. 80, August 1978, pp. 11-18.
89. R.H. Hilton, *Bond Men Made Free*, pp. 85ff.
90. Ibid.; G. Duby, *Rural Economy*, pp. 332-5.
91. Peter Blickle, 'Peasant revolts in the German empire in the late Middle Ages', *Social History*, Vol. IV, No. 2, May 1979, pp. 223-39.
92. Perry Anderson, *Passages*, p. 199 and n.
93. R.H. Hilton appears to be astonished that 'the impoverished and badly harassed area to the south-west of the city—precisely where one would expect an explosion of pure misery—was virtually untouched by the rebellion', *Bond Men Made Free*, p. 117.
94. Ibid., pp. 82, 89-90, 94.
95. Perry Anderson, *Passages*, p. 293.
96. Maurice Dobb justly considers the fifteenth and the sixteenth centuries 'transitional' between feudalism and capitalism, *Studies*, p. 20.
97. V.I. Kalyanov and I.P. Baikov cited in B.N.S. Yadava, 'Some Aspects of Changing order in India, during the Saka-Kusana Age', in G.R. Sharma,

ed., *Kusana Studies*, Allahabad, 1968, p. 80. For Baikov the exploitation of the two lower varnas or castes by the higher ones constituted feudalism.

98. R.S. Sharma, *Indian Feudalism*, pp. 1-76, 210-62.
99. B.N.S. Yadava, *Society and Culture*, pp. 172-3.
100. Daniel Thorner, 'Feudalism in India', in R. Coulborn, ed., op. cit., pp. 143-5.
101. D.D. Kosambi, *An Introduction to the Study of Indian History*, 2nd revd. edn., Bombay 1975 (first published 1956), pp. 391-2.
102. Col. James Tod, *Annals and Antiquities of Rajasthan*, ed. W. Crooke, Vol. I, London, 1920, pp. 155-6, 182-3 190.
103. Tod, op. cit., p. 154. Interestingly, Hallam's work still provides the reference point at least to D.C. Sircar, *Landlordism and Tenancy in Ancient and Medieval India as Revealed by Epigraphic Records*, Lucknow, 1969, p. 36.
104. Tod, op. cit., p. 190.
105. D.D. Kosambi, *An Introduction*, pp. 353-5 and 403 n. See also his *The Culture and Civilization of Ancient India in Historical Outline*, rpt, New Delhi 1972 (first published 1970), pp. 23-4.
106. R.S. Sharma, *Indian Feudalism*, pp. 1-2, 16, 34, 63-4, 84, 154, 208, etc., B.N.S. Yadava, *Society and Culture*, pp. 171-2, 175-80, etc.
107. Satish Chandra, 'Some Aspects of Indian Village Society in Northern India During the Eighteenth Century', *Indian Historical Review*, Vol. I, No. 1, March, 1974, p. 51.
108. D.D. Kosambi, *An Introduction*, Chaps. 9 and 10.
109. For a critique of this concept see Irfan Habib, 'Marxist Interpretation', *Seminar*, 39, Nov. 1962, pp. 36-7.
110. R.S. Sharma, *Indian Feudalism*; 'Problem of Transition', op. cit.; 'Origins of Feudalism in India', *Journal of the Economic and Social History of the Orient*, Vol. I, 1957-8, pp. 297-328; 'Indian Feudalism Retouched' (review article), *Indian Historical Review*, Vol. I, No. 2, Sept. 1974, pp. 320-30, etc.
111. B.N.S. Yadava, *Society and Culture*. Yadava's numerous articles rarely go beyond the arguments and evidence of his book.
112. Thus the decline of trade—both internal and international—and, following it, the decline of urban centres is seen by R.S. Sharma as evidence of the rise of feudalism in post-Gupta times, and the revival of trade and city life, of feudalism's decline, *Indian Feudalism*, pp. 65-73 and 242-62. For a similar assumption of a trade-feudalism dichotomy in B.N.S. Yadava's work see his *Society and Culture*, pp. 172-3 and 'Immobility and Subjection of Indian Peasantry in Early Medieval Complex', *Indian Historical Review*, Vol. I, No. I, p. 27. Unfortunately, Yadava has misunderstood Moreland's phrase 'peasants' payments' in cash as 'the regular practice of payment *to* the peasants in cash', which contributed to the growth of economic mobility; Moreland was referring to the revenue paid *by* the peasants to the state or its agents. See W.H. Moreland, *Agrarian System of Moslem India*, Allahabad, 1929, p. 204 and Yadava, 'Immobility and Subjection', p. 27 (emphasis added).

113. *Indian Feudalism*, pp. 53-9, 118 and *passim*.
114. Ibid., pp. 74, 271.
115. Ibid., pp. 71, 242, 271.
116. Ibid., pp. 238-41.
117. For revival of trade and towns, ibid., pp. 242-62; flight of peasants to towns p. 244; commutation, pp. 243-4, 262.
118. Ibid., p. 74.
119. B.N.S. Yadava, *Society and Culture*, pp. 137-9.
120. R.S. Sharma, *Indian Feudalism*, pp. 50-3, 121-2, 243, 283; R.S. Sharma, *Light on Early Indian Society and Economy*, Bombay, 1966, p. 73; B.N.S. Yadava, *Society and Culture*, pp. 163-73; Yadava, 'Immobility and Subjection', pp. 21-3.
121. D.C. Sircar, 'Landlordism Confused with Feudalism', in Sircar, ed., *Land System and Feudalism in Ancient India*, Calcutta, 1966, pp. 58-61; Chattopadhyaya, 'Trade and Urban Centres in Early Medieval North India', *Indian Historical Review*, Vol. I, No. 2, Sept. 1974, pp. 203-19. See also M.R. Tarafdar, 'Trade and Society in Early Medieval Bengal', *Indian Historical Review*, Vol. IV, No. 2, Jan. 1978, pp. 274-86.
122. Perry Anderson, *Passages*, p. 128.
123. Forced labour rendered gratis appears to have been absent in the pre-Mauryan period, P.C. Jain, *Labour in Ancient India*, New Delhi, 1971, pp. 242-3; in the Mauryan period compulsory labour was used for purposes like the construction of state buildings, though it is not clear whether it was paid for or unpaid, ibid., and G.K. Rai, 'Forced Labour in Ancient and Early Medieval India', *Indian Historical Review*, Vol. III, No. 1, July 1976, pp. 26, 37. By the first century AD *visti* had acquired the characteristics of unpaid compulsory labour. Its scope began to expand even as a wider section of the people was subjected to the exactions under this heading; forced labour came to acquire a permanence in Indian society that is exceeded only by the caste-system, for we find continuing reference to it throughout the ancient and medieval periods; see R.S. Sharma, *Indian Feudalism*, pp. 48-53, 121-2, 242-3; Irfan Habib, *Agrarian System of Mughal India*, Bombay, 1963, pp. 150, 239, 248; H. Fukazawa, 'A Note on the Corvee System (Vethbegar) in Eighteenth Century Maratha Kingdom', in *Science and Human Progress* (Essays in Honour of the late Professor D.D. Kosambi), Bombay, 1974; Harbans Mukhia 'Illegal Extortions from Peasants, Artisans and Menials in Eighteenth Century Eastern Rajasthan', *Indian Economic and Social History Review*, Vol. XIV, No. 2, April-June 1977, pp. 231-45; Henry Elliot, *Memoirs of the History, Folk-lore and Distribution of the Race of the North-Western Provinces of India*, ed. John Beames, Vol. II, London, 1859, p. 232. While forced labour was used for a variety of purposes like the construction of forts, repair of roads, carting of goods of the King's officials, etc., there is very meagre evidence of its use for agricultural production. R.S. Sharma cites only one source—the *Kamasutra*—where peasant women are required to work on the

village headman's fields, apart from cleaning his house, carrying things from and into his house, etc., *Indian Feudalism*, pp. 51-2. But quite apart from the vagueness of the reference to peasant women working in the village headman's fields, one of a whole range of their tasks, even the interpretation that those women were rendering forced and unpaid labour has been questioned by G.K. Rai, 'Forced labour', op. cit., p. 30.

There is some primary evidence for the existence of forced labour for agricultural production such as in the *Bhagavata Purana* (not later than AD 800) cited in G.K. Rai, op. cit., p. 33, and some village level documents in Rajasthan cited in Harbans Mukhia, 'Illegal Extortions', p. 233. But on the whole its incidence is quite marginal and even Sharma agrees that serfdom had not become 'a common trait of the Indian agrarian system in medieval times', 'Indian Feudalism Retouched', op. cit., p. 328.

Curiously, it is the artisans who were continually subjected to forced labour from the post-Gupta period. In the *Arthasastra* they are treated as independent, Kautilya's *Arthasastra*, tr. R. Shamasastry, Mysore, 8th edn., 1967 (first published 1915), Book IV, Chap. 1, pp. 229-32; but from the post-Gupta period, particularly from the sixth century, the artisans were attached to merchants and were liable to render forced labour, R.S. Sharma, *Indian Feudalism*, pp. 69-73. In the seventeenth century we still find them being subjected to forced labour, this time by the nobles: F. Bernier, *Travels in the Mogul Empire 1656-68*, tr. A. Constable, London, 1916, pp. 228-9 and Ali Muhammad Khan, *Mirat-Ahmadi*, Vol. I, ed. Nawab Ali, Baroda, 1928, p. 260. The phenomenon is somewhat curious because there is little evidence of the scarcity of artisan labour. Of course, forced labour was not necessarily unpaid labour and there is a considerable amount of evidence of wages being paid to artisans. See, for example, F. Pelsaert, *Jahangir's India*, tr. W.H. Moreland and Peter Geyl, Cambridge, 1925, p. 60, and *Waqai-Ajmer-wa-Ranthambor*, transcript, Andhra State Archives, Hyderabad, p. 227.

124. Elliot, for once championing the cause of India against a compatriot, argued in 1859 that the average produce of the Province of Allahabad was *double the average* of the scientific cultivators of England; he also noted the decline in soil fertility in his own day, *Memoirs*, Vol. II, p. 341 and n. (emphasis original).

125. Thus, while Abul Fazl speaks in glowing terms of the fertility of the *suba* of Lahore, he is far less enthusiastic about the provinces of Gujarat and Ajmer, see *Ain-i-Akbari*, ed. Blochmann, Calcutta, 1867-77, Vol. I, pp. 538, 485 and 505 respectively.

126. The *Taittiriya Samhita* makes a clear reference to the harvesting of two crops of corn in a year from the same piece of land apart from beans and sesamum; this would naturally imply crop-rotation, see S.P. Raychaudhuri, L. Gopal and B.V. Subbarayappa, 'Agriculture', in D.M. Bose, S.N. Sen and B.V. Subbarayappa, eds., *A Concise History of Science in India*, New Delhi, 1971, p. 353 (hereafter *History of Science*); P.C. Jain, *Labour in Ancient India*, pp. 35-

6. A.K. Ghosh and S.N. Sen accept the two crops but are less certain about rotation, 'Botany: Vedic and Post-Vedic period', *History of Science*, pp. 377-8. References to two crops can be found continually since the *Taittiriya Samhita*: in Megasthenes' account, Puspa Niyogi, *Contributions to the Economic History of Northern India*, Calcutta, 1962, p. 20; in Kautilya's *Arthasastra*, pp. 131-2; in the *Brhatsamhita* of the Gupta period, S.P. Raychaudhuri, et al., 'Agriculture', op. cit., p. 361; in the *Ain*, Vol. I, pp. 304-36 where all the revenue rates of Akbar's reign are mentioned for two crops—the winter and the spring.

127. Panini (c. 400 BC) refers to three annual crops, see P.C. Jain, op. cit., p. 50; *Ain*, Vol. I, p. 389 (*suba* Bengal where rice was harvested thrice), p. 473 (*suba* Khandesh where *jowar*—a millet—was similarly reaped thrice and p. 513 (*suba* Delhi). The sources that leave one in no doubt regarding the cultivation of two or three crops in a year in the same field are: *Taittiriya Samhita* and *Ain*, Vol. I, p. 389 (Bengal *suba*). The *Arthasastra*, on the other hand, suggests the use of compulsion by the state to grow a second crop on the field if the state's interest so required, p. 273.

128. Thus in the law-book of Narada (Gupta period) a tract of land that had not been cultivated for a year is defined as *ardhakhila*, Puspa Niyogi, *Contributions*, p. 21, and as *Khila* if it had been uncultivated for three years, R.S. Sharma, *Indian Feudalism*, p. 35. *Khila* is then rendered as 'fallow' by Sharma, though Niyogi prefers 'half-waste' for her *ardhakhila*. Sharma also renders *bhumicchidra* as fallow, *Indian Feudalism*, p. 36, though the context clearly points to virgin land. R.P. Kangle in fact translates *bhumicchidra* as 'land which cannot be used for agriculture because it is unsuited for it', *The Kautilya Arthasastra*, part III, Bombay, 1965, p. 174. See also Niyogi, *Contributions*, p. 69. D.C. Sircar has a section entitled 'Reclamation of Fallow Land' which would appear curious but for the fact that 'fallow' denotes virgin or deserted land to most historians of ancient India. See Sircar, *Landlordism and Tenancy*, p. 4; P. Niyogi, *Contributions*, p. 1; B.P. Mazumdar, *The Socio-Economic History of Northern India* (AD 1030-1194), Calcutta, 1960, p. 175. See also D.C. Sircar, *Indian Epigraphical Glossary*, Delhi, 1966, for *Khila* (rendered: uncultivated land, fallow land), p. 157 and *Khila-Ksetra* (rendered: fallow land) p. 157. To S.P. Raychaudhuri it appears that the system of fallowing was known in the age of the *Yajurveda*, though, unluckily, he says nothing more about it, in Raychaudhuri, ed., *Agriculture in Ancient India*, New Delhi, 1964, p. 81. However, even some of the later works dealing exclusively or partly with agricultural practices make no mention of the genuine fallow. See, for example, the *Arthasastra*, the *Krsi-Parasara*, ed. and tr. G.P. Majumdar and S.C. Banerji, Calcutta, 1960, and Sarngadhara, *Upavana-Vinoda*, ed. and tr. G.P. Majumdar, Calcutta, 1936. The estimates of the date of *Krsi-Parasara* vary widely between 1300 BC, the post-Vedic but pre-Christian era, and between AD 100 and 600; see S.P. Raychaudhuri, 'Land Classification in Ancient India', *Indian Journal of the History of Science*, Vol. I, No. 2, Nov. 1966,

p. 107; A.K. Ghosh and S.N. Sen, 'Botany: Vedic and Post-Vedic Period', *History of Science*, p. 379, and G.P. Majumdar, 'Introduction', *Krsi-Parasara*, p. vi, respectively. Some of the recent secondary works also discuss the whole range of agricultural operations in ancient India but do not refer to fallow; see, for example, B.N.S. Yadava, *Society and Culture*, pp. 256-62. If modern historians have used the term 'fallow' for virgin or deserted lands, or for the lea, it is obviously because the genuine fallow hardly existed.

129. William Tennant, *Indian Recreations; consisting chiefly of strictures on the Domestic and Rural Economy of the Mahomedans and Hindoos*, Vol. II, Edinburgh, 1804, p. 16.

130. *Ain*, Vol. I, p. 297. This category is named *parauti*. However, the third category, *chachar*, is so classified when it falls out of cultivation 'owing to excessive rain or inundation', ibid., p. 301; and the last, *banjar*, land when it loses its productive capacity through inundation, ibid. Thus, barring *parauti*, the forced exclusion from cultivation of the other categories of land is due to circumstances extraneous to the cycle of production. Indeed, the first class of land, *polaj*, is that which is never allowed to lie uncultivated, ibid., p. 297 and the other lands are to be slowly encouraged to develop into the *polaj* class, by means of progressive taxation keeping pace with the diminishing period of their non-cultivation, ibid., pp. 301-2.

131. *Risala-i Ziraat*, Edinburgh University Library, Persian MS. No. 144, fols. 6b-7a.

132. Irfan Habib, *Agrarian System*, p. 23 and n. Irfan Habib's source speaks of the cutomary practice in Gorakhpur, eastern U.P., of reclamation of new land once the old soil had spent its fertility. The period is early nineteenth century. Mufti Ghulam Hazart, the informant, however, makes it a point to highlight the low fertility of the region where the practice prevailed.

133. Irfan Habib suggests the following logic: Since in Mughal times between one-half and three-quarters of the land was cultivated compared to the area of such land at the beginning of the twentieth century, keeping in view regional variations, the medieval Indian peasant should have had at his disposal extensive wastelands and forests and therefore more cattle and draught animals. He could also have burnt firewood and used animal dung for manure. See Irfan Habib, *Agrarian System*, pp. 53-4, 55-6, 116, and 'Potentialities of Capitalistic Development in the Economy of Mughal India', *Enquiry*, new series, Vol. III, No. 3, Winter 1971, p. 4. If this were so of medieval India, it should have been truer of the earlier period.

134. A.K. Ghosh and S.N. Sen appear to be doubtful, 'Botany: Vedic and Post-Vedic Period', *History of Science*, p. 377.

135. Page 132.

136. B.N.S. Yadava, *Society and Culture*, p. 257.

137. Pages 74, 78.

138. Pages 81-3.

139. *Arthasastra*, p. 132.

140. P.C. Jain, op. cit., pp. 60–1.
141. B.B. Lal. 'Perhaps the Earliest Ploughed Field So Far Excavated Anywhere in the World', *Purattatva*, No. 4, 1970–1, pp. 1-3. Romila Thapar drew my attention to this evidence, for which I am extremely grateful.
142. P.C. Jain, op. cit., pp. 32, 34; S.P. Raychaudhuri, et al., 'Agriculture', *History of Science*, p. 352; R.S. Sharma, *Light on Early Indian Society*, pp. 55-6.
143. The *Atharvaveda* refers to ploughs driven by six and twelve oxen, P.C. Jain, op. cit., p. 35. There are references to the yoking of 6, 8, 12 and even 24 oxen to the plough, R.S. Sharma, *Light on Early Indian Society*, p. 57. The *Krsi-Parasara* in a colourful verse suggests that 'a plough is said to have eight bulls, six for the ordinary use, four for the cruel and two for the cow-killers', p. 73. Abul Fazl implies that a peasant having four oxen for his plough was too poor to be taxed, *Ain*, Vol. I, 287.

    The regional variation in the shape of the plough as used today has been recorded by Jaya Datta Gupta and B.N. Saraswati, 'Ploughs and Husking Implements', in *Peasant Life in India*, Memoir No. 8, Anthropological Survey of India, Calcutta, 1961, pp. 25-9. The regional variation in the weight of the plough was noted by N.G. Mukherji, *Handbook of Indian Agriculture*, Calcutta, 1915, pp. 93 and 99 where the ploughs of Bengal and Bundelkhand are respectively estimated at 1.25 and 3.5 maunds. It is perhaps not unreasonable to assume that these variations are a legacy of the distant past.

    Panini divides agriculturists into three classes according to the type of plough they used and whether the plough belonged to them or not, P.C. Jain, op. cit., pp. 48-9.
144. Elliot, *Memoirs*, Vol. II, pp. 340-1.
145. This was the conclusion reached by the Royal Commission on Agriculture in India, *Report*, London, 1928, pp. 110-12, cited in Irfan Habib, *Agrarian System*, p. 24 n.
146. Elliot, *Memoirs*, p. 340 n.
147. S.P. Raychaudhuri, et al., 'Agriculture', *History of Science*, p. 352.
148. D.R. Chanana, 'The Spread of Agriculture in the Ganges Valley', *Contributions to Indian Economic History*, No. 2, 1963, p. 115 n. The Pali texts also refer to the spade, P.C. Jain, op. cit., p. 43.
149. S.P. Raychaudhuri et al., 'Agriculture', *History of Science*, p. 360.
150. Op. cit., pp. 74-5.
151. R.S. Sharma, *Light on Early Indian Society*, pp. 57, 60-1.
152. Elliot, *Memoirs*, Vol. II, pp. 341-2.
153. According to Panini, the field was at times ploughed twice and at others thrice. P.C. Jain, op. cit., p. 49; Kautilya suggested ploughing the field 'often', *Arthasastra*, p. 129; The *Krsi-Parasara* recommends five ploughings for abundant crops, p. 77.
154. Grierson, *Bihar Peasant Life*, 2nd edn., Patna, 1926, p. 172, cited in A.K. Chaudhuri, *Early Medieval Village in Northern-Eastern India (AD 600-1200)*, Calcutta, 1971, pp. 153-4.

155. *Krsi-Parasara*, p. 82.
156. Irfan Habib, *Agrarian System*, p. 26; also B.N.S. Yadava, *Society and Culture*, p. 257.
157. *Krsi-Parasara*, pp. 80, 81.
158. The *Vrksayurveda*, also attributed to Parasara, author of *Krsi-Parasara*, deals with the treatment of plants, as the title suggests, A.K. Ghosh and S.N. Sen, op. cit., p. 379.
159. S.P. Raychaudhuri et al., 'Agriculture', op. cit., pp. 353-4.
160. Page 131.
161. Ibid.
162. R.P. Kangle, op. cit., p. 174.
163. Irfan Habib, 'Presidential Address', *Proceedings of Indian History Congress*, 31st Session, Varanasi, 1969, pp. 149-55.
164. *Ain*, Vol. I, p. 538.
165. Zia ud-din Barani, *Tarikh-i Firuz Shahi*, ed. Saiyad Ahmad Khan, Calcutta, 1862, pp. 367-71; Shams-i Siraj Afif, *Tarikh-i Firuz Shahi*, ed. M. Wilayat Hussain, Calcutta, 1888-91, p. 127.
166. Sujan Rai Bhandari, *Khulasat al-Tawarikh*, ed. Zafar Hasan, Delhi, 1918, pp. 29-30, 36-7.
167. Baudhayana suggests a holding of six *nivartanas* for the purpose, R.S. Sharma, *Light on Early Indian Society*, p. 62. A *nivartana*, according to Sharma, comprised roughly an acre and a half, ibid., p. 73. Puspa Niyogi on the other hand suggests, on the basis of a longish discussion with many impressive details, that a *nivartana* was equal to 40,000 cubits, *Contributions*, p. 97 and n. That would bring it close to 2.3 acres.
168. The Malabar Kannamkar, for example, tied to the land and working for the *janmi* landowners, could come near the category of serfs.
169. R.S. Sharma: 'On the whole while a great part of the time and energy of European peasants was consumed by their work on their master's fields the peasantry in India gave most of their time to their own fields, of the produce of which a considerable share went to the holders of the grants and other intermediaries; on the contrary, the number of free peasantry seems to have been far greater', *Indian Feudalism*, p. 75; also *Light on Early Indian Society*, p. 83. B.N.S. Yadava: 'Thus the Sudra peasants cannot be equated with the unfree serf of Medieval Europe', in D.C. Sircar, ed., *Land System and Feudalism*, p. 94; also *Society and Culture*, p. 171 and 'Immobility and Subjection', op. cit., p. 25.
170. The State farms of the Mauryas were cultivated by slaves, amongst others, *Arthasastra*, p. 129; artisans were enslaved by the Sultanate of Delhi during the thirteenth and fourteenth centuries, Zia ud-din Barani, *Tarikh-i Firuz Shahi*, pp. 313-14. See also Irfan Habib, 'Economic History of the Delhi Sultanate—An Essay in Interpretation', *Indian Historical Review*, Vol. IV, No. 2, Jan. 1978, pp. 292-4, 297.
171. R.S. Sharma, *Indian Feudalism*, pp. 56, 118-24. In a recent article Sharma

describes the Indian peasants as having been reduced to the position of 'semi-serfs as a result of numerous impositions made on them', 'Indian Feudalism Retouched', op. cit., p. 327.

172. Irfan Habib, *Agrarian System*, pp. 115-16, 118; 'Economic History of the Delhi Sultanate', p. 298. Irfan Habib does not consider forced labour an important element in this situation.
173. Page 46.
174. Page 197.
175. Page 273.
176. Cited in B.P. Mazumdar, op. cit., p. 171.
177. *Arthasastra*, p. 197.
178. R.S. Sharma, *Indian Feudalism*, pp. 149-50.
179. Ali Muhammad Khan, *Mirat-i Ahmadi*, pp. 268-72.
180. Ibid., article III.
181. Ibid., articles XIII and XVI.
182. Zafarul Islam reasonably questions Irfan Habib's suspicion of the testimony of the *firman*. While Irfan Habib thought the order had little relevance to the agrarian conditions in India for it was expressly drafted to set out the laws of the Shariat, *Agrarian System*, p. 113, Zafarul Islam, comparing its provisions with those of Islamic law, suggests its specific late seventeenth century relevance to India, 'Aurangzeb's Farman on Land Tax—An Analysis in the Light of the Fatawa-i-Alamgiri', *Islamic Culture*, Vol. 52, No. 2, April 1978, pp. 117-26. It is possible to trace these provisions back to the *Arthasastra* and to late Hindu law-books.
183. Aurangzeb's *firman* to Muhammad Hashim, article II.
184. Besides the *firman* to Muhammad Hashim, article II, B.R. Grover has brought to light pieces of evidence from Shah Jahan's reign wherein the Desais were charged with resettling in their original homes tenants who had migrated to some other villages, 'The Position of the Desai in the Pargana Administration of Subah Gujarat under the Mughals', *Proceedings of Indian History Congress*, 24th Session, Delhi, 1961, p. 152. Grover's evidence comes from some Persian documents located in Paris. The Desais, however, used persuasion and reassurance rather than coercion in carrying out their duties; but then the line between the two is very thin.
185. *Arthasastra*, p. 213; P.C. Jain, op. cit., pp. 236-9 for regulation of wage-payments by law-giver of the Gupta age; Irfan Habib, *Agrarian System*, p. 120. For sale of land, see *Arthasastra*, p. 197; D.C. Sircar, *Land System and Feudalism*, p. 12; R.S. Sharma, *Indian Feudalism*, pp. 36, 149; B.R. Grover, 'Nature of Dehat-i-Talluqa (Zamindari villages) and the Evolution of the Taaluqdari System During the Mughal Age', *I.E.S.H.R*, Vol. II, Nos. 2 and 3, April and July 1965, p. 261.
186. R.S. Sharma, 'Indian Feudalism Retouched', p. 329: 'In fact even without compulsion peasants and artisans had no option but to stick to the village

for the set up being the same everywhere, migration to another village could not materially change the situation.' B.N.S. Yadava stresses the role of ideology more than of law in enforcing immobility, *Society and Culture,* p. 166.

187. R.S. Sharma and B.N.S. Yadava have merely *inferred* that the state's grant of villages, enumerating a number of rights transferred to the intermediaries, should have led to the creation of dependence of the peasants on them. This is by no means certain. Villages, according to Sharma's own evidence, were donated even by private individuals, *Indian Feudalism*, p. 61; these individuals were clearly in no position to change class relations in the countryside. As D.D. Kosambi remarks with characteristic perception, 'The recipients of a whole village gained at most the rights the state would normally claim. That is, they collected the taxes already fixed by usage. No portion of the tax was to be passed on to the state or any state official, but the donee had not the right to increase such taxes, nor any property rights over land and cattle', *An Introduction,* p. 321. At any rate the creation of peasant's dependence implies changes in the processes and relations of production and these can hardly be brought about by administrative fiat.

188. D.D. Kosambi, *An Introduction*, p. 323; Irfan Habib, *Agrarian System,* p. 115; S. Nurul Hasan, *Thoughts*, p. 3.

189. Historians, too numerous to be referred to here, have discussed the question of landownership confining the options by and large to the State and the peasant. Communal ownership is definitively ruled out by all. Various combinations of the State's and the peasant's rights have also been suggested. Thus D.C. Sircar urges that it was the king who in theory owned the land and the cultivators were his tenants. However, they held permanent occupancy rights and the king was not expected to evict them, *Landlordism and Tenancy*, pp. 1-3. B.N.S. Yadava believes that royal ownership and private individual ownership of land were not mutually exclusive in the context of the land system of the twelfth century, *Society and Culture*, p. 254. For medieval India, B.R. Grover has strongly argued in favour of peasant-proprietorship of land, 'Nature of Land-Rights in Mughal India', *I.E.S.H.R.*, Vol. I, No. 1, 1963, pp. 2-5; 'Dehat-i-Taaluqa', pp. 261-2. Irfan Habib, on the other hand, while accepting the notion of private property in land, qualifies it with the absence of the right to free alienation etc., as we have noted earlier. Noman A. Siddiqi goes to the extent of denying to the peasants the right to sell or mortgage land, *Land Revenue Administration under the Mughals*, Bombay, 1970, pp. 11, 16.

190. P.C. Jain, op. cit., pp. 44-5.

191. Page 129.

192. R.S. Sharma, *Indian Feudalism*, pp. 61-3. Elsewhere, Sharma remarks of the post-Gupta period: 'Perhaps the major portion of land continued to be in the possession of free peasants, who paid revenue directly to the State', *Light on Early Indian Society*, p. 83. Sharma, of course, appears to derive his

definition of free peasantry from Fa-hsein who states that 'only those who till the king's land pay a land tax' and that they are free to go and stay as they please, ibid.

193. *Arthasastra*, p. 45.
194. Manu, cited in P.C. Jain. op. cit., p. 51.
195. Irfan Habib, 'Jatts of Punjab and Sind', in Harbans Singh and N.G. Barrier, eds., *Essays in Honour of Dr Ganda Singh*, Patiala, 1976, pp. 92-103.
196. *Ain*, Vol. I, p. 199.
197. Ibid., pp. 285-6.
198. Abdul Qudir Badauni, *Muntakhab ut-Tawarikh*, Vol. II, Bib. Ind., p. 189.
199. B.R. Grover, 'Dehat-i-Taalluqa', p. 262.
200. See the 'Yaddasht-i-izafa-i-dehat' (memorandum regarding newly settled villages) of Shah Jahan's time in Ziauddin Ahmed Shakeb, ed., *Mughal Archives*, Vol. I, Hyderabad, 1977, p. 295; also pp. 36-45. The fact that such memoranda were to be submitted enumerating the number and location of newly settled villages suggests that the official injunction to extend cultivation had to be taken seriously.
201. Article V: 'whoever turns (wasteland) into cultivable land should be recognized as its owner (malik) and should not be deprived (of land)'.
202. Irfan Habib, *Agrarian System*, pp. 121-2.
203. R.S. Sharma, *Indian Feudalism*, p. 75; R.S. Sharma, *Light on Early Indian Society*, p. 83; B.N.S. Yadava, *Society and Culture*, p. 171; S. Nurul Hasan, *Thoughts*, p. 18.
204. P.C. Jain, op. cit., p. 43.
205. *Arthasastra*, p. 131.
206. Op. cit., p. 174.
207. B.N.S. Yadava, *Society and Culture*, pp. 297-8.
208. Puspa Niyogi, *Contributions*, p. 180.
209. D.D. Kosambi, *An Introduction*, p. 365; D.C. Sircar, *Land System and Feudalism*, p. 21. For Balban's similar advice see Zia ud-din Barani, op. cit., pp. 100-1.
210. Sircar, *Landlordism and Tenancy*, pp. 66-79; Yadava, *Society and Culture*, pp. 288-301.
211. *Society and Culture*, p. 301.
212. Irfan Habib, 'Potentialities of Capitalistic Development' pp. 11-12, 27; *Agrarian System*, pp. 192-6. Irfan Habib suggests a major new argument that the Delhi Sultanate created 'an entirely new kind of agrarian taxation in India. Once implanted, the single massive land-tax was to last in India till practically the first half of this century. The State would henceforth regularly claim the bulk of the peasants' surplus . . .', 'Economic History of the Delhi Sultanate', p. 297. The bulk of the surplus was, indeed, claimed by the Sultans, but in view of the evidence available for the pre-Sultanate period, particularly for the eleventh and twelfth centuries, we need really to be more certain whether they were doing anything unprecedented.

213. Even if we took only foodgrains into account, the increase in their number over the centuries has been very impressive. Thus, while barley, wheat and rice are referred to in the Vedic literature, R.S. Sharma, *Light on Early Indian Society*, pp. 56, 58, the *Arthasastra* enumerates many crops, some of which remain unidentified, and the number of grains comes to about ten, p. 131. A twelfth-century work refers to twenty-four kinds of food-grains, P. Niyogi, *Contributions*, pp. 23-4. The *Ain* has revenue-rates against twenty-nine varieties of grains and fourteen vegetables, Vol. I, pp. 298-301. Even of the same grain, a large number of varieties gradually began to be cultivated. We are informed that around the twelfth century fifty varieties of rice were grown in Bengal, B.N.S. Yadava, *Society and Culture*, p. 258. Abul Fazl makes nearly the same point when he remarks that if a single grain of each kind of Bengal rice were collected, a large vase would be filled up, *Ain*, Vol. I, p. 389.

214. The water-wheel might have had a three-rather than a two-stage history which Irfan Habib has so painstakingly reconstructed. The *arghatta* (or the noria) had buckets attached to its rim and was thus functional only on surface water—in a pool or on the bank of a river. It also had to be manually operated. The fully developed Persian wheel, on the other hand, was an animal-powered, geared machine which collected water from a well in its bucket chain attached to the rim. A technologically intermediate stage appears to have consisted of the water-wheel with a bucket chain but without the gear. It was manually operated and drew water from wells. A three-stage history of the water-wheel, if valid, should suggest not only a longer period of development of this irrigation device but also a wider social participation in the process of its development, for a larger number of peasants could perhaps afford the wheel available in a wider range. The consequent rise in the productivity of land should also have had its impact on the process of state-formation between the seventh-eighth and the fourteenth century. The establishment of a highly centralized state-structure, collecting at times as much as a half of the peasants' produce as revenue in the thirteenth and early fourteenth century, was perhaps not an act of conquest but the culmination of a process that started during the seventh century or thereabout. The first to notice the rise in productivity, owing to the spread of irrigation, were the village potentates and they might also have been the first to demand a greater amount of the peasants' produce in revenue. The state would take its own time to wake up to this new reality; but once it did, it introduced an element of systematization in the appropriation of the peasants' increased surplus, through a relatively efficient, and highly centralized administrative apparatus. The establishment of this state can thus be seen as the culmination of a process that developed from the bottom upwards rather than from top downwards.

Clearly, this is still the very initial outline of a hypothesis and much research is called for to arrive at a conclusion.

215. Irfan Habib, *Agrarian System*, p. 257. Irfan Habib makes this remark in the context of medieval India, but this would as well be true of the earlier period irrespective of direct collection of revenue by the state-officials or on its behalf by assignees.

216. Bhimsen, a late seventeenth-century chronicler, grasped this point in his description of Tanjore: in the whole world nowhere else are there so many temples, he says. The cause of the building of these temples he assigns to the very high fertility of land—producing four crops a year—and the abysmal standard of peasants' subsistence which he describes in detail and 'without exaggeration'. Consequently, 'a large revenue is raised, the amount of which is known only to the Recording Angel', *Nuskha-i Dilkusha*, tr. Jadu Nath Sarkar, Bombay, 1972, pp. 193-4.

217. In the *Mahabharata*, Bhisma says, 'If the king disregards agriculturists, they become lost to him, and abandoning his dominions betake themselves to the woods', cited in P.C. Jain, op. cit., p. 54; in the eleventh century Ksemendra bemoans the fact that the poor, with malice towards the property of the rich, were turning violent, B.N.S. Yadava, 'Problem of Interaction between Socio-economic Classes in the Early Medieval Complex', *Indian Historical Review*, Vol. III, No. 1, July 1976, p. 55; the Kaivarttas in east Bengal took to arms to resist the increasing state oppression in the last years of the eleventh century, R.S. Sharma, *Indian Feudalism*, p. 268; the peasantry of Doab revolted in the second quarter of the fourteenth century against the state's excessive exactions, Zia ud-din Barani, op. cit., pp. 472-3; for the documentation of the widespread peasant rebellions of the second half of the seventeenth century, see Irfan Habib, *Agrarian System*, pp. 330-51.

218. It has been argued that Indian feudalism comes closest to European feudalism of the twelfth century, B.N.S. Yadava, *Society and Culture*, p. 171. Quite apart from the validity of this comparison in terms of historical evidence which is by no means conclusive, even if such evidence were conceded, a momentary convergence between two social systems following independent paths of historical development can hardly justify the conclusion that they were both marked by the same characteristics.

219. The major part of Muzaffar Alam, *The Crisis of Empire in Mughal North India: Awadh and the Punjab, 1707-1748*, Delhi, 1986, demonstrates the resurgence of zamindars in the debris of the Empire, even as Alam locates unfulfilled potential change in this resurgence. See also Shaukat Ullah Khan, 'Zamindars in the Mughal *Subah* of Gujarat during the first half of the Eighteenth Century', unpublished doctoral thesis, Jawaharlal Nehru University, 1993.

220. For a persuasive argument regarding the absence of any potential for capitalist development in the Mughal economy, see Irfan Habib, 'Potentialities of Capitalistic Development'.

221. Irfan Habib vehemently questions the validity of the notion of the Asiatic mode of production; see his 'Problems of Marxist Historical Analysis', *Enquiry*, n.s., Vol. VIII, No. 2, Monsoon 1969, pp. 52-67. For a recent re-

statement of the rejection of this notion see Bipan Chandra, 'Karl Marx, His Theories of Asian Societies and Colonial Rule' (mimeo). Unfortunately, in Bipan Chandra's discussion of ancient and medieval Indian history there is hardly a statement that can go uncontested. Marian Sawer has, in her *Marxism and the Question of the Asiatic Mode of Production*, referred to earlier, made a very interesting study of the history of this concept and the recent political context in which it has been discussed.

222. R.A.L.H. Gunawardana suggests that Marx had at some point abandoned the notion of the absence of private property in land in India, 'The Analysis of Pre-Colonial Social Formations in Asia in the Writings of Karl Marx', *Indian Historical Review*, Vol. II, No. 2, Jan. 1976, pp. 365-88. Gunawardana has in this connection drawn attention to evidence hitherto overlooked by historians. It remains true, however, that this evidence belongs to the period between 1853 and 1858; on the other hand in his writings of the latter phase of this period and afterwards Marx continued to insist on the absence of private property in land in that he spoke of its communal ownership: *Grundrisse*, tr. Martin Nicolaus, London, 1973, pp. 472-3; *A Contribution to the Critique of Political Economy*, Moscow, 1970, p. 33 n. (where Marx says that 'primitive communal property . . . is still in existence in India'); *Capital*, Vol. I, pp. 357-8.
223. 'Problems of Marxist Historical Analysis'.
224. 'Economic History of Delhi Sultanate', p. 298.
225. Whenever we discuss the question of feudalism in any country and in any period, medieval Western Europe inevitably provides the point of reference for such a discussion, whatever be our answer to this question. One can, of course, see the justice of comparing the history of other countries with that of Western Europe in modern times for it was, after all, in Western Europe that capitalism arose which was later to encompass the whole world; but it is difficult to see the logic of such a comparison in the ancient and medieval periods when it might only persuade us to ask questions which have so little relevance to our history.

It is possible, of course, to speak of regional variations of feualism. One could thus argue in favour of an Indian feudalism, a Chinese feudalism, a West Asian feudalism, etc., apart from the West European and the Japanese one. However, I visualize two reservations with respect to this argument. First, the use of a common denominator for the whole range of regionally and temporally variant socio-economic systems could hardly be justified unless one could establish a fundamental similarity underlying these variations—a similarity that was precisely defined. Second, quite apart from the fact that feudalism as a category achieves universality only through the looseness of its definition, the very search for a universal category, equally applicable to different medieval regions, is based on the assumption that the medieval world was one world sharing a common socio-economic system. We thus attribute to the medieval world characteristics which more appropriately belong to the nineteenth and twentieth centuries.

How Feudal was Indian Feudalism?

R.S. Sharma

Several scholars have questioned the use of the term feudalism to characterize the early medieval socio-economic formation in India.[1] But the points raised by Harbans Mukhia[2] deserve serious attention. He rightly suggests that unlike capitalism, feudalism is not a universal phenomenon. Yet in our view tribalism, the stone age, the metal age, and the advent of a food-producing economy are universal phenomena. They do indicate some laws conditioning the process and pattern of change.

Tribalism may continue or be followed by different forms of state and class society, but it appears universally. Tribal society has many variations. It can be connected with any of the modes of subsistence such as cattle pastoralism, other types of pastoralism, hoe agriculture, plough agriculture, and so on. The advent of agriculture requires cooperation and settlement at one place, and creates a lasting base for the tribal set-up. Many tribal societies practise shifting cultivation or swidden cultivation. But an advanced type of agriculture produces substantial surplus and creates dents in tribal homogeneity. Conditions appear for the rise of classes based on status and wealth and above all on the large-scale exploitation of the bulk of the kinsmen by a few people on top. In such a situation the tribal system becomes heavily corroded.

Similarly, although the tribal society is organized on the principle of kinship, this organization could have large variations. Some form of organization, inherited from the band society, would be developed further in the tribal stage. Cooperation in production efforts would be needed; division of labour would be required. But this could be on a matriarchal basis, patriarchal basis, on the basis of a combination of the two, and in fact could rest on an organization based on all kinds of kinship combinations and permutations. Marriage practices and laws of 'property' inheritance might differ from one tribal society to another, and may differ even in the same tribe. But, in spite of these variations, tribal society has been found on a universal scale. Therefore the concept of tribe is useful even for the understanding of social formations known from written texts.

It is not necessary to posit diffusion of tribal society although this may have taken place in certain cases. Although feudalism does not seem to be as universal as tribalism, in the Old World it was undoubtedly more widespread than the slave system. The concept of peasant society is still in a nebulous state. But if peasant society means a system in which the orders of priests and warriors live on the surplus produced by peasants and augmented by the activities of the artisans, such a society existed in a good part of the Old World. Tribalism, peasant society or slave system could originate due to internal or external factors, or both. Similarly it is not necessary to think in terms of the diffusion of the feudal system, although this happened in certain cases. For instance, Norman feudalism in England was a result of the Norman conquest.

THE ESSENCE OF FEUDALISM

Just as there could be enormous variations in tribal society so also there could be enormous variations in the nature of feudal societies. It is rightly stated by Marx that feudalism 'assumes different aspects, and runs through its various phases in different orders of succession'.[3] But certain universals remain the same. This is admitted even by critics of Indian feudalism who think of the variants of feudalism.[4] Feudalism has to be seen as a mode of the distribution of the means of production and of the appropriation of the surplus. It may have certain broad universal features and it may have certain traits typical of a territory. Obviously land and agricultural products play a decisive role in pre-capitalist class societies, but the specific situation in relation to land distribution and the appropriation of agricultural products will differ from region to region. No one could argue that what developed in pre-capitalist Western Europe was found in India and elsewhere. Historical laws, as far as they are known, do not work in this manner, but neither could one say that feudalism was the monopoly of Western Europe. It is not possible to have any neat, cut and dried formula about feudalism. The utmost that one could say about the universals of feudalism would be largely on the lines of Marc Bloch and E.K. Kosminsky.[5] Feudalism appears in a predominantly agrarian economy which is characterized by a class of landlords and a class of servile peasantry. In this system the landlords extract surplus through social, religious or political methods, which are called extra-economic. This seems to be more or less the current Marxist view of feudalism, which considers serfdom, 'scalar property' and 'parcellized sovereignty' as features of the West European version of the feudal system. The lord-peasant relationship is the core of the matter, and the exploitation of the estate by its owner, controller, enjoyer or beneficiary is its essential ingredient.

With these minimum universals, feudalism may have several variations. The particularities of the system in some West European countries do not apply to the various types of feudalism found in other areas. For example, evidence for peasant struggles against landlords in other countries has not been produced in sufficient degree. Similarly, artisan and capitalist growth within the womb of feudalism seems to be typical of the West European situation where agricultural growth and substantial commodity production created major structural contradictions. The nature of religious beneficiaries, who grabbed a major portion of land, also differed from country to country. Thus the Church was a great landlord in Portugal. Buddhist and Confucian establishments controlled land in Korea. Buddhist monasteries were also important in eastern India. Temples emerged as estates in south India, and many brahmanas enjoyed a similar position in the upper and middle Gangetic basins, central India, the Deccan, and Assam. Non-religious landed intermediaries also appear in different forms in different parts of India and outside the country. In certain parts of the country, for example in Orissa, we find tribal chiefs being elevated to the position of landlords. In other parts many administrative officials enjoyed land taxes from the peasants. But in spite of all these variations the basic factor, namely the presence of a controlling class of landlords and a subject peasantry, remained the same at least in early medieval times.

Again the degree of the servility of the peasants to the landlords might differ from region to region; so also the composition of the cultivating class. The development of agriculture, handicrafts, commodity production, trade and commerce and of urbanization could create conditions for differentiation in the ranks of the peasantry. Those peasants who produce a little over and above their subsistence needs might buy their freedom by payment of money in lieu of labour service provided such a practice was favoured by the state and provided a reasonable extent of market economy was available. Several peasants might be reduced to a state of further penury and rich peasants might grow at their expense. But where such developments do not appear a more or less homogeneous peasantry might continue. However, differences in the techniques of farming and the nature of the soil might affect the agricultural yield and create variations.

Similarly, peasants might be compelled to work as serfs on landlords' farms in addition to working on their own farms. This was a common practice in Western Europe. But serfdom should not be considered to be identical with feudalism.[6] It was, after all, a form of servility which kept the peasant tied to the soil and made him work on the farm of his lord. Those peasants who were compelled to pay heavy rents in cash and kind to the landlords or required to provide rent as well as labour were as servile as those who supplied only labour. It also makes some difference to his servility if a peasant has to bear allegiance only to the landlord. If he has to be loyal to both the state and the landlord then it could be either a case of double servility or divided loyalty. But the fundamental point is the subjection of the peasantry, and that subjection is found in all the possible situations to which we have referred earlier. There is no doubt that this subjection is a characteristic of early medieval Indian social structure.

It is argued by Mukhia that the peasant in medieval India enjoyed autonomy of production because he had 'complete' control over the means of production.[7] But what is the significance of owning the means of production? Does it signify an ability to use the fruits of production? Do the fruits stay with the peasant or are these substantially appropriated by the landlord? How does this appropriation become possible? What is the mechanism that enables the landlord to appropriate the surplus, a part of that fruit? Is it merely because of his control over the means of production or because of his coercive power? Or is it extracted through an ideological weapon such as the peasant's belief that he is duty bound to pay? The latter ideology, that the landlords are the parents of the peasants,[8] is reminiscent of the tribal outlook. This idea may have been further fostered by the priestly landlords in medieval times. At present we will try not to answer all of these questions but concentrate upon the problem of the distribution of the resources of production in early medieval India

THE DISTRIBUTION OF RESOURCES IN EARLY MEDIEVAL INDIA

Obviously land was the primary means of production. But the real difficulty in understanding the distribution of land arises when we think in terms of exclusive control over land by one party or another. It should be made clear that in early medieval times in the same piece of land the peasant held inferior rights and the landlords held superior rights. One may possess land, labour, oxen, other animals and agricultural implements. But we have to find out how effective is this 'control' over the means of production. Do other conditions such as taxes, forced labour, constant interference by ever-present on-the-spot beneficiaries make the peasant's control really operational? Obviously nobody would kill a hen that lays eggs. So peasants would be allowed to stay alive. But that should not be understood as their having effective control over the means of production.

In fact, land grants leave hardly any doubt that the landlords enjoyed a good measure of general control in the means of production. Why did the landlords claim various types of rents from the peasants and how could they collect their demands? Clearly they did so on the strength of royal charters which conferred on them the villages or pieces of land or various types of taxes. Why did the king claim taxes? Formerly the king claimed taxes on the ground that he afforded protection to the people. In early medieval law-books he claimed taxes on the ground that he was the owner of the land.[9] Numerous epithets indicate that the king was the owner of the land in early medieval times.[10] By the charter he delegated this royal authority to the beneficiary, and on this strength the beneficiary claimed taxes. The king was called *bhumidah*, giver of land. It was repeatedly said that the merit of giving land accrues to him who possesses it.[11]

Generally the early charters give the beneficiary usufructuary rights. But the later charters grant such concessions as render the beneficiary the *de facto* owner of the village land. The donated village/villages constitute his estate. For example, the beneficiary is entitled to collect taxes, all kinds of income, all kinds of occasional taxes, and this 'all' (*sarva*)[12] is never specified. Similarly he is entitled to collect proper and improper taxes,[13] fixed and not fixed taxes,[14] and at the end of the list of the taxes the term et cetera (*adi, adikam*)[15] is used. All this adds enormously to the power of the beneficiary. These extraordinary provisions could serve as a self-regulating mechanism as and when production increased,[16] but they could also interfere with the expansion of production. Some provisions clearly created the superior rights of the beneficiary in the land of the peasants. For example, the land charters of Madhya Pradesh, northern Maharashtra, Konkan and Gujarat in Gupta and post-Gupta times empower the beneficiary to evict the old peasants and introduce new ones; he could assign lands to others. Such concessions leave no doubt that the beneficiary was armed with superior rights in land, which of course was in actual occupation of the cultivator. Most grants after the seventh century AD give away the village along with low land, fertile land, water reservoirs, all kinds of trees and bushes, pathways and pasture grounds. In eastern India grants, the village was granted along with mango trees, *mahua* (*Bassia datifolia*) trees and jack-fruit trees and various other agrarian resources. Cotton, hemp, coconut and arecanut trees are also given away in grants, but this happens mostly after the tenth century when cash crops assume importance. Such provisions connect agrarian production directly with the beneficiary and, more importantly, transfer almost all communal agrarian resources to him. If a peasant does not have free access to various agrarian resources his autonomy in production is substantially crippled. Only a free exercise of the agrarian rights mentioned above can make his unit effective in production. Until recent times the powerful landlords barred and blocked the access of the weak and helpless peasants to such rights and could make their life impossible. Of course the caste system helped this process. The untouchables had no access to public tanks, wells, etc. Even if they possessed their bits of land, how could they function independently in production?

Most charters ask the peasants to carry out the orders of the beneficiaries.[17] These orders may relate not only to the payment of taxes which will be concerned with the fruits of production, but also to the means and processes of production. In a way the blanket authority to extract obedience places the peasant at the beck and call of the beneficiary. It implies general control over the labour power of the peasants, and undoubtedly labour is an essential ingredient of the means of production. This labour may be used either in the fields cultivated by the peasant or in those directly managed by the beneficiary. The beneficiaries may insist on having certain types of produce for their ostentatious and unproductive consumption, and with all the seigniorial rights that they possess they can compel the peasants to produce those cereals or cash crops which they need.

We may also note that the law-books of Yajnavalkya, Brhaspati and Vyasa specify four-graded stages of land rights in the same piece of land. Thus we hear of *mahipati, ksetrasvamin, karsaka* and the sub-tenant or leaseholder.[18] It is important that the medieval jurists understood *svamitva* in the sense of ownership and *svata* in the sense of property, and this was considered to be a significant distinction in Hindu law.[19] The *svamin* therefore could be equated with the landed beneficiary and the *karsaka* or the *ksetrika* with the rent-paying tenant peasant. Multiple, hierarchical rights and interests in land, which was the chief means of production, can be inferred even from Gupta land sale transactions. These transactions mention the interest not only of the king but also of the local administrative body (*adhikarana*) dominated by big men; we also hear of the beneficiaries and of the rights of the occupant of the plot.[20] Of course in several Gupta transactions no occupant is mentioned, and it further appears that money for the purchases of the land is paid not only to the *adhikarana* but also probably to the occupant. These typical land transactions are found in Bangladesh. But in the grant system which became widespread in post-Gupta times the local *adhikarana* disappeared, and was generally not consulted in matters of land grants.

Hierarchical control over land was created by large-scale subinfeudation, especially from the eighth century onwards.[21] Subinfeudation gave rise to graded types of landlords, different from the actual tillers of the soil. Such a process seems to be in line with a significant generalization made by Marx about feudalism. According to him, 'feudal production is characterized by division of soil amongst the greatest possible number of subfeudatories'.[22]

The peasantry was divested more and more of its homogeneous and egalitarian character. Many indications of unequal distribution of land in the village are available. We hear not only of brahmanas but also of the chief brahmana, *mahattama, uttama, krsivala, karsaka, ksetrakara, kutumbin* and *karuka*, land-endowed brahmanas and *agraharas*. We also hear of *ksudra prakrti* or petty peasants, not to speak of Meda, Andhra and *candala*. It is obvious that certain people in the villages had a greater share in the sources of production and apparently possessed more than they could manage directly. It is also obvious that such people got their lands cultivated by petty peasants through lease holding or through sharecropping or through the system of serfdom. We have therefore no means of establishing that most peasants living in the villages were in 'complete' control of the means of production.

Terminological studies throw interesting and revealing light on the relation of the peasant to the land in early India. The English term peasant, which literally means rustic or countryman, can be translated into *janapada*, which means an inhabitant of the countryside. That the *janapada* or the territorial unit formed by the countryside was considered to be a source of revenues is well known. Among the other qualities of a *janapada* are those of possessing active peasants capable of bearing taxes and fines (punishments).[23] Naturally when the peasantry was oppressed it led to the revolt of the peasants (*janapada-kopa*), which term occurs in the *Arthasastra* of Kautilya.[24] Curiously, the term *janapada* is not in much use in medieval Sanskrit literature although it occurs in early medieval inscriptions. In medieval times *jana* came to mean a dependant who was valued and acquired because of his labour power. Thus he could be a servile peasant. More significant is that in several Indo-Aryan dialects of Bihar the term means field labourer. In practice some of these labourers are given small patches of land to earn their subsistence. This practice is apparently a survival of the medieval system according to which *jana* or field workers were possessed by and transferred to landed magnates, as can be inferred not only from inscriptions but also from works on horoscopy.[25] This would show that the tribal *jana* with egalitarian ethos is reduced to almost a serf.

The terms for the peasant used in medieval texts, and particularly in inscriptions, indicate the change in the nature of the peasant's relation to the land he cultivated. From the age of the Buddha to the advent of the Gupta period tax-paying vaisyas continued as an omnibus order, comprising mostly peasants. But by early medieval times they were reduced to the position of the sudras, who in spite of having acquired peasanthood, continued to bear the hallmark of servitude.[26] *Gahapati*, literally head of the household, was the term used for the landowning peasant in early Pali texts[27] typical of the middle Gangetic plains which witnessed the rise of the first large states. He seems to have enjoyed substantial autonomy in his unit of production. But the term almost disappears in land grant inscriptions. *Gahapati* or *grhapati* becomes village headman in later texts.[28] A clear term for peasant is *ksetrika* or *ksetrin*,[29] which means controller of land, but even this is sometimes understood as an agriculturist or cultivator in later texts and lexicons. From *ksetrika* in Assamese is derived *khetiyaka*,[30] which means cultivator or husbandman, and who is not necessarily the owner of the field. A common term used for the peasant in many grants, especially in those from eastern India, is *ksetrakara*,[31] which literally means cultivator. The term *seti* in Marathi is probably derived from it,[32] and does not always mean the owner of the land. Some other terms used in inscriptions are *karsaka*[33] and *kutumbin*.[34] The term *kutumbin* gives some indication of an autonomous peasant family, but it occurs mainly in early land records from eastern India and Madhya Pradesh. In later grants from eastern India it is replaced by *ksetrakara* or *karsaka*. In Gujarat and Rajasthan the *kutumbika* loses his status, for he is sometimes transferred to the beneficairy along with the land.[35] According to Yajnavalkya (*c*. AD 300) the *karsaka* is a mere cultivator in the service of the landowner or *ksetrasvamin*, whose field lies under the general control of the king (*mahipati*).[36] In the Candella grants in eastern Madhya Pradesh the *karsaka* was made over to the assignee along with the village.[37] Land grants also use the term *halika*[38] or ploughman. Sharecroppers are indicated by *arddhika*, *arddhasirika* or *ardhasirin*. In literature the word *kinasa* is also used.[39] Evidently these terms have nothing to do with control over land. The term *kisan*, so common now in India, is derived from *krsana* or one who ploughs. The word *krsivala*[40] or cultivator is also frequently used in medieval texts. The term *langalopajivin* or one who lives by ploughing is used in the *Brhatsamhita*.[41]

A review of the terms used for the peasant in medieval inscriptions and literature fails to present the peasant's image as a controller of land. On the other hand, such technical terms as *bhokta, bhogi, bhogika, bhogijana, bhogapati, bhogapatika, bhogikapalaka, bhogirupa, mahabhogi, brhadbhogi, brhadhogika*, and so on, are used generally for those who enjoyed landed estates.[42] Here we have not taken into account many other terms connected with *raja, ranaka, samanta, mandalesvara*, and so on, who happened to be large landed intermediaries. The contrast between the two types of terms is obvious. Some people are meant for cultivating, and some meant for enjoying the fruits of production. There is nothing to show that the peasants who produced were in firm and independent control over their holdings. And finally there was the state, symbolized by the king, whose general authority over land was recognized by numerous epithets used for him in early medieval records.[43]

CONTROL OVER LAND AND SEIGNIORIAL RIGHTS

The point that there were superior and inferior rights in the same piece of land was made much earlier,[44] but the common phrase 'means of production' was not used in that context. It may be added now that the practice of granting a village with all possible taxes and impositions and with all its resources created a kind of feudal property in contrast to peasant property and communal rights. The new phenomenon caused headache to medieval jurists and law commentators, who found neither much of a sanction nor a precedent in the early law-books. Therefore, Vijnanesvara, the famous author of the *Mitaksara*, which enjoyed authority in a large part of the country in legal matters, propounded the principle of the popular recognition of property. He and his followers, including Mitra Misra, maintained that property has its basis in popular recognition without any dependence on the Sastras.[45] Commenting on a passage of Gautama,[46] Haradatta of about the twelfth century expressed a similar view. According to him even short enjoyment of *bhumi*, which is explained as cultivated field (*ksetra*) and orchards, gardens, etc. (*aramadika*), confers property rights on the enjoyer.[47] Short enjoyment probably means a period of less than ten years.[48] The complexities caused by the superimposition of new rights on the means of production hitherto effectively controlled by the peasants, also because of their free access to various village resources, baffled the medieval jurists who had to recognize the multiplicity of rights in the same piece of land. It is worth reproducing a quotation, which I used earlier: 'The Indian jurists took it for granted that the incidents of particular manifestations of ownership might differ, while the *svatva* (rights)[49] of the king, the *svatva* of the landowner, the *svatva* of the tenant-farmer, and in an extreme case, even the *svatva* of the mortgagee in possession (as against a trespasser) were all comprehensible under the single term of property.'[50] It has been shown that in law as well as in actual practice these rights were graded. In the Indian context one could therefore talk of the varying degrees of control over land, which was the primary means of production, and not of exclusive rights of either the landlord or the peasant. But the grants show an increasing tendency to establish the superior rights of the landlord at the cost of both the king and the peasantry, so much so that ultimately assignments are converted into virtual estates.

More effective control over the means of production obtained in such cases as transferred plots of land to the beneficiaries. Many big plots of land in Vidarbha and Maharashtra were assigned to gods and brahmanas under the Vakatakas and also under the Rastrakutas. For example, eight thousand *nivartanas* of land were granted to one thousand brahmanas by Pravarasena.[51] Similarly four hundred *nivartanas* of land were granted to a single brahmana.[52] Again the same measure of land was granted to a god.[53] Further, 2052 *nivartanas* of land were granted to brahmanas.[54] We learn from earlier authorities that in the Deccan, land measuring six *nivartanas* was considered to be sufficient to maintain a family of a brahmana which may have consisted of five to eight members. But the instances given above refer to large stretches of land, which could not be cultivated by the brahmana beneficiaries themselves. Even if labour in a brahmana family was available for smaller pieces of land, they would not actually cultivate it because of social inhibitions. But, more importantly, grants of large plots introduced an element of direct control of the beneficiary over the means of production.

An important factor which gave the beneficiaries general control over the means of production was the conferment of seigniorial rights on them. The charters authorized the beneficiaries to punish people guilty of ten offences,[55] including those against family, property, person, and so on, and to try civil cases.[56] Further, royal officers were not allowed to enter their territory[57] and cause any kind of obstruction in their functioning.[58] All these are as good as manorial rights, and might even enable the beneficiary to force the peasant to work in his field. It would appear that the right to try cases on the spot involving the imposition of fines could seriously interfere with the process of production. It is therefore obvious that the political and judicial rights, which were non-economic rights, helped the beneficiaries to carry out effectively the economic exploitation of the peasants living in his estate. This may have been a successful way of governing the vast population because crimes could be nipped in the bud on the spot. But, at the same time, these non-economic rights served to enforce the general economic authority of the beneficiaries over both the means and the processes of production. It may further be noted that in many cases the beneficiary was empowered to adopt all measures to enjoy the village, and the term used for this was *sarvopaya-samyuktam*.[59] He was also authorized to enjoy the fruits according to his sweet will. If we carefully examine the phrase *sambhogya yavadichcha kriyaphalam*[60] it would mean that the donee could even intervene in the process of production. If a person is entitled to the enjoyment of the fruits of the process of production according to his discretion, he may develop a natural tendency to control the process (*kriya*) itself on which the nature and the amount of yield depend. Sometimes, whatever belonged to the village (*svasambhoga sametah*) was to be enjoyed by the beneficiary.[61] The beneficiary was also granted the village along with all its products (*sarvotpattisahitah*).[62] The Candella charters from eastern Madhya Pradesh name the crops that were produced in the donated villages. Does this mean that the peasant could not alter the pattern of crops? At any rate all such provisions could create the interest of the landed beneficiary in the means and process of production. It would be really extraordinary if the beneficiary did not keep an eye over the resources, processes and fruits of production in such cases.

It is not clear how the peasants were provided with agricultural implements. The charters authorize the beneficiaries to enjoy all that is hidden under the earth. This amounts to giving the mining rights to the beneficiaries. It is well known that the mining rights belonged exclusively to the king. The king may have acquired this monopoly at the initial stage as the head of the tribe or the community. Once this exclusive control over iron and other types of mines passed into the hands of the beneficiaries, they could also control the supply of agricultural implements to the peasants. But in pre-feudal times the big landowners did not have such rights in lands. Mining rights belonged to the king who symbolized the community, and the peasants may not have experienced difficulties in procuring agricultural implements.

Not only are the successors of the king and people in power asked to observe the terms of the grants[63] but also all those who would upset the grant are threatened with the use of force.[64] In some warnings corporal punishment (*sariradandam*) is clearly mentioned.[65] The threat to use force is found mostly in the grants from Madhya Pradesh, Maharashtra, Andhra and Karnataka, and the earliest example belongs to the fourth century in a Pallava grant from Guntur district. In addition, the enemies of the land grant were invested with all kinds of curses and most heinous sins. The idea that a peasant was the complete master of the means of production is also belied by the philosophical teachings found at the end of most grants. The grants underline the instability of life. Apparently this instability of life is based not merely on the idea of death which ultimately overtakes everybody but also on the fickleness of fortune. The concept of the fickleness of fortune (i.e. mobility of Laksmi) is mainly derived from the frequent transfer of control over the means of production from one hand to the other. It would therefore appear that ideology, derived from the relations of production, strengthened the general control of the beneficiaries over the means of production. Ideology was also used for indoctrinating the producers in ancient times. Through ideology and administration, the priests and warriors regulated production and distribution in pre-feudal times, but now they acquired an effective hand in the mode of production because of their general, superior control over land, which was the chief means of production. The beneficiary started with the state-sanctioned title to various types of dues delivered by the peasants to the state, but in course of time his claims were made so comprehensive that because of his local presence and delegated administrative powers he could convert his title into possession and could treat the donated village as his estate. It is clear that the peasants had to reckon with the control of the donee over the village resources.

The real problem, therefore, is not to demonstrate the autonomy of peasant production, which in any case was drastically curtailed in the land grant areas. It is, rather, to determine the extent and impact of peasant population working in the land grant areas and that of similar people working in the non-land grant areas in medieval times.[66] Since references to palm-leaf (*talapatra*) and birch-bark (*bhurjapatra*) *sasanas* charters even for religious purposes are found in Assam and Madhya Pradesh it is likely that many such grants were issued in favour of both religious and secular parties. We learn how these *patra* grants were burnt and replaced by copper plate charters in Assam[67] and Madhya Pradesh.[68] Another important problem is to identify and plot on maps the donated villages or plots of land region-wise within a short time bracket (say, within half a century or so). We have shown earlier that in the donated villages the beneficiaries enjoyed superior authority in the means of production. Donated fields, many of them very large in area, were without doubt under the direct and complete control of the beneficiaries, who manipulated their production resources and processes.

SURPLUS COLLECTION AND THE PATTERN OF PRODUCTION

It is argued that landed beneficiaries were mainly concerned with the problem of surplus collection. But the question of surplus collection/distribution cannot be viewed in isolation from that of the pattern of production. In a feudal system of production we expect to find a lord's share called rent, in labour and cash/kind, coupled with a patron-client system of distribution, primarily between the peasant and the landlord. For surplus collection superior rights in the land of the peasants become the precondition. More surplus seems to have been extracted because of more product. In pre-Gupta times the surplus was mainly collected by the agents of the state in the form of taxes, or by priests in the form of gifts. There were a few landowners working with the help of slave and hired labourers in the age of the Buddha. We hear of state farms in the *Arthasastra* of Kautilya. But state control could operate only in small areas. By and large the settled part of the country had independent peasant units of production and was also blessed with some amount of market economy. But market economy was not so strong as would enable the rich landowner to invest his capital in new enterprises and work for profits, which might eventually lead him to the capitalist path. At best a millionaire such as Anathapindika would purchase land for donation to the Buddha. There could be other such examples. Payment in cash could be made for the sale of cereals and for the purchase of petty commodities by the peasants. Generally in pre-feudal times the priests, warriors and administrators were entitled to the surplus in the form of taxes and gifts for services rendered, but a good deal of these payments was made in cash.

Peasant units of production first appeared in the age of the Buddha and not in post-Maurya times. Slavery was neither preponderant nor negligible in production. Large holdings including Maurya state farms, were worked by slaves and hired labourers, in the middle Gangetic plains, but big landowners were swamped by peasants. The vaisya, who was almost identical with the peasant, was the principal taxpayer. His counterpart in the Buddhist idiom was a peasant householder who contributed to the increase in cereals and paid taxes to the state (*gahapatiko karkarako rasivaddhako*). Thus the peasant units of production functioned more or less effectively in pre-Gupta times. But after that the authority of the peasants over these units suffered erosion because of the appearance of landed beneficiaries supplemented by large disappearance of trade and urban centres. In India the problem of the rise of the landed magnates is not connected with 'the decomposition of the slave mode of production' but with the decreasing control of the peasant over his unit of production coupled with his restricted access to communal agrarian resources. As will be shown later, over-taxation and imposition of forced labour by the state created such problems as called for new remedies.

To think that the fight for a share in the cake does not necessarily affect the production of the cake is to ignore historical examples. It is true even of capitalist societies in which such fights eventually lead to structural changes. In conditions of early medieval times the beneficiary demanded his pound of flesh because he claimed superior rights in land. If the object of the grant was the maintenance of the beneficiary and the provision of requirements either for worship or for domestic purposes the peasant could be compelled to produce certain cereals which were badly needed by the donee.

If parts of the products are placed at the disposal of the grantee, what is the difference between enjoying the means of production, that is land, and the fruits of production? Land does not mean anything without products. Whoever seizes land rich with crops (*sasyasamrdham vasundharam*) is guilty of great sins—so goes the medieval saying. Thus land carried meaning in the context of its products. Surplus was collected not only after production but also in the course of production. On-the-spot collection and quick administration could be the most effective way of managing a large population.

THE QUESTION OF SERFDOM

On the basis of the land charters we can say that in the donated areas the landed beneficiaries enjoyed general control over production resources. Of course they did not enjoy specific control over every plot of land that the peasant cultivated. But there is nothing to question their control over the plots of lands that were directly donated to them by the king, sometimes along with the sharecroppers[69] and weavers and sometimes along with the cultivators.[70] This raises the problems of serfdom. It is thought that feudalism was identical with serfdom, and there seems to be an assumption that serfdom was the only potent method of exploiting the peasants. It may be very effective, but other forms of servitude imposed on the peasantry did not prove inoperative and unproductive. After all what is the essence of serfdom? In this system small farm units are attached to big farm units, and the two are interdependent for purposes of production. Big farms are directly managed by manorial magnates but cultivated by those who possess small plots. Therefore serfdom means giving more surplus labour than surplus produce. But in the Indian case surplus produce is extracted more through the general control exercised by the landed intermediaries than by their employment of serfs. A serf also occupies some land and provides his family with subsistence. However he not only pays rent in cash or kind for exploiting his unit of production but also spends extra hours labouring on the field of his lord. Nevertheless, if these extra hours of his are used on the field occupied by him the extra yield does not necessarily stay with the cultivator. On the other hand it enables him to pay more rent in cash or kind to his lord.

It is argued by Mukhia that serfdom is an incidental feature in the case of India.[71] But the evidence cited so far would show that it is more than incidental.[72] In any case if the lord gets his share without reducing too many people to serfdom, what basic difference does it make to him or to the social pattern? Both systems are concerned with extracting the lord's share; in both the cultivator is a dependent peasant under the exploitation of his lord, and in both cases the social structure is beset with the internal contradiction between the landlord and the actual tiller. A beneficiary may not possess big plots, but he possesses too many plots which make management difficult. In fact, laws of partition of land became effective in Gupta and post-Gupta times,[73] and they may have contributed to the fragmentation of land. Fragmentation of land is also indicated by epigraphic sale transactions found in Bangladesh.[74] Therefore, if a landlord possesses too many plots, tenanting and sharecropping may be more convenient than getting the land cultivated through the deployment of serfs.

Mukhia argues that because soil in India was very fertile there was no scope for the rise of serfdom or forced labour.[75] But we have indications of forced labour in the middle Gangetic basin where the soil is most fertile. Till recent times poor tenants, belonging to lower castes, were forced by landlords from upper castes to work in the fields at meagre wages.[76] Peasants were compelled to plough the land of the landlords and do various odd jobs for the sake of the landlords in other fertile areas. This is known as *hari* and *begari* in the whole Gangetic basin area. The medieval term for the first is *halikakara*,[77] and for the second is *visti*, from which *bethbegari* is derived. The Pala charters found in Monghyr, Bhagalpur, Saharsa and Nalanda districts, all forming parts of the middle Gangetic plains, mention the term *sarvapidaparihrta*. This means that the peasants were subjected to all types of forced labour and oppression, but when the village was transferred to a beneficiary he became entitled to these advantages without the interference of the state. Forced labour may have originated in less populated areas but not necessarily in less fertile parts.

In any case, once its usefulness was recognized it spread to more populated parts.

Feudalism flourished in paddy producing areas. Paddy production requires 50 per cent more man hours than wheat production. According to a popular saying in Patna and Gaya districts, wheat cultivation can be undertaken even by a widow, who represents an image of helplessness in the countryside. Evidently wheat requires less and barley requires least labour. Therefore paddy transplantation would mean scarcity of labour in peak season; and it could be necessary to take to forced labour. We need not add that the term *sotpadyamanavisti* is used frequently.[78] It has been translated to mean the use of forced labour as occasions arise. But since the term qualifies the donated land or village, it might mean the labour generated or produced by the village in future.[79] This was a significant development in a good part of the country. It would imply that besides customary sources of forced labour new sources could be exploited by the beneficiaries according to their needs. Unfortunately these sources are not specified in medieval records. That there were various types of forced labour is clear from the use of the terms *sarvavisti*[80] in many land grants, particularly in Vakataka grants. It is obvious that these many types may have included the use of labour in the fields. The evidence from the *Skanda Purana* produced by B.N.S.Yadava leaves little doubt that hundreds of people were compelled to do forced labour, and this was evidently meant for production.[81] Hence serfdom cannot be dismissed as an incidental feature.

If serfdom is understood as compulsory attachment of the peasants to the soil, it prevailed in good parts of Madhya Pradesh, eastern India, Chamba and Rajasthan. In many cases the charters clearly transfer the peasants, artisans and even traders to the beneficiaries.[82] In most charters they ask the villagers, the peasants and other inhabitants of the villages to stay in their villages and to carry out the orders of the beneficiaries. This fact of immobility of peasants and artisans has not been contested by anybody so far. However it is argued by Mukhia that, even if these people were allowed to move, what purpose would it serve? If such a view is taken, what is the point in underlining the absence of serfdom in the Indian context? After all in conditions of serfdom a peasant has to be tied to his piece of land and when that piece of land is transferred the peasant is automatically transferred. This practice prevailed widely in early medieval times. Nevertheless, the peasants were not engaged widely in agricultural operations in the fields of their landlords. If it is argued that peasants were not employed in production but in building forts, roads, temples, massive and impressive structures, then we may say that all such grandiose projects were undertaken by the landed aristocracy, chiefs and princes, to strike the people with awe at their majesty. They could be of great indirect help in collecting taxes and presents from the peasantry. Some of the projects, such as building roads, could eventually be useful from the point of production. The employment of forced labour, therefore, did not depend on the rate of the fertility of the soil but on the realization of its usefulness by the landlords. There is no doubt that the rural aristocracy led an ostentatious and luxurious life requiring much consumption. Although we cannot measure the rising expectations of the landlords we notice indications of growing luxurious living.

The practices of forced labour, sharecropping or leasing the land were promoted and supported by social institutions and inhibitions. The law-books ask the brahmanas not to take to the plough. It seems that the upper caste people could not transplant paddy.[83] Naturally, even in a small holding which could be managed by their family labour, such people would need some labour which could be either forced labour or sharecropping. In such cases it is immaterial whether the soil is less fertile or more fertile, for at any rate labour would have to be drafted from outside the family unit. Lack of labour power and plenty of land create conditions for introducing an element of compulsion. But this can happen only in a particular socio-economic formation. We may have lack of labour in socialist or capitalist countries, but that does not necessarily lead to forced labour.

The idea that the gap between the labour potential of the family and the land that it has leads to feudal conditions may be far from true. Under-utilization of labour capacity may not necessarily produce demand for such labour in the form of forced labour. This labour can also be invested in auxiliary crafts in response to agricultural and domestic demands. But what is more important is that, if the needs of the landlords are met otherwise through rents and presents, why should he assume direct and onerous responsibility for cultivation and mobilize labour power for that purpose? At present we have no means to measure the needs, demands and expectations of the landlord, which may vary region-wise. These needs could be easily met by the landlords because of the provisions of the charters empowering them to depart from customary and established taxes and to impose and introduce new levies and new forms of forced labour.

SOCIAL CRISIS AS THE ORIGIN OF LAND GRANTS

It is repeatedly stated that no new mode of socio-economic formation can appear as a result of political, administrative and juridical measures.[84] Yet the colonial system in India owed its origin largely to such measures. The king in ancient India symbolised state authority, and the state was backed by priests and warriors who lived on the surplus produced by the peasants and further supplied by the artisans. This kind of state and society appeared in the age of the Buddha. It continued to function more or less smoothly till the third century AD. But there are many passages in the epics and the Puranas which speak of a kind of social crisis symbolized by the Kali age. These passages are ascribed to the second half of the third century AD and the beginning of the fourth century AD. They depict a state of affairs in which rural people were oppressed with taxes and forced labour,[85] which was considered an important element of the military power. The oppressions of the state coupled with the havoc caused by natural calamities created a state of chaos, and the lower orders, particularly the vaisyas and the sudras, refused to perform the functions assigned to them. On top of this the peasants refused to pay taxes.[86] The *Manu Smrti, Santi Parva* and other texts suggested two measures to overcome this social crisis. One was the use of force or *danda*, which is glorified in these texts. The other was the restoration of the *varnasramadharma* which was considered to be the bedrock of the class-based and state-based society. Obviously these measures alone could not cope with the critical situation. Since it became difficult to collect taxes it was not possible to run the state and to pay the priests, administrators, the army and numerous officials. Apparently, as an alternative, the practice of land grants, which was not unknown in early times, was adopted on a wide scale in a major part of the country, particularly from the fourth to fifth centuries AD onwards.

It would therefore appear that we have an indication of a crisis in production relations, which may not be unconnected with changes in the mode of production. The fact cannot be discounted that trade[87] and urbanism[88] suffered a distinct decline, and the absence of gold coins for three centuries between the seventh and the tenth centuries and paucity of other types of coins[89] are well known. There is practically no indication of the use of slaves in production. All these are presages of changes in the methods and relations of production. Hence the production system as a whole was afflicted with certain maladies, which compelled the state to convert land/land revenues into a general mode of payment for religious and administrative services. The grant system relieved the state of the heavy responsibility of getting the taxes collected all over the countryside by its agents and then of disbursing them in cash or kind. On the other hand priests, warriors and administrators were asked to fend for themselves in the villages they were assigned for their enjoyment. The system also relieved the state of the responsibility of maintaining law and order in the donated villages which now became almost the sole concern of the beneficiaries. Therefore it would be wrong to assume that political, administrative and juridical measures, which created new property relations in land, were undertaken by the state entirely on its own.

The social crisis apparently led to the withdrawal of slaves from production, and provision of land for them as tenants and sharecroppers. This explains to a good extent the elevation of sudras to peasanthood and their participation in rituals. It seems that landowners converted sudra labourers into peasants and themselves became landlords living on rents. The substantial *gahapatis* of the age of the Buddha probably turned landlords. That the village headman tended to become landlord has already been shown,[90] although the causes of this transformation need investigation.

CONFLICTS WITHIN THE NEW FORMATION

The new socio-economic formation that emerged as a result of the appearance of a class of landlords and a class of subject peasantry had its own limitations. The peasants were accustomed to give certain taxes and services to the state and, if the demand of the beneficiary was confined to those claims, in normal times the routine payment could continue. But the beneficiaries would impose proper and improper taxes, fixed and unfixed taxes, would collect 'all kinds of taxes', and, what is worse, they could make additional impositions which were covered by the term *adi*, i.e. 'etc.'. In certain areas they could also introduce new forms of forced labour. On top of this, all communal and agrarian resources hitherto enjoyed by the peasants were transferred to the landed beneficiaries who were always present on the spot. This situation caused constant conflict between those who claimed rent on the strength of their royal charters and others who claimed immunity on the basis of customary and immemorial rights which would certainly be known to local people but because of their illiteracy could not be shown in black and white. Hence there were bound to be constant friction, tensions and struggles between the landed beneficiaries and the servile peasantry. This might lead to litigation between the beneficiaries, and also between the beneficiary and the peasants.[91] Because of the common practice of land grants and the enormous advantages derived from them the brahmanas forged many charters (*kuta-sasana*) and claimed enjoyment of villages on that basis. But there were so many valid charters that the conflict between the landlord and the peasant was an ever-present possibility. In order to settle this conflict *Narada, Brhaspati, Agni Purana* and other authorities give the final authority to the royal charter in a case of dispute. They lay down that if there is a conflict between the religious right (*dharma*), contract (*vyavahara*) right, customary (*carita*) right and the right derived from the royal charter (*rajasasana*) the royal charter will override all the other sources of the law or authority.[92]

But it seems that this overriding power of the royal charter did not work in all cases. We have the case of the Kaivartas, a fishing and cultivating community in Bangladesh, who rose against Ramapala in the eleventh century AD. They fought with bamboo sticks riding on buffaloes. So powerful was their revolt that two dozen vassals had to be mobilized by Ramapala in order to put down the Kaivarta rebellion. This is an important example of peasant revolt.[93] The possibility of clash is also indicated in some Bengal grants which mention the term *karasanavirodhi sthana*.[94] At least two grants take pains to show that they do not clash with the existing cultivating rights of the peasants. Therefore the possibility of clash between the peasants and the incoming beneficiaries is clearly visualized. Similarly in many grants from Madhya Pradesh and Maharashtra the people are warned that if they try to upset the grant in any manner they will be punished with force.[95] This point is stated repeatedly[96] in many inscriptions. In some cases this threat is directed towards royal officials, but mostly it is a general threat meant for all. Again in the texts of this period, *brahmahatya*, that is killing of brahmanas, is considered to be a great sin and it occurs in many Puranas. Why does the murder of brahmana become so important in early medieval times? Apparently it is because of his becoming a landed beneficiary and therefore an oppressor. If we look at the distribution of hero stones in Karnataka and other parts of south India it would appear that some of them are found in the *agrahara* areas.[97] This would again suggest that open friction appeared between the beneficiary of the *agrahara* and the peasants living there. In the case of Karnataka, R.N. Nandi has collected certain evidence which suggests some kind of collaboration between the brahmanas and the peasants in the beginning, but eventually shows open conflict between the two.[98] D.N. Jha refers to several instances of conflict between the peasants and the beneficiary landlords in Cola inscriptions, particularly after 1000.[99]

Although we can see and visualize polarity between the central state and smaller states, polarity between various types of beneficiaries, and polarity between landed magnates and the cultivator, the human factor operating in these polarities does not come out clearly in our sources. It is thought that the peasant's independent control over the process of production prevented acute social tensions.[100] But as shown earlier, this control was more dependent than independent. The multiplication of the existing units of production in new areas could obviate occasions for open conflicts leading to changes. But to a good degree the seeming stability was promoted by other factors which were closely linked with the system of production, especially with production relations. First the caste system with the features of hierarchy and superiority, not to speak of untouchability, provided ritualistic sanction for the production and distribution system. It seems that the *jajmani* system developed in this period and was a part of more or less self-sufficient economy. At the end of harvesting, on the threshing floor portions of paddy were given to gods, brahmanas, rulers and various kinds of labourers, indicated by the term *bhrtyavargaposanam*.[101] The brahmanas, who controlled many 'estates', played a crucial ideological role in penetrating the consciousness of the peasantry and making them behave as they liked them to do. Some medieval religious reform movements apparently sought to improve the status of those who really produced and suffered, but those movements were manipulated to contain the conflicts and scotch the tensions; they could not rouse the peasantry to realities. In certain parts of the country survival of bonds of kinship also helped to keep people together. This may have particularly happened in Rajasthan and Himalayan areas. Classes with conflicting interests were kept together through the performance of *puja, japa, vratas, tirthas, samskaras, prayascittas* and through prospects of heaven and hell. The all-pervasive influence of astrology (*jyotisa*) and that of the doctrine of Vedanta kept the people reconciled to their lot. All these factors brought people of opposite interests together.

AGRICULTURAL EXPANSION

It is held that lack of 'concentrated social effort' blocked changes in the means, methods and relations of production.[102] We may not have much idea about the social effort, but we can certainly identify significant changes in the mode of production in early medieval times. This period was undoubtedly an age of larger yield and of great agrarian expansion. It is possible to count hundreds of states, particularly in those areas which had never witnessed the rise of full-fledged states. A state presupposes an assured source of income which would enable it to maintain a good number of managerial staff. This could not be possible unless the agrarian base was strong enough to pay for the priests, officers, army men, and so on.

A few technological innovations contributed to rural expansion. Apart from the use of the *araghatta*, the Persian wheel, the early Middle Ages saw several changes in agriculture. The importance attached to agriculture in this period is indicated by the fact that several texts were composed on it such as *Krsi-Parasara* in the north and Kamban's book in the south. Kasyapa's *Krsisukti* has been found in the south,[103] but it may have belonged to some paddy producing area in either the north or the south. It prescribes three methods of lifting water (i.e. using the *ghati-yantra*), by men, oxen and elephants.[104] That certain persons were engaged in working the 'Persian' water-wheel can be inferred from the use of the term *arahattiyanara* in a lexicon of the twelfth century.[105] The *Vrksa Ayurveda* of about the tenth century recommends recipes for treating the diseases affecting plants.[106] Apart from special attention being given to horses,[107] because they were used by chiefs and princes, animal husbandry was improved because of care given to the treatment of cattle diseases.[108] In addition, detailed instructions regarding agriculture appear in the *Brhatsamhita* of Varahamihira, the *Agni Purana* and the *Visnudharmottara Purana*.[109] Three crops, first mentioned by Panini, were known widely,[110] and better seeds were produced.[111] Meteorological knowledge, based on observation, was far advanced in the *Krsi-Parasara*. The knowledge of fertilizers improved immensely and the use of compost was known;[112] and, more importantly, irrigation facilities were expanded. The law-books lay down severe punishments for those who cause damage to tanks, wells, ponds, embankments, and so on.[113] The construction of *vapi* became very popular in Rajasthan and Gujarat. Its importance is also underlined in the work of Kasyapa.[114] In his doctoral thesis V.K. Jain has prepared a map in which he has shown the distribution of the *vapis* (step wells) in western India in the eleventh to thirteenth centuries.[115] It is interesting to note that the term *vapi* is derived from the Sanskrit root *vap* which means to sow. So it is clear that step wells were meant for irrigating the fields.

Of course, the use of iron implements attained a new peak in this period. In the *Paryayamuktavali*, a medieval lexicon whose manuscripts have been found in West Bengal and Orissa, as many as half a dozen types or grades of iron are mentioned.[116] The use of iron became so common that it began to be employed for non-utilitarian purposes. Several pillars, including the Mehrauli Pillar in Delhi, were erected to mark the conquest of victorious princes. The increase in the number of varieties of cereals including rice, wheat and lentils as well as in fruits, vegetables, legumes, and so on, is striking. These can be inferred not only from the *Amarakosa* but more so from the *Paryayamuktavali*.[117] According to the *Sunya Purana* more than 50 kinds of paddy were cultivated in Bengal.[118]

Apart from the foundation of numerous states the various medieval texts suggest an enormous increase in agricultural production. Therefore agricultural technology in terms of a single major break may not be striking[119] but the overall effect of various measures and improvements seems to have been substantial. However, mere increases in production may lead neither to stability nor to structural changes. For this certain other conditions including the rousing of the necessary consciousness may be needed.

CONCLUDING OBSERVATIONS

Feudalism in India, therefore, was characterized by a class of landlords and by a class of subject peasantry, the two living in a predominantly agrarian economy marked by decline of trade and urbanism and by drastic reduction in metal currency. The superior state got its taxes collected and authority recognized by creating a number of inferior power blocs or even states (that is, landed priests, *mathas, viharas, basadis,* temples, *agraharas, brahmadeyas*, etc.) which generated the necessary social and ideological climate for this purpose. Unlike the European system, most of the power structures within the state did not have to pay taxes. West European feudal lords granted land to their serfs in order to get their own occupied land cultivated. But Indian kings made land grants to get the taxes (surplus) collected. In their turn the grantees collected rents from their tenant peasants who could be evicted and even subjected to forced labour.

Our comments are sometimes couched in terms of probabilities and reservations, because the nature of sources does not admit of clear and categorical statements. Nevertheless, they raise some theoretical issues. The position of class is to be located in the overall system of production. But if a class covers either those who exclusively control the means of production or those who are completely deprived of such control, such a thing can happen only in a full-fledged capitalist system. The application of such a concept to pre-capitalist societies is riddled with difficulties, for even in the feudal society of Western Europe the serf enjoyed day-to-day control over his bit of the means of production.[120] In such a society, class is best seen in the context of the unequal distribution of the surplus, which was eventually given a lasting basis by the unequal distribution of the means of production and strengthened by ideological and juridical factors. Second, ecological factors influence the development of material culture. However we find several countries with similar climatic conditions but dissimilar social structures. Therefore, to attribute such structural phenomena as the absence of serfdom or the longevity of peasant autonomy to the carrying capacity of the soil would be to go too far.

NOTES

1. D.C. Sircar, *Landlordism and Tenancy in Ancient and Medieval India as Revealed by Epigraphical Records*, Lucknow, 1969. Also see *Journal of Indian History*, XLIV, 1966, 351-7; LI, 1973, 56-9; *Journal of Ancient Indian History*, VI, 1972-3, 337-9; D.C. Sircar, ed., *Land System and Feudalism in Ancient India*, Calcutta, 1966, pp. 11-23. Irfan Habib discusses 'Indian Feudalism', in *The Peasant in Indian History*, Presidential Address, The Indian History Congress, 43rd Session, Kurukshetra, 1982.
2. Harbans Mukhia, 'Was There Feudalism in Indian History?', *The Journal of Peasant Studies*, 8(3), April 1981, 273-310. In this paper the whole medieval period is discussed but I will confine myself primarily to early medieval times (fifth to twelfth centuries), about which I have some idea. My task has been made easier because Mukhia's criticisms have been effectively met by B.N.S. Yadava in *The Problem of the Emergence of Feudal Relations in Early India*, Presidential Address for Ancient Indian Section of The Indian History Congress, 41st Session, Bombay, 1980. In a similar address delivered at the 40th Session of the Indian History Congress held at Waltair in 1979, D.N. Jha anticipated and answered many of these objections in *Early Indian Feudalism: A Historiographical Critique*. Also see Suvira Jaiswal, 'Studies in Early Indian Social History', *Indian Historic Review*, VI, 1979-80, 18-21.
3. Karl Marx and Fredrich Engels, *Pre-Capitalist Socio-Economic Formations*, Moscow, 1979, p. 23.
4. Mukhia, op. cit., p. 310, fn. 225. In the discussion on variants Indian feudalism is seen as a distinct possibility.
5. E.K. Kosminsky's views based on Marx and expressed in his *Studies in the Agrarian History of England in the Thirteenth Century*, Oxford, 1956, are summarized and discussed in Barry Hindess and Paul Q. Hirst, *Pre-Capitalist Modes of Production*, London, 1975, pp. 222-3, 234-5.
6. Marx considers tenants to be an object of feudal exploitation. According to him the feudal lord differs from the bourgeois in that he 'does not try to extract the utmost advantage from his land. Rather he consumes what is there and calmly leaves the worry of producing to the serfs and tenants'. Marx and Engels, op. cit., p. 20. In the 1880s Engels also concluded that serfdom is not solely a 'peculiarly medieval-feudal form', ibid., p. 23. This implies that the feudal formation could have other features.
7. Mukhia, op. cit., pp. 275, 290, 291, 293.
8. I owe this to Ranajit Guha.
9. The king is called *bhusvamin* by Katyayana, a lawgiver of about the sixth century (P.V. Kane, ed., verse 16).
10. R.S. Sharma, 'From Gopati to Bhupati' (a review of the changing position of the king), *Studies in History*, II(2), 1980, 6-8.
11. *Yasya yasya yada bhumih, tasya tasya tada phalam*, D.C. Sircar, ed., *Select Inscriptions Bearing on Indian History and Civilization*, Vol. I, University of

Calcutta, 1965 (hereafter as *Sel. Inscrr.*), Bk. III, No. 49, line 26.

12. The terms used are *sarvoparikarakaradanasametah, sarvakarasametah, sarvakaravisarjitah,* etc. See Balchandra Jain, *Utkirna-Lekha,* Raipur, 1961, pp. 56-7. The terms *samastapratyaya* and *sarvayasameta* also occur (R.S. Sharma, *Indian Feudalism,* 2nd edn., Delhi, 1980, p. 100). Also see *Sarvadanasamgrahya, Epigraphia Indica* (hereafter *EI*), V, No. 5, line 14.
13. Sharma, *Indian Feudalism,* 2nd edn., p. 98.
14. The phrase used is *niyataniyatasamastadaya,* all specified and unspecified dues. *EI,* No. 21, line 26.
15. *Epigraphia Indica,* XXIX, No. 7, line 42; Jain, op. cit., p. 52.
16. Mukhia rightly postulates that the village potentates would be the first to notice the rise in productivity and the first to demand a greater share in the peasant's produce. Op. cit., p. 309, fn. 214.
17. The phrase *ajnasravanavidheyibhuya* is common in north Indian grants.
18. The point has been discussed in Sharma, *Indian Feudalism,* 2nd edn., pp. 38-9.
19. The distinction is brought out clearly in P.N. Sen, *The General Principles of Hindu Jurisprudence, Tagore law Lectures,* 1909, University of Calcutta, 1918, p. 42.
20. *Sel. Inscrr.,* Bk. III, Nos., 16, 18, 19, 41, 42, 43, etc.
21. Sharma, *Indian Feudalism,* 2nd edn., pp. 73-5, 185-7.
22. Marx and Engels, op. cit., p. 22.
23. ... *sadandakarasahah karmasilakarsako'balisasvamyavaravarnaprayo janapadasampat. Arthasastra* (of Kautilya), R.P. Kangle's edn. (hereafter *As.*), VI.1.
24. *As.*, I.13. The term *prakrtikopa* or revolt of the subjects is used in V. 6 and VII. 6.
25. Yadava, *The Problem of the Emergence of Feudal Relations in Early India,* p. 7, contains several references to the acquisition of *jana.*
26. R.S. Sharma, *Sudras in Ancient India,* 2nd edn., Delhi, 1980, Chap. VII.
27. The term used is *kassako gahapati,* cultivating family head. *Anguttara Nikaya* (Pali Text Society, London), i, 239-40. But *gahapati* in the sense of substantial peasants is used in Pali texts at many places.
28. s.v. *griha,* Monier Monier-Williams, *A Sanskrit-English Dictionary,* Oxford, 1951.
29. R.L. Turner, *A Comparative Dictionary of the Indo-Aryan Languages,* Oxford, 1973, No. 3736.
30. Ibid.
31. R. Mukerji and S.K. Maity, *Corpus of Bengal Inscriptions bearing on History and Civilization of Bengal,* Calcutta, 1967, No. 18, line 45; No. 22, line 46; No. 28, line 52; No. 30, line 48; No. 36, line 36; No. 37, line 32.
32. Turner, op. cit., No. 3736.
33. Mukerji and Maity, op. cit., No. 47, line 50.
34. Ibid., No. 7, line 3; No. 9, line 3 (p. 59).
35. Sharma, *Indian Feudalism,* 2nd edn., pp. 188-9.

36. Ibid., p. 38.
37. Ibid., p. 188.
38. Ibid., p. 98, fn. 3, 99.
39. It is taken in the sense of a ploughman. See Yadava, *The Problem of the Emergence of Feudal Relations in Early India*, p. 25.
40. s.v. *krsivala*, Monier-Williams, op. cit.
41. Yadava, *The Problem of the Emergence of Feudal Relations in Early India*, p. 32.
42. Sharma, *Indian Feudalism*, 2nd edn., pp. 12-13, 216.
43. These terms are *avanisa, avanindra, ksitipati, ksitendra, ksitisa, ksiteradhipa, parthiva, prthivipati, parthivendra, prthivinatha, bhupa, bhupati, bhubhuj, bhumipa, bhumisvara, mahipa, mahipati, mahipala, mahindra, mahamahendra, urvipati, vasudhadhipa, vasudhesvara, samanta-bhumisvara*, etc. R.S. Sharma, 'From Gopati to Bhupati', *Studies in History*, II(2), 1980, p. 8 with fns. 81-2.
44. R.S. Sharma, *Indian Feudalism*, Calcutta, 1965, Chap. IV.
45. Sen, op. cit., pp. 42-3, 46. The theory of popular recognition, which gives preference to unwritten laws, is known as *laukika svatvavada* (ibid., p. 42). Several logicians such as Guru, Kumarila Svami and Parthasarathi Misra, who interpreted the Dharmasastras according to the canons of *mimamsa* also supported the popular recognition theory. Jimutavahana, Dharesvara, etc., supported the sastric view (ibid., p. 42), The difference does reflect conflicting claims to land control in early medieval times.
46. *Gautama Dharmasutra*, Varanasi, 1966, II.3.36. The passage reads *pasu bhumistrinamanatibhogah*.
47. *Alpenapi bhogena bhoktuh svam bhavati*. Comm. on *Gautama* II.3.36 By this interpretation cattle and women slaves are also covered. It is interesting that a ten-year limit of enjoyment is set for acquiring ownership over the property of others in several cases by the commentator. Comm. on *Gautama* II.3.34-5.
48. Comm. on *Gautama* II.3.34-5.
49. *Svatva* should be taken in the sense of property rights, as has been done by Sen., op. cit., p. 42.
50. J.D.M. Derrett in *Bulletin of the School of Oriental and African Studies*, XVIII, 489.
51. V.V. Mirashi, *Inscriptions of the Vakatakas, Corpus Inscriptionum Indicarum*, Vol. V, Ootacamund, 1955, No. 6, lines 19-20.
52. Ibid., No. 12, lines 20-1.
53. Ibid., No. 13, lines 22-3.
54. Ibid., No. 14, lines 22-32.
55. Sharma, *Indian Feudalism*, 2nd edn., p. 3; the common term used is *sadandadasparadhah*.
56. Ibid. The term *abhyantarasiddhi* is used.
57. Ibid., p. 2.
58. *Sel. Inscrr.*, Bk. III, No. 62, lines 21-2.
59. Mukeriji and Maity, op. cit., No. 47, line, 62.

60. Ibid., line 63.
61. Ibid., No. 46, line 22.
62. *EI*, V, No. 20, line 54. The village, situated near Nagpur, was granted by Krsna III in 940-1.
63. *Sel. Inscrr.*, Bk. III, No. 49, lines 18-28; No. 50, lines 15-23.
64. . . . *sadandanigraham karisyamah*. This phrase is found, with slight variations in many charters. Ibid., No. 61, 11.22-4; No. 62, 11.32-4; No. 64, 11.21-4; No. 65, 11.39-41; No. 67, 11.24-5.
65. Ibid., No. 67, 11.24-5.
66. In the context of slave society it is held that if 20 per cent of people are engaged in production as slaves in a society, it should be considered a slave society. Five such societies have been identified. Keith Hopkins, *Conquerors and Slaves*, Cambridge, 1978, pp. 99-100. But the qualitative place of slaves or other categories of servile people in the total mode of production deserves equal consideration.
67. D.C. Sircar, *Indian Epiography*, Delhi, 1965, p. 97 fn. 2.
68. Balchandra Jain, op. cit., No. 3, 11.6-11 (p. 8).
69. *Sel. Inscrr.*, Bk. III, No. 65, 11.38-9.
70. Ibid., no. 61, 1.15.
71. Mukhia, op. cit., p. 286.
72. R.S. Sharma, *Indian Feudalism*, Delhi, 1980, pp. 19, 31, 40-3, 56, 60, 67-8, 99-101, 109, 195-8; B.N.S. Yadava, *Society and Culture*, pp. 164-9; 'Immobility and Subjection of Indian Peasantry in Early Medieval Complex', *The Indian Historical Review*, I, 1974, 18-27. A good deal of evidence can be obtained from G.K. Rai, *Involuntary Labour in Ancient India*, Allahabad, 1981, but the passage from Vatsyayana's *Kamasutra* (V. 5.5) is inaccurately construed and translated.
73. Sharma, *Indian Feudalism*, 2nd edn., pp. 118-19.
74. Ibid., p. 49.
75. Mukhia, op. cit., pp. 286, 289, 303 fn. 124.
76. This was the case in my own village Barauni (District Begusarai, Bihar) till 1950 when the Permanent Settlement was abolished.
77. Y.B. Singh, 'Halika-kara: Crystallization of a Practice into a Tax', paper (unpublished) presented to the 43rd Session of The Indian History Congress, Kurukshetra, 1982.
78. Sharma, *Indian Feudalism*, 2nd edn., pp. 99-100.
79. The term *utpatsyamana* would suit this interpretation better, although even *utpadyamana* means the same thing. I owe this suggestion to Professor R.C. Pandeya. Palaeographically there is very little difference between the two terms.
80. *Sel. Inscrr.*, Bk. III, No. 61, line 19; No. 62, line 28.
81. Yadava, *Society and Culture in Northern India*, pp. 164-6.
82. Sharma, *Indian Feudalism*, 2nd edn., p. 188 with fn. 6.
83. The passage *panktisah panktiso bhrtyaih vinyaset samabhumike* (verse No. 431)

occurs in the context of paddy transplantation in the *Kasyapiyakrsisukti*, Gy. Wojtilla, ed., *Acta Orientalia Academiae Saentiarum Hung.*, XXXIII (2), 1979, 209-52. The frequent use of the term *krsivala* for the peasant shows that the text belongs to some paddy producing area either in south India or in some other part of the country, and contains much medieval material. Verse No. 450 speaks of the employment of the classes of agricultural labourers in weeding operations: *trnakosthan nirasyatha panktisah panktisah kramat, bhrtyavargaih praty aham va vairicchedah prasasyate.* If we look at the survival of the transplantation practice, it would appear that this use of labour was made by the upper caste people in medieval times.

84. Mukhia, op. cit., pp. 274, 286.
85. This Kali passage in the Cr. edn., of the *Mahabharata* (III. 188.71), amended by me on the basis of the Gita Press edn., reads: *nirvisesa janapada kara-vistibhirarditah.* Apparently taxes (*kara*) affected the vaisyas and forced labour (*visti*) the sudras.
86. I discussed the Kali problem in some detail three years ago in a paper 'The Kali Age: A Period of Social Crisis', in S.N. Mukherjee, ed., *India: History and Thought: Essays in Honour of A.L. Basham*, Calcutta, 1982, pp. 186-203. But see my *Sudras in Ancient India*, 2nd edn., Delhi, 1980, pp. 233-9.
87. In addition to the material presented concerning the decline of trade in my *Indian Feudalism*, 2nd edn., Chaps. I and III, further evidence appears in Yadava, *Society and Culture in Northern India in the Twelfth Century*, pp. 270-5. Speaking of early medieval Bengal, M.R. Tarafdar says: 'the period between the eleventh and thirteenth centuries shows distinct signs of the decay of trade and urban centres, a process which must have started earlier' ('Trade and Society in Early Medieval Bengal', *Indian Historical Review*, IV, January 1978, 282). However in western India trade shows revival in this period (V.K. Jain, 'Trade and Traders in Western India', Ph. D. thesis, Delhi University, 1983); so also seems to be the case with south India (Kenneth R. Hall, *Trade and State Craft in the Age of the Colas*, New Delhi, 1980). We postulate decline of trade mainly in the seventh to tenth centuries.
88. Although the decline of urbanism has been sometimes doubted (B.D. Chattopadhyaya, 'Trade and Urban Centres in Early Medieval North India', *Indian Historical Review*, I, 1974, 203-19), progress in historical archaeology in the Gangetic zone and elsewhere since 1971 coupled with further research in literary texts confirms what I stated earlier ('Decay of Gangetic Towns in Gupta and Post-Gupta Times', *Journal of Indian History*, Golden Jubilee Volume, 1973, pp. 135-50). Almost all Satavahana towns decay and disappear after the third century AD. A.H. Dani informs me of a similar fate of the Kusana towns in Pakistan, and the Soviet archaeologist V. Masson tells me that five central Asian urban centres of about the first to fourth centuries AD become either villages or castles afterwards. In two Patna University doctoral theses (Om Prakash Prasad, 'Towns in Early Medieval Karnataka', 1978, and B.P.N. Pathak, 'Society and Culture in Early Bihar', 1983) the

phenomenon of decay comes out very clearly. R.N. Nandi convincingly shows that many of these decaying towns were converted into *tirthas* or places of pilgrimage in early medieval times. 'Client, Ritual and Conflict in Early Brahmanical Order', *Indian Historical Review*, VI, 1979-80, 100, 103-9. Additional evidence has been collected on the decay of towns (Ibid., 74-80).

89. R.S. Sharma, 'Indian Feudalism Retouched' (review paper), *Indian Historical Review*, I, 1974, 320-30. For additional evidence regarding paucity of coinage see Tarafdar, op. cit.
90. Sharma, *Indian Feudalism*, 2nd edn., pp. 41-2.
91. In 1214 a temple in Karnataka claimed the land of its neighbours, but the local authorities decided against the temple. S. Settar and G.D. Sontheimer, eds., *Memorial Stones*, Dharwar, 1982, p. 303.
92. R.S. Sharma, '*Rajasasana*: Meaning, Scope and Application', *Proceedings of the Indian History Congress*, 37th Session, Calicut, 1976.
93. Sharma, *Indian Feudalism*, 2nd edn., p. 220.
94. Mukherji and Maity, op. cit., No. 6, line 18; No. 7, line 19.
95. *Sel. Inscrr.*, Bk. II, No. 61, lines 22-4.
96. Ibid., No. 62, lines 32-4; No. 634, lines 21-4; No. 67, lines 24-5.
97. Settar and Sontheimer, eds., op. cit., p. 223.
98. R.N. Nandi, *Ancient India Presidential Address*, The Indian History Congress, XLV Session, Annamalai University, Annamalai Nagar, pp. 64-70.
99. D.N. Jha, *Section I: Ancient India Presidential Address*, The Indian History Congress, XL Session, Andhra University, Waltair, 1979, p. 18.
100. Mukhia, op. cit., p. 293.
101. Gy. Wojtilla, ed., *Kasyapiyakrsisukti*, op. cit., verses 491-2.
102. Mukhia, op. cit., p. 292. However this statement is qualified by the phrase 'change completely' (ibid).
103. Wojtilla, ed., op. cit. The usual term for cultivator in this text is *krsivala*, which occurs in early medieval texts and inscriptions. Most material in this text probably belongs to medieval times.
104. Ibid., verses 167-8. The *ghati-yantra* operated by oxen is considered to be the best, that by men to be the worst, and that by elephants to be of the middling quality.
105. Yadava, *Society and Culture in Northern India in the Twelfth Century*, p. 259.
106. D.M. Bose et al., eds., *A Concise History of Science in India*, New Delhi, 1971, p. 362.
107. Ibid., p. 255.
108. Ibid., pp. 363-4.
109. Ibid., pp. 358, 361, 363.
110. Ibid., pp. 356, 361.
111. Ibid., pp. 358-9.
112. Ibid., pp. 358-60.
113. These texts belong to the early centuries of the Christian era. See R.S.

Sharma, *Light on Early Indian Society and Economy,* Bombay, 1966, pp. 90-111.

114. Wojtilla, ed., op. cit., pp. 219-20.
115. V.K. Jain, op. cit.,
116. The text was edited by T. Chowdhury in *Journal of Bihar Research Society,* XXXI (1945) and XXXII (1946). The earliest ms. used by him belongs to 1851-2. Composed by Haricaranasana, the text is based on the *Paryayaratnamala* of Madhavakara (*JBRS,* XXXI, 1945, Introduction, p. i). Since it is strikingly indebted to Amara in Chaps. 22 and 23 (ibid.) and since potato and tobacco are not mentioned in it, it seems to be pre-Mughal. The synonyms for iron and other metals are found in Chap. (*varga*) 6 (*JBRS,* XXXI, 1945).
117. Chap. 18 (*JBRS,* XXXI, 1945, 31-3) speaks of 24 types of *simbisukadhanyagana* (p. 33), but the varieties, when counted, come to nearly 110 types of cereals including wheat, barley, lentils, etc., Chap. 19 (ibid., 33-4) speaks of 10 types of *salidhanya* (transplanted paddy) and 19 types of *trnasalidhanya* (un-transplanted? paddy), but counting various types of paddy and allied cereals, it come to nearly 64.
118. T.C. Dasgupta, *Aspects of Bengali Society,* Calcutta, 1935, pp. 249-50, quoted in Yadava, op. cit., pp. 258, 305 fn. Yadava has cited several other pieces of evidence, op. cit., pp. 258-9.
119. Mukhia, op. cit., p. 292.
120. Yadava, *The Problems of the Emergence of Feudal Relations in Early India,* p. 46, fn. 1, draws attention to the position of the serf as stated by E.J. Hobsbawm on the basis of Karl Marx: 'The serf, though under the control of the lord, is in fact an economically independent producer', *Karl Marx: Pre-Capitalist Economic Formations,* London, 1964, p. 42.

The Uniqueness of the East

Chris Wickham

Harbans Mukhia, in his stimulating article, 'Was There Feudalism in Indian History?', rejects the use of the Marxist concept of feudalism outside restricted areas of the world, principally Europe. He is not the first to do this; another recent discussion, Perry Anderson's at the end of his *Lineages of the Absolutist State*, does so equally forcefully, if on different grounds. This article, a critical response to such a limitation of feudalism, draws primarily on my experiences in attempting to reformulate the problem of the fall of the Roman Empire in the West in Marxist terms. Here I porpose to discuss the contrast between the Roman Empire and its failure on the one hand, and the remarkable continuity of some of the Asian empires on the other, concentrating on those of China and of the Islamic world (Arab, Persian, and Turkish). I leave out India, which is covered in other articles here. I write as a Western medievalist, without any pretensions to expertise in the areas or the languages: I have, that is to say, followed Anderson's example in moving into everyone else's field. It would in fact be churlish not to admit my debt to Anderson at the start, though I will disagree with him; I started with his analysis—and with his bibliography—even if I have finished elsewhere.[1]

There are two typical ways of seeing Asia in current Marxist historiography. The first is to take the modes of production from Marx's published and unpublished writings and try to fit the peculiar patterns of Asian history to them: the feudal mode of production, the Asiatic mode, even the slave mode sometimes, with particularly unhappy results. This method has led to the straitjacketing of Asian historical development and sometimes to serious misunderstandings of whole socio-economic processes. The second method is to abandon Marx's systems altogether and to formulate new modes or categories of analysis that are, in effect, nothing more than claims in traditional historical fashion for the historical uniqueness of specific areas: 'I study Byzantium, or some part of Africa, or India, or the Mediterranean; it is empirically different from the medieval West or the Roman Empire; therefore I can establish a new mode'—the Byzantine, or African, or Indian mode. Irfan Habib's 'Indian medieval economy' and Gunther Lewin's refusal to categorize the medieval Chinese economic system at all are other variants of this, put into different terminology.[2] Harbans Mukhia and Perry Anderson are also very firmly in this second group. It seems to me that, whereas the first method is overschematic, the second is defeatist. Often defeatist, too, is a third method, the habit of some historians to say, in effect, that there must be some undefined sort of mixture of modes inside the social formations of different places in Asia, that can explain the Asian divergences from European 'norms'. This often leads once again to a refusal to categorize at all: Maxime Rodinson's *Islam and Capitalism*, though providing a succinct critique of a variety of analyses of medieval Islam, is an example of this tendency. Modes of production are ideal constructs; social formations are real societies in all their complexity, and thus in practice virtually irreducible to formal categories. This argument is little more than an excuse for the absence of analysis. But the method none the less seems to me to be the most useful to pursue. There have been close on no societies in human history, after the development of classes, with a single mode of production in them. What matters is to find out *how* different modes articulate together, a procedure that has generally been neglected, not least by the philosophers who have set out the complicated patterns in which mythic modes might behave.[3]

Why do we try to categorize world history in Marxist terms at all? Leaving aside the devotional elements in such categorizations—an element that is, as is well known, still strong—the only answer can be Marx's own: that we understand the world better by so doing, so that we can change it. Such categorizations must set out and make comprehensible the more, or less, latent socio-economic processes that underly the social formations, social systems, societies, which we study and whose ruling classes (usually) have produced the surviving material at our disposal. Marx's great achievement was to lay bare the economic logic underlying capitalism, while making it clear that this logic was specific *to* the capitalist mode of production, rather than a timeless historical given. Marx's own musings on pre-capitalist systems were virtually all side-effects produced by this insight. But while this has given all of us our clues, it also, for pre-capitalist historians, produces a problem: what sorts of economic logic did pre-capitalist modes actually possess?

Marx's list of pre-capitalist modes of production varies through his—and Engels's—lifetimes, and it is absurd to assume *a priori* that it has to have been complete, or even properly thought out. But economic systems with their own procedures and logics of development cannot be unlimited. It is quite notable how few attempts there have been since Marx to invent new modes of production outside the individual contexts that historians have found themselves studying; and how such modes work, what their specificity is, is seldom explained. There are of course the non-exploitative modes, where combinations and recombinations seems to be endless (nomadic or seminomadic/transhumant or settled exploitation of resources; communal or collective or private ownership; clan/kin-group or village or household cooperation, etc.), and these elements indeed also underlie exploitative modes in a complex array that, in the absence of serious study, sometimes at first sight seems random. But what distinguishes exploitative modes is that their social relations of production contain, and are largely defined by, specific systems of the appropriation of the surplus; and there are certainly not a limitless number of these. Methods of surplus-appropriation in practice seem to be restricted to a few basic types—slavery, rent-taking (either 'feudal', i.e. backed up by coercion, or determined by market forces), tribute and taxation, wage-labour, the manipulation of the petty commodity market. There may be others, but there are not a lot of others. And it is in the difference between these elements, in my view, that the differences between modes of production lie.[4]

Barry Hindess and Paul Hirst have pursued some of this line of argument—though they would certainly not agree with my formulation of it—in their acute (if somewhat criticized) book, *Pre-Capitalist Modes of Production*. They laid down some strict criteria about what constituted a mode of production; over-strict, it is true, particularly in their insistence on a one-to-one correspondence of given sets of productive forces and relations of production (see pp. 183ff.), and sometimes contradicted by their own practice, but useful as a critique of many more sloppy formulations.[5] Their demonstration that the core of the feudal mode of production lies less in the political-juridical aspects of serfdom than in the rent extraction relationships intrinsic to all pre-capitalist landlordship is particularly important for us here. Such a relationship is defined and backed up by non-economic coercive force, of course, but it is not dependent on peasant unfreedom, for tenants can perfectly easily be legally free; it is their rent-paying (or labour-service) that defines their economic world as feudal, not their political subjection.

This definition of feudalism is certainly one that would be opposed by Mukhia. He sees feudalism as almost wholly specific to Europe, because he defines it as constituted in earlier paragraphs all by labour-service. Such a characterization is too restrictive, however. Apart from the fact that very little of medieval Europe would be feudal if it were so, it presupposes that labour-service constituted a landlordly control over the work-process different in *type* from that involved in the specification, say, of precise types of produce required as rent in kind. In fact, landlords did not often regard their demesnes as the places *par excellence* where they could closely direct the work-process of subjected labourers; peasants performed their labour-services according to the same locally-determined procedures that they used in cultivating their own land. (Attempted control by landlords tended to be at the level of trying to dominate the process of determining such procedures; see pp. 135ff.) There is a lot of interplay in Western history between different forms of rent—labour, kind, money; there is nothing to show that these were different economic systems. But the *set* of relations between landlord and tenant gives an analytical coherence to feudalism as an independent mode, and it is Hindess and Hirst's definition that I will use in what follows.[6]

It seems to me that feudalism was a world system. That is, not in the sense that it had to be because of some extra-historical teleology; but because *empirically* there have been few if any class societies that have not experienced some form of landowning and coercive rent-taking. This experience unifies Capetian France and *ancien régime* France and Russia and Sung China and Qajar Iran and the late Roman Empire and modern Guatemala. Anyone who looks at analyses of the experiences of tenants in different places and times in world history must recognize the similarities—not just existential ones, but in the logics of the economic system of rent-taking compared. Sung China is *not* unfamiliar, unrecognizable, to Western economic historians; not in this respect, at least.

The standard counter-argument is the clear and irrefutable statement that in all other respects these latter societies are rather unlike Capetian France; so their modes of production cannot be the same, that is, cannot be feudal. Anderson has made the point at some length, and perhaps in the clearest manner; he is paralleled by many others, particularly by historians of the individual societies concerned. Sometimes the argument is beside the point, for the definition of feudalism is simply taken as being the existence of fiefs, vassals, and military service based on contract; this is not and never has been a Marxist definition, and arguments of this kind are based on a simple misunderstanding. Anderson is more sophisticated; he certainly recognizes that a 'minimal' definition of feudalism, such as the one I have outlined earlier, could indeed cover wideish tracts of world history. What worries him, however, is only in part the inexactness of analysis he says results; it is that the unique Western development towards capitalism becomes inexplicable. He resolves the problem by *defining* a mode of production in terms of its superstructure—for feudalism, therefore, the political-military systems of vassalage and the rest. Paul Hirst has effectively analysed the sleight of hand through which Anderson does this; in his words, 'This means that there can be as many modes of production as there are distinct legal-political constitutions and forms of extra-economic sanction which follow from them.' Anderson is here abandoning Marxism—indeed, abandoning systematic economic analysis (I'll leave it to the reader to decide which is worse).[7]

But the problem need never have arisen. All these writers know and state that a single mode of production almost never defines a whole society (i.e. social formation).[8] All of them as regularly forget it in their actual analyses, whether Hindess and Hirst on the Roman Empire or Anderson on China (contrast Anderson's skilful discussion of the relationship between modes in Russia, though). If feudalism is not necessarily the dominant mode everywhere that it is present, then the notable differences, especially in political system, between the vast range of societies where feudalism can be found, are more easily explained. Anderson's problem of the West's uniqueness (or primacy) is a lot less difficult to solve if his world is reformulated: the medieval and post-medieval West was one of the few societies where feudalism has *dominated.* Not that I am going to discuss, still less explain, the problem of the origin of capitalism here. Instead, as a realistic alternative to the task of characterizing all world history in 10,000 words, I shall restrict myself to a relatively narrow question: the relationship between two modes of production, characterized respectively by rent-taking and tax-raising, in a number of pre-capitalist state societies stretching West-East from Rome to China. I shall discuss the relationship between these two modes at two levels, that of the economy itself and that of politics and the state; I will thus for the most part exclude the problem of ideology. My other exclusion will be any discussion of other modes and their role in these societies, even the capitalist mode (potentially nascent in most of the societies I shall discuss), despite its evident importance for the classic problem of their 'blocked development'; indeed, I shall not dwell on problems of distribution at all. Often more significant an omission, however, will be the array of more primitive modes that these societies also contained, and which have often been of considerable relevance to their historical development (particularly what has sometimes been called the 'nomadic' mode; nomads conquered every Asian state I shall discuss at least once, and often several times; nomadism, in both exploitative and non-exploitative forms, is still an economic and social system of some importance and political weight in, for example, Iran).[9] Rent and tax have, however, been until the present century the major forms of surplus extraction everywhere in the states of Asia, and the relationship between the two is historically and analytically crucial; here must be the place to start.

Coercive rent-taking is the feudal mode of production; it represents the exploitative relationship between tenant and landlord, and it has been extensively discussed by generations of experts.[10] What is tax? What it is not is the traditionally defined Asiatic mode of production. There is no space to repeat the varying criticisms levelled against this category of analysis and its less or (recently) more sophisticated advocates; it is sufficient here to state that one or other or both of autarkic village communes, and a tax-raising state owning all landed property and carrying out large-scale necessary public works, are actually rather rare. Indeed, the absolute predominance of state landed property, as we shall see, is a feature of societies so developed that village autarky and communality are effectively excluded, and the absence of classes, another traditional feature, is nonsensical. State irrigation, state landed property, and a tax-rent equivalence are present in different places at different times, but are rarely together. The Asiatic mode as it has always been formulated cannot be regarded as having any analytical validity.[11]

The real problem about the Asiatic mode is that it is too politically and legally specific. Like the private-justice-and-serfdom-and-labour-service version of the feudal mode, it has too many institutions arbitrarily attached to it for it to be of much help as an economic category. But the simpler relationship represented by a state bureaucracy taxing a peasantry is another matter. Samir Amin uses an alternative term, the 'tributary mode of production', and this gives him *carte blanche* to reformulate its elements without going eternally back to what Marx thought of Bernier and Kovalevsky; I will follow his example. (It will give me, too, *carte blanche* to depart where necessary from Amin.)[12] A 'state class' based on a public institution, with political rights to extract surplus from a peasantry that it does not tenurially control, is certainly common enough in Asia, and not only in Asia. Since the Asiatic mode lost credibility, this pattern has often simply been regarded as a state version of feudalism, particularly by Soviet historians; but it is important to recognize that it normally *co-exists* with more typical feudal relations, those of landowners taking rent from tenants, and that taxation is always in an explicitly antagonistic relationship to such rent-taking—landowners do not want to pay taxes any more than peasants do. Tax and rent are thus frequently perceived as in opposition. That they are also opposed in their economic logics, as different modes must necessarily be, is less obvious; I will return to the question at the end, in my third section and try to set out how such an opposition works. In the intervening section I will take the tax *vs.* rent antagonism for granted, and show how it is useful in explaining some specific societies and their developments; this will give me a firmer heuristic position from which to discuss some of the problems that are left.

II

I started with an attempt to explain the fall of the Roman Empire in the West, a full discussion of which I have published elsewhere. I posited the relationship between tax and rent there as being one between 'ancient' and feudal modes, the ancient mode in its class form being seen as a city-based subtype of the tributary mode (see pp. 137ff.). The ancient mode predominated over feudalism in the good days of the late Roman Empire, through the fact that tax at times actually took more from peasants than rent, and (more important), through the dominance that the hierarchies of state office, and state financial handouts, had over the social relationships of the landed aristocracy, and even the relations between the latter and the peasantry. But the two modes were structurally antagonistic, even though the aristocracy participated in (and took the benefits from) both: in an underdeveloped economy, there is not much to do with wealth except put it into land, and land carried tax liability. As the aristocracy increased their landholdings, the state was less a benefit to them, and more and more a burden. When the state was threatened by Germanic invasion and settlement, the aristocracy and peasantry were unprepared to pay increasing taxes in return for less and less defence; the state simply broke up. The Germans found no tax-raising infrastructure left that was sufficient to allow them to maintain the major Roman expense, the standing army. The German armies settled on the land, becoming aristocracies and peasantries in their turn; although taxation took a century and more to disappear entirely, feudal relations dominated in Western Europe henceforth.[13]

The key feature—one could indeed say peculiarity or particularity—of this account is the ultimate *failure* of the Roman state in the West when opposed directly to the landed aristocracy. It seems obvious to Westernists: the civic aristocracies were closer to the land than the state was; they were locally powerful enough to sabotage tax-collecting by the state's functionaries—who were usually other aristocrats, in fact, in collusion; they extended their *de facto* protection against taxation to any free peasants prepared to become their tenants, and so on. The state was starved of funds and collapsed; perhaps the economy was too undeveloped to allow for large powerful states. But this did not happen even in the Eastern empire (soon to become Byzantium), not to speak of Iran, China, and the innumerable Arab successor-states in the Middle East. Individual states had their bad times, or were replaced by others, but the state *itself* did not go away. Why not?

Let us start with China. One of the most striking features of Chinese history is by no means its uniqueness; it is, rather, its almost exact homology, often phrase for phrase in the books, with much of the development I have just outlined for late Rome. The difference is, of course, that the Chinese state did not collapse; to be more precise, it eclipsed, sometimes temporarily broke up, and then reformed, several times in the two millennia or so since unification in 211 BC. The 'dynastic cycle' occurred under the Ch'in and Han (221 BC–AD 220), Sui and T'ang (581-907), Sung (960-1127/1279), Ming (1368-1644), and Ch'ing (1644-1911).[14] The recurrent nature of this cycle has always formed the basis for the false image of static Chinese history, which in reality, anyway until the Ming, showed a steady development in the political and ideological coherence of state structures, as well as in agricultural expansion and commerce (especially under the Sung and early Ming). But our concern here is the relationship between the aristocracy and the state, insofar as it can be sketched out in its full complexity from documentation that almost exclusively, until at least the Sung, comes from the state itself.

Recently, a considerable body of high quality socio-economic historiography on China has appeared in Western languages, above all in English, and this makes our task a lot easier, if a little difficult to summarize in a few pages. One development during the whole of Chinese history that is now increasingly clear is the slow political absorption of the landed aristocracy in the state, which carries on across dynastic boundaries and times of trouble, independent of the expansion and contraction of aristocratic landowning in general. The aristocracy were older than the unified state, and the Han recognized the independent powers at least of the greatest aristocratic clans of the north. Such independence was certainly in part an ideological feature, in that such aristocrats did not depend on state office-holding for their self-definition; but we have reference to the effective political control they had locally, as well. The T'ang still recognized this ideological autonomy, in the aristocracies of both the north (the Yellow River) and the south (the Yangtse valley), but on the other hand they succeeded in recruiting the old northern aristocracies to the Imperial court as officials; so much so, that the great families of aristocrats actually died out when the T'ang fell after the 870s, and before the Sung recentralized China in the 960s-70s.[15] Under the T'ang, smaller local aristocracies all over China began to be systematically involved in state service (and thus the state financial patronage network), through the pseudo-meritocratic examination system; under the Sung, these became the whole ruling aristocracy, the 'bureaucrat-gentry' stratum, a vast (if fairly thinly spread) field of small to medium landowners, ready for state patronage, and in general dependent on state recognition as officials for the establishment of their places in local aristocratic hierarchies.

The pattern persisted and perfected itself. As late as the Ch'ing, when the Western world was already closing in on China, its force can be seen in Chang Chung-li's calculations that the nineteenth-century gentry globally got nearly half its income from official pay and services, and only a third from land (the rest was from commerce). Here, the gentry look like a real state class, financially dependent on tax-raising, rather than an aristocracy. But these figures are only valid for the officials themselves, and not, for example, for their non-degree-holding kin. It would, indeed, be wrong to see the gentry of any period between Sung and Ch'ing as defined exclusively by their office, either in economic or political terms. Office-holders—even, or especially, those few who had risen from the peasantry—typically and consistently used their wealth, as in the Roman Empire, to buy land. The Sung period, the first period where the state really controlled the ideology and social hierarchies of the aristocracy, was also the great age of the establishment of large estates, mostly by officials using their new wealth while they had it and before they were replaced by other officials. A recent study of T'ung-Ch'eng county, part of the lower Yangtse plain, under the Ming and Ch'ing shows how such official families came to have real local power as a result of their landowning (and, of course, of the patronage possibilities of office), which persisted whether the family-members were in office or not. Even when subsumed into the state, these office-holding aristocracies valued local control that was essentially based on the feudal relationships functional to landowning. Indeed, when aristocracies became linked too tightly to the state, as were the old northern families of the T'ang, they could founder when the state did, as they had *lost* such a feudal base. Aristocracies in China, then, never ceased to be feudal, no matter how firmly attached they were to the state class and its vast cultural/ideological apparatus (Confucianism, the literary ethic of 'mandarinism', etc.); or, if they did, they fell.[16]

Over time, again regardless of the dynastic cycle, the state became more powerful. The early (seventh-century) T'ang state was relatively small-scale, based on landed peasant armies and with light taxation. This must indeed partly explain why the T'ang emperors (with some notable exceptions) recognized that the old aristocracy were necessary to the state even on the aristocracy's own terms; the T'ang did not have the strength to usurp, or even overawe, them. But—largely as the nomad threat to China built up, not for the first time—armies became salaried, and taxation rose. The bureaucracy, in other words the patronage-network that was beginning to incorporate the local aristocracies into the state, was also expanding fast; taxation rose further. This then ran into the classic pattern of the dynastic cycle: raised taxes resulted in networks of clientage, protection, tax-evasion, the weakening of the state. But the trend was slowly upward; the Sung reestablishment presupposed taxes that, though perhaps lower than in the late T'ang, were certainly higher (and better collected) than in the early T'ang; the late T'ang, Sung and Ming also benefited from systematic large-scale taxes on trade and minerals extraction. On the other hand, the scale of taxation can be exaggerated. By Western standards, formal taxes were never high: under the Ming, seldom over 10 per cent of crop even in the fertile Yangtse, where landlords could take 50 per cent of the crop as rent (though tax came out of this). The state had financial drawing-power because it took taxes from so vast an area, not because it took a lot of tax. And locally, even at the height of dynastic power, its officials had in practice to negotiate with powerful interests; government could not always be uncompromisingly coercive ('despotic'), even if potentially backed up by force.[17]

China is a big country, with a lot of mountain land obstructing communications. Even though it should be recognized that my descriptions relate very largely to the two interlocking basins of the Yellow River and Yangtse, linked after 600 by a canal system, the size of the area is still vast, and difficulties of control were enormous right into the present century. This is clearly seen in the early centuries of central government, with long (if lessening) periods of breakdown in the face of foreign invasion and internal disorder, particularly in 220-589 and *c.* 880-979. But even these years were ones of more or less effective *regional* states, not of the total breakdown of the state itself and the tax system. The collapse of the tributary mode, so visible, almost inevitable, in Rome, did not occur.[18]

The chief reason for this must have been the existence, in particular over much of the North China Plain, of a free land-holding peasantry. In the north, even in the Ch'ing period, there was relatively little landlordship; the stronghold of estates has always been the more fertile Yangtse valley. Though there were certainly strong aristocratic families in the north at least until the T'ang, the trend of scholarship is to stress the dominance of a free peasantry in the Yellow River valley throughout historical times. The northern plain was perhaps too poor to attract the concentration of estates of the Yangtse delta. But, as a result, it has always offered an easier locus for state exploitation; there are fewer landlords to undermine the tributary mode. The state, even at its weakest, even when fragmented into warring provinces as after the Han and after the T'ang, was always able to tax.[19]

The dynastic cycles, when they are looked at more closely, thus take on a slightly different form: not the rise and fall of strong government, but the expansion and contraction of the scale of centralized government. The political core of the Chinese state was always in the poorer and more 'egalitarian' north; the post-Han and post-T'ang periods see the shrunken 'legitimate' state surviving there, and one might almost say experimenting with new forms of state organization that might act as a springboard for the reconquest of the richer and more feudal south. The Toba Turks of the fourth-to sixth-century north began to generalize the so-called *chün-t'ien* or equal-field system, the state-sponsored land redistribution that underlay the landed armies of the early T'ang; the Five Dynasties (907-60) reshaped the sclerotic late T'ang bureaucracy and recentralized the provincial armies of the north, to serve as the basis for Sung reunification. When the emperors reconquered the south, on each occasion they discovered that the south had developed economically in its independence, which they were then able to exploit; the Sung takeover and exploitation of southern development clinched central government power for nearly a millennium.[20]

So: which mode was dominant? Some historians have tended to stress the lightness and weakness of central government, and attribute the failure of China to break up in a feudal manner entirely to the force of Confucian ideology among the upper classes. But, although it may seem that central government was by no means financially onerous in world terms (even if the poor of the north would have found even 10 per cent of crop excessive), individual private ownership was never, in any period, able to destroy its structure. Landlords, however extortionate, only ever controlled a minority of China's peasants, concentrated in the centre-south, and they too were in world terms quite notably small-scale owners. There were few aristocrats (after 880 perhaps) large enough to envisage a firm feudal alternative to the public tax-raising of the tributary state—although they were certainly always happy to evade or expropriate it on a small scale where they could. Even when central government broke down, often in the face of generalized peasant revolts, aimed at state and landlords alike (the 880s, the 1350s, the 1630s),[21] government and taxation still survived in the north. One might expect the breakdown of the tributary mode in front of the feudal mode to be found, if anywhere, in the independent tenth-century kingdoms of the Yangtse delta, where feudal power was strongest; it would be interesting to have a study of the states of Wu and

Nan T'ang, for example. But otherwise, the tributary mode remained dominant—ideologically, certainly; economically, probably (indeed, total tax perhaps surpassed total rent in all periods); politically, without doubt, for the landlord class was always too divided, and over the centuries became even more so, as average aristocratic holdings tended gradually to diminish in size. The state could thus always give aristocrats more than they could get on their own. The tributary mode dominated the social relations of production: the peasantry were always nominally-free tax-payers, and the aristocracy and gentry accepted the ground-rules of the hierarchies of the state. But the feudal mode was always there, ready when appropriate to undermine it.[22]

This underlying framework to Chinese historical development shows the pattern I want to explore very clearly. The dominance of the tributary mode over the feudal mode characterizes, in my view, the relation between state and landowners/peasants in most traditional state societies. Let us pursue it in the case of our second example, the Arab empire and its successors in the medieval period. I shall in fact focus less on the period of the Arab empire proper (636-945) than on its Iranian and Turkish heirs in the tenth to twelfth centuries, for the latter period is a relatively low point for state power in general, and is quite well documented and studied; there are thus some good test cases for the problem of state survival. I shall concentrate on the kingdoms of the Buyids (945-1055) in western Iran and Iraq, the Ghaznavids (994-1040) in north-eastern Iran (Khurasan), and the Saljuqs (1037-1157), rulers of the whole Middle East, and survivors after the mid-twelfth century in several areas of western Iran and Turkey until their final supersession in the thirteenth century by the Mongol Ilkhans.[23] These states, different enough in detail, had one socio-political feature in common that is of relevance here: unlike in the Roman and Chinese empires, where a roughly homogeneous aristocratic class participated in the profits of both state and landownership, in most of these 'Islamic' states a state class clearly stood in opposition to an aristocratic class of local landowners. There was certainly overlap, but the two were socially and often ethnically distinguishable, and frequently antagonistic in ideology, as well as in their economic base.

The origins of this counter-position are easy enough to explain: they are the product of conquest, first by Arabs, then by various waves of Turks, and eventually Mongols. Each new regime had a new armed backing which represented the military power of that state for the century or so of its rule over some part of the Arab empire. It is always, then, the army that is most clearly distinguishable from the local civil aristocracy. Central government in its civil sense, by contrast, the bureaucracy that ran the states and their taxation, was more continuous. Though this too was seen in opposition to local power, there was here rather more overlap in personnel; civil bureaucrats had to come from somewhere. Thus Nizam al-Mulk, the great vizir of the Saljuqs (1063-92), and the greatest lay theorist of government of his century, was of a local landowner (*dihqan*) family from Baihaq in Khurasan, rising through Khurasani civic office to central (and almost absolute) power. Such roots are normal. But the military elites were not so rooted, or not so often, and it is this fact that gives the period its flavour.[24]

The Arabs conquered parts of the east Roman (Byzantine) Empire and the whole of the Persian (Sassanian) empire, both states with a long tradition of tax *vs.* rent, and of military and civil officials who were themselves landowners. The Byzantine Empire had been institutionally decentralized in the Roman sense (see pp. 137ff.), but the Arabs changed that; like the Sassanians (and like the Byzantines themselves from now on), their Empire was administered and taxed centrally, from the capital. Exactly how the Sassanian state worked socio-economically is very obscure; it seems that tax was collected by the lowest stratum of the aristocracy, the *dihqans*, who ranged in wealth from rich peasants to substantial local landowners. Presumably they had the force to collect tax from the free peasantry, still a considerable group, but not from the *de facto* exempt greater nobility, who could be very large owners indeed (with dependent tenants, both slave and free). The Arabs settled their ethnic armies, with some tensions, but left the *dihqans* alone. Indeed, they still used them as tax-collectors, especially in Khurasan, although the organization of taxation was eventually bureaucratized. There were considerable local differences in the extent to which the Arabs left the social structure alone, particularly as regards the position of the upper nobility (in noble-dominated Iran, almost totally; by contrast, the equally rich aristocracy in Egypt soon vanished, its lands falling to the state). But the major changes were in central government and the army; traditional private landowning remained the basis of *local* power into the tenth to eleventh centuries, and beyond. The Arab rulers maintained substantial state lands, too, though these fluctuated in size, as some were handed out in small blocs in effectively full ownership, *qati'a,* mostly to ethnic Arabs (a feature of the early period), and as others were seized back at times of dynastic change.[25]

Few large centrally-run pre-capitalist states have been able to do without tax-farming, and that of the Arabs was certainly no exception. Tax-farming, however, is dangerous to central government, as it can too easily be turned into private power. So it was with the Arabs. And increasingly, from the ninth century on, the concept of tax-farming was extended to the army. In the tenth century the Buyids began to adopt the procedure of granting their soldiers *iqta'*, the right to exact tax from particular areas, instead of part or all of their pay. This was generalized under the Saljuqs, and became the predominant governing principle for the remuneration of the army in the whole Islamic world for many centuries. Much has been written about the *iqta'*. There is a long argument about whether it is 'feudal' or not, for example, in the sense of Western military feudalism (answer: yes, sometimes, but it depends on time and place).[26] Claude Cahen, who dominates the historiography, discussed at some length its classic development; he pointed out the easy procedures by which a *muqta'* (*iqta'*-holder) could usurp all the powers of the state, privatise them, and turn the tax payable from estates to him as *muqta'* into rent paid to him as landlord, especially as *iqta'* became hereditary in the twelfth century or so. Indeed, in a classic Western-style development, a *muqta'* was able to extend his non-taxpaying privileges by persuasion or coercion to his neighbours, in exchange for their land. Cahen tends to assume in his discussions that all taxpayers are peasants, even though we know that there were many private landlords who could presumably have resisted the privatization of *muqta'* powers more effectively. Nevertheless, the development (or its potentialities) is clear: the tributary state was tending towards feudalism, this time meant in Marxist terms.

States, of course, resisted. They often redistributed *iqta'* and made sure for as long as possible that they were not hereditary; they kept the bureaucracy of tax-assessment in their own hands. *Muqta'* did not reside on their estates, so this, at least, decreased the immediacy of their possession. Nevertheless, the failure of states lay in their growing incapacity to maintain such controls. Hereditary *iqta'*, as in twelfth-century Syria or the fourteenth-century Ilkhanate, is a sure sign that the state is weak.[27] If we read the laments of central government bureaucrats in such periods, we might marvel that the state ever survived at all. Tax no longer comes into the exchequer; central authority over far-off provinces is growing weak. Tax is turning into rent; private and local lordship is replacing public power. There are even hierarchies of *muqta'*, linked by private bonds of loyalty. We can see the same process, indeed, in the late (thirteenth- to fifteenth-century) Byzantine Empire, where it is in fact better documented. There, it is arguable that the state was falling to feudal patterns by the time of the Ottoman conquest. But the Islamic states did not. Possession of *iqta'* never became ideologically separated from a recognition of the tax system; it never became *simply* landholding.

Partly, this is because the scale of *iqta'* concessions has sometimes been exaggerated; rulers kept a sizeable proportion of tax-raising in their own hands and those of their more dependent civilian tax-farmers.[28] But it is also because Middle Eastern society was more locally complex and diverse than central government documents admit.

Recently, there have been some good studies of local elites in the cities of northern Iran and Khurasan in the tenth to eleventh centuries, particularly Nishapur, based on local urban and lineage histories. The city focus of these histories is not misleading, for the areas were very urbanocentric: all important landowners, and many less important ones, lived in cities. (The religious focus of the histories is more misleading, but cannot be helped.) From these, it is clear how decentralized social life in a wide-spaced and thinly-populated society such as Iran actually was. Urban patrician elites (*a'yan*) genuinely controlled Nishapur, Bayhaq, Qazvin. Though not formally self-governing, they were at least legally autonomous in the sense that there was no appeal from the local judge, the *qaḍi*, who was almost always chosen by and/or from the local elite. There is dispute as to how organized local government was (the urban headman or *ra'is* is a particularly shadowy figure, though of crucial importance to the city and its relation to the state, and again almost always from the *a'yan*), but it is clear that local power was sufficiently coherent to be worth fighting for—local factionalism was rife in all these cities. And the state, even in the figures of the strongest rulers like Mahmud of Ghazni or Nizam al-Mulk, had to respect the cities and their factions—heavy intervention led to disloyalty. These elites were based very largely on landowning; although religion and commercial wealth were also status indicators and indeed ladders up into the patriciate, landowning was the base that every *a'yan* family had, or obtained as soon as possible. Landowning and local power were inseparable; every major local owner was in a position to be an important figure in one of the factions of the urban arena. Economic and social power in these cities was thus ultimately feudal, despite a considerable commercial (and ideological) element. But it was all civilian. The *iqta'* developments described above do not visibly enter into it at all.[29]

In part, this division must be because there are as yet no systematic analyses of the political interrelation between the central power-structure and the local elites. It is as if they belonged to two separate worlds. They cannot have done, of course; the central elites cannot have been quite as deracinated as they sometimes seem. But we do none the less have two separate tendencies to feudalism in the one society, one the decentralization and privatization of central government tax-raising, and the other the continuing independence of private civilian landowning. They were distinct, and in structural rivalry. The state actually benefited, as 'honest broker' between factions.[30] This on its own cannot explain the state's survival, of course; it is too contingent an explanation. As I have said, a major element in the political survival of states has to have been their continuing control over at least some of the tax wealth of their localities. The local angle on the Iranian political system does, however, show that the picture of total dominance by *muqta'* is incomplete, for local differences, and local elites, are left out of account. And, on the other hand, the break between land and central government (military) power in the successor states meant that land on its own did not bring automatic rights to direct rule. There was less incentive to reject the opportunities and responsibilities of civil or military office and go it alone as a landowner: power was still defined in central government terms, and office (or more *iqta'*) was still in the gift of the state. Local power was in the hands of the urban elites, but few of them attempted independence—they had no armies. The only solution for the disloyal was to re-invent central government locally (a development aided when, as became common, whole provinces and their administration were handed out in *iqta'* to governors). Central government breakdown in Iran and its neighbours, as in China, thus meant the establishment of regional states on the Baghdad model, not the end of the state (and its tributary underpinning) itself.[31]

Tax rates varied greatly. In ninth-century Iraq, Adams calculates that one-quarter to one-third of gross grain crop went in tax, a considerable figure; in the thirteenth century, tenants still paid this, and another third to their landlords. In neighbouring Khuzistan in the latter period, though, tax was apparently only at 10 per cent and rent up to 50 per cent. We cannot produce global figures for each, for, quite apart from the chance nature of the survival of these rates, we cannot even guess at how much land was held by landlords at any period; we can thus draw no general conclusions about the relationship.[32] This is unfortunate, for the global extent of aristocratic landowning and the general relation between rent and taxation is of obvious importance for the power of the state, as the contrasting experience of Rome and China shows. In Iran, we must accept that this quantitative aspect of the analysis is closed to us. But the key qualitative aspect for state survival is the state's continuing control over the terms of the relationship between aristocrat and peasant; this, as we have seen, can be studied, and it is arguably more important.

Whether peasants themselves ever saw tax and rent as separable, especially as it was the responsibility of the landowner to divide them and pass the tax on, is in doubt; the implications of this I shall return later. But on one type of land, peasant perception would have been correct: on state land there cannot have been any structural difference between tax and rent at all. And in one area of the Middle East, Saljuq and Ottoman Turkey, this becomes a crucial fact, for there, unlike anywhere else, almost all the land belonged directly to the state. How the state came to take over all the land is not fully clear, but it certainly lay in the chance circumstances of conquest, and is thus not relevant here as a problem.[33] It is a theoretical possibility, of course, in any state society. Indeed, many societies regard all land as nominally owned by God (= the community = the state), as the Arab legists did, as the Saljuqs did even outside Turkey, and as indeed Zoroastrian and Confucian ideology enjoined. Under normal circumstances, however, this has no meaning, for private landowning persists without interruption. It certainly does not mean that such societies are 'Asiatic', as is often said; William the Conqueror claimed no less full ultimate ownership, and indeed exercised his eminent rights rather more seriously, without being any less the emblematic feudal monarch, in all senses. But the Saljuqs in Turkey, and, still more, the Ottomans, went beyond this: they did not merely have eminent rights; they owned. This difference does not turn on legal prerogatives; it turns on *power*.[34] In Turkey, the state had the political strength to maintain its rights to all land as the state *and* as the immediate landowner, real and uncontested for centuries. In its doing so, all relationships that can be called feudal in Marxist terms withered; it is in many ways legitimate to see post-eleventh-century Turkey as the purest tributary society. I shall end my descriptive section with a discussion of how this seems to have worked.

The Ottoman state owned more-or-less all the land of Anatolia and the Balkans: at its height, in 1528, some 87 per cent (of Anatolia only?), on Inalcik's figures.[35] Ottoman peasants paid no rent; only tax to the state. But the fifteenth- to sixteenth-century state assigned over half of this back, in *timars*, to their *sipahi* cavalry, called in the fiscal context *timariots*. Whether the *timar* was direct descendent of the *iqta'*, or of the *prónoia*, the parallel Byzantine institution, is not important; the function of the *timar* was the same as both (names proliferate after *c.* 1500: the Mongol-Iranian *tuyul* and the Mughal *jagir* are the same institution). *Sipahis* lived on the land, however, on their *timars*. *Timars* were not hereditary, and could be transferred; such transferrals became less and less common, however, especially after 1550 or so. The fact that the *sipahis* lived locally and took crops directly produced an unusually close link between them and their tied (but 'free') peasants, reinforced by the wide powers delegated to *timariots*: local justice and policing, the right to exact private corvée service, control over land and produce sales. *Timars* were, however, never entirely privatized, or even immune from central government; the state always kept up its fiscal registers.

The Ottomans doubtless realized the feudalizing dangers of the *timar* system, and, when military technology changed, making the *sipahi* system less useful, they moved away from it. After the late sixteenth century, therefore, the Ottomans began to use a salaried army; *sipahis* declined in importance (not without the occasional revolt, with peasant support, in the early seventeenth). The state farmed out taxes to civic entrepreneurs instead. Tax-farmers were, initially, less hereditary, more civilian; this soon began to change, as indeed it had to—unarmed tax-farmers were not always able to collect taxes at all. By the end of the seventeenth century they too could have private armies, and be *de facto* hereditary. Their most spectacular representatives became in the eighteenth century *derebeys*, valley lords, controlling entire provinces and often groups of provinces, in effect as hereditary princes of mini-states. More significant, though, was the importance given by tax-farming and local influence to an entire urban stratum, the local rich, still called *a'yan*, notables; this stratum in the late seventeenth to nineteenth centuries was autonomous from the state, maintaining its traditional intermediary role between state and civil society. The *a'yan* were also the first to adapt to the possibilities of capitalism in the outside (Western) world. Under their influence, the concept of the landed estate, *çiftlik*, reappeared in the Balkans and western Anatolia in the eighteenth century, after centuries of eclipse, as an organizing device, oriented towards commerce: a notable concession to privatized control, and, significantly, in the areas most open to the West. But the state had not given up. Mahmud II in the 1820s to 1830s moved against these decentralizing forces; he overthrew or curbed the *derebeys*, he confiscated much *a'yan* land, he reassumed all surviving *timars*. His success was not complete (Muhammad 'Ali, himself from the *a'yan*, was almost completely successful in a similar politics in Egypt, by contrast), but it was substantial. The nineteenth century proceeded with a continual struggle between state and notables as to how far private property law should be accepted, and whom it should benefit; but even the weakened (and commercially undermined) Ottoman state of the late nineteenth century could at least hold notables to a standoff until World War I.[36]

Of course, the feudal elements in this are obvious. The Ottomans could not hold on to an entirely centralized power-network in so underdeveloped an empire, even in the Turkish heartlands. The tendency to privatization implicit in all decentralized local power was a tendency, as elsewhere, towards direct personal control of the land, the feudal mode. But it was not complete; in fact, genuine feudal appropriation barely began before the late eighteenth century. And the Ottoman state was always strong and sophisticated enough to be able to reassert its power, in the late fifteenth century, the mid-seventeenth, the early nineteenth. It never lost its control over the rules of political legitimacy. Its local rivals, though strong, never managed to establish local power-structures that were anything other than versions and perversions of the powers delegated to them by central government. The classic article on nineteenth-century urban notables by Hourani, though it emphasizes their substantial autonomy, also points up the informality and ambiguity of the political arena in which they were operating, in between the 'state class' and the urban commoners and peasantry. Their power was the manipulation of the state; it did not establish itself with its own political terrain, unlike notable power in Saljuq Khurasan, or gentry power on the Yangtse. Feudal landed power was too weak; the patronage potential of the state too vast to allow deviation from it. Real local independence was once again only possible by usurping the powers of *central* government—and, in Muhammad 'Ali's Egypt, actually using them more effectively.[37]

That this was a matter of power rather than legal form is best seen by looking to nineteenth-century (Qajar) Iran. The Safavids and Qajars also seriously claimed rights to the ownership of all land, though their legal justification for this ran back to an increasingly hard interpretation of Islamic law, rather than to the state's occupation of all the land, as in Turkey. But they could not maintain it. Iran was too underdeveloped; its communications were too sketchy. Aristocracies, based on *tuyuls*, could rise or be pulled down, but the state always in practice had to recognize them as real landowning aristocracies, and they acted themselves as if they were. The politics of urban notables, as a recent study of Maragheh in Azerbaijan shows, were in principle independent of the state and, quite simply, functional to landowning. Even *tuyuldars* were now often seen as landowners not tax-farmers, and the sources show that there had also, somehow, by the nineteenth century come to be landowners with close to full private title once more. The state had to negotiate; it could not dominate, for its army and bureaucracy were too weak. One has to recognize that the Qajars, and even their shortlived eighteenth-century predecessors, did this rather well, controlling local elites with intelligent brokerage, and maintaining the existence and influence of central power and taxation through a period of increasing penetration of capitalism, and right into the twentieth century; but the pattern of relationships is more reminiscent of Iran in the eleventh century than Turkey in the nineteenth.

Legal title or no, the Iranian rulers had to recognize that landlorship was feudal, and defend their tributary power-base accordingly.[38]

Turkey and, to a lesser extent, Iran were the Asian states best known to Marx's predecessors. Marx knew India better, and indeed India seems to me to fit into this array of patterns without difficulty. But Marx's conception of Asian state power was largely formed from the second-hand images he received of Ottoman power and legal rights. The absence of private property in land seemed to him an extraordinary representation of the most primitive of social forms. And so, maybe, it is. But it should be clear that only an unusually *developed* economic and political system was actually capable of maintaining it. Only the 'Islamic state' at its most centralized and sophisticated, as its most uncompromising, was able even to try to stop landed property from being *de facto* privatized, from falling back into feudalism. The Ottomans could do it; the Qajar state, far less politically and economically developed, could not. Tributary states thus normally co-existed with feudal ownership; they had no choice. The extreme social forms of the Ottoman world that underlay what Marx sometimes called the 'Asiatic' mode were in fact at the opposite end of the run of human history from where he supposed. 'Static' is the least adequate adjective for the development towards the Ottoman state.

III

I have so far concentrated broadly on 'socio-political' history, rather than 'socio-economic'. Peasants have not appeared as often as they might. This is not because historical development *lies* in the history of the state, as Anderson would sometimes imply. It is because, first, the problem of characterizing Asia has always lain in the remarkable coherence of its state structures ('despotism', as it is still, astonishingly, often called, without any pretence of analysis of what this might mean—indeed, the very word represents an abstention from sociological analysis). It is because, second, the problematic of the tributary mode of course concentrates on the state; and because, third, the way state exploitative mechanisms persisted amazes me as a Westernist, and it is the reasons for this that I originally sought to explore. I have tried to characterize one particular opposition, between tax (the state) and rent (private feudal landowning), principally at the political level of my various social formations. The rest has gone by the board, in particular, the real productive and commercial developments in these very different societies that give the lie to most of them being economically static in any sense.[39] Neglected, too, has been the ideological level of state dominance, over what is now often called 'reproduction'. This is unfortunate, but inevitable in view of the space it would take to describe such articulations; it would anyway be presumptuous of me to try to dot the t's of descriptions of societies all of whose primary evidence, and an increasing amount of whose secondary analysis, is written in languages I cannot read. I will finish with two problems. The first is the real difference between tax and rent, as keys to the characterization of modes with separate economic logics; the second is the general one of the survival of the state. The first is the presupposition for my whole argument, of course; the second is the locus of my original interest.

The problem of tax *vs.* rent is twofold. The first is their surface aspect: the two are sometimes difficult to tell apart, and sometimes, as in the Ottoman state, even fused. The second is the latent reason for this: that both are modes of surplus extraction based on peasant production, individual or collective. Seen existentially from the peasant standpoint, there might seem not to be a lot of difference between them in that they are both unnecessary outgoings enforced, ultimately, by extra-economic coercion of various kinds. The peasant's perception of this equivalence is most evident when he is also the tenant of a landlord, for in most tax-raising societies (though not all), tax under these circumstances is passed on by the landowner, who has extracted it in the rent-taking process. As a result, there is a strong if varied body of experts who do not distinguish between tax and rent at all, or, to be more exact, who see them as centralized and decentralized (public and private) variants of the same economic system, which most of them call feudal. A good percentage of Soviet scholars would say this, for example; so would Amin, though he calls the whole mode tributary; so, from different positions, would the French Byzantinist Éveline Patlagean.[40] This is certainly a better stance than that of those who have a much more Western-based definition of feudalism, and try and fit Asia to it, even though almost all of world history would thus come under the same heading. But the major problem about this formulation is that its pre-supposition is that all extra-economic surplus extraction from a peasantry has to have the same economic form; has to be the same mode of production. Is this really true?

I have excluded and will continue to exclude political and legal definitions from my counterpositions. Public *vs.* private is a convenient shorthand, but it derives from the ideological superstructures of a social formation, and cannot define an *economic* opposition (tenth-century Western Europe, for example, surely the society where the feudal mode was more overwhelmingly dominant over all rivals than ever before or after, certainly maintained a clear notion of the public). The formal constitution of the state, and the legal characterization of landed property, are equally superstructural, although they can at least give us guides as to where to look. What matters for the constitution of states, as I have emphasized, is not so much law as power, and its origin, the nature of the state's economic resources; only by studying this can the separate identity of state (/tax) *vis-a-vis* landlords (/rent) be explored.

States do not only tax peasants; they characteristically tax landlord has too, at least in that they take a percentage from the surplus the landlord has extracted (not always a massive one, we may recall). One arena in which tax is thus very definitely opposed to rent lies in the structural antagonism there is between the state (unless it is itself a feudal state[41]) and the landed aristocracy, or—with the Ottomans—the would-be landed aristocracy. Take a very small tributary state, a city-state, say, and a large private landed estate. Social relations in these two are very different—indeed, ironically, the reverse of the traditional Asiatic: feudal opposition. It is in the latter that there is one sole owner and power-focus; in the former, there will characteristically be independent exploitative powers, landowners, inside and subject to the tax-raising state apparatus and its associated state class. A tributary state is thus both economically and socio-politically more complex than a feudal estate. This is at least a more solid contrast than the legal one. The feudal mode can exist without the tributary mode, but the tributary mode cannot exist without the feudal mode, except in extreme circumstances, when it continually has to fight off the feudalization of some of its local institutions; its history is the history of the resultant antagonisms.

The political contrast between East and West could even stop here. But if we are to establish a *modal* difference between tax and rent, then it must lie in the relationship between the alternate exploiting groups and the peasantry. (This is a rough restatement of the classic formulation that the mode of production is an articulation of productive forces and social relations of production, though the level is a little different: peasant production and peasant society certainly cannot be reduced to the level of technique and the simple appropriation of the products of the soil, that constitute the productive forces.[42]) The contrasts in such relationships lie in social distance and in control.

Taxation by a state is mediated and formalized. The state needs surplus, but in a fairly abstract manner. That is, not so abstracted that any surplus will do: cash is now needed, and now kind. The state may intervene to keep peasants on the land, cultivating and paying taxes; but it is not in the state's purview to control the process of production. If it does, it does so in a very generalized way: the semi-mythical 'hydraulic state', for example, or the organization of colonization and clearance, or the periodic redistribution of land that underpinned the armies of the early T'ang in China. The actual *production process* is not touched by these: neither what is grown, nor the social organization of production. The lack of structural relationship between the state and the presuppositions of production is well illustrated by the state irrigation system of Sassanian Iraq, maintained by the early Arab state, but allowed to fall into disuse from *c.* 900 onward, with the resultant abandonment of large parts of the region. The state, here actually the creator of the conditions of existence of a peasantry, seems to have ceased to care, as a contemporary put it, whether or not the land was in cultivation.[43] The distance of the state from civil society is here clear. States can sometimes benefit the lives of subject peasantries; equally, and more often, they may tax so heavily, or (as in tenth-century Iraq) administrate so ineptly that the country is laid waste, without their coming close enough to their subjects to notice it, or without their understanding global economic processes well enough to realize that it is ultimately counter-productive.

Hindess and Hirst attacked the 'Asiatic mode' as a concept, largely criticizing traditional elements of the mode, such as the absence of property-owning, which I have already rejected. But they are particularly hostile to the idea that a mode can be coherent if it allows for more than one set of productive forces to articulate with a set of relations of production (or *vice versa*). This definition of a mode must be rejected as too restrictive. (Indeed, it caused them so many problems that they now oppose the concept of mode of production altogether.) The tributary mode as I define it certainly allows peasants in their villages to organize production however they like, in the same way as it allows landlords to co-exist with it. There can thus be a whole variety of types of cooperation persisting in such villages, arrays of organization of production from the individual to the totally communal that could often have pre-existed class exploitation, but are now systems in articulation with, and dominated by, the tributary state, as part of the whole social formation. The state does not need to control the economic and social lives of its subjects; it just needs the funding that enables it to pursue its chosen objectives. It is in this area that we find class struggle between the state and its peasantry (and indeed its landowners): in the amount of tax payable, especially when it is felt that there are no adequate returns.[44]

Landowners relate to peasants more closely. Their interest is not just in the amount of surplus, though this is important enough; it is in the recognition of local power, local control. Indeed, the major test for whether the local representatives of a state class have become feudal is whether this local control has become more important for their wealth and self-definition than has their relationship upwards to the state. But this control is not just political, i.e. coercive; it extends to involvement in production itself. This involvement is structural rather than necessarily conscious; landlords are not always, or even frequently, *interested* in production. But their control very typically extends to some of the crucial presuppositions for production—mills, sometimes plough teams, in the West; canals in Iran or China. Sometimes, surplus-product is extracted under quite tight supervision, e.g. through demesne-farming, although this supervision tends to be counter-balanced by peasant customary practice. And, everywhere, landlords control access to the land, even if in practice how much power this gives them is very variable, and largely dependent on the strength or weakness of peasant resistance. These last two points show that landlords do not have uncontested powers over their peasants. Indeed, when they do try to influence production, they do not always succeed; it is the peasant, after all, who actually does the producing under feudalism. Recent work tends rather to emphasize the autonomy of peasants and village communities *vis-a-vis* landlords, even—and especially—with respect to the process of production. But the peasants have to fight for it. It is thus in this arena that class struggle tends to happen between peasants and landlords; over the control of the productive processes, and, at a more mediated level, over the conditions in which one side or the other might be able to exert such control: protection of local customs on the one hand, judicial subjection on the other.[45] Sometimes they fight over the amount of rent, too, as in the arena of tax; but it is over the control of production that the dynamic of class struggle in feudalism is most acute. In fact, at points of economic conjuncture for other reasons, such struggle can lead out of feudalism altogether. When peasants lose, they can be reduced to the total subjection of plantation slavery, or the total economic control represented by capitalist agriculture based on wage-labour (or, in the latter context, they can be expelled from the land altogether, to form the proletariat of the expanding cities of eighteenth-century England); when they win, as in twentieth-century Albania or China or Cuba, socialist relations can ensue (in the earlier period, peasant victory was rare; in late medieval Switzerland, success resulted in a partial return to *pre*-class, not *post*-class, relations of production).

The focus of class struggle is a pointer to the internal economic logic of modes. The state under pressure will attempt to increase the intensity of exploitation; the landlord is as, or more, likely to attempt to increase his influence over the productive process. Landlords are also more likely to respond to opportunities, as well as pressures, by increasing surplus extraction—so in Kula's Poland, early modern lords responded to a developed grain market by maintaining as high a degree of control over agriculture as they could, through demesne farming. (Pre-capitalist states were, by contrast, very reluctant to expropriate surplus so as to put it on the market, except for redistributive purposes, such as when both Rome and China moved grain around to alleviate famine, not always very effectively.)[46] In one sense, one can say that the difference between the ruling classes of the feudal and the tributary modes is between the relative separation of the former and the near-total separation of the latter from the processes of production (just as, on the other side, the capitalist mode entails total control by owners over such processes). But this does not mean that the tributary mode involves no economic relationship at all between ruler and ruled; the link is not just arbitrary, based on the motiveless extraction of surplus. The state has economic objects, and its taxation can increase or decrease according to its success in achieving them. Warfare is one of the most obvious examples. Offensive war is, as has often been pointed out, an economically productive resource for a successful state; defensive war is one of the few activities of the state that is genuinely regarded as useful and necessary by its subjects. And indeed, it is after military failure that struggles over tax-paying tend to be the most acute; when, that is to say, the state is not fulfilling a major function. The difference between feudal and tributary is not, then, one between presence and absence of structural relationships, economic logic *vs.* lack of economic logic; there is a *positive* contrast in the methods and aims of economic interventions inside the two modes. And it is for this reason, too, that state tax-raising and coercive rent-taking by landlords cannot be conflated. They represent two different economic systems, even if they can come together in some exceptional circumstances. Their differences, their antagonisms, lie in their divergent interventions in the peasant economy, just as their convergencies lie in the fact that both are rooted in it. The same productive forces, however, can be seen as giving rise to two separate modes of production.

Finally, let us return to the survival of the state in Asia: to the maintenance of the dominance of the tributary mode in various social formations, despite its continual undermining by feudal relations. We have seen how in China a reserve of free peasantry to whose surplus only the state had access is one of the keys to how tax-raising could survive even in adversity; otherwise, it largely dominated through the fact that landowning was small-scale (although in many areas globally extensive), so that the patronage network and military protection of the state was always of greater value to local gentry than any uncertain local independence might have been. The Arab and post-Arab states were perhaps more complex, and explanations are anyway not helped by a greater vagueness in the modern historiography; but, as we have seen, decentralization certainly led to an accumulation of states on a smaller scale rather than to the abolition of state structures themselves. Even though the processes of tax-raising devolved to local tax-farmers, states always maintained the power to recentralize them periodically, or at least to ensure that they were not privatized out of existence. Some states found this a lot easier than others (Mamluk Egypt, sixteenth-century Turkey, nineteenth-century Egypt, as against Iran in most periods), but all found it *possible*.

I have not discussed the origins of these various versions of tributary social formations, and the problem would not be closely relevant to the patterns I have been trying to delineate. But origins may be of relevance to the one obvious failure among these secular successes, the Roman Empire in the West. The historical origins of the Roman Empire lay in the difference between the city as an institution and the countryside, expressed initially, in the early Republic, in the existence of public landed property, to be enjoyed by all citizens, in opposition to the private property they also possessed. This is the core of the ancient mode, which was (at least ideally) a pre-class economic system; but when the Romans began to conquer everybody else, the public part of the state, originally largely in land, came to include tribute as well. In the context of Mediterranean economic history, this can be treated as the ancient mode in its class aspect, the city exploiting the countryside and, indeed, other cities, who were exploiting their countrysides in turn.[47] But from an Asian standpoint, there is certainly no structural, modal, difference between this and the classic tributary states. The only organizational difference is that in the ancient mode tax-raising was devolved to local public bodies, the nominally independent cities of the Roman Empire. The specific city-state origins of the tributary mode in the Roman Empire thus left their trace in a particular institutional identity, which is sufficient for the characterization of the ancient mode as an identifiable subtype. The decentralized city society of the empire was the key not only to tax-raising, but to the whole society and ideology of the ruling classes, straddled between their access to state patronage and their local land-owning, which in the West could be very great indeed. Cities were the foci of taxation; and also the centres of all aristocratic life, with formal institutional autonomy. In all these respects they were very unlike Chinese cities, or indeed Arab and Iranian cities, which, although major social foci, had no autonomy or tax functions.

In these respects, even the most autocratic of Roman systems, the later Empire of the third to sixth centuries, was more decentralized than any eastern state. And it is these respects, in particular the local control over taxation, that were most fatal to the Roman Empire. When it hit military crisis, in the fifth century, the Empire in the West broke up, in effect, into its urban components; and each component was controlled by aristocrats who no longer had the economic interest to participate in raising taxation that did not benefit them (for Roman armies were being defeated) and which was being taken largely from their own estates. Late Roman urban aristocracies in Western Europe were civilian and conquerable, once the central government of the Empire began to fail, just like eleventh-century aristocracies were in Khurasan, by Germans and Turks respectively. But local Roman aristocracies as organized bodies, that is as a (feudal) class, had their hands on the very structures of tax-raising; local Iranian aristocracies, despite some individual involvement in tax-farming, did not. The Romans sabotaged the whole system; by the time the Germans established organized successor-states, taxation was barely possible. The feudal mode *had* to dominate henceforth. It is scarcely surprising that when the surviving east Roman (Byzantine) state faced its own crisis in the seventh century and held it off, at least partly because its landowners were smaller, one of the casualties in reorganization was the decentralized city-based tax network. Byzantium henceforth headed down a road more like that of the Arab states, with the antagonism between tax and rent expressed in terms of centre *vs.* periphery; and this enabled it to survive for centuries. Tax-farming was dangerous to states, because of its localizing feudal potential; but it was not as ultimately fatal to their survival as the *institutional* decentralization of taxation, and the consequent entrusting of tax-raising powers, autonomously, to the very people most structurally opposed to it, the feudal aristocracy.

In returning to the problem of the survival of states, through a recognition of the differences inherent in the Roman Empire, I have put the problem in a different perspective from that standard for Westernists: it is survival that is the norm, failure that is the deviation. Indeed, Westernists must respect the empires of Asia for their recuperative powers, against the extraordinary inbuilt disadvantages of their vast size and appalling communications; we are not entitled to use this as a stick to beat them with ('Oriental despotism', 'stasis', 'stagnancy'). What their peasantries thought is a different matter, of course. But the basis for their survival was their continuing force as motors of surplus extraction, even in the presence of structurally antagonistic feudal aristocracies, more or less ready to replace them in a hierarchy of dominance, if it ever became possible (and it seldom did). It is at the posing of this antagonism that my analysis has been directed.

NOTES

I am grateful to Paulo Farias, Rodney Hilton, Stephanie White, and especially Joanna de Groot for reading and commenting on an earlier draft; and to Anthony Bryer, Michael Cook, Mark Elvin, John Haldon, Martin Hinds and Sam Lieu, for bibliographical help and discussion.

1. Mukhia (1981); Anderson (1974). For the Roman Empire and its problems, Wickham (1984).
2. Habib (1978: 298); Lewin (1973: 260-2—an appendix in English).
3. Rodinson (1974:58-68). Some Soviet scholars tend to nod towards such formulations, too; e.g. a number of comments in *Soviet Studies in History* (1966). These are now given context, and indeed endorsed, by Dunn (1982: see especially 81-4, 123-4). The problem of articulation is confronted by relatively few people; good (contrasted) instances are Islamoglu and Keyder (1977), and Hilton (1979).
4. Varying economic logics: see, for example, the substantivist analyses in Sahlins (1974), Godelier (1972: esp. 303-18), or the more mainstream discussion in Kula (1976). Non-exploitative modes: no fully coherent categorizations exist, as far as I know, despite much discussion of some aspects. (Nomadism, note, is not necessarily non-exploitative: see n. 9.) For some useful general comments on defining modes, see E.J. Hobsbawm's introduction to Marx (1964). I stress social relations of production, as against, e.g. Cohen (1978: 134-74); productive forces can be rather more various. But there is of course a mutual conditioning and interrelation between them: see pp. 135ff. For a lapidary statement of the basic position I am taking up, see Marx (1971: 791-2).
5. Hindess and Hirst (1975). Useful critiques are in Carandini (1979a: 354-75); Cook (1976-7); Asad and Wolpe (1976). Their theory of knowledge is particularly unacceptable to historians; it is almost comforting to reflect how irritated they must be at the uses I and others put their models to.
6. Hindess and Hirst (1975: 221-55) (it is worth noting that they discuss labour rent extensively, but explicitly exclude that it *defines* the feudal mode—so pp. 254f.); Mukhia (1981: 273-80). Mukhia has been criticized for his definitions and has defended them in *Compte rendu des séances de la societé d'étude du féodalisme* (1979-80: 59f.). Capitalist rent is of course different, for it is market-determined; more and more of the peasantry of the world are coming into this sector. See Marx (1971: 614-39, 782-813) for the classic account.

7. Anderson (1974: 401-31); criticized in Hirst's review, Hirst (1975: 462). Feudalism as fiefs, etc.: see especially the discussion on 'Islamic feudalism', below nn. 26, 38.
8. Anderson [1974: 421, 428f. (and 348-60)]; Hindess and Hirst (1975: 13-15)—but see Asad and Wolpe (1976: 501-5).
9. See the journal *Iranian Studies* for some current discussions; empirically, Lambton (1969: 140-4, 157-64, 283-94) is the starting point, together with a substantial anthropological literature. Asad (1979) attacks the concept of the nomadic mode as an independent category, pretty effectively. Nomads as conquerors—see conspectus and references in Crone (1980: 18-26, 215-23), and the warnings against over-enthusiastic use of Ibn Khaldun in Asad (1980: 456ff.).
10. Its economic logic is most clearly explicit in Kula (1976), though parts of this study are only specific to Polish feudalism; a brisk characterization can be found in Bois (1976: 351-6).
11. The vast historiography is best analysed in Sofri (1973) and Bailey and Llobera, eds. (1981); Dunn (1982) analyses and explicates the Soviet discussions. Attacks: Anderson (1974: 484-95, 548-9); Hindess and Hirst (1975: 178-206); and many empirical criticisms. One useful note (for the 'village autarky' aspect) is Owen [1975: 109f. (cf. also Anderson, 1974: 489f.)].
12. Amin (1976: 13-58); cf. also Amin (1974). The only general discussion of taxation I know (Ardant, 1965), is of curiously little use for its length—1200 pages.
13. See Wickham (1984). I exclude the slave mode, which had almost totally vanished by the late Empire; I doubt it ever existed in the Old World as a mode outside the ancient Mediterranean.
14. I shall not go back further than unification. The Yüan (Mongol) period (1263-1368) is a special case. I use the traditional Wade-Giles transliteration, as does all the English-language historiography; the French and Germans have sensibly adopted the more accurate pin-yin transcription used now by the Chinese. A good brief traditionalist discussion of cycles can be found in Wu (1952).
15. For this survey, I have focused on the T'ang historiography, based firmly on three generations of great Japanese historians, whose work is inaccessible to me: see, for a basic guide, *The Cambridge History of China* (*CHC*) (1979, Vol. 3), the political history of the Sui and T'ang (Vol. 4 will be on other aspects of the period). For the aristocracy, see Twitchett's introduction to *CHC* (8-31); Twitchett (1962, 1966, 1973); Ebrey (1978); and the older general economic survey in Maspéro (1959).
16. On Sung change and the fall of the old aristocracy see: Ebrey (1978: 87-119) (for the Po-ling Ts'ui); Johnson (1977: 50-102) (for the Chao-chün Li); both of these authors stress ideological changes more than I would. Post-Sung:

Eberhard (1977: 205-16), for introduction; and especially Beattie (1979) on T'ung-Ch'eng, against Chang (1962).

17. The basic T'ang taxation book is Twitchett (1970). For the skeleton early T'ang state, ibid. (11, 104-6, 229-30); *CHC* (12ff., 203-10)—though (134-8) the Sui in the preceding decades were organized enough to complete the Grand Canal with corvée labour. Note, too, that the Han and their pre-unification predecessors regarded 10 per cent as a minimum, and 20 per cent was common; the formal rate of exploitation and the power of the state did not necessarily go hand in hand. See Hsu (1965: 108-13), with caution. On low formal taxation under the Ming, see: Beattie (1979: 56-87 (cf. 135-7)), and Huang (1974: esp. 182-8). Officials frequently extorted rather higher rates, however. Taxation may even have got lower: see Perkins (1969: 175-8). On government by negotiation, see, for example, Beattie (1979: 67-80); for the T'ang, Twitchett (1976: 93ff.); for the small personnel of Sung bureaucracy and the resultant reliance on local elites to keep order, see McKnight (1971: esp. 3-10, 183-5).
18. The problematic is best expressed in Elvin (1973: 17-110). Cf. also Perkins (1969: 169-82).
19. For figures for the last century or so see Perkins (1969: 85-110), and Chang (1962: 144-5). I over-generalize in my counter-position of 'north' and 'south'—there were many exceptions. On estates in the Yangtse, see: Lewin (1973: 66-150); Elvin (1973: 69-83); Beattie (1979: *passim*). On the state always being able to tax, see: *CHC* (514-22) (C.A. Peterson on provincial government *c.* 750-880); Wang (1963); and the fairly awful Schafer (1954), on tenth-century Fukien. The latter two *show* state and provincial taxation, rather than analysing how it survived.
20. On Toba (Northern Wei) and other northern dynasties, see: Ebrey (1978: 17-20, 24-9); Elvin (1973: 34-61). On Five Dynasties, see: Wang (1963: *passim*); Twitchett (1973: 79); Eberhard (1977: 195-204), building on his idiosyncratic *Conquerors and Rulers* (1952).
21. *CHC* (i.e. R.M. Somers) is unhelpful on the 870s-80s risings (for example, p. 723): they aren't 'peasant rebels', but 'bandits' (cf. Eberhard, 1952: 54-64). It would be a bit much to expect twentieth-century social consciousness in the ninth century, though (cf. Hobsbawm, 1972). They terrorized everyone, perhaps, but they certainly killed many landlords. This is one of the points at which the absence of Chinese historians in *CHC* becomes particularly obvious.
22. Vietnam fits into this pattern, too, following Le Tranh Khoi (1972).
23. Dates are approximate. I shall in what follows stick to Arabic spellings and terminology, for greater consistency, rather than their Persian/Turkish/Mongol variants, except when it would be ridiculous.
24. Nizam al-Mulk: Aubin (1966: 325). Military elites: see, for example, Crone (1980: esp. 82-9); Shaban (1976).

25. On taxation, see: Løkkegaard (1950: 168-72) for survival of *dihqans. Dihqans,* etc., under the Sasanians: Christensen (1944: 111-13); Pigulevskaja (1963: 133-58); Lambton in *Encylopaedia of Islam* (*EI*[2]) (1960-), *s.v.* Complexity of Arab conquest: Dennett (1950); Shaban (1970: 5, 19-21, 91f., 96f., 129f.); cf. Asad (1980: 464-7). *Qati'a*: Cahen (1953: 26-8). Landowning patterns after the conquest: Cahen (1954); Lambton (1947-8), a reference I owe to Martin Hinds. Kennedy (1981), which I only read at a late stage of preparing this article, is the most sophisticated discussion of the real complexities of the pre-tenth-century state power I have seen.
26. Cahen (1953) is still the touchstone after thirty years. See also idem in *EI*[2], *s.v.*; Lambton (1969: 31-76 and *passim*; 1967); Poliak (1936), among many general surveys. I will use *iqta'* as both singular and plural, and likewise other words in Arabic.
27. Egypt is the exception: here, the Ayyubid and Mamluk state from the late twelfth century onward maintained *iqta'* as entirely fiscal (Cahen, 1953: 45-8; Rabie 1972). Egypt is easily controlled politically, being all flat; state landowning was high.
28. Cahen (1953: 50f.) There were taxes on commerce too, that the state held on to better. *Muqta'* elites in fact were constantly replaced, as states recovered their power or were overthrown by new ones (cf. n. 31). This is not because *iqta'* were legally precarious, though they were—so were European fiefs, after all—but because states could obtain (i.e. pay for) sufficient armed strength to do so. It is an expression of state power, not its cause. It should anyway be remembered that the turnover in individual aristocratic *families* in Western Europe was almost as great, without threatening global feudal dominance.
29. Aubin (1966); Bosworth (1973: 163-200) (the Ghaznavids did not use *iqta'*); Bulliet (1972)—cf. review by Mottahadeh (1975); Mottahadeh on Qazvin and Bulliet on Nishapur in Richards, ed. (1973: 33-45, 79-91); Bulliet (1978), the neatest survey. Cf. also Kennedy (1981) for an earlier period. Note that in the late Mamluk state, where local landowning was in the hands of *muqta'*, the state's men (and under considerable central control), cities were far less independent, and heavily subject to local state (emir) patronage: (Lapidus, 1967).
30. Mottahadeh (1980) is the only systematic analyst of Buyid state *vis-à-vis* civil society, almost entirely from the standpoint of ideology. He claims that people needed the state (175-90), against, for example, the implications of some of Bulliet's work. He also stresses the informality of many of the structures of local power (123-74); but I suspect he may be too influenced by Lapidus's work, which is dealing with a rather different socio-political power structure (see n. 29). Later parallels for the state as broker: see Abrahamian (1974).
31. Continual conquests from the steppe and the deserts, though contingent, did help periodically to reestablish the state in the Middle East, especially Iran, and to undermine independent landowning. The deserts *were* close, after

all (as they were not in Western Europe). An extreme is Ibn Khaldun, in fourteenth-century North Africa, who states flatly that landowning is *worthless* without state protection (1958, Vol. 2: 283-6 = Bk. IV §§ 15-16). But North Africa is particularly exposed to nomad pressures—Ibn Khaldun's whole theory of history is based on this fact.

32. Adams (1965: 101-2); Petrushevsky (1968: 525-6). This latter is the basic analysis of the peasantry, a marvellous article, shortened from his book in Russian (1960); cf. also F. Nomani (1976; 1977). Peasants were tied, but free; no other 'feudal' controls were put on them—there were no demesne labour services; all corvées were for the state. There were no general statistics in Iran as late as the twentieth century (Lambton, 1969: 266).
33. See Turan (1948) Cahen (1954-5; 1968: 173-89); Beldiceanu-Steinherr (1976).
34. *Contra* Anderson (1974: 424-6, 497-9, 522), for whom the tight legal forms of Roman property law are a real cause of capitalist development, against feudal, Islamic, Chinese vagueness. The Ottomans would sin here, more than anyone else (cf. ibid.: 387f.)—and, indeed, Western representatives in the nineteenth century worked hard to introduce private property into the Turkish empire. But the expropriation of rivals, and its converse, security of property, depend less on legal rights than on power—ask any Russian landowner after 1917. Limits to the powers of rulers do exist, but they are seldom delineated by the legal system. Cf. also n. 38.
35. Inalcik (1973: 110). The rest was mostly *waqf*, charitable estates incorporated by Islamic law for religious purposes, though in practice often acting as lineage foci for the aristocratic families that controlled them (like Chinese lineage charities and Western proprietary monasteries). This, at least, was feudal; but *waqf* remained a minority element in Ottoman landholding, even after their eighteenth-century expansion. They were relatively numerous in the Balkans, and were something of a basis for the survival of ethnic landowners (Zakythinos, 1976: 38-42, 110-4; Demetriades, 1981; these references I owe to A.A.M. Bryer). However see Anderson's warning footnote (1974: 386).
36. The analysis closest to mine is that of Islamoglu and Keyder (1977), who also stress ideology and commerce, themes I am ignoring. They see the Ottomans as 'Asiatic', as does the more quirky Divitçioglu (1969). General social development: Inalcik (1973: 104-18); Gibb and Bowen (1950, I.i: 235-75); Beldiceanu (1980: 743-53); Inalcik (1977); articles on *A'yan*, Derebey, Kara 'Othman-oghli, in *EI*[2], *s.u.v.*; Owen (1981: 10-44, 58-64; Karpat (1968).
37. Hourani (1968). Inalcik, too, for the previous century, stresses that *a'yan* are informal—when given official posts, they cease to be *a 'yan* (1977: 32). Cf. also Owen (1981: passim), e.g. for Egyptian contrasts.
38. This analysis, I have to admit, is contested; I am using Lambton (1969: 105-77; 1977); Abrahamian (1974); M.-J. DelVecchio Good's local study (1977); and, for the similar problems of the Safavids in the sixteenth century, Aubin

(1959). Against, there are the 'anti-feudal' analyses, varying in approach, of Ashraf (1970), and Katouzian (1981: 7-26), an extreme proponent of the 'all property is precarious' school (and why do so many people, studying all parts of Asia, harp on about partible inheritance inhibiting the establishment of aristocracies—thus here, p. 15?—it didn't stop anyone in early medieval Western Europe). I owe much insight on Iran, as well as references for nn. 36-8, to discussions with Joanna de Groot.

39. Cf. Elvin (1973) and Anderson (1974: 520-46), for China and the points raised by Hirst (1975: 452-3). Feudalism did not produce capitalism; it produced capitalism *first*. But the dominance of the feudal mode lasted well over a millennium; to allow the tributary mode two millennia or more does not seem to prove that it is static in any absolute sense. (Let us hope that these timescales do not represent some unrecognised economic law for the dominance of all modes.)
40. Dunn (1982: esp. 20-2), a warning against this tendency by Kovalev as early as 1931; Petrushevsky (1968: 514f., 536f.); Amin (1976: 15-16); Patlagean (1975). Cf. Hindess and Hirst (1975: 223-5), who see the equivalence, but show that it is different from their feudal mode. Wolf (1982: 79-88) sees the differences between centralized and decentralized state systems, but too easily subsumes them into a single tributary mode covering Europe, Asia and much of the rest of the world. His analysis is highly sophisticated, however, and is strong on commerce, which I have left out of this article.
41. As the Absolutist states were in the early modern West, on which see the sharp synthesis of Anderson (1974: 15-59). They taxed, of course, as did many feudal states from late Saxon England and the Italian communes onwards. Such taxation is generally regarded as a concentrated version of feudal rent, and no one doubts the general dominance of the feudal mode in such societies, but it seems to me inescapable that some of my discussions should be relevant to them.
42. Cohen (1978: 28-62), for the clearest definitions of productive forces.
43. Adams (1965: 71-89; 87-9) for contemporary analyses.
44. Hindess and Hirst (1975: 193-200); cf. Hindess and Hirst (1977), and Asad and Wolpe (1976: 482-4). The state absorbing and exploiting pre-class relationships is nicely discussed for the Incas in Godelier (1977: 63-9)—setting aside the problem of the exactness of Godelier's empirical categorization of the Incas, which is contentious.
45. Hilton (1973: *passim*); Brenner (1976); cf. Hindess and Hirst (1975: 233-55).
46. Kula (1976). So feudal lords were more receptive to market forces than were tributary states. They were also less able to control and ideologically englobe merchants and the artisanate than Asian states were, though they certainly tried to do so when they could. These factors have obvious links to the classic issues around the rise of capitalism.
47. Hindess and Hirst (1975: 106-8); Wickham (1984) for all that follows.

REFERENCES

Abrahamian, E., 1974, 'Oriental Despotism: The Case of Qajar Iran', *International Journal of Middle East Studies*, Vol. 5, pp. 3-31.

Adams, R.M., 1965, *Land Behind Baghdad*, Chicago.

Amin, S., 1974, 'Modes of Production and Social Formations', *Ufahamu*, Vol. 4, No. 3, pp. 57-85.

———, 1976, *Unequal Development*, Hassocks.

Anderson, P., 1974, *Lineages of the Absolutist State*, London.

Ardant, G., 1965, *Théorie sociologique de l'impot*, 2 vols., Paris.

Asad, T., 1979, 'Equality in Nomadic Social Systems? Notes Towards the Dissolution of an Anthropological Category', in *Pastoral Production and Society*, Cambridge, pp. 419-28.

———, 1980, 'Ideology, Class, and the Origin of the Islamic State', *Economy and Society*, Vol. 9, pp. 450-73.

Asad, T., and H. Wolpe, 1976, review of Hindess and Hirst (1973), *Economy and Society*, Vol. 5, pp. 470-506.

Ashraf, A., 1970, 'Historical Obstacles to the Development of a Bourgeoisie in Iran', in M.A. Cook, ed., *Studies in the Economic History of the Middle East*, London, pp. 308-32.

Aubin, J., 1959, 'Études safavides I. Sah Isma'il et les notables de l'Iraq persan', *Journal of the Economic and Social History of the Orient*, Vol. 2, pp. 37-81.

———, 1966, 'L'Aristocratie urbaine dans l'Iran seldjukide: l'exemple de Sabzavar', *Mélanges R. Crozet*, 2 vols., Poitiers, Vol. 1, pp. 323-32.

Bailey, A.M., and J. Llobera, eds., 1981, *The Asiatic Mode of Production*, London.

Beattie, H.J., 1979, *Land and Lineage in China*, Cambridge.

Beldiceanu, N., 1980, 'Le Timar dans l'etat ottoman', in *Structures féodales et féodalisme dans l'occident méditerranéen*, Rome, pp. 743-53.

Beldiceanu-Steinherr, I., 1976, 'Fiscalité et formes de possession de la terre arable dans l'Anatolie préottomane', *Journal of the Economic and Social History of the Orient*, Vol. 19, pp. 233-322.

Bois, G., 1976, *Crise du féodalisme*, Paris.

Bosworth, C.E., 1973, *The Ghaznavids*, 2nd edn., Beirut.

Brenner, R., 1976, 'Agrarian Class Structure and Economic Development in Pre-Industrial Europe', *Past and Present*, No. 70, pp. 30-75.

Bulliet, R.W. 1972, *The Patricians of Nishapur*, Cambridge, MA.

———, 1978, 'Local Politics in Eastern Iran under the Ghaznavids and Seljuks', *Iranian Studies*, Vol. 11, pp. 35-56.

Cahen, C., 1953, 'L' évolution de l'iqta' du IXe au XIIIé siécle, *Annales E.S.C.*, Vol. 8, pp. 25-52.

———, 1954, 'Fiscalité, proprieté, antagonismes sociaux en haute-Mesopotamie', *Arabica*, Vol. I, pp. 136-52.

———, 1954-5, 'Le Regime de la terre et l'occupation turque en Anatolie', *Cahiers d'histoire mondiale*, Vol. 2, pp. 566-80.

———, 1968, *Pre-Ottoman Turkey*, London.

The Cambridge History of China, 1979 (*CHC*), Vol. 3, D.C. Twitchett, ed., Cambridge.

Carandini, A., 1979a, *Archeologia e cultura materiale*, 2nd edn., Bari.

———, 1979b, *L'Anatomia della scimmia*, Rome.

Chang Chung-li, 1962, *The Income of the Chinese Gentry*, Seattle.

Christensen, A., 1944, *L'Iran sous les Sassanides*, 2nd edn., Copenhagen.

Cohen, G.A., 1978, *Karl Marx's Theory of History, A Defence*, Oxford.

Compte rendu des séances de la société d'étude du féodalisme, 1979-80, Nos. 3-4.

Cook, S., 1976-7, review of Hindess and Hirst (1973), *Journal of Peasant Studies*, Vol. 4, No. 4, pp. 360-89.

Crone, P., 1980, *Slaves on Horses*, Cambridge.

DelVecchio Good, M.-J., 1977, 'Social Hierarchy in Provincial Iran: The Case of Qajar Maragheh', *Iranian Studies*, Vol. 10, pp. 129-63.

Demetriades, V., 1981, 'Problems of Landowning and Population in the Area of Gazi Evrenos Bey's Waqf', *Balkan Studies*, Vol. 22, pp. 43-57.

Dennett, D.C., 1950, *Conversion and the Poll Tax in Early Islam*, Cambridge, MA.

Divitcioglu, S., 1969, 'Modele economique de la société ottomane', *La Pensée*, Vol. 144, pp. 41-60.

Dunn, S.P., 1982, *The Fall and Rise of the Asiatic Mode of Production*, London.

Eberhard, W., 1952, *Conquerors and Rulers*, Leiden.

———, 1977, *History of China*, 4th edn., London.

Ebrey, P.B., 1978, *The Aristocratic Families of Early Imperial China*, Cambridge.

Elvin, M., 1973, *The Pattern of the Chinese Past*, London.

Encyclopaedia of Islam, 1960- (*EI*[2]), Leiden.

Gibb, H.A.R., and H. Bowen, 1950, *Islamic Society and the West*, Oxford.

Godelier, M., 1972, *Rationality and Irrationality in Economics*, London.

———, 1977, *Perspectives in Marxist Anthropology*, Cambridge.

Habib, I., 1978, 'Economic History of the Delhi Sultanate', *Indian Historical Review*, Vol. 4, pp. 287-303.

Hilton, R.H., 1973, *Bond Men Made Free*, London.

———, 1979, 'Towns in English Feudal Society', *Review*, Vol. 3, No. 1, pp. 3-20.

Hindess, B., and P.Q. Hirst, 1975, *Pre-Capitalist Modes of Production*, London.

———, 1977, *Modes of Production and Social Formations*, London.

Hirst, P.Q., 1975, 'The Uniqueness of the West', *Economy and Society*, Vol. 4, pp. 446-75.

Hobsbawm, E.J., 1972, *Bandits*, 2nd edn., London.

Hourani, A., 1968, 'Ottoman Reform and the Politics of Notables', in Polk and Chambers, pp. 41-68.

Hsu Cho-yun, 1965, *Ancient China in Transition*, Stanford.

Huang, R., 1974, *Taxation and Governmental Finance in 16th Century Ming China*, Cambridge.

Ibn Khaldun, 1958, *The Muqaddimah* (tr. F. Rosenthal), 3 vols., London.

Inalcik, H., 1973, *The Ottoman Empire*, London.

———, 1977, 'Centralisation and Decentralization in Ottoman Administration', in Naff and Owen, pp. 27-52.

Islamoğlu, H. and C. Keyder, 1977, 'Agenda for Ottoman History', *Review*, Vol. 1, No. 1, pp. 37-55.

Johnson, D., 1977, 'The Last Years of a Great Clan', *Harvard Journal of Asiatic Studies*, Vol. 37, pp. 50-102.

Karpat, K.H., 1968, 'The Land Regime, Social Structure and Modernisation in the Ottoman Empire', in Polk and Chambers, pp. 69-90.

Katouzian, M.A.H., 1981, *The Political Economy of Modern Iran*, London.

Kennedy, H., 1981, 'Central Government and Provincial Elites in the early "Abbasid Caliphate"', *Bulletin of the School of Oriental and African Studies*, Vol. 44, pp. 26-38.

Kula, W., 1976, *An Economic Theory of the Feudal System*, London.

Lambton, A.K.S., 1947-8, 'An Account of the Tarikhi Qumm', *Bulletin of the School of Oriental and African Studies*, Vol. 12, pp. 586-96.

———, 1967, 'The Evolution of the Iqta' in Medieval Iran', *Iran*, Vol. 5, pp. 41-50.

———, 1969, *Landlord and Peasant in Persia*, 2nd edn., Oxford.

———, 1977, 'Tribal Resurgence and the Decline of the Bureaucracy in the 18th Century', in Naff and Owen, pp. 108-29.

Lapidus, I.M., 1967, *Muslim Cities in the Later Middle Ages*, Cambridge, MA.

Le Tranh Khoi, 1972, 'Contribution à l'étude du mode de production asiatique: le Viêt Nam ancien', *Studi storici*, Vol. 13, pp. 231-48.

Lewin, G., 1973, *Die ersten fünfzig Jahre der Song-Dynastie in China*, Berlin.

Løkkegaard, F., 1950, *Islamic Taxation in the Classic Period*, Copenhagen.

McKnight, B.E., 1971, *Village and Bureaucracy in Southern Sung China*, Chicago.

Marx, K., 1964, *Pre-Capitalist Economic Formations*, London.

Marx, K., 1971, *Capital*, Vol. 3, London.

Maspéro, H., 1959, 'Les régimes fonciers en Chine', *Recueils de la société Jean Bodin*, Vol. 2, 2nd edn., pp. 275-323.

Mottahadeh, R.P., 1975, Review of Bulliet (1972), *Journal of the American Oriental Society*, Vol. 95, pp. 491-5.

———, 1980, *Loyalty and Leadership in an Early Islamic Society*, Princeton.

Mukhia, H., 1981, 'Was There Feudalism in Indian History?', *Journal of Peasant Studies*, Vol. 8, No. 3, pp. 273-310.

Naff, T. and R. Owen, eds., 1977, *Studies in 18th Century Islamic History*, Carbondale.

Nomani, F., 1976, 'Notes on the Origins and Development of the Extra-Economic Obligations of Peasants in Iran, 300-1600', *Iranian Studies*, Vol. 9, pp. 121-41.

———, 1977, 'Notes on the Economic Obligations of Peasants in Iran, 300-1600', *Iranian Studies*, Vol. 10, pp. 62-83.

Owen, R., 1975, 'The Middle East in the 18th Century', *Review of Middle Eastern Studies*, Vol. 1, pp. 101-12.

———, 1981, *The Middle East in the World Economy 1800-1914*, London.

Patlagean, E., 1975, 'Économie paysanne et "féodalite byzantine"', *Annales E.S.C.*, Vol. 30, pp. 1371-96.

Perkins, D.H., 1969, *Agricultural Development in China 1368-1968*, Edinburgh.

Petrushevsky, I.P., 1960, *Zemledeliye i agrarnyye otnoseniya v Irane XIII-XIV vv.*, Moscow.

———, 1968, 'The Socio-Economic Condition of Iran under the Il-Khans', in J.A. Boyle, ed., *Cambridge History of Iran*, Vol. 5, Cambridge, pp. 483-537.

Pigulevskaja, N., 1963, *Les villes de l'etat iranien*, Paris.

Poliak, A.N., 1936, 'La féodalité islamique', *Revue des études islamiques*, Vol. 10, pp. 247-65.

Polk, W.R., and R.L. Chambers, eds., 1968, *The Beginnings of Modernisation in the Middle East*, Chicago.

Rabie, H., 1972, *The Financial System of Egypt 1167-1341*, London.

Richards, D.S., ed., 1973, *Islamic Civilisation 900-1150*, Oxford.

Rodinson, M., 1974, *Islam and Capitalism*, London.

Sahlins, M., 1974, *Stone Age Economics*, London.

Schafer, E.H., 1954, *The Empire of Min*, Tokyo.

Shaban, M.A., 1970, *The 'Abbasid Revolution*, Cambridge.

———, 1976, *Islamic History: A New Interpretation*, Vol. 2, Cambridge.

Sofri, G., 1973, *Il modo di produzione asiatico*, 2nd edn., Turin.

Soviet Studies in History, 1966, Vol. 4, No. 4.

Turan, O., 1948, 'Le Droit terrien sous les seldjoukides de Turquie', *Revue des études islamiques*, Vol. 16, pp. 25-49.

Twitchett, D.C., 1962, *Land Tenure and the Social Order in T'ang and Sung China*, London.

———, 1966, 'Chinese Social History from the 7th to the 10th Centuries', *Past and Present*, No. 35, pp. 28-53.

———, 1970, *Financial Administration under the T'ang Dynasty*, 2nd edn., Cambridge.

———, 1973, 'The Composition of the T'ang Ruling Class', in A.F. Wright and D.C. Twitchett, eds., *Perspectives on the T'ang*, New Haven, pp. 47-85.

———, 1976, 'Varied Patterns of Psrovincial Autonomy in the T'ang Dynasty', in J.C. Perry and B.L. Smith, eds., *Essays on T'ang Society*, Leiden, pp. 90-109.

Wang Gungwu, 1963, *The Structure of Power in North China during the Five Dynasties*, Kuala Lumpur.

Wickham, C.J., 1984, 'The Other Transition: From the Ancient World to Feudalism', *Past and Present*, No. 103, pp. 3-36.

Wolf, E.R., 1982, *Europe and the Peoples without History*, Berkeley.

Wu Ta-k'un, 1952, 'An Interpretation of Chinese Economic History', *Past and Present*, No. 1, pp. 1-12.

Zakythinos, D.A., 1976, *The Making of Modern Greece*, Oxford.

The Universalization of a Concept: 'feudalism' to 'Feudalism' in Chinese Marxist Historiography

Arif Dirlik

This article is not about feudalism in Chinese history, but about feudalism in Chinese historical thinking. For reasons that should become obvious in the course of the discussion, my goal is not to evaluate the relative merit of individual historians' claims concerning feudalism in China. Rather, I seek to identify themes in Chinese discussions of feudalism which, taken together as a historical discourse,[1] yield insights into Chinese historians' understanding of feudalism, as well as into the meaning of the search for feudalism in China's past. Judgements on empirical questions, or even the question of whether or not there was feudalism in Chinese history, must be placed within the broader contexts of this discourse which is implicated deep in modern Chinese historical and political consciousness.

In this particular sense, the problem of feudalism in Chinese historical thinking presents problems common to discussions of feudalism everywhere. To discuss feudalism is to enter a universal discourse on history, its meaning and its place on our consciousness. This discourse is universal in two senses. Firstly, it is worldwide. There is scarcely an area of the world today where the issue of feudalism is not an issue in discussions of the past (or the present). That this discourse is worldwide, however, does not imply that it is global. The material constraints on a global discourse do not require much elaboration. Linguistic, political and economic factors delimit access to such a global discourse or obstruct active participation in it. This is evident in the case of Chinese historians whose discussions of feudalism have taken place within a Chinese framework, isolated from similar discussions elsewhere. While in the 1920s and 1930s Chinese discussions of feudalism were fed by, and fed into, discussions in Japan and Russia; since then, especially since the 1950s, discussions of feudalism in China have taken place within an exclusively Chinese 'tradition of discourse'. Nevertheless, as in much of the Third World, the Chinese 'tradition of discourse' is tied to the worldwide discourse through the texts that provide its point of departure: the works of Marx, Engels and Lenin. Its assumptions on history, on the issues of feudalism, and even the contemporary significance of the study of feudalism are common to the discourse worldwide.

Secondly, the discourse on feudalism is universal in the sense that it is a consequence of a modern consciousness of history as universal history, which takes as its object of understanding not particular peoples and cultures but the world as a whole. Even where the scope of this consciousness is not global, it is universal because is presupposes the existence in history of regularities that cut across cultural and political boundaries, and seeks to uncover systematic forces that explain the dynamics of history on a worldwide basis. This historical consciousness is but a projection into the past of the globalized consciousness that has arisen with the material unification of the world with capitalism. The concept of feudalism is a case in point. While the term feudal had specific institutional associations in its origins in medieval Europe, in modern historical discourse it has served as a representation of European society prior to capitalism, deriving its meaning, not from descriptive association with historically specific institutions, but from the contrast with capitalism of a diffuse set of pre-capitalist economic and political structures. As capitalism has spread out of Europe to encompass the globe, the concept of feudalism has followed in its footsteps to depict the pre-capitalist societies that confronted capitalism and, more often than not, obstructed its assimilation. And as capitalism has brought these societies out into the stage of world history, so has feudalism been made into a component of universal history. A judgement on feudalism in any society's past, consequently, is not simply a historiographical judgement (the correspondence between concept and history) but a judgement on that society's location in history.

Chinese conceptualization of feudalism is best understood as a Third World variant of the Marxist discourse on feudalism. Being on the receiving end of the modern universalization of historical consciousness, the Chinese have responded with ambivalence to the universalization of a model of historical development patterned after European history. They have, however, remained within the boundaries of Marxist discourse. The problem is to identify the location of Chinese thinking on feudalism in its discourse, and the implications of Chinese thinking for the discourse in its universality. This requires examination of the manifestations in Chinese historical thinking of what I consider to be the three constitutent elements of this discourse: the representation of feudalism as a social formation, the location of feudalism as a stage in history, and the political attributes that have been bestowed upon the concept in the course of its history.

First, feudalism in Chinese historiography does not refer to specific institutions but to a social formation, with all the totalistic implications of that concept. Since the late 1920s, Marxist historians in China have described Chinese society for a varying but large part of its history as a feudal society. While the term they have used as the equivalent for feudal, *fengjian*, has a long history in Chinese political discourse as the description of a decentralized political organization where the ruler would share power with a hereditary local elite, the reference in twentieth-century historiography is not to any real or ideal system out of China's past, but to the economic and political organization of medieval Europe (Guo, 1930: 309–10). The associations of the Chinese term may have influenced some historians' understanding of medieval European feudalism, but the term in its usage in contemporary historiography is clearly of Euopean origin in its depiction of a 'universal' social formation. It is conceived of not only as a mode of political organization but as a mode of production with a corresponding class structure, political organization and ideology. its theoretical features, as well as its concrete historical referents, are derivative of Marxist texts. Chinese history has indeed informed the Chinese understanding of feudalism, but this is more a consequence of the attempt to fit the concept to Chinese history than of the hold on historical thinking of native concept. On the contrary, the concept of feudalism has been used over the years to evaluate the historical development of Chinese society.

Second, feudalism does not depict merely a social formation but a social formation that is a stage in a universal pattern of historical development. The problem of feudalism, therefore, is not simply a problem of correspondence between one or another period of Chinese history and medieval European history, but has implications for Chinese history as a whole. As a stage in history, feudalism demands the *a priori* determination of its antecedent and consequent stages: how one stage is conceived must shape how the remainder of history is conceived. Conversely, how these antecedent and consequent stages, namely, slavery and capitalism, are conceived determine the location and nature of feudalism in China.

Chinese historians have found it difficult to reconcile the received conception of feudalism with the historical development of Chinese society. On the other hand, the paucity of alternatives to feudalism as a historical formation has limited confrontation of the problems that arise from the inconsistency between theory and history. To deny feudalism has usually meant falling back upon the so-called 'Asiatic mode of production', which has proven undesirable to Chinese historians for a variety of reasons. Furthermore, since the status in China's historical development of the antecedent and consequent stages of feudalism is highly ambiguous, Chinese historians have had to stretch the received conception of feudalism to accommodate disparate historical formations, or to judge Chinese history a 'failure' in historical development on the basis of abstract historical criteria. Hence, the historical treatment of feudalism presents a discursive problem that transcends simple historiographical questions. To appreciate the problem, we must consider not only what it means to describe Chinese society as feudal, but more importantly what it means not to do so.[2]

Finally, the question of feudalism is not an abstract intellectual question but a question that is embedded in Chinese political consciousness. Marxist historiography in China was in its origins intimately bound up with the problem of revolution in Chinese society. The location of Chinese society within the universal pattern of development first emerged as a problem in Chinese historiography amidst polemics on the revolutionary strategy most appropriate to the liberation of China within the context of world capitalism. The question of revolution has lost much of its urgency since the Communist victory in 1949. Nevertheless, it has emerged repeatedly in connection with the formulation of a strategy of development most appropriate to carrying China into socialism. The political implications of historical choice must ultimately provide the context within which feudalism as a historical problem must be viewed. If a statement on feudalism constitutes a statement on China's place in world history, as I have noted above, it is also a statement on China's future; the discourse on history, in other words, is also a discourse on politics. Much of the meaning of the Chinese conception of feudalism is lost if the question of feudalism is taken merely as a historiographical question, isolated from this broader discourse.

My goal, ultimately, is to examine Chinese historiography as an illustration of some of the basic problems of the materialist conception of history. While Chinese conceptions of Marxism and Marxist historical categories are no doubt products of concrete historical and intellectual experiences, Chinese thinking on history must be incomprehensible outside of the Marxist tradition of discourse. The peculiarities of Chinese thinking, rather than representing deviations from Marxism, bring into sharp relief fundamental problems of Marxist thinking on history. I will point to some of these problems in the concluding section of this article.

FEUDALISM IN CHINESE HISTORIOGRAPHY

Over the past half century, debates over feudalism in Chinese Marxist historiography have revolved around three main versions of feudalism in Chinese history. The feudal period in Chinese history, according to these three versions, covered: (a) the early part of the Zhou period (1122-255 BC), roughly the first half of the first millennium BC; (b) the imperial period, covering roughly the period from the late third century BC into the early twentieth century; (c) the three-thousand-year period from around 1000 BC to the twentieth century.[3]

While one or another of these versions has dominated historical interpretation at different times, no one version has achieved sufficient dominance to drive competing versions into oblivion for long. Indeed, in spite of the establishment of a politically sanctioned historical orthodoxy in the late 1930s, the issues raised in the initial years of Marxist historical writing have persisted to the present, albeit in somewhat disguised form to conform to the demands of orthodoxy. Current debates on feudalism in Chinese historiography are a great deal more sophisticated than debates in the past both in the questions they raise and in their coverage of historical data; but the basic issues remain the same, and are firmly within the discourse established in Marxist historical writing at its origins in the late 1920s and early 1930s. The historians whose interpretations have set the tone for historical writing got their initiation into history in this initial period. Their basic views, and the polemics these views have generated, are as old as the history of Marxist historiography in China.[4] These polemics represent a struggle for hegemony over historical discourse and, by implication, over the historical profession. Given the ideological significance of historical interpretation, moreover, these struggles also represent struggles over alternative conceptions of revolution and revolutionary strategy in China.

The different versions of feudalism in Chinese history appear at first sight to differ only in historical scope, that is the period of Chinese history they describe as feudal. Closer analysis reveals, however, that they also imply different conceptualizations of feudalism, since the definition of feudalism must vary in order to render feudalism applicable to stretches of Chinese history that display significant differences in economic, social and political forms. The debate over feudalism, in other words, is both a debate over the meaning of feudalism and over the path Chinese society followed in the course of history.

The view that feudalism in China was a phenomenon of the early Zhou period was widely held among Chinese Marxist historians in the late 1920s and early 1930s. While these historians did not necessarily agree on all the particulars of feudalism or early Zhou society, their arguments shared certain basic features. These features may be illustrated through the arguments of Tao Xisheng, a Guomindang Marxist, who exerted considerable influence on Marxist historiography during these years as historian and teacher.[5]

Tao argued that early Zhou society displayed all the basic characteristics of feudal society as it had existed in the medieval West. These were as follows: (a) The manorial organization of production as represented by the 'well-field' (*jingtian*) system.[7] The manor (*zhuangyuan*) was made up of farm land, pastures and hunting grounds surrounding the fortress of the lord. Part of the land was divided among the serfs and constituted their private holdings; the rest was public land. The serf had three obligations to the lord: rent in the form of a fraction of the produce (rent in kind), forced labour, and occasional tributes of diverse articles of consumption such as wine or poultry. (b) The hierarchical nature of land rights—that is, the division of the land according to the political rank of the landholder. Theoretically, all land was the property of the Zhou kings and the lords held their land in trust as fiefs; practically, military power and rank were the chief determinants of power over land. (c) The existence of a class of free peasants and landlords who did not pay rent to the lords but owed only military obligations. (d) A rigid adherence to the hierarchical system with periodic enforcement of its rules.

It is worth emphasizing the elements that Tao perceived to be essential to feudalism, for the absence of these elements provided him with the basis for his rejections of feudalism in imperial China. Economically, he stressed the self-sufficient manorial organization of production as the foundation of the feudal system. Agriculture and cottage industries constituted the primary economic activity in such society, and labour devolved upon the shoulders of peasants attached to the manor, in other words, serfs. The owners of property were those who also monopolized the functions of government, the feudal lords who were organized in a hierarchical structure of power. The latter, a feature peculiar to feudalism, also accounted for the decentralization of power under the feudal system. Tao emphasized repeatedly the concentration of political and economic power in the same class as the distinctive feature of feudalism. These economic, social and political characteristics, he believed, characterized both medieval European and early Zhou societies.

In a book he wrote in 1930, Tao offered the definition of feudalism that informed his analysis of feudalism in China:

> The feudal system is founded upon agriculture and handicrafts conducted within the boundaries of the local community (*difang gongtongti*). A single village or a number of villages constituted the local community which possessed in common forest and pasture land, water resources, and arable land. In this local community, the common land and the fields which were distributed among the peasant households provided the necessities of life; for instance, the fields, hunting and fishing, and domestic animals (provided the necessities for consumption) while materials such a timber and sheep wool provided the raw materials for household industries. This kind of local community was ordinarily *a self-sufficient economic organism and had little economic interchange with the outside world.* The local lord nurtured within the community awe for his powers. The king was only an elevated lord and did not have the power to subject other lords to his will; hence the feudal state had an extremely loose organization. (emphasis in the original)

According to Tao, the feudal system in China began to disintegrate by the middle of the Zhou period (around the fifth century BC). Increase in population rendered the feudal organization of production unfeasible. Population increase was in turn made possible by advances in production, chief among which was the sophistication of land irrigation, and the emergence of new agrarian techniques. Increased production also contributed to the emergence of a commercialized economy, which put an end to the natural economy of the early Zhou.

These changes had revolutionary consequences for Chinese society. With increased commercialization of the economy, land lost its characteristic as a privilege of political power and was converted into a commodity subject to the market. Socially, the result was the appearance of a new class of landlords and merchants who challenged the power of the Zhou nobility. By the end of the Zhou period, the concentration of political and economic power in the same class was a thing of the past. Political power came to be concentrated in the hands of bureaucrats who served the now centralized Chinese state. Economic power, on the other hand, rested with landlords and merchants. Bureaucrats and the new economic class were interrelated, but they no longer represented a single class as they had during Zhou feudalism. The resultant social structure retained feudal elements in ideology, but it could no longer be described as a feudal society.

For Tao, Chinese society had retained this basic social structure for the ensuing two thousand years. The transition to capitalism which was implicit in the changes of late Zhou was aborted due to two features of this society. Firstly, the state and the bureaucracy, with its feudal ideology, had obstructed the emergence to dominance of the social forces that had emerged with the commercialization of the economy. Secondly, and more fundamentally, capital in China had taken the form of commercial capital which had been destructive of the natural economy of feudalism, but was incapable on its own of establishing a new mode of production.

Taking his cue from Marx, Tao argued that the 'independent development' of commercial capital (that is, divorced from production) obstructed the development of productive forces by diverting surplus capital to unproductive uses, chief among which was investment in land. Since the overall backwardness of the Chinese economy and the poverty of the peasantry impeded the maturation of commerce into a force capable of fusing the various regions into an organically integrated national market governed by a network of urban centres, commerce and cities were themselves condemned to play a negative role as parasitic exploiters of the countryside. Commercial capital (combination of merchant's capital and usury) impoverished the peasantry and, more seriously, undercut agrarian livelihood by encroaching upon the land. Since commerce remained marginal to the economy, merchants never acquired sufficient power to demand the establishment of an economic environment more conducive to the conduct of business or even to defend their wealth and interest against arbitrary usurpation by the political elite. In response, they resorted to investing in land to guarantee their financial security, thereby causing the periodic concentration of land. Land concentration not only deprived large numbers of peasants of their livelihood, stirring unrest in the country; it also ate into government revenues, as landlords (or merchant-landlords) successfully exploited their legal and illegal privileges to take their lands off the tax rolls. The result was not development into capitalism but periodic destabilization of a weak agrarian economy.

The view was challenged from the beginning by proponents of the third alternative cited above; in other words, those who assigned to feudalism a much larger place in Chinese history. The difference between the two views did not lie in their evaluation of Zhou feudalism. Both held that China had entered the feudal stage in history with the early Zhou. Rather, they disagreed on the nature of post-Zhou society. Whereas Tao argued that feudalism had come to an end by late Zhou, proponents of this alternative view argued that Chinese society had remained feudal throughout the imperial period. Their argument called for a fundamentally different definition of feudalism (Dirlik, 1978: 121-9).

The most extensive arguments in favour of this view were advanced by Zhu Peiwo who explained many of his own views in his prolonged polemics against Tao's interpretations. Zhu's theoretical rejection of a significant role for commercial capital in the dynamics of Chinese history was based on the same section in Marx (quoted here) employed by Tao. Zhu argued that commercial capital was powerless in the creation of a new society which depended on changes in the mode of production; Tao was really suggesting, he pointed out, that the opposite was true even if he tried to cover his real position by calling the new society transitional. Zhu conceded the undeniable existence of commercial capital in traditional Chinese society but minimized its disintegrative power: commercial capital had existed in China and had even infiltrated the village economy, but its disintegrative effects had worked so slowly that at the end of two thousand years of disintegration, China had still not experienced the transformation of its feudal basis. Besides, Zhu contended, commercial capital was itself not a mode of production but assumed the features of the social formation within which it functioned. The presence of commerce in feudal society did not signify change in that society; rather commercial capital in feudal society served the feudal mode of production, intensifying feudal exploitation.

Zhu also denied that the changes in the pattern of land-ownership and political superstructure added up to a transformation of feudal society since neither of these signified a change in the mode of production and exploitation. Land may have changed hands, but neither the method by which it was worked nor the exploitation of the peasant by the landlord had changed. As for the separation of political from economic power, this was illusory because the officialdom which had replaced the nobility could hardly be distinguished from landlord interests.

At the basis of these arguments lay a definition of feudalism Zhu derived from Marx. Feudalism as he interpreted it had two essential features, a natural economy (self-sufficient, non-commodity) and the non-economic (*fei jingji di*) or extra-economic (*chao jingji di*) exploitation of the peasant, with the latter foremost in his mind. In dealing with the relationship between western Zhou feudalism (which he did not elaborate on) and imperial China, two questions guided his enquiry: first, did the nominal owner of the land use non-economic exploitation against the direct producers after the Warring States period (475-221 BC)? and second, did natural economy remain dominant in the post-Qin (221-207 BC) period? The answer to the first of these disposed of the difference between the feudal lord of western (1122-771 BC) Zhu and the landlord of imperial China; the answer to the second implied a rejection of any important role for commercial capital.

Evidence of non-economic exploitation, according to Zhu, were first, high rents equalling 50 to 80 per cent of the yield; second, tribute obligations of the peasant to the lord; third, coercive legal and political power of the landlord over the peasant; and fourth, status differences (hierarchiacal relations) between the two. With respect to land rent, Zhu also took the persistence of rent in kind as further evidence of the persistence of feudal relations.

Primary evidence of the dominance of natural economy was to be found in the primitive development of a cash economy and the continued use of barter in trade. Ironically, using facts unearthed by Tao Xisheng, Zhu argued that, although the low development of a cash nexus did not mean the absence of trade, it demonstrated that trade was small in volume and restricted to commodities locally unavailable. Such trade was not capable of motivating the accumulation of capital and the improvement of production.

With land as the economic foundation of society, one would expect the dominance of landed interests in the political superstructure. Zhu argued, in support of this position, that the suppression of merchants by the Chinese government and the primacy given to agriculture in government ideology were the most conspicuous manifestations of this power balance. The Chinese government did not emphasize agriculture out of altruism but only in order to perpetuate feudal exploitation of the peasants as its needs demanded. Aside from landlord control of the government, the feudal superstructure displayed two additional features, decentralization and hierarchy. The imperial government did not differ from the Zhou state in these respects either. Centrifugal forces persisted into the Qing period (AD 1644–1911); Qing governors and viceroys commanded such financial and political power over their localities that the authority of the emperor was only nominal. As for hierarchy, it continued intact, the only difference between the two periods being the change in the titles employed.

Zhu regarded imperial Chinese society and the feudal state of Zhou as essentially similar. Curiously enough, the key to China's non-emergence from feudalism in Zhu's analysis was the stagnation of commerce, a factor he theoretically assumed to be of little consequence in social development. In Europe, capitalism had developed through the primitive accumulation of capital and the need to expand production in order to supply the foreign markets commerce opened up. The search for new markets itself was not accidental; the internal markets of European countries were limited and proved to be of insufficient scope with the advance of handicrafts, which produced a saleable surplus, and of exchange. China's 'curse', on the other hand, had been her natural wealth! The various regions of the country had been largely self-sufficient, and the national market was capacious enough to absorb whatever trade there had been. A major motivation for improving the forces of production, the need for foreign markets, had been absent. Also, since the Chinese soil was rich, the peasants had been able to survive despite heavy exploitation; an unemployed labour force, the second condition for the growth of capitalism aside from capital, had never come into being.

The third important version of feudalism in China to emerge from these early debates was one that was based on a literal reading of Marx's preface to *An Introduction to the Critique of Political Economy*. The author of this view, Guo Moruo, rejected the interpretation of early Zhou as a feudal society on the grounds that his interpretation departed from the universal scheme of development outlined by Marx (Dirlik, 1978: 140-6, 149, 170-1). 'Zhou society has historically been regarded as a feudal system', Guo wrote in his seminal work on Chinese history, *Researches in Ancient Chinese Society* (1930), 'but this view does not accord with the order of social development. The fall of gens society must be followed by the stage of the slave system—which is also when the state emerges—before society can proceed to feudalism.'

Guo's depiction of early Zhou society as a slave society is a matter of debate to this day. What is important for our purposes here are the implications of this view for feudalism in China. The model of historical development Guo adopted, the description of early Zhou as a slave society, required the relegation of feudalism to the imperial period of Chinese history. Guo justified this conclusion with a definition of feudalism that rendered any connection of the term with medieval European society irrelevant, and foreshadowed a view of feudalism that was to become increasingly important in Chinese historiography. In a work he wrote in 1945, where he defended his views against his critics, Guo explained:

> *My* feudalism is a stage that has evolved out of slave society. The producers are no longer slaves but liberated peasants and artisans. The important means of production in agriculture is the formally divided land which is now under the ownership of an exploitative class of landlords. Crafts and trades are free of official control and organized according to guild enterprises. The state that is founded upon these classes subsists on the taxes paid by landlords, craftsmen and merchants. This is the feudal society we speak of now. (emphasis mine)

While Guo had earlier stressed the manorial organization of agriculture and guild organization of industry, as well as the division of society into feudal lords and serfs, as the chief characteristics of feudalism that distinguished the latter from slave society, he had from the beginning held a notion of feudalism that equated the feudal system with the characteristics of imperial Chinese society. As early as 1930, in *Researches in Ancient Chinese Society*, he had characterized social relations under feudalism as relations between officials and people, landlords and peasants and masters and apprentices. His 1945 statement merely formalized these earlier notions.

Guo's equation of feudalism with agrarian society, as well as the possessive tone—'*My* feudalism'—of the definition given earlier were to become commonplace in Chinese thinking on feudalism in later years, as I will argue later. Suffice it to say that in spite of his schematic appreciation of Marxist modes of production, his underlying technological determinism, and the vagueness in his use of concepts, Guo resolved a problem that had been glossed over in the other two versions of feudalism in Chinese history.

Marxist historians of China have all along agreed that the late Zhou period was a period of crucial changes in Chinese society. Guo's was the first periodization of Chinese history to present these changes as change from one mode of production to another. He was thus able to avoid the pitfalls, on the one hand, of the 'long feudalism' view which recognized these changes only to dismiss their significance, and the 'long transition' view which presented a major portion of Chinese history as a period of stagnation. The latter, in particular, smacked too much of the stagnant Asiatic mode of production which did not find much favour among Chinese historians. Guo's periodization of Chinese history, whatever its weaknesses, placed China within an unambiguously universal pattern of historical development.

This last view, according to a contemporary account, was on the way to achieving dominance in Chinese historiography by the mid-1930s. Whether or not such was the case is questionable. What is more evident is that the first version of feudalism cited above began to lose ground in these years. This was due, to an extent, to the attraction of an increasing number of historians to a model of historical development in five stages from primitive through slave, feudal, bourgeois and socialist societies. Tao Xisheng, the foremost proponent of the first view, himself switched to the five-stage model in the mid-1930s. His analyses of this time placed feudalism in the third to the eighth centuries AD, during the imperial period, preceded by slave and gens societies respectively.

More important, however, were the political implications of the view that had confined feudalism to the early Zhou period (Dirlik, 1978: Chap. 3). Communist revolutionary strategy in China was based all along on the assumption that the Chinese revolution was an anti-feudal revolution. After the revolutionary débâcle of 1927, when the Guomindang suppressed the Communists, this view came under attack from both the Marxist right and the Marxist left. On the left, Trotsky and Chinese Trotskyists blamed the failure of revolution on the erroneousness of the Stalinist diagnosis of China as a feudal society. They countered with their own argument that China was already a capitalist society, some going so far as to suggest that capitalism had determined Chinese social structure for a long time. Guomindang Marxists who as a rule denounced class conflict, on the other hand, argued that the Communist pursuit of an anti-feudal revolution was misguided because feudalism had ceased to exist in China millennia earlier. They believed, however, that the fall of feudalism had not been accompanied by the rise of capitalism, as in the case of Europe, but had resulted in a prolonged period of stagnation during which political and commercial forces had obstructed the emergence of a new mode of production. Tao's arguments had been formulated initially to challenge Communist claims, and even after he revised his periodization in the mid-1930s, his analysis of late imperial social structure remained the same. This argument was in retreat by the mid-1930s as Communist affiliated historians achieved dominance in Marxist historiography. These historians rejected any view of Chinese history that denied the persistence of a feudal or feudalistic structure into the twentieth century.

The second and third versions of feudalism met this requirement, and have set the boundaries for discussions of feudalism since the late 1930s. With the establishment of the five-stage orthodoxy in the Soviet Union after 1938, Chinese historiography too came to be confined within the bounds set by this schematic interpretation of Marxism. After 1949, when historians came under direct official control, Guo Moruo's version of Chinese history received official sanction. Though Guo's views did not go unchallenged, his prestige as an intellectual, his status as the head of the Chinese Academy of Sciences, and his political connections guaranteed to his views a power over historical discourse that was out of all proportion to the intellectual persuasiveness of his arguments. For almost three decades after 1949, his views were to dominate official historiography in China.

The confinement of history within officially sanctioned boundaries guaranteed orthodoxy, but it did not eliminate the problems raised by historians earlier. Before 1937, discussions of feudalism in China had been part of a broader discussion over the claims to universality of alternative models of historical development. With the establishment of a single model, these problems reappeared as problems within this model, manifested in disagreements over the timing of changes in Chinese history. Two problems were especially significant, and reveal the tensions created by the restriction of historical alternatives.

First was the problem of the transition from slavery to feudalism. The view that feudalism had prevailed in China for three thousand years, from early Zhou to the twentieth century, remained an important current in historical thinking. Influential historians who had advocated this view in the 1930s continued to uphold their views. These historians, for the most part, accepted the five-stage periodization of Chinese history but disagreed with the interpretation of early Zhou as a slave society. When and how to draw the dividing line between slavery and feudalism remains an important issue in Chinese historiography to this day. The timing of this transition has varied from around 1000 BC to the third century AD and sometimes even later. Guo himself changed his timing of the transition a number of times. Despite intense controversy over this issue, however, Chinese historians have not added much to the theoretical problems that had been raised earlier.[6]

The second issue concerns the latter part of feudalism. With the elimination of views that had challenged the feudalism of imperial Chinese society, Chinese historians have had to deal with the question of how to explain economic and social changes of imperial China that did not fit within accepted views of an unchanging feudalism, and that had led historians earlier to describe imperial China as a pre- or proto-capitalist society. Out of this problem emerged the controversy over the 'sprouts of capitalism' which continues to occupy Chinese historians. In accordance with the premises of the established model, Chinese historians accept that China never made the transition from feudalism into capitalism, but many hold the view that the seeds of capitalism had begun to sprout within the womb of feudal society long before Western intrusion in the nineteenth century. The major controversy is over the timing of the 'sprouts', which ranges from the Tang Dynasty (AD 618–906) to the last few centuries of the imperial period. Most advocates of the sprouts of capitalism seem to agree, however, that it was only with the late Ming (sixteenth century) that Chinese society began to show signs of the growth of capitalist elements in the economy. This controversy has been significantly more fruitful than the controversy over slavery in the empirical findings it has generated, but as in the case of the other controversy, it has not led to any significant theoretical breakthroughs.[7]

A CONTEMPORARY VIEW OF FEUDALISM IN CHINESE HISTORY

Contemporary discussions of feudalism continue to be bound by the discourse established in the early 1930s. A brief look at a recently published study of feudalism in Chinese history by the eminent economic historian Fu Zhufu should illustrate this point. Fu, whose career as economic historian coincides with the history of Marxist historiography in China, reveals in his work the hold of this discourse in Chinese historical thinking. Chinese historians still continue to debate problems similar to those discussed above. My choice of Fu is not simply because of his prestige, or any assumption that his views are accepted universally by contemporary historians. Still, there is some evidence, however indirect, that Fu's interpretations have been given official sanction. Second, in its explicit articulation of the meaning Chinese historians have long bestowed on the concept of feudalism, Fu's work clearly indicates the transformation of the meaning of the concept in its universalization.

Fu stands within the historiographical tradition that assigns to feudalism a three-thousand-year history in China. What gives his argument distinction are two features of his work. First is his meticulousness in the choice of problems relevant to analysis and the data he musters to argue out his case. His *Collection of Essays in Chinese Economic History* (Fu, 1980) breaks the problem of feudalism into a number of constituent problems such as the development of landownership in Chinese history, urbanization, the guild system, money, policies toward commerce, and the sprouts of capitalism. Through careful analysis, he traces the historical development of these elements and their relationship to one another, comparing Chinese developments to developments in Europe at every point. As a result, his work elucidates the significant changes that have taken place in Chinese social and economic structure over three thousand years, as well as the elements that have persisted over time to subvert development in the direction implied by these changes.

Second, Fu enunciates clearly conceptual premises that have guided the historiographical tradition implicitly since its beginnings. Fu's meticulous analysis, and his findings, lead him not to question these premises but to reaffirm them. As in the case of his predecessors in this tradition, Fu views feudalism in China as a special case in history, with its own laws of development within the universal history of feudalism. These special laws, however, are to him not a sign of Chinese parochialism or of China's departure from a universal course of development. On the contrary, they show a universality of their own: Chinese history does not just reveal a difference of course from a universalized European model; rather, it becomes a case from which to draw conclusions of universal relevance concerning feudal society in general.

According to Fu, feudal society in China came into being with the Zhou conquest of Shang around the turn of the first millennium BC. This feudal system exhibited all the characteristics of the medieval European feudal system. Political and economic power resided with a class of hereditary military nobility organized hierarchically; land, the basis of economic power, was distributed among the nobility according to this hierarchy; agricultural production was organized in a manorial system, and carried out by serfs attached to the land; surplus labour was exploited through labour services imposed upon the serfs; and the economy was a natural economy directed towards manorial consumption with little in the way of commerce (Fu, 1980, I: 67–84).

This system disintegrated in the latter part of Zhou, mainly under the impact of rising commerce. In Europe, the fall of feudalism was accompanied by the emergence of capitalism. The result had been different in China where, in this early period of history, conditions for capitalism, did not yet exist. What emerged in China was a 'landlord' economy or system (*dizhu jingji* or *dizhu zhidu*) that was to last for two thousand years. Not only did a new mode of production not come into being, but the landlord system did not differ in 'quality' (*zhi*) from 'noble lord' system (*lingzhu zhidu*) of the early Zhou (Fu, 1980, I: 243). As Fu put it, 'the change was not one of the mode of production, but merely a change of the pattern of organization and of the form of exploitation. The mode of production remained feudal.'[8]

The main tendency of this new organization of production was the chronic accumulation of land, since land remained as the basis for production and economic power, and those who accumulated wealth invested in land for lack of any other significant outlet for accumulated wealth. This resulted in the chronic disintegration of the economy and the stagnation of China's economic development. Government efforts to prevent this tendency were of no avail as the tendency was rooted in the laws of China's feudal economy (Fu, 1980, I: Chap. 3 esp. 100, 141).

Fu, however, also described the changes of late Zhou as 'revolutionary' changes that produced 'qualitative' changes in Chinese economic structure (Fu, 1980, I: 198). And, by his own evidence, they were indeed revolutionary changes. For one thing, land became a commodity from the late Zhou and wealth, rather than rank, was the source of landownership. The landlord class under the empire ranged from the emperor to merchants who invested in land; for all, it was the command of wealth that was the starting point of land accumulation. In his introduction, Fu described land during this period as 'a kind of interest-bearing capital'.[9]

As the nature of landownership and the landowning class changed, so did the nature of labour and the expropriation of surplus value. Serfs became free peasants with the changes in late Zhou and, for the most part, remained so. Whereas early Zhou had a dual economy, the economy of the lord and the economy of the serf, the economy was now unified. Landlords and peasants were competitors in the same economy, not different economies. Landlord exploitation of labour, too, changed with the emergence of a free peasantry. The relationship between lord and peasant in early Zhou had been a relationship of dependency; the relationship between landlord and peasant in the landlord system was contractual (Fu, 1980, I: 198-9). Peasants served landlords now as tenants and hired labour. The expropriation of surplus, accordingly, took the form of payment in kind and, later, cash payments.

This feudal society, moreover, was highly commercialized, even if its economy remained basically a self-sufficient natural economy. According to Fu, commerce and commodity production began to emerge in late Zhou and so did wage labour. With the T'ang Dynasty, the sprouts of capitalism began to appear with the rise of regional specialization, large-scale production of commodities, urbanization, merchants' and artisans' guilds and long-range (including international) trade. By the Song Dynasty (AD 960-1275) China had become a fully commercialized society. In late empire, even agricultural products assumed the form of commodities (Fu, 1980, II: 669-708).

Nevertheless, according to Fu, China never made the transition to capitalism. The sprouts of capitalism, he argued, do not necessary lead to a capitalist mode of production without other conditions. The reasons were intrinsic to the Chinese economy. Land remained as the source of economic power and, therefore, the object of investment. Commerce itself developed independently of production. Commercial capital did not enter the process of production but remained restricted to the inter-regional movement of commodities. Its effect on production was negative. It ate into the productive sector of the economy and periodically undermined it (Fu, 1980, II: 678-9).

Fu also stressed the importance of social and political factors in impeding the development of capitalism. Unlike in Europe, cities in China were under direct political control and were unable to change into centres of commerce. Guilds, which had played a crucial role in Europe, remained weak in China. This might have been beneficial to the rise of capitalism because it prevented guilds from establishing monopolies over production and commerce; but it also rendered merchants and artisans weak because they were unable to resist political interference and control (Fu, 1981: 22-6).

Some historians of China might take issue with these arguments, and Fu himself documents meticulously variations in landownership and labour over the two thousand years of imperial China. The important question here, however, is not agreement or disagreement over specific issues, but the way in which the concept of feudalism has come to encompass two (or more) entirely different societies (by Fu's own admission). To Fu, imperial China is not a case of stagnant transition, or merely a continuation of early Zhou society, but a social formation in its own right.[10] He nevertheless encompasses both this 'landlord system' and the 'noble lord system' of the early Zhou within the concept of feudalism. Accordingly, China's 'special' laws of development are no longer 'special' but are laws in their own right.

Fu's place in the Chinese discourse on feudalism should be evident from the outline of his arguments presented earlier. The defence of the position that feudalism in China lasted from early Zhou through the imperial period has long rested on two premises. First is that capitalism as a mode of production did not appear in China until the twentieth century. Most historians of China have recognized that Chinese society went through significant changes in late Zhou, and again during the T'ang-Song period, with less spectacular changes throughout Chinese history. However, the fact that it is not possible to speak of the emergence of the capitalist mode of production before the twentieth century has left historians little choice but to minimize the structural effects of these changes.

Second, this denial of change in the mode of production has been justified by an essentialist (in contrast to structural) definition of feudalism. The form of a society, in this view, is significant only insofar as it provides clues to its essence. It is this essence, therefore, that must ultimately serve as the criterion for judgement on historical change. The essence of feudalism has been taken variously as a natural self-sufficient economy, 'extra-economic' exploitation, or simply as an economy where land is the primary means of production, a class of landlords controls this means of production, and labour is any form of labour between (and excluding) slave labour up to (and including) wage labour, in other words, a post-slavery pre-capitalist agrarian economy.

For all the sophistication of its empirical basis, Fu's view of feudalism is in this essentialist vein. Referring to changes in late Zhou, Fu states,

> . . . the result of changes in the land system was only to produce changes in the form of economic structure; it could not induce transformation of the entire mode of production; in other words, following the changes, the mode of production was still the feudal system. (Fu, 1980, I: 91)

The mode of production in this statement is distinguished from the form of the economic structure; conversely, different economic forms may be accommodated within the same mode of production. Though Fu does not clearly define the distinguishing features of the feudal mode of production, there is some suggestion of a definition in his view that, under feudalism, landlords completely control the means of production (land) but only incompletely control the producer. This 'definition', which he offers to distinguish feudalism from slave society, could obviously refer to a whole range of societies with different economic, social and political characteristics. Not only do 'superstructural' elements, such as the form of the state, legal relationships and ideology, not enter the definition, but basic features of the economy—such as the organization of production, forms of labour, exchange relationships (including the market), the sources and nature of landownership, class relations and the nature of exploitation, and even economic structure—are eliminated as criteria in establishing boundaries for the concept.

Fu has incorporated into his identification of feudalism in Chinese history objections raised to this version of feudalism by proponents of alternative views of Chinese history such as Tao Xisheng and other advocates of pre-capitalist society for imperial China. Tao argued earlier that, after the fall of feudalism, Chinese society had entered a pre-capitalist transitional phase. Many of the characteristics Fu assigns to the landlord system phase of his feudalism are indeed identical to the characteristics Tao had adduced to argue that imperial China was *not* a feudal society. Fu's essentialism represents the culmination of a long-standing tendency among advocates of feudalism of long duration: the reduction of feudalism to an essence, in order to accommodate disparate economic and social structures, has culminated in the claiming of these structures for feudalism.

The argument for a feudalism of long duration had remained strong even when Guo Moruo's views dominated officially sanctioned historical interpretation. With Guo's recent demise, it seems that this view might emerge as a new orthodoxy. Fu's views on feudalism are echoed in the recently published *Dictionary of Political Economy*, edited by the prominent official economist Xu Dixin under the auspices of the Academy of Social

Sciences (Xu, ed., 1980). The definitions of feudalism, noble lord economy and landlord economy in this dictionary are quite revealing, especially the two latter definitions. Noble lord economy, according to the dictionary, 'is a form of the feudal mode of production, often used in contrast to another form, the landlord system economy. The distinction between the noble lord system and the landlord system is relative; they are both based upon feudal productive relations where landlords completely control the land and only incompletely control the peasants.' The 'classic' case of the noble lord system, according to the dictionary, was realized in medieval European feudalism, the 'classic' case of the landlord system is to be found in the 'middle and latter phases of Chinese feudal society' (Xu, ed., 1980: 216-17).

European feudalism, in these definitions, is no longer the source of the concept of feudalism but merely one case of a universal concept. Similarly, feudalism in China no longer represents a deviation from a norm based on European feudalism, but a 'classic' case of feudalism in its own right. This same tendency to the universalization of the concept that presents Chinese and European feudalisms as equally parochial, or equally universal, cases of feudalism is suggested in another important study of Chinese feudalism published in recent years, Hu Rulei's *History of Feudal Society in China*. In apologizing for the limitations on his comparative method, Hu states:

> In order to recognize the peculiarities of the feudal social formation in China, it is necessary to compare Chinese and other histories. Such comparison is best undertaken with the broadest scope. But due to individual limitations, (I) know little of conditions in countries of regions outside of Western Europe, and have been unable to undertake a broader comparison. The peculiarities of the Chinese feudal social formation to which this book points are consequences of comparison with medieval European history and are, therefore, of a very limited nature. If in the future I develop a better understanding of the history of counties outside of Europe, I would like to continue work on this subject. (Hu, 1979: 3)

The more cases of feudalism the comparison covers, in other words, the more the likelihood of grasping the essence of feudalism and, therefore, the peculiarities in its manifestations around the world, including in medieval Europe.

This universalization of the concept presents basic problems. But we must note one of its byproducts that may be considered quite beneficial to historical analysis. In universalizing the concept of feudalism, Chinese historians have simultaneously particularized the case of medieval Europe. This points to the possibility of taking account of the peculiarities of

European history which led to results in Europe that were not replicated elsewhere in the world, a possibility that is ruled out by the alternative of making Europe and feudalism into a universal model. Unfortunately, rather than work out the implications of their analysis, Chinese historians, in their loyalty to a universal teleology, continue to introduce by the back door standards of development derived from European history. This is most evident in the preoccupation with the 'sprouts of capitalism' which implies that even if China had its own 'special' laws of development, Chinese development nevertheless anticipated the universal goal of historical development: capitalism. In spite of its 'special' development, therefore, feudalism in China is portrayed as the stage prior to capitalism in a universal model of development. The result has been to enlarge the concept to encompass all pre-capitalist agrarian society.

CONCLUSION: CHINESE HISTORIOGRAPHY AND THE MARXIST HISTORICAL DISCOURSE

The concept of feudalism in Chinese usage no longer derives its meaning from a specific social formation but is used to represent structurally different societies. The meaning of the concept in this usage must be determined anew in every case because it no longer provides direct clues to the concrete referents of the concept. The questions raised by the concept, therefore, are not empirical but hermeneutic questions: relations between part and whole, substance and from, form and function, the concretely historical and the abstractly theoretical. These questions are not likely to be answered by further historical research or the generation of new definitions of feudalism.

Problems of the Chinese conceptualization of feudalism are not peculiar to Chinese historical discourse but are universal problems of the discourse on feudalism. These problems are products of what Isaiah Berlin has described as the 'inflation' of concepts, the accretion of new meanings to a concept as the concept is made to correspond to the different realities which it is used to represent. Feudalism certainly has undergone such inflation as it has had to accommodate widely different realities in its worldwide diffusion. These problems exist no matter whether we speak of Chinese feudalism, Japanese feudalism, Latin American feudalism, African feudalism, Russian feudalism or whatever. In order to describe these societies as feudal, it has been necessary, on the one hand, to ignore significant structural differences among them, and, on the other hand, to inflate the meaning of feudalism to accommodate such structural differences. Feudalism has come to describe anything from a specific

European political-economic institution to all post-slave pre-capitalist agrarian economies.

As I noted earlier, Chinese discourse on feudalism is a Third World variant of the Marxist discourse on the subject and, as in the case of other Third World usages, it raises central questions on Marxist thinking on history. Nevertheless, these questions are not necessarily peculiar to Marxist discourse or products of that discourse. The problem of feudalism has existed as a problem since the beginnings of modern historical discussions of feudalism. As historians of Europe point out, feudalism had a residual character as a concept in its earliest usage in the seventeenth and eighteenth centuries, when it was employed to distinguish pre-capitalist from capitalist legal concepts, especially in relationship to legal definition of property rights (Cheyette, ed., 1968: 5). Non-Marxist historians of Europe have not done much better than Marxist historians in agreeing upon an acceptable definition of the concept. The more historicist-minded historians have gone so far as to advocate the abolition of the concept as a hindrance to historical research (Brown, 1979). While Marxist usage has created its own problems, in other words, it is necessary to keep in mind that, as a product of the modern discourse on history, Marxism also shares many problems in common with non-Marxist historiography.

As a product of the Marxist discourse on history, Chinese discussions of feudalism point to basic problems in this discourse. It might be argued that problems of Chinese historiography are due to the foreignness of the concept to Chinese history, rather than to any problems intrinsic to Marxism. The thesis here is based on the opposite premise: that the very foreignness of the concept in Chinese historiography helps bring into relief problems of Marxism that are easily glossed over within the context of European historiography where the concept had its origins, and feudal institutions dominated a stage in historical development. This is quite evident in the three basic elements of the discourse enumerated in the introduction to this essay: feudalism as a mode of production, feudalism as a stage in history, and feudalism as a component of historical and political consciousness.

The feudal mode of production in Chinese historical usage covers social organizations that vary greatly not only in their political and ideological constitution but even with regard to the technological basis of production, the organization of production and the expropriation of surplus labour, and even in class structure. While the Chinese case may seem an extreme example of the inflation of the concept, this kind of inflation is not peculiar to Chinese historians or the application of the concept outside of Europe. The much-acclaimed *An Economic Theory of the Feudal System* by Witold Kula adopts a definition of feudalism that does not differ significantly from Chinese usage:

> . . . the term 'feudalism' refers here to a socio-economic system which is predominantly agrarian and characterized by a low level of productive forces and commercialization; at the same time it refers to a corporate system in which the basic unit of production is a large landed estate surrounded by the small plots of peasants who are dependent on the former both economically and juridically, and who have to furnish various services to the lord and submit to his authority. (Kula, 1976)

Such inflation in the use of feudalism raises basic questions concerning the theoretical coherence and historical validity of feudalism as a mode of production and, by implication, the concept of a mode of production itself. While the idea of a series of modes of production succeeding one another in history has been crucial to the Marxist conception in history, as Hobsbawm has argued, the concept of the mode of production remains vague in Marxist theory. In Marxist historical discourse (including Marx's own work), mode of production refers to anything from a particular organization of production, that articulates a particular relationship between forces and relations of production, to whole social formations that encompass entire societies over long stretches in history, as in Marx's use of the term in his Preface to the *Introduction to the Critique of Political Economy*. The confusion between mode of production and social formation (which includes the entire social, political and ideological structure) is not fortuitous; it is a product of the functionalist theoretical premise that a mode of production shapes the structure and constitution of society as a whole.

It is this confusion that lies at the heart of many of the problems in the Marxist analyses of social formations and modes of production. It has resulted, on the one hand, in a functionalist reduction of social, political and even economic relations to a mere formal expression of some 'substantial' essence that is so vaguely defined that it may serve logically as the determinant of widely different, and, in some cases, disparate social structures. Such is the case with the definition of the feudal mode of production in terms of a natural economy, extra-economic exploitation, or landownership all of which may characterize diverse societies in history. On the other hand, it has created blindness to the possibility that a social formation may accommodate more than one mode of production, if the latter is defined with precision as a particular form of the organization of production and the expropriation of surplus labour.[11] Such is the case with the definition of feudalism as a social formation in terms of a specific relationship between a landowning nobility and a dependent peasantry, embodied in manorial organization, which ignores not only the existence of a free peasantry but all the relations of commodity production and exchange which provide the context for the particular mode of production described as feudal, and shape its form and substance. As George Lefebvre once pointed out, the manor is not an exclusive characteristic of feudalism but has existed in all types of societies (Lefebvre, 1956: 242); the important question is to demonstrate the distinguishing feature of the manor under feudalism—and this requires, we might add, analysis of the manor within the context of feudal society. Some type or other of the manorial organization of production existed throughout Chinese history, but this organization acquired a differnt form and played a different function depending on the broader social and economic context. The manor (as embodied in the 'well-field' system) of early Zhou existed within the context of a possibly self-sufficient economy and served as remuneration for military and official service; the manor of the Song Dynasty existed within the context of a highly commercialized economy, and its purpose was not self-sufficiency but the maximization of production and exploitation (Elvin, 1973: Chap. 6). Banaji has suggested in the case of Europe that the 'feudal' manor reached its full development not during the 'classical' feudalism of twelfth-century Western Europe but within the context of a commercialized economy in Eastern Europe of the sixteenth to eighteenth centuries (Banaji, 1976: 311–12). Analysis that does not take such variations in the relationship between a mode of production and its broader context in the social formation is not only theoretically deficient but obscures the historical substance and function of economic forms.

One could raise similar questions with other basic economic elements, such as serfdom, wage-labour, or petty production, that cut across social formations as defined in Marxist discourse. The point is that the separation of form from essence, and function from substance, has inevitably led to an oversimplification of history and a theoretical involution that is the source of much confusion within Marxist historical discourse. The result is a situation where the general 'laws' of history can be salvaged only through the creation of special 'laws' for each society, an enterprise which only negates its own premises. The problem, once again, is not peculiar to Chinese historiography. Kula's remarks on the relationship between history and theory illustrate the fundamental nature of the problem:

> If the elaboration of a theory is not to be a mere intellectual game, the premises taken as a whole must correspond to the existing conditions in the societies

under examination. Such a theory, once constructed, will be valid only in relation to the societies (known today or to be discovered tomorrow) in which the elements comprising our model are actually present. The more elements we introduce into the model, the richer will be the theory we construct; but the number of societies to which this theory could be applied will decline commensurately. (Kula, 1976: 20)

The price to be paid for the creation of a widely applicable theory, in other words, is not just historical irrelevance but the poverty of theory as well!

This must be the fate of a historical theory that separates form from essence, and reduces the form to a mere shell of the essence without a substantial historical significance of its own. This may have the advantage of making possible cross-historical generalization; generalization that ignores significant formal differences between societies, however, only creates the need for the formulation of 'special' laws to explain why societies supposedly identical in essence did not assume the same form, or follow the same course of development in history. In other words, such generalizations undermine their own underlying intention to discover general laws to explain historical development. Indeed, it may be suggested that the effort to formulate such general laws would possibly be more successful if it recognized the particularity of social forms in history. A systematic analysis of modes of production must remain beyond reach unless it is recognized that the conditions for the existence of such modes of production—not simply the ecological conditions but political and ideological ones as well—are not merely of an essence but historically significant conditions in their own right. This has been undertaken with considerable success by historians such as Perry Anderson and Georges Duby, who have shown how feudal institutions, in their diffusion in Europe, were adapted to the conditions of particular regions at the same time as playing a transformative social and political role themselves.[12]

An analysis such as Fu Zhufu's also promises a more historical approach to the problems of Chinese society. Because of his conceptual framework, however, the author proceeds to look for special laws where in fact there might be the possibility of discovering sociological principles of universal relevance. Fu's analysis of the relationship between landownership, commerce, cities, money, the guild system in China, the role of political and ideological authority could be revealing to the dynamic interrelationship of these elements in social development. Instead, having cast his analysis within the framework of 'feudalism', the author remains concerned exclusively with discovering differences of Chinese feudalism from European feudalism.

Furthermore, Fu, like his predecessors, devotes little attention to regional variations in the Chinese economic structure, or to variations within the same region.[13] Just because the subcontinent that is China has been encompassed for most of its history within a single political boundary does not justify analysis that assumes it to be a single economic entity. This is obviously not due to any lack of awareness of regional variations in the Chinese economy, for most historians of China have seen in regional specialization a dynamic source of economic development within the 'feudal' economy. Nevertheless, the tendency to deduce a single, or dominant, mode of production from the relatively homogeneous social and political structure (the social formation) has been a strong one—that is, a tendency towards internal sociological 'universalization' that corresponds to the global universalization of the concept of mode of production. The most fruitful work on European feudalism has been that which has taken into account regional variations, and the implications of regional variation for feudal institutions or a feudal mode of production. It is possible, of course, to fetishize regionalism to the point where all extra-regional phenomena are ignored, as is the case with those historicist approaches that view with suspicion any analysis that claims generalizations which transcend any but the most minute local boundaries. The point, however, is not to restrict analysis to regions or periods isolated from one another, but to account for regional differences over time in order to elucidate regional variations in the mode of production, the interrelationship between different regions, and the structure that is the product of such relationships. Such analysis promises a more precise understanding of the relationship between modes of production and social formations as wholes, as well as the dynamic forces at work in the overall structure.

The history of Marxism, it may well be argued, has been the history of progressive departure away from the materialist premises of the theory—the activities of '[illegible]al' people—to a scientistic idealism that feeds upon itself by creating ever novel abstractions. This is not to deny the importance of abstraction in social and historical analysis, but only of those abstractions that are so far removed from concrete existence that they serve no purpose either in understanding the world or in changing it. This sort of abstraction has taken over all the fundamental concepts of Marxism, including class, mode of production and social formation. As many Marxists preach but few practise, it is important to return theory to its roots in material existence, and seek to create a Marxist discourse that retains its ties to concrete historical experience. A mode of production is, ultimately, a mode of producing that not only transforms the world, but embodies in its process all the material and spiritual constituents of its social context. What is essential is to understand this process, its implications for class relations and social and political relations in general. Chinese historians who deem even the organization of production irrelevant to the definition of mode of production may have carried the abstraction to a caricaturized extreme, but they appear relatively circumspect when placed against Marxist theoreticians who point with pride to the irrelevance of their speculations to history.[14]

Were the problem simply one of labelling social formations, this preoccupation with abstract definitions of feudalism might easily be dismissed as irrelevant to the substance of historical analysis. It is the second element of the discourse, the assumption of a universal teleology, that makes the preoccupation with feudalism an obstacle to understanding. The affirmation of 'special' laws for Chinese feudalism has not led Chinese historians to challenge this teleology; rather, Chinese historians have proceeded to incorporate 'special' phenomena into a universal scheme of development. This has led, on one hand, to the distortion of Chinese society into a 'special' case of feudalism and, on the other hand, to a reductionist definition of feudalism. Ultimately, the problems of the Chinese analysis of feudalism are traceable to the urge to package history into well-defined stages that succeed one another in orderly progression.

Fu's analysis once again illustrates the problems created by this teleology. According to Fu, capitalism began to sprout in China before it did in Europe, but it never fulfilled its growth into the capitalist mode of production because of the special features of Chinese society. Unlike many other advocates of the sprouts of capitalism in China, Fu has acknowledged that sprouts did not guarantee the emergence of capitalism. But like others, he assumes that capitalism must succeed feudalism in history. Many of the contradictions in his analysis of feudalism are products of his recognition that capitalist sprouts existed side by side with the feudal system, without ever reaching their historically promised fulfilment.

This claim to the sprouts of capitalism could be dismissed as an expression of a chauvinism that will not permit to China a second place to Europe in historical development. Though perhaps not entirely unfounded, such an explanation is one-sided. Important theorists of capitalist development such as Max Weber have been intrigued with this same question, and Japanese Marxist historians have made similar observations on China's historical development.[15] Fu's assessment of Chinese history, like that of other Marxist historians in China, rests rather upon the assumption that historical development must culminate in capitalism, an assumption that is imbedded deep in Marxist historical discourse, and the modern consciousness of history of which Marxism is an integral expression. The universality of capitalism, as I suggested earlier, is the starting point in historical consciousness of the universalization of historical development.

In the case of Marxism, however, the assumption that history must develop through a number of stages imposes more serious restrictions on historical analysis. Since feudalism must precede capitalism as a stage, a society that exhibits 'capitalist' elements but cannot be categorized a capitalist must by definition be a feudal society. This lack of alternatives lies at the root of the circular, and contradictory, arguments that while China was a 'special' feudal society because it never made the transition to capitalism, it was a special feudal society because it contained important capitalist elements.

This is a general problem of the Marxist conception of history as a succession of internally related modes of production culminating in capitalism and, ultimately, socialism. Whether or not Marx intended European development to be universalized into a global model of development, which is debatable, Marxist discourse has been guided by this assumption. The only alternative to this unilinear scheme of development has been provided by the notion of Asiatic society which, as Western and non-Western Marxists have recognized, is the product less of theory than of a Europe-centred culturalism. Whether because of the imposition of a European model upon the rest of the world, or because of the culturalist exclusion of non-European societies from general theoretical considerations, Marxist models of development have proven deficient outside of Europe.

The insufficiency of these models in explaining the diversity and complexity of global historical development is evident in the efforts of Marxist historians and social scientists to generate new modes of production, which seek to account for diversity while retaining the coherence of theory. In Chinese historiography before the establishment of Stalinist orthodoxy, some historians protrayed the 'pre-capitalist' society of imperial China as a historical stage. Others spoke of 'despotic feudalism', which has remained alive in the notion of a 'bureaucratic feudalism'. By and large, however, historians sensitive to the insufficiency of Marxist categories to encompass China's development resorted to the idea of transition to cover the differences.

These universalist assumptions have important theoretical implications. To take the case of a special feudal society in China, the idea of a special path of development necessarily implies that historical development must follow different paths in different societies, and that not all societies must evolve towards capitalism. And yet Chinese historians, with the exception of a few advocates of Asiatic society, have not considered this issue seriously. If history develops out of inner necessity, as the materialist conception of history suggests, in other words, if the course of history is determined by forces immanent in society, different societies must of necessity develop in different directions. This basic theoretical premise is at odds with the forced conclusions of Chinese historians that, even if Chinese society had its own special laws, the course of development of Chinese society was in the direction of capitalism. Fu Zhufu's caveat that the sprouts of capitalism did not necessarily imply the development of the capitalist mode of production bypasses this issue but does not resolve it. After all, if there was no implicit development towards capitalism, it is not very meaningful to speak of the sprouts of capitalism!

The multiplication of available modes of production in order to account for the complexity of historical development would seem to be a possible answer to this problem. This, too, must require revision of the theoretical premises of Marxism, and especially revision of the assumption that historical development follows a universal course. The abandonment of this assumption, however, is not merely a theoretical matter, but impinges upon fundamental political assumptions of Marxism, including the assumption that historical development can be neatly packaged into a series of class formations characterized by opposition between two major classes.[16] It is this third element of the discourse, and the questions it raises concerning socialism as the end of history, that provides the context within which we must view theoretical issues of the materialist conception of history.

The importance of politics for history is quite evident in the case of Marxist historiography in China which grew out of polemics half a century ago over the nature and the future of the Chinese Revolution. The conceptualization of Marxist historical categories such as feudalism in the Chinese historical discourse is often traceable to the way these concepts were employed, often very loosely, in connection with discussions of revolutionary strategy. On the other hand, historical discussion took as its ultimate goal the validation of a revolutionary strategy based on such conceptualization. The revolutionary roots of Marxist historiography in China continued to shape historical discourse even after revolution ceased to be a problem, for these initial conceptualizations of Marxist categories have been constituent elements of Chinese thinking on the past. Furthermore, the political implications of historical analysis have continued to be issues in historical interpretation. Some historians who spoke of the 'sprouts of capitalism' were accused in the late 1950s of reviving the counter-revolutionary ideas of Tao Xisheng. The idea of Asiatic society, long a dead issue, has been revived recently to explain why the 'Gang of Four' could achieve the power it did. And some of the policies of the post-Mao regime, including its emphasis on rapid development, have been justified by reference to the need to extinguish the 'feudal' outlook and practices that persist in Chinese society.

The Chinese case once again points to broader questions within the Marxist tradition of discourse. Obviously, for a revolutionary theory which rests on the assumption that revolution is a product of forces immanent in society, the question of the nature of a society at the moment of revolution is of the utmost significance. Whether a society is diagnosed as bourgeois, feudal or Asiatic is not an academic question, but a question fundamental to the formulation of revolutionary strategy—in terms of both the targets and the objectives of revolution.

The questions raised by the ideas of a 'special' society, an alternative mode of production, or of the particularity of historical development gain an additional significance when viewed in this context. In Marxist politics, socialism is the product of a historical development that culminates in capitalism, which in turn is the condition for socialism. Denial of universality to historical development has inevitably raised questions about the universality of socialism, or at the very least about the necessity of identity for socialism everywhere. In other words, if societies differ historically, there is no reason to think that they must all converge to socialism, or, if they do so, that socialism must assume the same form everywhere.

It may be argued that the achievement of socialism depends solely on capitalism, not on pre-capitalist society. There are good grounds for such an argument within the Marxist tradition. It is valid to argue, as Mukhia does, that Marx viewed only capitalism to be a universal social formation, subject to the same laws regardless of historical context (Mukhia, 1981: 273). But the implications of this argument are ambiguous. In the first place, it suggests that capitalism was an exclusive product of European society and spread around the globe out of Europe. One need not disagree with this proposition to argue that a socialism that is a product of the response to the intrusion of capitalism from the outside, rather than an outgrowth of the immanent development of capitalism, is certainly not the same socialism that Marx had in mind in the formulation of his ideas. Moreover, if capitalism is a foreign implant, the pre-capitalist pasts of these societies must enter into the making of their socialist future. To the extent that societies have differed historically, their socialisms must show evidence, for better or for worse, of the burden of their pre-capitalist pasts.

Second, capitalism may have universal laws of its own in the abstract, but the impact of the capitalist mode of production on different societies has varied according to their inherited constitution. In other words, capitalism, too, must be viewed historically in order to account for the different results it has produced in different social contexts. Capital may have unified the world, but it has not transformed the world in its image. While it is possible to speak today of a universal history that is the product of capitalism, it is not possible to speak of a global identity among societies. The history of capitalism is as much a history of resistance to capitalism as it is of the capitalist transformation of the world. The political implications of this recognition must be obvious. If societies differ significantly even in the era of capitalism, Marxists must learn to speak not of socialism but of socialisms, socialisms that do not bear the same relationship to their immediate capitalist pasts. The inability, or the unwillingness to do so, accounts to a large extent for the perpetuation of the myth of universality in history. The political emergence of the Third World has obviously created a crisis in Marxist historical and political discourse. While the assumption of universality has disguised this crisis, it is itself at the root of the crisis. Whether or not the crisis generates a new discourse must depend on the willingness of Marxist to confront fundamental assumptions of Marxism.

To sum up, then, the problems Chinese historians have encountered in employing the concept of feudalism within Chinese history are not empirical problems imbedded in the Chinese discourse on history. Some Chinese historians have suggested, at least to justify their own particular views, that unless historians address theoretical questions of the materialist conception of history, more data will not resolve disagreements among historians (Wu, 1962: 116). Their own criticism, however, remain within the prevailing tradition of discourse. The analysis here suggests that theoretical adjustments (such as new definitions of feudalism) are not likely to resolve these problems either, for the basic problems are discursive ones, imbedded in the discourse that informs theory.

Most of the basic problems of the Chinese historiography of feudalism, moreover, are common to Marxist discussions of feudalism elsewhere. Certain claims of Chinese historians, such as the presentation of imperial Chinese 'feudalism' as a 'classic' case, may be disconcerting to historians of Europe who suffer from their own brand of parochialism; nevertheless, these claims are the culmination of a historical discourse guided throughout by the Marxist conceptualization of history. Problems in Chinese history, in other words, offer significant clues to fundamental problems of the Marxist discourse on history as a universal discourse.

If these problems are to be resolved, it is important for Marxists to reconsider the guiding assumptions of this discourse, rather than to engage in empirical quibbles or theoretical adjustments that only add to the confusion of a concept that has long outgrown its original empirical boundaries. It is necessary above all to re-evaluate the Marxist conceptualization of history in terms of a limited series of vaguely conceived modes of production that either are theoretically incoherent or fail to account for concrete historical phenomena of significance, the myth of universality in history that restricts historical diversity within the boundaries established by these modes of production, and the ideology of unilinearity that imprisons the future in the strait-jacket of a political blueprint that is purportedly derived from the 'scientific' study of the past but which in fact remakes the past in its own image. Such re-evaluation must start with the demystification of a consciousness which limits the possibility of diversity in the past in order to rationalize its denial to the present of imagining alternative possibilities for the future.[17]

NOTES

1. My use of discourse in this essay owes much to M. Foucault's presentation of this idea (Foucault, 1970; 1972; 1980). Foucault himself endows this idea with more than one meaning. I mean by the term, first, that a concept is 'constituted by all that was said in all the statements that named it' (1972: 32) and, second, that there is a 'regularity' to be found in all such statements that gives the discourse its unity and meaning.
2. Harbans Mukhia in his 'Was There Feudalism in Indian History?' (Mukhia, 1981) raises this question but does not pursue, it, which is a serious weakness of his discussion. It is interesting that the one Chinese historian Mukhia cites to back up his argument that feudalism be restricted to European history, Wu Dakun, has been an advocate of an Asiatic society in China (Dakun, 1980). I should also explain here that though the conclusions of the present article do not differ from Mukhia's, at least with regard to the use of the term outside of Europe, the reasoning underlying my conclusions is significantly different from Mukhia's. Mukhia offers a new definition of feudalism to sustain his arguments against an Indian feudalism. The problems with this definition are as follows. (a) It simplifies Europe by reducing it to a unit to contrast it with India. This simplification ignores the problems that attend the Marxist (and non-Marxist) analyses of a feudal system in Europe. (b) Mukhia's characterization of the feudal mode of production in terms of 'a hiatus between the labour potential of a peasant family and its resources (used for production)' seems to

me to refer not to the 'distinctive characteristic' of the feudal mode of production but to a condition for feudalism. This characterization is, at any rate, too vague to be useful. The more important question is why and how this hiatus was created and sustained. The statement as is stated may be applicable to any society where one class denies to another the resources for production. (c) Mukhia's definition of feudalism at another place as 'the structured dependence of the entire peasantry on the lords' is equally vague, since it is not accompanied by an analysis of the particular structure at issue. As in the case of the Chinese historians who have based their arguments for feudalism on an 'essentialist' definition of feudalism (see later), Mukhia cavalierly refuses to incorporate into his definition any of the formal characteristics of feudalism that he considers to be superstructural. These, I think, are crucial to the discussion of structures and 'structured dependence'. This, I will argue later, is a feature of Marxist discourse that had long obstructed the articulation of some of the most valuable theoretical insights of Marxism.

3. For variation on these periodization see the table on pp. 187-90 in Dirlik (1978). This work also discusses extensively the sources that were available to Chinese historians in the 1920s and 1930s.
4. The most prominent historians of post-1949 China started their careers as historians in the 1930s (Dirlik, 1978: 223-4). Their views dominate Chinese historiography to this day. Fu Zhufu, whose views are discussed below, published his first analyses of Chinese history in 1934. His early work was clearly part of the first Marxist discussions of Chinese history.
5. The discussions of Chinese history in early Marxist historiography are derived from my work cited earlier (Dirlik, 1978). Rather than cite the Chinese sources, I will refer later only to the appropriate sections of the book where these arguments are elaborated in greater detail. Those interested in the sources are referred to the citations in that study. For Tao's views, see Dirlik (1978: 110-19).
6. For these discussions, see *Zhongguo di nuli zhi yo fengjian zhi fenqi wenti lunwen xuanji* (*Selected Essays on the Problems of Periodising the Slave and Feudal Systems in China*) (1962), and *Zhongguo gudai shi fenqi wenti luncong* (*Essays on the Problems of Periodising Ancient Chinese History*) (1957).
7. For a discussion of this problem, see Dirlik (1982: 105-32).
8. Fu's introduction (to Fu, 1980), translated in *Modern China* (Fu, 1981). For the quotation, see p. 10.
9. Fu (1981: 15). Fu is remarkably cavalier in including social groups in the landed class which are in potential, if not actual, conflict with one another. His list includes the Emperor, nobles, high and low officials, merchants and all 'those who commanded wealth' (Fu, 1980, I: 99).
10. In Fu (1980, I: 196). Fu describes imperial Chinese society as 'entirely different' from Zhou society. It is also noteworty that in his earliest studies of Chinese history that I have been able to locate, Fu restricted feudalism in

China to the Zhou period, and identified it with the noble old (*lingzhu*) economy. At the time, he attacked Tao Xisheng for extending feudalism in China all the way to the twentieth century (which was off the mark), and described the landlord economy of imperial China as a transition period: '. . . this very long transitional period was neither feudal nor capitalist; if I were to name it, I would name it a period of oscillatory economy', meaning that the economy advanced at times and regressed at other times, but remained on the whole in a stage of stagnant transition. See Fu (1934b; also 1934a: 1-42). Many of the reasons for China's inability to advance to capitalism that Fu has given in his recent work, including the nature of the economy as well as external factors such as 'barbarian' invasions, were first enunciated in these essays. The continuity reflects the persistence of the discourse; the changes may reflect adjustment to political orthodoxy, or to the carrying of the discourse to its 'logical' conclusions.

11. The theoretical speculation over modes of production and their 'articulation' is yet to be translated into historical analysis. Part of the reason for the gap between theory and practice is the abstruseness of much of this theoretical speculation. More important, I think, are the questions it raises, in particular questions concerning class relations peculiar to any social formation: a multiplicity of modes of production in a social formation clutters neat divisions of society into two antagonistic classes. For some recent discussions of the problem, see n. 14. Marx, of course, was quite explicit about the multiplicity of modes of production in any social formation: 'In all forms of society there is one specific kind of production which predominated over the rest, whose relations thus assign rank and influence to the others. It is a general illumination which bathes all the other colours and modifies their particularity. It is a particular ether which determines the specific gravity of every being which has materialized within it' (Marx, 1973: 106-7). The poetic eloquence of the statement, however, disguises the many problems to which it points.
12. See Anderson (1978), and Duby (1978). The task in these works is rendered easier by the fact that the feudal institution and its economic, social and political products are European in origin. The problem, therefore, appears as a historical rather than a theoretical problem. But the theoretical implications of these historical approaches are quite evident.
13. For seminal discussions of this problem, see Skinner (1977 and 1971). For a discussion of the problem with reference to the 'sprouts of capitalism', see Dirlik (1982: 115). Most of Skinner's works deal with this problem.
14. See Hindess and Hirst (1977: 312). For a discussion of recent Marxist writings on modes of production, see Foster-Carter (1978).
15. For a discussion of Japanese historians' view of China, see Grove and Esherick (1980).
16. See Dirlik (1978: 245-8) for further discussion of this problem.
17. I would like to add a note here on a report on a recent conference held in

China over the problem of studying feudalism that came to my attention after I concluded the writing of this article (see 'Zhongguo fengjian zhuyi yanjiu fangfa lun wenti taolunhui zongshu' ('Report on a Conference on the Methodological Problems of Investigation into Chinese Feudalism') (1982). This report shows the continued 'lively' interest in the question of feudalism in Chinese historical studies. According to the report, this conference, attended by scholars from all over China, addressed the question of methodologies that might be useful in resolving the problems Chinese historians have encountered over the past fifty years in dealing with the issue of feudalism. The conference focused especially on the problem of how to explain the 'prolonged' duration of feudal society in China. It addressed questions concerning the relevance of the methods of natural science to social science, Marxism and its relationship to the methods of analysis that have appeared in the West since World War II (with stress on cybernetics, systems theory, etc.), the uses of the comparative method, as well as the relevance of local studies to studies of the whole.

The revealing aspect of this conference is its concern with methodological questions, as the conferees agreed that the problem of feudalism rested not with historical materials but with the fundamental question of how to approach this problem. The conference recognized the political origins of discussions of feudalism in China, and the need to move away from the restrictions imposed upon discussion by those origins. These concerns reveal a refreshing recognition of the problems that have long plagued Chinese studies of feudalism. Especially interesting is the reported concern over structural approaches (emphasizing interaction between parts as well as the parts and the whole) *vs.* approaches in terms of ultimate causes (forces and relations of production). What all this might mean is another matter. The report gives no hint of questions concerning the concept itself. The conference presupposed the 'prolonged persistence of feudal society in China' and, rather than question this presupposition, focused its attention on ways to explain the reasons for this phenomenon. Its goal, following in the tradition of discourse discussed in this article, would seem to be to elucidate the special features of Chinese society as well as the ways in which Chinese society followed the 'universal' laws of feudalism. Feudalism, as far as is possible to tell, is still taken as a universal concept in the sense in which I have presented it earlier: the report cited the conferees' agreement that it is necessary through comparison 'to seek out the similarities and differences of feudal society in China with feudal society in other countries', and their injunction that 'when engaging in comparison, it is necessary not to take any one region as the standard against which to measure China, but to consider carefully the traditions and peculiarities of each state and people' (p. 90).

Perhaps the best illustration for the thesis that has been argued already is provided by the title of an article published in a recent issue of *Lishi Yanjiu*: 'Fundamental Reasons for the Relatively Brief Duration of Feudalism in

Western Europe' (Pang, 1983: 107-21). The author, Pang Zhuoheng, argues that the successful struggle of the serfs against the feudal lords brought feudalism to an early end in Europe. The opening up of new lands by agricultural workers helped increase production, advance trade, and strengthen the cities, which facilitated the liberation of the serfs. This article suggests perhaps that European feudalism was not even 'a classical case' of feudalism but an exception to it!

REFERENCES

Anderson, P., 1978, *Passages from Antiquity to Feudalism*, London: New Left Books, Verso Editions.

Banaji, J., 1976, 'The Peasantry and the Feudal Mode of Production: Towards an Economic Model', *Journal of Peasant Studies*, Vol. 3, No. 3.

Brown, E.A.R., ed., 1979, 'The Tyranny of a Construct: Feudalism and Historians of Medieval Europe', *American Historical Review*, Vol. 79, No. 4.

Cheyette, F.L., ed., 1968, *Lordship and Community in Europe*, New York: Holt, Rinehart & Winston.

Dirlik, A., 1978, *Revolution and History: Origins of Marxist Historiography in China, 1919-1937*, Berkeley: University of California Press.

Dirlik, A., 1982, 'Chinese Historians and the Marxist Concept of Capitalism: A Critical Examination', *Modern China*, Vol. 8, No. 1 (January).

Duby, G., 1978, *The Early Growth of the European Economy: Warriors and Peasants from the Seventh to the Twelfth Century*, Ithaca: Cornell University Press.

Elvin, M., 1973, *The Pattern of the Chinese Past*, Stanford: Stanford University Press.

Foster-Carter, A., 1978, 'Can we Articulate "Articulation"?', in J. Clammer, ed., *The New Economic Anthropology*, New York: St. Martin's Press. Also published in 1978, with slight alterations, as 'The Modes of Production Debate', *New Left Review*, No. 107 (January-February).

Foucault, M., 1970, *The Order of Things*, New York: Vintage.

———, 1972, *The Archeology of Knowledge*, New York: Pantheon.

———, 1980, *Power/Knowledge*, New York: Pantheon.

Fu Zhufu, 1934a, 'You jingji shang kaocha Zhongguo fengjian zhidu shengcheng yu huimie di shidai wenti' ('An Examination of the Rise and Fall of the Feudal System in China from an Economic Perspective'), *Shehui kexue congkan* (*Social Science Journal*), Vol. 1, No. 1 (May).

———, 1934b, 'Zhongguo jingji jiegou zhi lishi di Jiantao' ('A Historical Examination of China's Economic Structure'), *Shehui kexue congkan* (*Social Science Journal*), Vol. 1, No. 2 (November).

———, 1980, *Zhongguo jingji shi luncong* (*Collection of Essays in Chinese Economic History*), 2 vols., Beijing.

———, 1981, 'Introduction' (to Fu, 1980), translated in *Modern China*, Vol. 7, No. 1, pp. 1-30.

Grove, L. and J. Esherick, 1980, 'From Feudalism to Capitalism: Japanese Scholarship on the Transformation of Chinese Rural Society', *Modern China*, Vol. 6, No. 4 (October).

Guo Moruo, 1930, *Zhongguo quaid shehui yanjiu* (*Researches in Ancient Chinese Society*), Shanghai.

Hindess, B. and P.Q. Hirst, 1977, *Pre-Capitalist Modes of Production*, Boston: Routledge & Kegan Paul.

Hu Rulei, 1979, *Zhongguo fengjian shehui xingtai yanjui* (*Researches in the Feudal Social Formation in China*), Beijing.

Kula, W., 1976, *An Economic Theory of the Feudal System*, London: New Left Books.

Lefebvre, G., 1956, 'A Historian's Remarks on the Transition from Feudalism to Capitalism', *Science and Society*, Vol. 20, No. 3 (Summer).

Marx, K., 1973, *Grundrisse* (trans. M. Nicolaus), New York: Vintage Books.

Mukhia, H., 1981, 'Was There Feudalism in Indian History?', *Journal of Peasant Studies*, Vol. 8, No. 3 (April).

Pang Zhuoheng, 1983, 'Xi ou fengjian shehui yanxu shijian jiaoduan di genben yuanyin' ('Fundamental Reasons for the Relatively Brief Duration of Feudalism in Western Europe'), *Lishi yanjiu* (*Historical Studies*), No. 1, pp. 107-21.

Skinner, G. Wiliam, 1971, 'Chinese Peasants and Closed Community: An Open and Shut Case', *Comparative Studies in Society and History*, Vol. 13, No. 3 (July).

———, 1977, 'Regional Systems in Late Imperial China', unpublished.

Wu Dakan, 1962, 'Yu Fan Wenlan tongzhi lun huafen Zhongguo nuli shehui yo fenjian shehui di biaozhun wenti' ('Discussion of the Criteria for Distinguishing Feudal from Slave Society with Comrade Fan Wenlan'), in *Zhongguo di nuli-zhi yu fengjian zhi fenqi wenti lunwen zuanji* (1962).

Wu Dakun, 1980, 'Guanyu yaxiya shenchan fangshi yanjiu di jige wenti' ('Some Problems in the Investigation of the Asiatic Mode of Production', *Qishi niandai* (*The Seventies*), Vol. 7.

Xu Dixin, ed., 1980, *Zhengzhi jingjixue cidian* (*Dictionary of Political Economy*), Vol. 1, Beijing.

Zhongguo di nuli zhi yu fengjian zhi fenqi wenti lunwen xuanji (*Selected Essays on the Problems of Periodising the Slave and Feudal Systems in China*), 1962, Beijing.

'Zhongguo fengjian zhuyi yanjiu fangfa lun wenti taolunhui zongshu' ('Report on a Conference on the Methodological Problems of Investigation into Chinese Feudalism'), 1982, *Lishi yanjiu* (*Historical Studies*), No. 5 (October), pp. 87-92.

Zhongguo gudai shi fenqi wenti luncong (*Essays on the Problems of Periodising Ancient Chinese History*), 1957, Beijing.

Classifying Pre-Colonial India

Irfan Habib

Any civilized society has such a vast number of features specific to it that the attempt to club it with any other in a single category of economic formations must begin by indicating what elements are deemed basic for such classification. In Marxist terms, there is, first, the form of the labour-process, which comprises the essential conditions in which the primary producer performs his or her function. Thus one distinguishes, in the classic line of succession, slavery, serfdom and wage-labour. One may say that where the social form of labour differs, the 'mode of production' cannot be the same (and the dominant mode of production defines the economic formation). But what seems often to be overlooked is that the converse is not necessarily true. Wage-labour remains the basic form of labour in socialism, but this does not entitle us to identify the capitalist and socialist modes. A second element, no less crucial, must therefore also be considered: this is the form in which the surplus extracted from the producer is distributed. It is clearly here that one major point of difference between the capitalist and socialist modes lies, apart from the control over production itself that is seized from the capitalists under socialism. It is true that the distributive system cannot be independent of the conditions of productive labour. Capitalism cannot subsist on serfdom, but only on wage-labour. Yet a particular form of labour can still conceivably exist within a varied range of economic formations. We have just given the example of wage-labour, alike found in capitalism and socialism; it is very likely that simple peasant production (peasant as a rent-paying petty producer) might be found to sustain an even wider range of formations. Moreover, if each economic formation is distinguished by its own specific laws of motion—and even a specific prime mover—it cannot simply stem from the conditions of labour alone, but must arise out of an interaction of these with the other elements of the property system, an interaction which cannot also remain unaffected by factors external to both.

These rather elementary observations are made here simply to stress the extreme unlikelihood of all pre-capitalist formations of class societies (that is, excluding primitive communities) having conformed to just two categories, namely, classical (based on slavery) and feudal (based on serfdom). Dobb (1946: 35) holds that feudalism is to be treated as 'virtually identical' with serfdom. But it was surely much more than that: its distributive system rested on the fief (with which the manor coalesced) and the entire fabric of vassalage. It is impossible to analyse its development and dissolution (in Western Europe) without considering these institutions. At the same time Dobb (1954: 26) dilutes his own definition by postulating a continuance of feudalism even after peasants had ceased to be serfs. From this, however, it cannot be argued that any society which had a peasantry of any kind of dependent status must be designated feudal, though it had no fief or vassalage, just as it is not easy to speak of a feudal mode of production wherever one finds institutions reminiscent of fief or vassalage but without serfdom. This is not a matter of excessive insistence on linguistic rigour. We are interested in feudalism (as in Western Europe) chiefly for elucidating the consequences of its breakdown which opened the way to the genesis and development of capitalism. For such purpose its 'laws of motion' are most important for us. These can only be inferred from what we know of all the three chief elements of feudalism (and not one only); and then we need also to study the influence on their mutual relationships exercised by external factors. These laws of motion are likely to be substantially different from those of societies which had only one of the three elements present: in that case to tar all such societies with the same brush will give us no illumination because we cannot read into them tendencies that we have established for an essentially different social order: if we did so, the result would hardly be of much use for historical analysis.

II

Marx was, therefore, clearly in the right when he thought that Indian society merited analysis on the basis of its own specific features. He found, first, that here the 'village community' rather than the individual peasant represented the basic object of subjection by the exploiting class. He recognized that cultivation was undertaken by peasant households separately, but that community and caste ties bound the peasant and village-artisan into a single social and economic unit (Marx and Engels, n.d.: 35-6; Marx, 1938: 351-2). As a result individual subjection, whether slavery or serfdom, could not become dominant. This he explicitly acknowledged in the *Grundrisse* (Marx, 1964: 91). But it is important to realize that Marx also attributed the lack of development of serfdom 'in

Asia' to be fact that, with the rent and tax coinciding, the state was the 'landlord'. In 'such circumstances there need exist no stronger political or economic pressure than that common to all subjection to that state' (Marx, 1959: 771-2). Near the end of his life Marx (1964: 58) again insisted on the absence of serfdom in India and on that basis rejected Kovalevsky's categorization of Indian property relations as feudal.[1]

There was yet another element in Indian society which demarcated it from the feudal in its characteristic medieval European form. In the latter 'only a relatively small portion of that part of the product which represents the landlord's revenue' entered 'the process of circulation' (Marx, 1959: 767). But in his classic description of the Indian community in Vol. I of *Capital*, Marx (1938: 351-2) presents the following picture of what happened to the surplus product in India:

> Hence, production here [within the village community] is independent of that division of labour brought about in Indian society as a whole, by means of exchange of commodities. It is the surplus alone that becomes a commodity, and a portion of even that, not until it has reached the hands of the State, into whose hands from time immemorial certain quantity of these products has found its way in the shape of rent in kind.

The assumption is here explicit that the surplus extracted from the village is converted into commodities: when it is paid in kind, the appropriator puts it on the market. Here we have extensive commodity circulation responsible for the division of labour outside the village; the extent of surplus alone sets the limits to its sway.[2]

A third feature further distinguished the Indian formation from the feudal. This was the positive role of the state in providing means of irrigation (canals, embanked tanks) for agriculture. Taking up a suggestion from Engels, Marx thought that this served as the economic basis for the state's claim to rent in 'Asiatic' societies (Marx and Engels, n.d.: 33-4, 278; Marx, 1964: 70-1; and 1938: 523n.). There was, again, nothing similar to this in the non-economic compulsion underlying feudal rent.

Marx was thus able to distinguish the pre-colonial Indian economy from the feudal formation of Western Europe. But his simultaneous relegation of it to a vast Asiatic system seems questionable. In the 1850s he seems to have believed that, in almost the whole of Asia, the social organization had remained unchanged from a time earlier than that of European classical antiquity down to the colonial era; and that the two pillars of this unchanging system were the village community and Oriental despotism (Marx and Engels, n.d.: 31-7, 76-7; Marx, 1964: 69-70). But what Marx himself wrote on India suggested that such a changeless system could hardly have existed. First, as he himself recognized, there had been a change from communal to individual agriculture, surely a fundamental alteration at the very heart of the system. Second, there had been the growth of the state's claim to rent, and Marx (Marx and Engels, n.d.: 290) was at one time ready to suppose that this might have come only with the rise of Islamic polities. Third, there was the growth of commodity circulation. Marx always considered money relations an important aspect of economic organization, and ascribed to money rent the capacity to change 'the character of the entire mode of production' (Marx, 1959: 777). Obviously, then, the stage of conversion of surplus product into commodities that Marx perceived in pre-colonial India could not have been reached without far-going social changes. Such a stream of changes in Indian society cannot be reconciled with the assumption of a single immutable formation from the beginning of civilization to the British conquests.

Given Marx's own delineation of certain features of the pre-colonial Indian economy, then, one is bound to think in terms of succession of social formations to explain the implicit but distinct stages in its evolution. This conviction is strengthened all the more when one comes to deal with the amount of information now available to us, which is naturally much larger than was accessible to Marx.

III

To appreciate where our enlarged knowledge leads us, let us take one of Marx's major premises about the Indian economy on the eve of the colonial conquest. His concept of the village community surely needs modification. The village was admittedly a separate, distinct economic and social unit: but its population was far more highly stratified than Marx appears to have allowed for. On the one hand, individual petty production necessarily generated economic differentiation. On the other, 'the great men', who controlled the village (or community) as tax-collectors, enriched themselves and could cultivate their land with hired labour (*khwud-kasht*, *mirasdars*, etc.) (Habib, 1963: 118-29; 1982: 39-41; H. Fukazawa, in *CEHI*, 1982, I: 253-4). Caste consolidated social differentiation notably by creating an enormous rural proletariat in the shape of the Untouchables.

Thus, collective subjection was accompanied by individual subjection in varied forms, existing principally through the framework of caste. This duality was reflected in the attitude of the state, which reserved the right to bypass the village headman and impose its land-tax on each individual peasant (*asami-war*), whenever this was to its advantage (Habib, 1963: 230-6). Moreover, since the state's claims were exercised through individual assignees of particular territories (*jagirs*), movements of peasants were subject to restraint, though in practice considerable mobility existed among the peasantry (cf. *pai kasht* peasants) (*CEHI*, I: 14; Habib, 1963: 115-16; Grover, 1961: 152-5; Chandra, 1974). These varied forms of subjection of different categories of the rural population have little in common with serfdom, nor with the classic image of the village community. They resulted from a historical process chiefly under the varied impact of the caste system, petty production and the rent-receiving state.

The second important modification one must introduce in Marx's picture is in respect of his notion that the surplus product of the village went entirely into the hands of the state (or its assignees). There was, in fact, a whole class of hereditary claimants to shares in rent, which in Mughal India came to attract the universal designation of zamindars. It is possible that something over one-tenth and up to one-quarter of the surplus was acquired by this class. In its claims and pretensions we can detect features of proprietary right; by the sixteenth century the zamindari right was saleable, as is attested by numerous sale deeds. According to one authority (*A'la, c.* 1700), the zamindars could also evict peasants, who treated them as the *maliks* or proprietors of the land. Still, the right had to be backed in most areas with armed power, and there was often a close association with local dominant higher castes. The state insisted that the right involved an obligation on the part of the zamindar to collect its tax from the peasants: it thus endeavoured to integrate the whole class in its fiscal apparatus.[3] Undoubtedly the existence of the zamindar class cannot fit any recognizable concept of the 'Asiatic' system, and suggests an element rather analogous to 'feudal' landownership subsequent to the disappearance of the fief and manor. But the zamindar's own very limited claim upon rent belies any existence of landed property properly speaking; in part, at least, it served as an instrument for the realization of the claims of the higher authority, the state.

The state, headed by a king who was apparently the fountainhead of all authority, comprised a ruling class, whose members held the right to the revenues of various territories at the pleasure of the king. It is a long time since Moreland (1929: 217-19) argued that these territorial assignments, styled *iqta's* or *jagirs*, were not 'fiefs' in any feudal sense. They were normally transferred from time to time, a practice which was essential for maintaining despotic centralized state. In the seventeenth century, Bernier (1916: 226-7) showed how the practice necessarily led to an increased pressure for immediate maximization of tax-revenue by the assigness. This was perhaps the most visible source of the major contradiction within society: the rent-receiving ruling class, on the one side, and the peasants and the intermediary classes (zamindars, etc.) on the other (Habib, 1963: 317-38).

The entire centralized fiscal structure was inconceivable without extensive commodity circulation. This explained the considerable development of commerce, banking and insurance, and growth of urban centres specializing in manufacture of commodities for distant markets (T. Raychaudhuri, in *CEHI*, I: 260-307, 325-59). But as far as we can see, Marx was right in stressing that it was by and large only the surplus which was converted into commodities, and the self-sufficiency of the peasant economy was not broken. The towns and their commerce were then entirely dependent on the system of state-enforced agrarian exploitation.

One factor on which Marx laid rather varying degrees of emphasis—namely, irrigation-works as the economic basis of the tax-rent—must perhaps be redefined and, in general, modified. The state in India seemed to act occasionally to help extend cultivation by measures such as *taqavi* loans, tax-remissions, repairing bunds, or excavating canals (Habib, 1963: 31-6, 249-56). But these did not constitute a very large portion of its total activity; nor was the effect of these measures more than marginal, at least in the north Indian Plains. It was, therefore, not that the peasants paid rent *because* the state enabled them by its bounty to cultivate the soil; but the state undertook these measures in the expectation that any extension of cultivation, howsoever marginal, would cause a disproportionate increase in rent. The basis of payment of tax-rent continued to be fundamentally non-economic compulsion.

Given these feature we can perhaps speculate on the main lines of movement of the system. Centralized despotism was essential for the extraction of tax-rent. But the only form in which it could acquire and retain its unified power—by keeping tax-assignments temporary—tended unceasingly to increase the fiscal pressure. This generated agrarian revolts, and so led to a breakdown of the imperial system. Two such cycles are noticeable, corresponding with the Delhi Sultanate in the thirteenth and fourteenth centuries and the Mughal Empire in the sixteenth and seventeenth centuries.[4] When the breakdown occurred, and the centralized despotism collapsed, towns and trade inevitably suffered—as Ashin Das Gupta (1979) has recently shown in his study of eighteenth-century Surat.

As the Empire collapsed, the zamindars generally enlarged their authority over the peasants (and so a seeming 'feudal' reaction), and regional powers struggled to retain the major part of the fiscal claims inherited from the Empire. This was a situation opposite to the one which grew out of the collapse of feudalism in Western Europe, leading to the nation-state, the expansion of commerce and the universality of the 'petty mode of production', out of which capitalism was to emerge.

Some of the impulse to designate the pre-colonial Indian formation as feudal seems to come from a belief that, like West European feudalism, it too could generate elements of capitalism [for example, Iqtidar Alam Khan (1976: 28-9)]. There can, perhaps, be two objections to this, apart from the lack of essential similarities between the two formations. First, as we have seen, the breakdown of the pre-colonial Indian formation had consequences very different from those of the feudal crisis. Second, even in Europe there was no direct transition from feudalism to capitalism. The feudal breakdown resulted, first of all, in a regime of private landownership and rent-paying free peasantry; and it was only out of the contradictions of this mode that capitalism developed.[5] India did not witness such a situation until the latter half of the nineteenth century, and then only as a result of colonial rule.

Mukhia (1981: 284-93) seems to take a different position altogether. He finds a 'free peasantry' already existing in pre-colonial India; so, of course, there could be no feudalism. But he finds no historical movement either: indeed, there was instead a 'relative stability in India's social and economic history'. Agrarian revolts were mere answers to imbalances, which a cautious state 'restored' soon enough. These conclusions presume a rather idyllic picture of pre-colonial India (without 'acute tensions') for which there is little justification. My own reading, which I have already set out, is that there were just as intense contradictions here as anywhere else; but that these were different in nature and consequence from the contradictions leading to capitalism in Europe [cf. Habib (1969)].

IV

The medieval Indian system—for such is the name I would give it until a better one is offered—can be traced in two phases or cycles, as we have seen. We may now consider the question of the formation or formations which, in turn, preceded this system, before the thirteenth century, when by our own dating its first cycle began.

D.D. Kosambi (1956: 275ff., esp. 326-8) and R.S. Sharma (1965: esp.

263-73) have made us familiar with the term 'Indian feudalism'. Sharma holds that the period of 'Indian feudalism' came to a close over most of northern India by the beginning of the thirteenth century, when the Ghorian-Turkish regime overthrew the old order. Kosambi, on the other hand, would include the succeeding period down to the British conquests within the phase of Indian feudalism. But the major part of the evidence he himself offers belongs to times preceding the thirteenth century. As for the beginning, both these scholars place it within the first millennium.

Of the specific characteristics that Kosambi and Sharma have assigned to this epoch, the first is political decentralization accompanied by the sovereign's alienation of fiscal resources through hereditary religious and secular grants. Ultimately a system of vassalage appears to have developed with a chain of potentates organized in some hierarchical order with the Indian 'knight' or *rajaputra* at the bottom as the basic unit of military and political power (Kosambi's 'feudalism from above' and Sharma's 'political feudalism').

Second, the economy of the period exhibited a steady contraction of money and commerce, a decay in towns, and the isolation of the self-sufficient village (Gopal, 1963a: 215-21; Sharma, 1974: 5; and Yadava, 1976: 44).[6] These conditions too seem analogous to what had happened in medieval Europe, after the fall of the Roman Empire.

There is no doubt that these features are important enough to demarcate this formation from its successor, which was marked by strong centralized power, and extensive commodity circulation, relegating the 'feudal' ruling class of the earlier period to the subordinate position of zamindars. The features contain sufficient similarity with some elements of European feudalism to justify the usage now established in writings on ancient India, in spite of dissentients such as D.C. Sircar (1969: 32-48). Indeed, support has come, rather unexpectedly, from Rushton Coulborn (1968), who, with his own unique definition of feudalism, still feels assured of its existence in exactly the same epoch where Sharma has placed it. It may therefore be churlish to contest the use of this term; but it would still perhaps be necessary to stress the first word in '*Indian* feudalism', so as to emphasize that it may well be a different kind of formation unless we are able to establish that the form of labour process in agriculture was akin to serfdom.

Sharma (1965: 57-8, 118-24) tends to use the term 'serfdom' for peasants who were under some restraint from leaving the land; and B.N.S. Yadava (1973: 163-73) reinforces the evidence regarding 'curbs' on the peasants' movements. Gopal (1963b: 296-309) accepts the presence of the constraints but relegates them to certain areas only, while D.C. Sircar (1969: 32-48) denies them, rather unconvincingly, *in toto.* Kosambi hesitates to propound the existence of full-fledged serfdom, though he points out that slavery 'took a new importance' in this period for the cultivation of land (Kosambi, 1956: 327). Quite possibly peasant cultivation and use of (semi-servile) hired labour existed as alternative means of rent-extraction. I-tsing (1896: 61-2), in the eighth century, could discuss the option the Buddhist monasteries had to lease out their lands to sharecroppers or till it through hired servants. In other texts we read of peasants, living in stratified communities, the richer exploiting their neighbours by exploying them on different tasks, the poor excluded from all voice in the affairs of the village (Habib, 1982: 23-5). The payment of taxes and claims of different superiors seemed to be the one major burden on the peasants at large. Beyond them were the menial ostracized castes, compelled to labour on the fields of others. From such varied evidence, to pick out serfdom alone as the universal or even a widespread form, would be a vulnerable proposition, though clearly the agricultural population was by no means free, but almost universally placed under a variety of forms of subjection. Kosambi (1956: 327) makes a perceptive remark when he says that the manorial system could hardly have been duplicated in India when the country had not had anything corresponding to the Roman villa.

Given such limitations of evidence, it is difficult to define the principal processes of movement within the 'Indian feudal' formation. It has been suggested that there was an influx of money and revival of commerce in the eleventh to twelfth centuries (Sharma, 1965: 242-62). But 'Indian feudalism' very obviously did not undergo a breakdown: it was overwhelmed by external conquest, which supplanted it by a new formation, in which its survivors had a definite, though subordinate, place. Such a radical consequence of an external intrusion may strike one as somehow non-dialectical; but such events are numerous in history. One cannot naturally use modern political frontiers to demarcate the external from the internal; but even to assume that all social change must come as a result of the internal contradictions of a formation alone would be a grave error. One may cite the influence of barbarian invasions in the evolution of West European feudalism; or of 1066 on English feudalism. By breaking up the 'strong elemental fief' (Coulborn, 1968: 372-3), the invaders destroyed the political structure of 'Indian feudalism'; by establishing the cash-nexus as early as the thirteenth century (Moreland, 1929: 37-8), the Sultanate generated such development of commodity production as could sustain a centralized rent-receiving despotism. These signified new relationships, which could only belong to a separate formation.

At the present stage of progress in the critical assessment of available evidence, it is difficult to go beyond the period of 'Indian feudalism' in the way of categorizing economic formations. However the fact that at least two distinct successive formations can be identified within 1,500 years preceding the colonial conquests underlines the truth that there is little real 'exceptionalism' in Indian history. It too is one of exploitation and class contradictions, generating cyclical movements, which Marx had postulated for social evolution in general.[7] The specificities lie in respect of the details of proerty relations and the pace at which contradictions matured, and still more in the realm of ideas, which we have not touched upon, but which could often be of decisive moment. All we can say, at present, is that the configurations have been dimly illumined; their precise delineation, and, indeed, the extension of our sights to areas beyond, would depend on the extent to which serious historical research is pursued in India.

NOTES

1. It is of interest that Marx cites other points of difference as well, including the lack of inalienability of land to 'non-members of the noble class' in India.
2. There are other statements, it is true, where Marx (1964: 80-1; 1959: 767) associates the village community with a natural economy; but either he had modified his view, or, by the 'natural economy' he was thinking of only the exchange-less system *within* the village. Cf. Irfan Habib (1983: 105-7).
3. The various statements made in this paragraph on the zamindar class are based on Irfan Habib (1963: 136-89). See also S.N. Hasan (1969), and *CEHI* (I: 244-7).
4. For the agrarian revolts in the Mughal Empire, see W.C. Smith (1946), and Irfan Habib (1963: 330-1; 1982: 43-7).
5. The clearest exposition of this point occurs in Marx (1938: 786-8), in the chapter in *Capital*, Vol. 1, on the 'Historical Tendency of Capitalist Accumulation'.
6. B.D. Chattopadhyaya (1974: 203-19) contests the thesis of the earlier urban decline; but it is difficult to agree with him merely on the basis of evidence of existence of certain towns or the establishment of some new ones.
7. 'The general theory of historical materialism requires only that there should be a succession of modes of production, though not necessarily any particular modes, and perhaps not in any particular predetermined order' (Hobsbawm in *Marx*, 1964: 19-20).

REFERENCES

A'la, Qazi Muhammad, *c.* 1700, *Risala-i Ahkam-i Arazi*, MS: Maulana Azad Library, Aligarh, Abdus Salam Coll., 'Arabiya (4) 331/101, ff. 43b-62a.

Bernier, Francois, 1916, *Travels in the Mogul Empire, A.D. 1656-1668* (tr. A Constable, ed. V.A. Smith), Oxford: Humphrey Milford.

Cambridge Economic History of India, 1982, Vol. I (*CEHI*, I), T. Raychaudhuri and Irfan Habib, eds., Cambridge: Cambridge University Press.

Chandra, Satish, 1974, 'Some Aspects of the Indian Village Society in Northern India during the 18th Century', *Indian Historical Review*, Vol. I, No. 1, pp. 51-64.

Chattopadhyaya, B.D., 1974, 'Trade and Urban Centres in Early Medieval North India', *Indian Historical Review*, Vol. I, No. 2, pp. 203-19.

Coulborn, Rushton, 1968, 'Feudalism, Brahmanism and the Intrusion of Islam upon Indian History', *Comparative Studies in Society and History*, Vol. X, No. 3.

Dobb, Maurice, 1946, *Studies in the Development of Capitalism*, London: George Routledge & Sons.

Dobb, Maurice, ed., 1954, *The Transition from Feudalism to Capitalism*, London: Fore Publications.

Gopal, Lallanji, 1963a, *Economic Life of Northern India, 700-1200*, Delhi.

———, 1963b, 'Quasi-Manorial Rights in Ancient India', *Journal of Economic and Social History of the Orient*, Vol. VI, Pt. 3.

Grover, B.R., 1961, 'The Position of Desai in the Pargana Administration of Suba Gujarat under the Mughals', *Proceedings of the Indian History Congress*, Delhi Session.

Gupta, Ashin, Das, 1979, *Indian Merchants and the Decline of Surat, c. 1700-1750*, Weisbaden: Franz Steiner Verlag.

Habib, Irfan, 1963, *Agrarian Systems of Mughal India, 1556-1707*, Bombay: Asia Publishing House.

———, 1969, 'Potentialities of Capitalistic Development in Mughal India', *Journal of Economic History*, Vol. 29, No. 1.

———, 1982, 'The Peasant in Indian History', Presidential Address, Indian History Congress, Kurukshetra Session.

———, 1983, 'Marx's Perceptions of India', *The Marxist*, Vol. I, No. 1, New Delhi.

Hasan, S. Nurul, 1969, 'Zamindars under the Mughals', *Land Control and Social Structure in Indian History* (ed. E.L. Frykenberg), London.

I-tsing, 1896, *A Record of the Buddhist Religion, & c.* (tr. T. Takakusu), Oxford: Oxford University Press.

Khan, Iqtidar Alam, 1976, 'The Middle Classes in the Mughal Empire', *Social Scientist*, No. 49 (August 1976).

Kosambi, D.D., 1956, *An Introduction to the Study of Indian History*, Bombay: Popular Book Depot.

Marx, Karl, 1938, *Capital*, Vol. I (Moore-Aveling translation, ed. Dona Torr), London: Allen & Unwin.

———, 1959, *Capital*, Vol. III, Eng. tr., Moscow: Foreign Language Publishing House.

———, 1964, *Pre-Capitalist Economic Formations* (tr. Jack Cohen, ed. E.J. Hobsbawm), London: Lawrence & Wishart.

Marx, Karl and Fredrich Engels, n.d., *On Colonialism*, Moscow: Foreign Languages Publishing House.

Moreland, W.H., 1929, *Agrarian System of Moslem India*, Cambridge: Cambridge University Press.

Mukhia, Harbans, 1981, 'Was there Feudalism in Indian History?', *Journal of Peasant Studies*, Vol. 8, No. 3.

Sharma, R.S., 1965, *Indian Feudalism, c. 300-1200*, Calcutta: University of Calcutta.

———, 1974, 'Problem of Transition from Ancient to Medieval in Indian History', *Indian Historical Review*, Vol. I, No. 1.

Sircar, D.C., 1969, *Landlordism and Tenancy in Ancient and Medieval India as Revealed by Epigraphical Records*, Lucknow: University of Lucknow.

Smith, W.C., 1946, 'Lower Class Uprisings in the Mughal Empire', *Islamic Culture*, pp. 21-40.

Yadava, B.N.S., 1973, *Society and Culture in Northern India in the Twelfth Century*, Allahabad.

———, 1976, 'Problem of the Interaction between Socio-Economic Classes in the Early Medieval Complex', *Indian Historical Review*, Vol. III, No. 1.

Politics, Peasants and the Deconstruction of Feudalism in Medieval India

Burton Stein

The reason for asking whether there was feudalism in India is to be satisfied that an epoch prior to the dominance of capitalism has in some manner been adequately characterized. That is, it is to be convinced that essential economic, political and cultural features of pre-modern India are seized by the concept 'feudalism' and, perhaps as importantly, that this conception provides a basis for comparisons of Indian and other pre-modern societies. No, says Harbans Mukhia,[1] that epoch has not been so characterized by 'feudalism' nor, he adds, by the Asiatic mode of production. Therefore, the task is before us still.

For many historians of pre-modern India who use feudal terminology ('vassal', 'feudatory', 'serf') without reflecting upon feudalism as a fundamental type of social organization nor upon the question of whether Indian historial conditions justify the use of the concept, Mukhia's argument, unphappily, will make little difference. To these historians, questions about comparative historical processes—within or beyond India—are not significant. For those fewer historians who have sought to justify their use of 'feudalism', Mukhia's argument is a very serious challenge. The latter understand that the purpose of constructing an adequate conceptual understanding of the broad character of pre-modern (that is, pre-colonial and pre-capitalist) India is not just for the sense of intellectual order which ensues, but because only by formulations at this level of abstraction can comparisons be made, larger historical processes be engaged, and more penetrating research questions on pre-modern Indian be framed. Mukhia's otherwise trenchant critique fails to notice how little research has been stimulated on medieval India as a result of the adoption of 'feudalism' by some historians.

The main contribution of his essay is that it is a challenge of a high order from an appositely materialistic perspective. Here, I wish to consider three propositions from this essay:

The characteristics of (Indian) agrarian history . . . high fertility of land, low subsistence level and free peasant production . . . explain the relative stability of India's social and economic history. (p. 58)

Thus with a high quantum of agrarian surplus available in the form of land-revenue and cesses etc. to the state—which formed the chief instrument of exploitation—because of the high fertility of land and low subsistence level of the peasant, a kind of equilibrium existed which facilitated the state's appropriation of the peasants' surplus in conditions of relative stability. (p. 58)

It is evident that a wide range of social formations have existed in the world prior to their subjection to the universality of capitalism, and this range cannot be exhausted with the concepts of feudalism and the Asiatic mode of production. (p. 59)

We may reduce these propositions to three issues; the configuring importance of Indian historical agrarian conditions and the 'relative stability' engendered by them; the nature and role of the Indian state; and the desirability of constructing socio-economic formations to replace 'feudal' or 'Asiatic' ones.

ON INDIAN AGRARIAN PRODUCTION AND 'RELATIVE STABILITY'

A major strength in Mukhia's deconstruction of an Indian feudalism is its anchoring in the agrarian base structure. His argument on the 'free peasantry' is compelling in its delineation of economic and non-economic notions about 'free', and it is salutary in asserting the primacy of productive features in the debate about feudalism. The charge that the base structure of agrarian relations has often been slighted, or ignored, by Marxist writers on European and Indian feudalism is a telling one. If, in analyses of feudal societies, political, juridical and other non-economic aspects of these societies have been accorded explanatory privilege, a fundamental question of Marxist analysis—that of determining precisely such things as politics, law, and ideology—is begged and with that the most ponetrating insight into the nature of societies and their transformations.

Having accorded primacy to an evaluation of the agrarian bases of European and Indian medieval societies, Mukhia's discussion is vexed by some old and some novel discursive problems. I do not attempt to pass detailed judgement on his reading of European feudalism which provides the model of feudalism for all. But two observations may be offered.

One is that the determination of whether or not feudalism existed in India can only doubtfully be made on the basis of a missing—albeit central—trait or property of feudalism, namely the absence of serfdom, or an unfree peasantry. Other defining properties can and have been discovered in medieval India: (1) private legal and political jurisdiction of many powerful men within parts of recognized polities or kingdoms based on (2) widely dispersed warrior groups who were recipients of tributary appropriations and independent of (3) central authorities which, when present, constrained weak state forms. It seems also the case that there was in most parts of India a uniform dependence of warriors (would-be 'feudatories') upon local, landed social groups, a condition which D.D. Kosambi called 'feudalism from below'. This could be conceived as an interesting variant of feudalism if the feudal model were favoured for more compelling reasons. My point here is that Mukhia's rejection, because it does not engage feudalism as a generalized structure, is a weak form of rejection, one that may persuade scholars who attached first importance to the question of coerced labour, but not others.

My second observation on Mukhia's comparative method leading to a rejection of feudalism for India is that he may not be comparing like with like. With most scholars, his treatment of feudalism in Europe as transitional (along with all pre-capitalist societies) inevitably tends to anticipate a time when feudal kingdoms were becoming stronger, when royal legal institutions, bureaucracies, and armies were becoming more effective instruments of centralizers, and mercantile interests were at once more independent of landed economic and political interests and more a potential (and potent) ally of centralizing political forces. The model of feudalism for such exotic comparisons as those with India is less often sought in the formative age of European feudalism—Merovingian or Carolingian times (fifth to tenth centuries)—when feudal institutions, while changing, comprised elements of a stable, general type of society. In contrast to this stable form (allowing for *within*-structure changes), later feudalism (*c.* tenth to fourteenth centuries) may be seen as evolving towards an unstable condition which, exacerbated by catastrophes in the fourteenth century, resulted in what is regarded as a generalized crisis and transformation to another structure, capitalism. Put another way, Mukhia compares a historical process (the transition to European capitalism) with a static structure ('relative stability'), a procedure which must weaken the power of the comparative argument. That Mukhia (and others who consider the question of feudalism in India) may be comparing unlike things need not be a very relevant matter since his basis of comparison is not systemic, but partial (the saliency of the economically free or unfree condition of the respective peasant populations). There is one way for even this narrow base of comparison to have been made more pointed: if under early European feudalism (that before the tenth century) it could be shown that the peasantry was, in the same sense proposed by Mukhia for India, 'free', that is, more masters over the means and processes of production than they were later to be.

'Stability' enters Mukhia's discussion in another, seemingly unrelated, way: in his proposed 'relative stability' of India's social and economic history. He asserts here that in India, unlike in post-fourteenth-century Europe, there was no need 'to change completely the means, methods, and relations of agrarian production' (p. 58). This assertion requires that we believe that there was no change in the means and relations of production for perhaps two thousand years, but nothing is said about these relations of production except that the chief (and only?) instrument of exploitation was the state. This is indeed stability, not 'relative', but quite absolute, a position which ought to trouble him as an historian; it troubles me!

If it is true that, apart from the Persian wheel, there were no fundamental changes in technical forces of production from Mauryan times, nor in relations of production of an economically 'free' Indian peasantry, how are the developments of that vast epoch before modernity in India to be explained? In denying the material base for feudalism in India, and affirming no other, has not the foundation for materialist explanations of a great historical age in India also been denied? Unless an argument privileging trade, urbanization, or some such process is made, then is it not the case that changes from post-Mauryan to Mughal times have to be explained by precisely the political, juridical and ideological forces that Mukhia excoriates in the interpretations of Indian feudalism?

Evidence on agrarian organization in medieval south India points to a way out of the predicament in which Mukhia has placed himself. For too long, the rich evidence and mature historiography of south India have been neglected in general discourse on Indian history, and it is with respect to agrarian matters in particular that south Indian history is most illuminating. In a recently published work, I have tried to present a view of south Indian agrarian history covering a period of about one thousand years, an epoch not as long as that treated by Mukhia, but one in which I have sought to treat peasant institutions and society systematically, as a process. In the light of this work, *Peasant State and Society in Medieval South India* (*PSSMSI*) (Stein, 1980), certain of the key issues raised by Mukhia may be examined.

Note has been taken of Mukhia's idea that the stability of Indian agrarian history stemmed from the high fertility of the soils and low subsistence requirements relative to Europe, as well as from 'free' peasant production. The point about soil fertility is misconceived. Surely here the issue is the difference in the growth seasons of the two environments. In most parts of the subcontinent, cultivation can take place throughout the year subject only to moisture availability. There are almost no soils in south India that could not be made and kept productive given adequate moisture. However, without that, yields from most Indian soils have been low and uncertain, worse perhaps than those of Europe.

Variation in cultivation regimes based upon moisture differentials can be shown to have had significant consequences in south Indian history. In *PSSMSI* (Stein, 1980), three sets of peasant ecotypes have been identified. As conceived, these sets of ecotypes possess social and political entailments derived from the commanding material base of each. In wet grain ecotypes of such places as the Palar, Kaveri and Vaigai basins, stable forms of rice cultivation may be seen in the Pallava period. Here, water management, labour organization, and cultivation techniques were articulated in an environment favoured by reliable moisture; high yields of food grains were produced from almost invariant cultivation regimes. Brahmans and the highest stratum of peasants occupied the apex of hierarchical social structures at whose bases was a larger population of landless workers. The latter, we can now say, were often treated as untouchables at least by Chola times when the term *tindachcheri* (untouchable hamlet) is encountered in inscriptions. A common feature of the hierarchial social systems in this most favoured of peasant environments was powerful chieftainships drawn from the leading, local lineages of territorially organized peasant subcastes. Representing the interests of the most powerful and wealthy stratum of the peasant population, these chiefs massed surplus resources (that is, resources beyond immediate productive and reproductive requirements) and redistributed them through the ranked social groupings of the chiefdom. There were kings, too, in a few places; after Pallava times, at least, these kings were also drawn from peasant groups dominating the most productive parts of the river basins, some anciently, such as the Pandyan kings, and others, such as the Cholas, conquerors from less-well endowed tracts around the basins. In addition to the appropriation and redistribution of resources, riverine chiefs and kings were responsible to their peasant constituencies for protecting existing tanks and distributaries upon which the wealth of these places depended.

The two other ecotypic regimes were not merely variants of the first. Stemming from the more vulnerable foundations of their agriculture which demanded the most flexible and skilful agriculture, the mixed wet/dry grain ecotypes were different. Different again were those ecotypes in which the risks of inadequate moisture were so great that they could scarcely be offset by skill; this resulted in agricultural practices as invariant as those of wet zones, but without their high productivity.

The mixed wet and dry ecotype included more variegated, often competitive social units which could not or would not be accommodated within a single hierarchy nor easily managed by august chiefs or kings. Here, except in a few places, there were fewer brahmans and brahman settlements (*brahmadeya*) and also fewer untouchables; here too there was more commodity production, especially of textiles and metalcraft, more articulated trade networks, and a tendency for local groups engaged in agricultural production and those engaged in commodity production to form hostile alliance formations, usually denominated castes of the right and castes of the left (*valangai* and *idangai*).

In the least favoured environments of the southern peninsula were the most backward peasant communities. Their defences against nature and humans alike took the form of highly segmented lineage-based societies with strong martial traditions.

While each of the three types of agrarian organizations was found concentrated in certain parts of the southern peninsula, no tract of the region was without some of each of the types. However, the modal type on any tract was obedient to environmental determinants and was thus, in greatest proportion, ecotypes of the mixed sort. Invariably these different ecotypes were linked together by politico-military relations as well as by exchange relations.

Ecoptypic variation and the social structural concomitants of such variety were probably no greater in south India than elsewhere in India. What seems different about south India was the vigour of local, often corporate, institutions over a large part of the southern peninsula during a substantial portion of the medieval period. Unless we are to understand (or rather misunderstand) such corporate institutions to be unconditioned cultural expressions manifesting the cultural diversity of pre-modern India (or a south Indian aberrance), the agrarian or material foundation of such institutions must be appreciated. Accordingly, south Indian agrarian organization is seen to be based upon a variety of adaptations by south Indian peasant groups to their environments, and corporate institutions for which we have evidence are seen to provide cooperation and continuity necessary for agrarian production. The 'relative stability' of agrarian history here was engendered, not by fertile soils and low subsistence needs, but by historically evolved and localized forms of co-operation among people with a high degree of social differentiation and with a level of living which, in general, cannot be considered as low (whatever that may mean).

It is at this level of production—the base of social and economic organization—that south Indian history appears capable of making a contribution to the delineation of a pre-modern Indian society. For, in south India, perhaps better than in north India, the extant evidence on local agrarian relations is relatively full. Thus, we may consider a thousand years of south Indian history—from the rise of the Pallavas of Kanchi to the decline of Vijayanagara institutions in the eighteenth century—with respect to that level of agrarian society most difficult to verify in north India. We may thereby be able to suggest forms of agrarian relations of generalized significance for defining a pan-Indian agrarian order presently missing from Mukhia's formulation, and from all others.

To carry such a comparative programme forward requires that evidence on south Indian historical agrarian relations be brought together with evidence from and interpretations about India as a whole. I believe that we have arrived at a point where such comparisons could be fruitful, as can be demonstrated with reference to Mughal agrarian historiography and its recent revisions.

Irfan Habib's *Agrarian System of Mughal India* (1963) set the terms of this discussion over twenty years ago. The agrarian foundation of that most impressive state of Indian history is seen to have been a major cause in its decline, an agrarian crisis engendered by peasant unrest. Compared with the voluminous documentation on Mughal politics and administration, Habib's thesis is sustained by quite fragile evidence. Indeed, his notion that there was a massive shift of peasants from the lands of Mughal grantees (jagirdars) to the lands of independent chiefs is based upon official Mughal explanations of a deepening political crisis seen to have been caused by the opportunism and perfidy of Hindu peasants and chiefs. More recent research has seemed to suggest that peasant unrest and flight was no less a problem in chiefly territories.

Some of Habib's subsequent writing on north Indian agrarian relations heightens rather than diminishes uncertainty about how to understand agrarian processes and problems of this period of medieval north India. His important essay on the distribution of landed property (Habib, 1967) reveals the great concentration of landed income in the hands of Mughal grandees in the middle of the seventeenth century. A minuscule group of nobles and princes commanded 36 per cent of the total revenue of the empire and controlled about the same proportion of arable land in their jagirs; a mere 445 mansabdars (including the above elite) controlled 61 per cent of land revenues and probably one half of the lands of the empire. The socio-economic consequences of this massive concentration of appropriation are by no means clear, and more recent work by others suggests why this lack of clarity may exist. The most important of these pertain to the relationships among three levels of the political structure in Mughal and post-Mughal times: imperial, provincial and local. Recent publications by D. Singh and M. Alam on Rajasthan, Punjab, and Awadh[2] add to earlier findings by N.A. Siddiqi (1970) to show that beneath the levels of Mughal court-oriented politics in central and provincial arenas, there were thousands of local systems of power and authority which were anything but passively engaged in the larger political and agrarian systems of the time. Yet, penetrating this locality level of politics and production in Mughal times has proven most difficult.

Can this level of agrarian relations in north India be illuminated by the more complete local records of medieval south India? One thing that can certainly be suggested here is that ancient forms of communal property and authority which existed in medieval north India as well as in the south were slow to yield to the demands and pressures of higher (or 'state') levels until these local communal systems had been prepared for this over an extended period. This process may be illustrated by consideration of south Indian agrarian history from the seventh to the eighteenth centuries.

South Indian, especially Tamil, society can be seen to have undergone several transformations which can only be grasped with reference to changes in agrarian relations. With respect to these transformations, we may trace—very schematically here—modifications of a *single* agrarian structure from Pallava times to the late Vijayanagara period. To this structure, the term 'socio-economic formation' can be applied in the sense, I believe, that Mukhia understands that concept in his essay. I mean by socio-economic formation that, as a society, a major portion of south India can be apprehended as arising from a particular material structure—economic and social relations manifesting particular property and productive relations—together with contingent political and ideological features, and that this set of elements comprised a structure (that is, that it was a self-regulating unity capable of transformation). I take it that a social formation refers to a society where 'society' is not defined as a people who share a culture and, incidentally, an economic organization and a polity, but as a people who share material interests which they manage politically and preserve over time through cultural forms which are best perceived as ideologies. I also take it that agrarian property and productive relations were the most significant material relations of the south Indian socio-economic formation.

The first phase of the long epoch of this formation covers the seventh to the tenth centuries. Contemporaneous with the Pallavas and early Cholas, this period witnessed the establishment of a new social formation in the southern peninsula. This was a formation in which peasant production and property was dominant. It was 'new' in being the successor to an earlier society, one in which several modes of production had co-existed for centuries. These several modes included an archaic urban-mercantile one, known from early Tamil and Western literary sources and from archaeological evidence, and two others—pastoral and peasant—known from the same Tamil literary sources and from some epigraphical ones as well. These different modes loosely co-existed in a polity which recognized three kingships—Chola, Chera, Pandya—and numerous warrior-chieftains. Kings and chiefs alike were celebrated in a corpus of bardic poetry in a language broadly shared by all, Tamil. Aryan religious forms—Buddhist, Jaina, Vedic—co-existed with indigenous cults. In about the sixth century, this multiplicity of social, economic and cultural forms was ended, and peasant societies rose to dominance everywhere. In the first phase of the now dominant peasant order, there was rapid expansion of the techniques of field agriculture developed previously in the riverine tracts of oldest peasant settlement especially in the Palar, Kaveri and Vaigai basins. The fundamental unit of society, of production, and of politics was the 'nadu', an ancient term which denoted a locality of cultivation in contrast to non-arable tracts called *kadu*. Nadu also denotes an assembly, a corporate body of sharers of communal property in fields and irrigation sources. Benefits from and protection of each were collective, though there were limited rights of individual alienation by chiefs and other notables (such rights of alienation usually to and sometimes by religious personages or institutions are often taken as 'private property', but are actually a limited form of individual possession with limited alienation possibilities). Multiple kingship had now given way to a single monarchy for all Tamils, and a new dynasty was introduced into the region with no previous, even poetic, existence. It, the Pallava kingdom, was established by outsiders, or at least by warriors from the northern part of Tamil country in contact with Aryanized kingdoms of the Deccan whose institutions the Pallavas adopted. By the ninth century Pallavas had completely adapted these borrowed, regal forms to Tamil conditions. They replaced Prakrit inscriptions with Sanskrit and Tamil language ones, along with contemporary northern kings they ceased the practice of Vedic sacrifices and adopted the more incorporating royal form of gifting (*mahadana*). With a single great kingdom over all Tamils came also adoption of devotional religious forms (*bhakti*) and the persecution of Jainas. Pallavas and early Cholas created the conditions for the emergence of a very sophisticated peasant society, that of the great Cholas, under Rajaraja I and his successors.

Hundreds of nadus are mentioned in the vastly increased inscriptions of the late tenth to twelfth centuries. Some were undoubtedly newly created under the aegis of the powerful Chola kings and chiefs as they expanded their control and peasant cultivation over Tamils and non-Tamils, but most nadus must be reckoned as older peasant localities whose chiefs were brought under the ritual hegemony of the Chola state (to be elaborated later). Conquering Tamil peasant militias carried with them a conception of land use and irrigation techniques from older core tracts that resulted in the maximum exploitation of hydro-agricultural potentials elsewhere. They also bore conceptions of communal property in which differentiation among local peasant groups was recognized, and in all of the localities of the Chola domain there were stratified peasant groups with dominance exercised by one group who were identified conspicuously with the nadu locality as *nattar*. From among the nattar one lineage provided chiefs (*araiyar*) of the locality.

Special settlements within a nadu were also established, some as centres for commerce, and some of brahmanical ritual. The former was designated as *nagaram* where traders involved with commodities of the locality were accorded privileges of self-government; the latter was the brahmadeya constituting gifts (*deya* = *dana*) to support the ritual, learned and educative functions of brahmans. It seems that all nadus had at least one of each of these kinds of settlements; it also seems that these settlements, while self-governing, in contrast to ordinary peasant settlements, were ultimately under the political control of the nattar and dependent, as all of the locality were, upon the latters' management of locality production.

To these local systems I have applied the term 'pyramidal', and to the larger Chola society of which each locality was a part, I have spoken of a system of 'pyramidal segmentation'. Complementary opposition among social constituents of every locality gave to each nadu the capacity, at once, to maintain a high degree of internal cohesion while simultaneously providing means for significant linkages with other localities. Bearing in mind that the social, economic, and political organization of the 500 or so nadus of which we have inscriptional evidence by the thirteenth century were shaped by the ecotypic conditions discussed earlier, we may speak of the elements of their internal coherence in the following way. We may, first, think of a double axis along which the various parts of unified, local societies can be disaggregated. One axis was categorical: the functional distinction between peasant and non-peasant. The other was dimensional: between high and low ranked groups. Of peasant groups the highest were the nattar, those families with acknowledged entitlements (*kani*) to a major share (*melvaram*) of agrarian production and local authority; next were perhaps several groups of ordinary peasant families with minor entitlements to a share of production (*kudivaram*); finally, there were field labourers with no fixed shares, only subsistence claims. These were ranked and endogamous groupings, the highest of which claimed a status of purity (*sat-sudra*), and learning, the lowest being regarded as polluting to the touch.

Of non-peasants, the most learned brahmans enjoyed the privilege of living in a brahmadeya. Governance of these 'free villages' (*taniyur*) through elected assemblies (*sabha*) with functional committees has been made famous in the works of Nilakanta Sastri, R.C. Majumdar, and others. However, contrary to the rhapsodic claims in some of these works about the 'democratic' or 'republican' character of villages of the time, brahmadeyas were dependent upon the protection as well as the resources of the nattar; and they were not only unique among villages in south India, but unique as well to south India. Most brahmans of this age (as in most others) lived in ordinary peasant villages and were subject to the same control of the nattar as other villagers.

Artisans and many traders appear to have been equally subordinated for the most part. Exceptions to this were the residents (*nagarattar*) of nagarams, trade centres with a degree of self-government (*tani-nagaram*) in many nadus. Special status for trade settlements resulted from commercial conditions of the time in which armed, itinerant trade groups (often called 'guilds' by historians) bearing commodities from afar were deliberately restricted in their local contracts to the nagaram of a locality. Petty commodity production in a locality required no such special arrangement. Most artisans, whether producing for local peasant consumption (for example, potters, carpenters, weavers) or producing other goods for local use (such as jewellery, iron tools, icons), lived within peasant villages where some were sequestered to separated hamlets (*kammach-cheri*) in the manner of untouchables.

Relations among the differentiated and ranked local groups of a nadu were in no sense simple. Neither rigorous and predictable hieratic relations based upon caste principles nor relations based upon the monolithic dominance of the nattar or their chiefs obtained. Rather, each was a system of balanced oppositions. This provided durability of these nadu societies and gave to them a prominence in south India for about six centuries until they were broken by internal strains and external stresses by the Vijayanagara period.

The working of oppositional tendencies within south Indian localities from the tenth to twelfth centuries (with one major exception) must be inferred from very fragmentary evidence. Between the dominant peasant lineage of a locality and other cultivating groups (excluding the lowest, perhaps) were contentions regarding the shares of production to be appropriated by each. One eleventh-century inscription from Avani in modern Kolar district in northern Tamil country meticulously enumerated the shares to be enjoyed by subordinate cultivators from regularly planted wet and dry fields as well as from swidden lands in the locality. This unique record refers to conflict about these matters and about other dues claimed by the locally dominant peasantry and sets out to resolve these conflicts. Alteration of the degraded status of artisan-traders (*kammalar* or *panchalattar*) with respect to the dominant peasantry is the subject of epigraphical records from several places, the issue being the right of these craftsmen to certain dignities (such as footwear and lime wash for their houses) previously denied. Conflicts among brahman groups are known from the sectarian history of the time, and those between brahmans and peasants over shares of production are also recorded.

Rather than to suppose that the nadu endured despite these tensions, it is argued that such oppositions contributed to its longevity. The nadu did not, in this period, dissolve into larger formations—economic or political—partly because there were no such formations and partly because each nadu was a historically adapted system of productive and social relationships. Its internal coherence was fortified by kinship and marriage ties that seldom went beyond the nadu and by ancient chieftainships inspiring local loyalty. Opposition within each nadu unit also limited (or minimized) the alternation of relations among its constituent parts, alterations caused, say, by the expansion of chiefly authority or the appropriation by the dominant peasantry of too great a share of local benefits. The balance of forces of unity and competition within a nadu—what provided durability and persistence to the nadu as an agrarian unit—was supported by two other institutions: the brahmadeya village and the division of lower castes into a right and left division (*valangai/idangai*).

Brahman settlements contributed to the constitution of the nadu in two ways. Simply in being in a particular nadu—and we know of none in which there was not a brahmadeya—marked that locality as complete; it signified that the nattar, who took a major role in the ceremonial establishment of these settlements as we know from numerous copper-plate inscriptions of the Chola period, understood and pursued dharmic ends (and were accordingly differentiated from other nadu groups). The second way in which the brahman village strengthened the nadu was in effecting important links beyond the nadu. One such link in which the brahmadeya figured was between the nadu chief and the Chola king, a signification of the righteous character of both as will be elaborated further below. Another link was that between brahmadeyas of different nadus which created networks of ritual specialists near and far thus fortifying in another way the standing of nattar upon whose patronage all of this depended. These linkages were ideological bonds operating to strengthen each nadu and comprised part of the ideological structure of the society as a whole.

More material linkages within as well as beyond many localities were those of the dual division of lower castes. Along with the prominent, prestigious brahman village, the dual division of peasant and non-peasant castes is known from considerable evidence and is distinctively south Indian; both are institutions which demarcate a macro region of the society being examined here. The dual division of castes is first noted in the eleventh century, suggesting an earlier history, though it is certainly not ancient. Theorizing about the dual division has gone on for a century, and still its meaning remains unclear. In Stein (1980), the division of the right (*valangai* in Tamil, *balagai* in Kannada) and the left (*idangai* in Tamil, *edagai* in Kannada) is characterized in two ways. First, it is taken as a division between agricultural groups (cultivators as well as some artisans and traders) and petty commodity producers. Second, it is taken as an occasional or potential action bloc rather than a corporate institution. In this, the dual division resembles the *sreni* of the dharmasastra tradition, a multicaste association based upon interest, especially of lower castes or occupations. Excluded from the divisions in almost all places were brahmans and dominant peasants.

As alliances, either division could be activated in some locality or in several contiguous localities to protect or to advance the interests of its constitutent groups. Violence was a frequent accompaniment from the first inscriptional reference we have in the eleventh century until the early nineteenth century when there were serious clashes between right and left castes in the towns of the Madras Presidency. But, during the period with which we are concerned here, violent confrontations were less important than the orderly and public incorporation of groups at the frontiers of an expanding peasant society to one or the other division, or the mobilization of lower peasant groups against older nattar dominance. A series of twelfth-century inscriptions from modern South Arcot district trace the process by which progenitors of the modern Palli peasant caste of that region were incorporated into the idangai, or left alliance. Involved here was what appears to have been the displacement of older peasant leadership by Pallis. This is the one major instance in which an agricultural people became affiliated with the left division which, in general, was a grouping of non-agricultural commodity producers and traders. The inscriptions referring to Pallis suggest that they were a recently peasantized people.

Many uncertainties remain in our understanding of the right-left division of medieval south India, but there is no question that this institution acted to provide a way for subordinate groups to reach across nadu boundaries and even to constitute military organizations. We know the last from references to valangai and idangai militias in Chola inscriptions. Within any nadu, the existence of the division could be relied on to bolster the interests of lower groups against the demands of the powerful nattar and the locality chiefs chosen from among their number.

Apart from introducing south Indian matters (some of which are admittedly particularistic to the region) into historical discourse on India and essaying to broaden that discourse to subcontinental scale, what of direct relevance to the agrarian history of north India can be suggested by the south? I think of three related issues. The first is that the decline of the Chola state and society and its supercession by those of Vijayanagara is perceived to be as much a disjunction in south Indian medieval history as the conquest of the Gangetic plain and the northern Deccan by Muslims is in north Indian historiography. In both cases, major attention has been given to political implications, not surprising given the political bias in most historiography. Among south Indian historians, however, considerably more attention has also been given to the impact of political changes on agrarian organization of the medieval period than in north Indian historiography. A second issue deserving notice is that, on the basis of this greater attention by historians of south India to agrarian consequences of political changes, the continuity of earlier agrarian forms has to some extent been recognized, that is the relative autonomy of extant productive systems from particular political changes of the time. The degree of independence of the agrarian from the political order has been a matter of debate among historians of the south, and this has had the salutary effect of stimulating research on agrarian processes between the twelfth and sixteenth centuries. Thirdly, there is an appreciation among scholars that the agrarian order of Chola times—among Tamils, Kannadiyans, and Telugus in the Chola macro region—provides a benchmark from which to assess the process of agrarian development for the next several centuries and thus a propensity to approach the social and economic history of post-

Chola times as a study of change and evolution affected by political changes, but not led by them.

My reading of contemporary north Indian agrarian history suggests that there has been less perceptive understanding of primary agrarian processes. Granted that there are reasons for this—I acknowledge differences in the quantity and quality of evidence on local, agrarian matters between north and south India in medieval times—it reduces our understanding of Indian society of that time. It also explains, to an extent, why Mukhia could so easily suppose extraordinary 'stability' and also why students of Maharashtrian agrarian history very often begin their historical analyses in the eighteenth century after positing, as R. Kumar (1968) did, some sort of prior system of unspecified antiquity. Whatever the quality that may be conceded to our reconstruction of the Chola-age agrarian order, it does provide a systematic basis for showing the changes which were to occur in the succeeding several centuries when forces were exerted in south India which are similar in many ways to those in the north.

A major line of interpretation of south Indian agrarian history has been that the Chola system of the tenth to the twelfth centuries endured until the fifteenth century when Vijayanagara power modified it. My own view is different. I hold that the agrarian system of the period of the great Cholas underwent internal changes before the Vijayanagara conquest and that these social changes were generated by contradictions within the existing system and resulted in important social and economic efforts.

In south India during the twelfth and thirteenth centuries a new agrarian institution came into being which extended the reach and dominance of ancient nattar chiefs from single, somewhat isolated localities to supralocal zones of power and authority. At that time the *periyanadu* and *periyanattar* are first encountered. Inscriptions of the periyanattar leave no doubt that they sought to extend the range of authority of the older, dominant peasantry. This is manifested in the use of the ploughshare (*meli*) as a decorative device on many of the periyanadu inscriptions and in the proud claim to being sudras. Consolidation of political authority at a higher level involved the cooperation of several nadus in some activity—usually temple endowments and protection. Such cooperation among nadus did not then result in the demise of these older locality bodies; each participating nadu is enumerated in many of the early records we have of the periyanadu.

Why the periyanadu arose in the late twelfth century can only be guessed. One factor may have been the increasingly effective organization of lower peasant and non-peasant groups of the right-left divisions. Their success could be countered by a matching nattar organization over several nadus. Another factor may have been the rising importance of temple towns serving the interests of several neighbouring nadus.

Inscriptions of the periyanattar deal with allocations of agrarian and trade resources to temples. There is nothing unusual in this of course, for such is the subject of most south Indian inscriptions. However, these twelfth- and thirteenth-century inscriptions record a shift in the locus of major ritual activity at this time from bramadeyas to bhakti-oriented temples and to the creation around temples of towns to serve temple functionaries and pilgrims. Endowments to create and to support temples were raised by appropriations from a larger surplus catchment area than a single nadu; often several nadus contributed and shared responsibilities for temples. And, along with appropriations from agrarian production, there were allocations of trade duties collected by the periyanadu in co-operation with local and supralocal trade bodies.

Certain older interests may be seen to have suffered from these activities of the periyanattar. One was the older, general dominance of agrarian over commercial interests in the society. The creation of temples and the provisioning of pilgrims meant an enhancement of the status and activities of skilled workmen and traders associated with the left division of castes. A series of inscriptions of the thirteenth century from Kongu (modern Coimbatore district of Tamilnadu) award to such groups (*kammalar*) sumptuary privileges long denied to them by dominant agrarian groups. Another loser was the brahmadeya. Bhakti temples became centres of popular religion in which most local and supralocal groups participated as donors and as recipients of temple honours. Whether it was because brahman villages were inimical to the exuberant and broadly participatory religion of bhakti, or other reasons, the ancient brahmadeya lost support and standing. New and competitive popular religious movements contributed to this decline. The Virasaivas in Karnataka and the Saiva Siddhanta movement in Tamil country are the best known of these. Each established sectarian organization was based upon seminaries (*matha*) under learned, non-brahman leaders that complemented the development of popular bhakti temples.

Another which lost as a result of these developments of the twelfth and thirteenth centuries was the Chola dynasty and state. Nothing has been said about the state here because it is to be treated more fully in the succeeding section. We may note that the Cholas were fatally weakened in the thirteenth century by challenges from great chieftains and were finally swept away by a revived Pandyan kingdom and by a vigorous Karnataka kingdom, the Hoysalas. In the conventional historiography of south India the rise of great chieftains is taken as a symptom of royal decay. Under the presumption that it was a centralized bureaucracy, the Chola state is given a Roman fate at the hands of newly emergent warrior chiefs emboldened by imperial weakness. I see the process differently. Chieftainship was continuous in the Chola macro region; chiefs and the most powerful peasantry they represented were government in most places, not the purportedly central state of the Cholas. What changed was the scope and scale of chieftainships during the Chola period. These changes corresponded with the enlarged zones of authority of the periyanattar, whose chiefs commanded ever larger agrarian bases, whose resources were enhanced by control of temple towns, and whose authority was enhanced through their patronage of temples. The double consequence of this transformation was, first, the inevitable, gradual decline of local nattar who came to be absorbed within larger evolving chieftainships and, second, the increased anomalousness of a kingship which never ruled (except in its Kaveri heartland) by superior force, but through a ritual hegemony. Great chiefs, now patrons of temples and pretenders to royal largesse and protection, were no longer dependent upon Chola hegemonic authority. Yet none, apparently, acted to usurp the Chola throne, which, with diminished ritual potency, had ceased to be the authoritative centre of the polity. This is yet another proof that there was no central state apparatus to entice usurpation of the Chola state by rival chieftains. A new and enduring political ordering, when it finally came to Tamil country in the fifteenth century, came by conquest from the north, but a strange conquest that of Vijayanagara was!

Persistently vexing in south Indian historiography has been the question of whether Vijayanagara rule caused the destruction of older social and economic institutions and principles (*purva mariyade*). Historians of medieval Karnataka say no; those of Tamil country say yes. To the extent that the latter suppose an unchanging agrarian order from Chola into post-Chola times, they are wrong, since the society of the great Chola age had undergone substantial change and no longer existed in the fifteenth century when Vijayanagara power was extended over Tamils. My view is that historians of Karanataka are the more convincing (though my assessment and theirs of what that ancient usage was differs). Vijayanagara power was extended over south Indian society without suddenly or fundamentally altering the society of the time. It was a conquest which only gradually caused changes in certain kinds of political and property relationships, and these were first manifested at a level of society that left local socio-economic relations communal, as they had long been.

The warriors under whom Vijayanagara power thrust southward from the Tungabhadra enduringly (rather than as periodic raids into southern Karanataka and Tamil country) were Telugus. Their lasting influence in the densely populated, advanced, and wealthy parts of south India can be measured and was achieved in two ways. First, we note the influx of Telugu cultivators and merchants who comprised or followed Vijayanagara armies and planted themselves (literally) in the black soil zone extending through the spine of Tamil country. Soon, these migrants converted themselves from an unreliable arm of Vijayanagara among the Tamils (unreliable because they opposed as often as advanced state ends) into permanent peasant communities and urban traders in Tamil country with no significant political role and hardly distinguishable from their Tamil neighbours. The second and certainly the major means by which Vijayanagara warriors became niched in Tamil society was their assumption of royal protection of Hindu institutions, especially their role as donors and protectors of temples. For historians of Tamil country who might be baffled by the ease of the Vijayanagara conquest, despite its purported destruction of ancient usage, the dharmic character of its rulers and their agents provides an explanation, however contradictory. More to the point is that Vijayanagara rule over non-Telugus neither sought nor attempted to achieve more than the recognition of the ritual hiegemony of the Vijayanagara and some sharing of chiefly resources. The latter were extracted from the communal base of agrarian and commodity production, but tapped in towns to an increasing degree.

That even as late as the Vijayanagara period the base agrarian structure maintained a high degree of communal organization is of importance though it is also important to recognize the changes that were in train. Over the numerous, local and still largely communal rural societies, a substantial superstructure had come into existence. Economic and political penetration of locality systems was occurring everywhere in the southern peninsula, and the agrarian structure was being transformed. We may here only summarize these penetrations and only suggest the shape of the emerging new agrarian structure.

With respect to economic relations, town-centred trade relations had created different conditions among cultivating groups and, of course, between cultivating and non-cultivating groups. Petty commodity production and exchange, limited to narrow localities before, now extended to town markets. Town-based merchants had replaced itinerant trading corporations such as 'the five hundred merchants of Aihole'. The latter may be considered another Chola period institution which, along with the nadu and brahmadeya, diminished in importance in the Vijayanagara period. Ancient itinerant trade bodies were displaced during the

Vijayanagara period for the same reason that the nadu was neglected and declined: their militarily supported activities—in the locality of the nattar and on the highways and in the forests of the itinerant traders—challenged the supralocal political and economic ambitions of those who ruled in the new age.

In all of this, money became increasingly evident and important. In contrast with the Chola period when most terms pertaining to appropriations from cultivators referred principally to those of labour and kind, Vijayanagara period extractions of agrarian surpluses were in money. This even included charges upon wet cropping which before had been collected in kind for local consumption. The increased production of dry crops of commercial value—cotton, dyes, garden food crops—was much in evidence. Textile production in those regions where cotton was grown—especially in the black soil tracts of what in British times were called 'the Ceded Districts' (modern Bellary, Anantapur, and Cuddapah districts) and its extension through the length of Tamil country to modern Tirunelveli—provided money income to cultivating families. One measure of increased monetization was the changed character of temple endowments. During the Vijayanagara period, money endowments in large volume signify not only its greater availability and used in the economy, but also the existence of procedures for creating income streams for the support of temple ritual. A major means for the accomplishment of this was investments in irrigation improvements and the disbursement of a portion of the enhanced production to the donor (as 'donor's share') and to the temple.

The temple in medieval south India was a major institution for extending money-mediated exchange. As the most important source of our knowledge of Vijayanagara society, temple inscriptions record a major shift in funding, but these same inscriptions and other evidence suggest, further, that temples may have generated much of the economic change of the age. Here, of course, we have a potential confounding of temples as institutions and urbanization as a general social process of the time. Temples were an important cause of urbanization in south India. In a recent, and still incomplete study I have made of 10,700 major and minor temples in the Ceded Districts of the Madras Presidency in about 1810, the number of temples in any taluk was more highly correlated with trade and industrial activities than with any other factors (such as population or irrigation). The causal relationship of town markets and textile and metal production with temples cannot be established from this analysis. However the connection seems to me significant, even though L.B. Alaev's recently published (1982) analysis of urban productive relations during the late Vijayanagara period contains no reference to temples, either as major consumers or as institutions for pooling resources for productive investment in irrigation. Pilgrimage and commodity circulations and the interrelations of the two are important in explaining the Vijayanagara economy. Differences and similarities between the urban situation in north India (arising from administrative and military factors) at the same time merit further attention.

Temples were also significant in the working of the political systems of the Vijayanagara age. A major deployment of resources drawn from production in the form of money tribute to great chiefs or agents of the Vijayanagara kings was to temples. Partly, this has been explained here as an investment by political outsiders in the supralocal polities in which they sought a place. The political elite of chiefs and royal agents (often the same person) were town dwellers in this age as they had been rural men in the Chola age. A lower stratum of powerful political men was called *palaiyakarar* (maintainers of military camps), and they, like the great chiefs to whom they were subordinated, and royal agents established small fortified towns as their headquarters. In both cases, a large, walled temple would likely be built—either anew or as additions of heavy walls and towering gopuram to existing, older shrines—as the central edifice of the town. Temples were 'central' in the sense of signifying dharmic rulership, by even small chieftains, as well as being defensible places. Great fortresses as such (*durga*) were state institutions; for major and minor chiefs, the temple added to local fortifications and symbolized proper, dharmic, chieftainship; finally, the temple was the focus of local groups who, in their worship of the deity of the place, constituted a community.

Towns and temples were no more new to south India in Vijayanagara times than were chiefs through whom south India had long been ruled. However, during the Vijayanagara age, these three institutions were orchestrated in ways that were different, and the structure of which they were parts, accordingly, must be considered as altered, though not superseded. Two characteristics of this altered structure stand out. One was a state capable of deeper penetration of local society, especailly agrarian relations, than any previous state; the other was a shift in the terms of dominance and trade between agrarian producers and non-agrarian, commodity producers in the towns. With respect to the first of these we may note greater coercive means and therefore greater capacities for appropriation by formal political personages (chiefs and royal agents), and with respect to the latter a corresponding change in the conceptions of property and other aspects of the relations of production.

State revenues were not in Vijayanagara times any more than in Chola times collected through some centralized apparatus, but Vijayanagara state agents often claimed some portion of chiefly dues from agriculture and trade. A minor portion of this was for the maintenance of fortifications in many parts of south India. More broadly, there was a claim of royal agents, usually denominated as *nayaka*, to a portion of the pooled resources of local and supralocal chiefs. This claim was entitled *amaram*, connoting a military charge, and claimants were called *amaranayakaran*. Resources intended for the creation or maintenance of fortifications, usually under the command of state-appointed brahmans (*durgadipati*), were designed by the term *bhandaravada*. This left a third category of appropriations covering a variety of charitable alienations designated as *manya*.

Amara, bhandaravada, and manya were superior entitlements to shares of agrarian production. These are not, strictly speaking, tenurial terms, since they are not concerned with conditions under which productive resources were held so much as they are with distribution, from the extant productive systems and these removed from the point of production, to where a political level of higher chiefly or state agency extraction was encountered. Still less are these general proprietorial terms; they do not seem to be used in the older, wet zone tracts of peasant agriculture, but in the dry, interior upland where the Telugu impact was greatest. These terms do not, either, pertain to different fields within a village or locality, but rather to charges upon entire villages. From the point of view of production, communal direction and a system of shares (*pangu*) continued; from the point of view of allocation of product, villages (taken as the productive unit from which shares were allocated, not as a unit in some larger administrative organization) were in some places categorized on the basis of whether some portion of their surplus production was alienated to religious or state purposes (the later being principally the maintenance of fortifications). The last category (bhandaravada) was the most rare, the amara category most frequent.

Amaram is taken by D.C. Sircar, and others, to be a feudal tenure, a grant of land by superior authority to a dependent warrior for his maintenance. This is held, despite Sircar's well-known opposition to the idea of an Indian feudalism. Contrarily, I take it to refer to the occasional appropriation—a tribute—by a superior authority, or *amaranayaka*, whose regular income came from appropriations within his own chiefdom. I also consider the term to be residual in the sense of pertaining to a portion of village surplus assests potentially alienable to superior local authority and not, therefore, to a temple, say, or to a state agent such as a fortress commander.

Where issues of property related to production arise and where the

Vijayanagara period revealed important changes had to do with divisions of product within villages. During this period, we hear for the first time of shares of village product allocated to a set of village functionaries called *ayagar* (from the Tamil, *ayam* for 'income'). Fields with ascertained income were held by persons on a hereditary basis in return for services to the village. These included the headman (or headmen), accountant(s), and watchmen; it also included purveyors of ritually marked services, including those of priests and washermen; it finally included those whose obligation it was to provide ancillary productive services or goods, including leather workers who made or mended buckets used in irrigation devices, potters, carpenters, water regulators, and even moneylenders. To each was accorded a fixed income share. There is no Vijayanagara evidence that these heritable income shares were saleable in the manner of the *watan* rights of eighteenth-century Maharashtra. Eighteenth-century evidence from the south suggests that the sale of village offices and shares occurred in some places such as the Nawab's territory of the Carnatic, but not in many other places.

We have few contemporary records which detail these new village property rights, but from early British records we are able to judge that these proprietorial claims comprised a substantial part of agrarian production, as much as perhaps one-third of the total revenue demanded by the British in the Ceded Districts in 1806. Then, so-called 'inam' lands were not saleable as were 'mirasi' share rights (in a very restricted way) in other parts of the Madras Presidency. While what obtained in the late eighteenth century may only be taken as an indicator of the specific arrangements of several centuries before, there are reasons to assume that general arrangements were the same, or very similar, in the two periods just as there are reasons for certainty that the agrarian order encountered by the first generation of British administrators in the late eighteenth century (and which they promptly set about modifying) was substantially that of the Vijayanagara period.

This survey of south Indian agrarian history can hardly be convincing in itself; for that, the evidence and arguments of Stein (1980) must be consulted. We may here only advance the following suggestive propositions. Mukhia's 'relative stability' is more like absolute stability and can only very doubtfully and partially hold for medieval India. Moreover, in advancing it, Mukhia is left either to suppose no disjunctions in the agrarian history of India to the late medieval period or to accept that societal changes over that period of long duration resulted from non-material causes: political, juridical or ideological. The evidence of south India reveals a set of transformations in a single agrarian structure which endured for a millennium. These transformations were most significant at the level of agrarian production involving patterns of surplus appropriation and altered systems of exchange. With Mukhia, I hold that there was little technical change and with him I also hold that the social relations of production at the productive base remained intact in late medieval times.

However, there is a potentially important difference between us on how the 'free' peasant was embodied in productive organization. I hold, with him, that the peasantry retained 'mastery' over the means and processes of production, but insist that this 'mastery' was within the social context of communal property relations at the productive base. It is precisely that communal base which the British encountered during the late eighteenth century, argued about in the mirasidar-ryotwar settlement debate of the early nineteenth century, and finally attacked without, for a long time, destroying. But even these communal-based agrarian relations were successively altered by the penetration of urban and state-level influences beginning in the thirteenth century.

A final suggestion pertains to the possible relevance of medieval south Indian agrarian history elsewhere in India. This I offer most tentatively. The major contribution which south Indian agrarian history makes is to the level of agrarian relations least fully understood in the historiography of the Gangetic plain and Maharashtra—that is, at the base of agrarian production. Mughal historians have only begun to penetrate the vast and differentiated world glossed by the word 'zamindar', and what seems to be revealed here is a system not greatly different from that of south India, a system in which older, local, communal forms were being transformed, but only very slowly, by relationships from without. In the absence of systemic reconstructions of this level or agrarian organization, our grasp of Mughal society and polity (upon which latter concern there has always been a fixation) must remain uncertain. Similarly, the Maharashtrian agrarian order, which appears fully blown in the eighteenth century, must be given a historical past and its *watan* relationships located in an agrarian process of sufficient time depth to be made comprehensible. South Indian agrarian history suggests that these are achievable objectives just as south Indian history has shed valuable light on the nature of the medieval Indian state.

ON THE ROLE OF THE STATE

There are rather obvious reasons to consider—or reconsider—the nature of the state in medieval India in connection with Mukhia's argument. One is that, having denied feudalism and some sort of feudal polity, it would appear to be necessary for Mukhia to specify, or at least to suggest, the sort of state that would be theoretically and empirically congruent with a 'free peasantry'. This he has not done; not has he stipulated the kind of state (or states, since he seems to cover almost two millennia) whose appropriation of 'peasant surplus' made it (or them) the 'chief instrument of exploitation'. Without such a stipulation, his assertions about appropriation and exploitation are unconvincing.

A second reason for reconsideration of the nature of the state is that there is a growing conviction among Marxist writers that political forces in any social formation possess a degree of privilege not to be accorded to other so-called 'superstructural' elements. Mukhia cites part of this growing literature which gives priority of political forms in relation to economic forces, not only under capitalism, but in pre-capitalist societies as well.

Questions about the south Indian medieval state became a part of the agenda of *PSSMSI* (Stein, 1980) as a result of my denial of the long prevailing notion that states of this period were centralized, bureaucratic polities. I sought to demonstrate that this conception was flawed in failing to recognize the profound incompatability of very local economic control, appropriation and allocation for a purportedly centralized political regime. Having shown this, it seemed necessary to propose an alternative state model, one that satisfied the conditions set by the deconstruction argument itself. The 'segmentary state' formulation was a first attempt at reconstructing the political system of the time. This formulation appeared (and appears yet) to satisfy major consequences of the deconstruction of the conventional conception of south Indian states [and also a less comprehensive critique of a presumed feudal polity in medieval south India, which was also rejected in Stein (1980)]. The segmentary state concept also satisfied other criteria of fitness arising from the mode of analysis in Stein (1980), especially the saliency of the peasant agrarian order and its economic processes and the nature and ideology of south Indian kingship and rule conveyed in the evidence of the time. What made the centralized, bureaucratic state impossible in medieval south India makes the segmentary state, or something like it, necessary.

The segmentary state is conceived as a 'peasant state' in the following sense. Even the greatest south Indian kings—Chola and Pandyan—presented themselves as of the place of the provenance of their power in the same way that chiefs of the dominant nattar peasantry did in their chiefdoms within the Chola and Pandyan kingdoms. Kings differed from peasant chiefs, and their realms from chiefdoms, in two ways: they underwent ritual annointment and their territories were larger, more populous and wealthy. These are not negligible but neither are they decisive differences between peasant chiefs and kings.

Moreover, the Chola, Pandyan and even later Vijayanagara monarchies were states only as and to the extent that their claims to sovereignty over large parts of the southern peninsula were acknowledged by peasant chieftains in particular coded contexts such as brahman villages and temples. South Indian political traditions preserve a notion of multiple and simultaneous kingships, large and small of which one, at any time, was seen to enjoy a hegemonic status. The state as a state was not perceived as an administrative or coercive fact as much as the expression of an idea of unity among many diverse peasant localities as actualized in ritual linkages between kings and chiefs. This defined the realm at any time.

Identifying these monarchies as peasant states draws attention to the commitment of formal political authority (kings and chiefs) to the protection of extant property relations. In south India (and I must suppose elsewhere in India) the major forms of property were improved arable land and the tools (including draft animals) for its exploitation. Proprietors were families, households differentiated according to their claims and entitlements as co-sharers in local production. Differentiated benefits and entitlements were correlated with membership in local, corporate kinship groups; the term *pangali*, co-sharer, also has the meaning of 'agnatic kinsman'. Such groupings were not, however, closed, or rigidly defined collectivities of classical caste theory, but relatively open formations in two senses. Dominant caste status was attainable for many families with substantial agrarian standing achieved by superior skill in the dry tracts of south India where agricultural skill and management were crucial for success, indeed for survival. In wet zones other criteria for achieved status (such as the military capabilities of Kallars in the Kaveri basin) might have been relevant. Families moved into high peasant statuses and dropped from them according to their fortunes, their membership being authenticated, or constituted, by their recognized claim of superior shares of production, by the appropriateness of their participation in worship of deities of the dominant peasant group of a locality, and by marriage relations with them. All locally dominant peasant groups, secondly, were members of regional peasant subcastes (for example, Kongu Vellalas, Oruganti or Warangal Reddis, or Gangadikara Vokkaligas). Such regional subcastes were as much political as they were nominally kinship groups; each had a capability for joint protection of their regional authority, joint maintenance of subcaste shrines, and each was further defined by joint recognition of regional chiefs.

Where south Indian peasants are concerned—those of the remote and the not-so-remote past—lineage and other solidarity principles are of great and neglected importance. To grasp this fact, it is necessary to begin where Mukhia left off his argument.

There can be no disagreement with his carefully specified sense of 'free peasantry' from evidence of south India during the medieval period. However, it is necessary to press further. What were the conditions in which this 'mastery' of productive forces were created and maintained? As there were neither developed land or labour markets nor proprietory rights in land and in its produce (in the modern or bourgeois senses), we may not think of individual peasants as productive agents. Is it not rather to local collectivities of peasants that we must look? Without a seigniorial or 'gentry' class, who but such local communities could stand as guarantors of the productive mastery of their fellows; who else could have protected it from the excessive demands of outsiders and those of certain privileged insiders? From these observations stem two requirements: the need to define those who did enjoy this mastery (for all did not) and the need to identify the organization of the means of that protection.

In medieval south India, the definition of those collectivities of peasants with 'mastery' was framed in the idiom of kinship, amounting to a sort of clanship. Dominant peasant groups in this region characteristically defined themselves with respect to ancestors who purportedly first settled their localities. These origin and charter explanations were usually expressed by a simple locality designation (such as Kongu, modern Coimbatore, as a branch of the Vellala caste) and in lineage myths.

Chieftains (*araiyar, udaiyar*) who came from such dominant lineages of peasants have tended to be submerged in the conventional historiography of the middle Chola period until they seem miraculously to burst forth as a major force in late Chola politics. These chieftains in fact are consistently recognizable in Chola inscriptions before that time. They can be seen to play a part in the most public of all activities for which there are records, those having to do with brahmadeyas and temples. It is moreover significant that such chiefs were almost invariably identified with their nadu. In the conventional historiography of the Cholas, certain of these chiefs—perhaps the greatest of them who are called *muvendavelar* (warriors who serve the three kings)—are without much warrant converted into 'state officials', or they are ignored. Yet, there is good reason to see these great chiefs and the numerous lesser ones as the political arm of the dominant peasantry in their respective nadus. This peasantry, from the earliest evidence we have on south India, maintained martial traditions, were praised for their bravery, and were memorialized in hero-stones everywhere in south India. For these various reasons, it is necessary to see such chiefs and their peasant constituencies as the basic blocs of the Chola state itself.

The configuration of local peasant lineages and wider, territorialized subcastes of which they were part is the result of historical processes about which we are not altogether pardonably ignorant. One such process is the already noted emergence of various Palli peasant groups in the Chola territory of Naduvil-nadu (modern South Arcot). Eleventh- and twelfth-century inscriptions reveal the beginnings of this cluster of peasant peoples who, in modern times, constitute the largest single peasant subcaste in Tamil country. They appear as a political movement in opposition to older, dominant peasants of their region whom they displaced in time.

The Chola state was the political embodiment of peasant agrarian and political relationships as they have been outlined earlier and more fully discussed in Stein (1980). The transformation of a small Chola kingdom of the Kaveri basin from one dangerously sited between the older Pandyan state in the Vaigai basin (Madurai) and the powerful Pallava state in Tondaimandalam (Kanchi) occurred in the tenth century. It was accomplished partly through conquest, by which all Indian kingships were enlarged, but, more significantly, it was accomplished through the development of a ruling ideology that accommodated the existing structure of peasant chiefly politics in much of Tamil country. Through what I have called a process of 'ritual sovereignty', Rajaraja the Great and his successors promoted a state ideology which simultaneously strengthened chiefly authority and the overall ascendency of the Chola kings at Tanjavur.

Clarification of the term 'ritual' invites extension of this political discussion to the Vijayanagara period. 'Ritual' consists here of three interrelated forms of connection between king and chief. One of these forms was kinship, in which the parity of ruling lineages—royal and chiefly—was expressed through a symmetrical exchange of women and the not uncommon giving of royal women as brides to chiefly families. Another form of connection in the kinship idiom was the well-known Vijayanagara institution of the *kumaravaragam* (lineage of princes) established at Madurai by its Nayaka kings of the seventeenth century. This involved a *mélange* of local chieftains of different places and subcaste affiliations in the Madurai region who became, by royal enactment, members of a single lineage. A second ritual form in the mutual incorporation of kings and chiefs was in the idiom of service. In Chola inscriptions, this idiom of connectedness is reiterated in the inscriptional term *muvendavelar*, already mentioned. In Vijayanagara inscriptions, this service idea was expressed regularly as an agency relationship, the local chief in his dealings with a temple calling himself an agent of the Raya. In this way, Vijayanagara kings were granted an immediate and personal presence in local affairs which Chola kings, as remote protectors of dharma, never attained. The third form of ritual was that of the gift (*mahadana*) in which, by constant cultural restatement, material gifts to brahmans and to gods were identified as the rightful possessions for chiefs and other donors, but the king was deemed a sharer of some merit as protector of the gift. In later, post-Vijayanagara times, as the research of Nicholas Dirks (1982) and others is making clear, gifts became a generalized form of exchange between kings and chiefs; the service of a chief was reciprocated by gifts of royal emblems. We may denote all of these as 'ritual' in that not only are they ceremonial enactments that publicized the relations of kings and chiefs, but they were deemed constitutive of these relationships. This ideology of 'ritual sovereignty' was attentive to sastric conventions, but not slavishly so, being, like much else in the medieval south Indian world, responsive to the exigent conditions and experiences of the time.

In any state-level political system, the ability to penetrate local systems of production and appropriate resources is a contingent one. Superior force facilitates this as does the perceived appropriateness of the demands of those with that force. The complementarity of these two contingencies is well illustrated in the Vijayanagara polity. Successive military incursions into Tamil country and southern Karnataka by Vijayanagara military forces from the very beginning of the first dynasty is not without precedence in south India, but these invasions remain impressive. It may be that this demonstration of military power reflected a technological advantage enjoyed by the armies of the founding dynasty in the fourteenth century, that is, their adoption of firearms then in use by Muslim forces of the region. This technical superiority was to be carefully enlarged in this and in succeeding dynasties of the state. Muslim and Protuguese soldiery experienced with firearms were recruited, and a monopoly over trade in military horses was established in the fifteenth century.

The weight of Vijayanagara military superiority was most felt by Hindu adversaries, notwithstanding the anti-Muslim ideology of the state. This superiority surely persuaded most Karnataka and Tamil country chieftains to cooperate rather than to oppose the northerners (*vadugan*). Another element of this concession of authority to the invaders must also have been the observation that Vijayanagara commanders or the Rayas themselves did not displace existing chiefs except when they contested the Vijayanagara overlordship. Hence, an important component of ritual sovereignty continued to be manifest in this state as it had during the period of the Chola state: a great monarchy which reigned over but did not directly rule most of its subjects. However, there was a crucial difference at least at higher levels of the political system and that is that the state, through its agents, was more immanent in its protection of dharma than had been the case earlier. And, corresponding with this more proximate power, was its greater potential for surplus appropriation from great and minor chiefs of the realm.

We are accustomed by the history of other civilizations to see the interests of local magnates and monarchies as opposed. We do not see that here. Chief and kings in south India appear to be engaged in the same process: that of freeing themselves from the restrictions of local corporateness, from their peasant roots. This they sought without benefit of clergy, feudalism, or incipient nationhood, and they achieved it through collaboration. In early Chola times, kings and chiefs collaborated in predations upon neighbouring kingdoms, including the Pallavas and Pandyans. Later they reached outward to the ancient Chalukyan domain in the Kistna-Godavari delta and even Sri Lanka and Malaysia. To this regime of conquest and looting was added an astute manipulation of rituals and symbols, more incorporative than those of the Pallavas or Pandyans. This was a new language of authority, one linking a variety of great and small magnates to the Chola kings while, at the same time, gradually strengthening ruling lineages against the opposition of other local peasant groups. Chola kings made the usual claims of being embodiments of dharma, protectors of brahmans, and divinely sanctioned conquerors. But, to the conventional royal rhetoric, they added a royal Siva cult centred upon the king's shrine (in Tanjavur during Rajaraja I's time and in Gangaikonda-cholapuram in the time of his successor, Rajendra I). Rajadharma here was not a royal monopoly, but a royal style accessible to all chiefs on condition of their recognition of the Chola overlordship and of their imitation of royal protection of dharma. In this process, what had been peasant chieftainships was extended in meaning to become a species of kingship itself, kingship of a subordinate sort that added to the grandeur of the Cholas.

This process, with some modifications, continued into the Vijayanagara period. Chieftains then continued to attempt to differentiate themselves from the communal base of their power by seeking new authority credentials from Vijayanagara kings, or, if they were minor chiefs, from yet greater ones. Agency—acting for the king in great public events, usually having to do with temple affairs—was one of the ways of accomplishing this. Other ways were dictated (or at least made possible) by changed socio-economic conditions of this late period.

In the urban headquarters of Vijayanagara chieftains, new opportunities for alliance with merchants and artisan-traders weakened the earlier reliance upon peasant groups, fiscally and politically. Chiefly pooling of resources facilitated this, and there is evidence that chiefs of this era conferred revenue and other privileges upon commodity producers—especially weavers—to lure them and thus to enrich their realms. Such autarchic measures, in addition to the political reasons for reducing military competition from armed itinerant trade groups, led to the decline of the latter in the Vijayanagara period. Larger Vijayanagara-period chiefs also imitated the Rayas (and their successors in Madurai and elsewhere) in incorporating lesser chieftains within their territories through ritual means. *Palaiyakarar*—as these lesser chieftains were frequently called—were granted emblems (*biruda*) and honours as tokens of their subordination and also their legitimacy as the dependents of 'little kings'; in return, these lesser chieflings supported their chiefly patrons militarily and paid them court. All of these relationships, along with the continued forms of acknowledgement of the ritual hegemony of the Vijayanagara rulers (until the late sixteenth century), were enacted and recorded in the major temples of south India. These various means of enhancing chiefly authority were intended to loose the bonds with their communal power base; it was never intended to break these bonds. Chiefs continued to call themselves sons of the soil and even sudras, and during the eighteenth century, in places, they could stir their rural followers to armed resistance, as the numerous 'poligars' opposing the British did, or they could, alternatively, dissolve into their rural constituencies as major landed families to survive the imposition of British control.

Several things must be emphasized in this necessarily schematic discussion of the Chola and Vijayanagara states and their agrarian bases. One was the determining character of the peasant order upon the nature of the state; a second was the evolution of state-level political demands upon the peasant base during the six centuries of their rule; the third was the establishment of those contradictions which not only ended the Chola state, but shaped the state and society of the later Vijayanagara period.

When considering the states of medieval south India (and perhaps states elsewhere in the subcontinent) it cannot be supposed that there was a single model of statecraft, inspired by dharma and constructed according to sastric injunctions. This is one of the false assumptions of some of the conventional historiography of south India, as well as of some western views of these states. The Chola state was a contingent formation; it was a form of monarchy which took its shape from the sub-strata of peasant societies of which it was the highest political expression. Reconstructions of state systems such as the Chola and Vijayanagara must be sensitive to their often great differences. The Vijayanagara state differed from the Chola with respect to its greater coercive capacity, its deeper penetration into local situations, and the changed character of the agrarian and commercial base of the society it governed.

The medieval south Indian state was an evolving political form. The Chola state was different from its predecessors in the Tamil country, and different, too, from the Vijayanagara kingship which succeeded to its hegemony over the same large portion of the south peninsula in the fifteenth century. It is claimed that these were segmentary states in the following several senses. They were monarchies which incorporated the chiefly polities of their realm without dissolving such polities; these states were primarily ideological manifestations of the pervasive and ambiguous conception of kingship which could be vested simultaneously in a large number of chieftains, as well as in a single ruling house whose hegemonic claims were conceded by all. The prevailing conception of rajadharma permitted chieftains to assume the responsibilities and dignities of supporting brahmans and gods and protecting them as well as the constituencies of peasant and non-peasant peoples of a chiefdom, just as kings did for the realm as whole. To king and chief alike was conceded the right to deploy resources which they—as kings and chiefs everywhere—massed and redistributed and thereby gave expression to the idea of a moral unity.

Thus, one way of understanding the demise of the Chola kingdom is to perceive that the initial advantages of the Chola kings—their most favoured environment and their adroit ideological innovations—were progressively eroded by two developments: the consolidation of advanced forms of agriculture elsewhere and the discovery by peasant chiefs that they too could transmute increased wealth into increased authority even to an extent approximating that of kings. As a result, the ritual sovereignty of the Chola kings was no longer tenable. Efforts by successors to the Cholas in Tamil country were incapable of resurrecting that system. A comparable reordering occurred only during the fifteenth century with the sovereignty of the Rayas of Vijayanagara. Theirs was a segmentary state of a different sort but, still, a segmentary state.

For this explanation of the role of the state in medieval south India to be persuasive, it is necessary to appreciate that the increase in agrarian resources by great chiefs of the Chola realm was mediated by changes in social and economic relationships and in religion and religious affiliations, that is, changes in interests and in ideology. Throughout the Chola period there was increasing differentiation of dominant peasant groups from subordinate ones, greater mobility and status, too, for commodity producers and mercantile groups. Finally, there was an emergent literary and religious sub-culture (e.g. the Saiva Siddhanta movement) led by men of peasant origins. This shifted the provenance of ruling ideology from the segregated brahman settlement and the universalizing royal cult of Siva to temple worship and forms of cult association which were more incorporative of local groups, of local cultic practices (e.g. devi-worship), and more responsive to sectarian leaders of the Saiva and Vaishnava bhakti orders which arose in the later Chola period. Taken together, these various developments—most clearly to be seen in Tamil country—exacerbated oppositions which in time became contradictions of such depth as to bring an end not only to the Chola state, but to an era during which peasant and non-peasant peoples, and their institutions, were transformed. These contradictions, further, set the conditions under which an altered agrarian order was consolidated, and with that an altered segmentary state.

ON PRE-CAPITALIST SOCIAL FORMATIONS AND THE ASIATIC MODE

The preceding sections delineated a social formation. It is not claimed that this was *the* social formation for south India during the pre-capitalist era, but only the construction of what seems appropriated for a part of that long era; obviously, also, there is no claim that it was the social formation for all of that vast and complex whole often designated as 'medieval India'.

Is what has already been sketched a social formation? If so, is it a single formation? Could it not be supposed that we are really considering three or even more social formations corresponding, say, to the basic modes of production which arise at any time from ecotypic variation in early south India? Or, minimally, should we not consider that the Vijayanagara socio-economic formation was different from that of the Chola period?

As to whether it would be correct to identify each of the three ecotypes discussed as the basis for a distinct social formation, we must recognize that one of the environmental contexts was primary within a unity consisting of all three. The wet zones of the southern peninsula are critical because here certain social principles (such as caste hierarchy) and political principles (such as ritual kingship) took their form and became culturally and ideologically normative in the other environments of the region. Few parts of even the most hostile agrarian landscapes were without a small area, often minuscule, in which the institutions of the most favoured agrarian contexts were not replicated in some degree nor in which peasant chieftains, to the extent that their resources permitted, did not emulate that of kings in the river basins, including their laborious capture of water of support a modest base of high chiefly culture.

On the question of whether there was a Chola social formation and a Vijayanagara one, one thing must be clarified at the outset. There should be no inference that designation such as 'Chola' and 'Vijayanagara' here are anything more than general dating labels. Neither a congruence of political and socio-economic periodization nor causation is supposed.

Two reasons may be offered for taking the medieval south Indian society of the tenth to the seventeenth centuries as a single socio-economic formation. One is that, for over 600 years, the basic system of agrarian production and property continued to be communal in the sense that productive resources vested in corporate peasant groups. Mastery over productive means was not individual: productive resources were pooled and distributed customarily by headmen, benefits were allocated by shares. A second reason for seeing continuity over these six centuries is that the political system remained a segmentary one: localized chieftainships ruling small polities were bound together as a state through ritual forms.

What then of such disjunctive developments of the age as urbanization, greater money use, and advances in military technology? Important as these elements were in distinguishing the earlier from the later part of these six centuries, they do not constitute a basis for positing a different social formation.

Towns and money, in themselves, may not simply be presumed to have altered fundamental agrarian relations. That there was an increase in the generalized use of money and in urban trade by agrarian producers to the seventeenth century is important. It was more important in some parts of south India than in others, however. There is no evidence in south India until the eighteenth century that money and urban trade connections resulted in the breakdown of communal relations of production, the widespread sale of shares of agrarian income (that is, beyond the very restricted exchanges by chiefs and brahmans which can be dated from Chola times), nor in the loss of control by dominant local peasant groups over agrarian production and distribution. During the eighteenth century, the penetration of fundamental, communal agrarian relations seems to have become more common in many parts of the region, but not, in general, before that time. It is the total configuration of economic, social, political, and ideological elements which must be considered, and the communal configuration of agrarian relations of production appears to me to have continued over the long period discussed here.

Can this proposed single social formation be taken as an appropriate response to Mukhia's call for consideration of a range of pre-capitalist social formations? If the answer is 'no', is it because I have not demonstrated a convincing fit of basic economic relations with social, political and cultural (that is, ideological) relations? Or, is it 'no' because the formation described is not inclusive enough, and something more extensive and perhaps more enduring is wanted? That is, if what I have outlined above is not a social formation in the sense suggested by Mukhia, is it because it is an imperfect structure by reason of its relations of parts and whole (or interior construction), or is it because this structure was itself part of what is as yet some unspecified 'medieval Indian social formation'?

It should be obvious that I believe that there may be such a generalized, pan-Indian social formation; that is assumed in some of the statements I have made earlier about north Indian agrarian historiography. Though I am unable to stipulate such a general construct, it seems to be a goal worthy of our attention. But would not such a pursuit take us back to an Indian feudalism or some equally vague conception? Not necessarily; and here we must pause to reflect upon the largely discredited notion of the Asiatic mode of production.

I believe that the concept of the Asiatic mode, as many of Marx's formulations, is based upon a profound perception which ought not to be lost, or consigned to the dustbin of historiography. Marx recognized that in the ancient cultures of Eurasia—those of the Fertile Crescent, India, and China—societies developed which were fundamentally different from those of Europe and incapable of being understood in terms of European historical processes. His notions about these differences are not, of course, his best work as even the most sympathetic Marxist writers seem to agree.

There are obvious reasons for the rejection of Marx's Asiatic mode of production concept, not least of which is the lumping of quite different societies as 'Asiatic'. Another reason pertains to India in particular. The hydraulic argument and its presumed consequence—despotic government—has no historical validity, and Marx's companion notion about the Indian peasant village—'small stereotype forms of social organism'—is even more distorted than the early nineteenth-century British view from which it is derived.

And yet, a profound idea remains. Ancient Eurasian peoples cannot but have developed social formations very different from those of Europe, not a single, unchanging formation as presumed in the Asiatic mode, but perhaps a great number of different formations.

It is understandable that Mukhia would not have looked at the Asiatic mode conception in this way. His purpose and his agenda were other. Also, of course, there is his assumption about the relative fertility of India soils in his argument against the feudal concept, an assumption which can hardly be reconciled with Marx's assumption of a requirement for massive irrigation works in 'Asiatic' agriculture. However, it should be pointed out that Mukhia has overstressed this purported characteristic of Indian agrarian production and neglected some others. In general the availability of water for cultivation and the labour required for its realization were quite central features in the historical ecotypes of south India, and south India did use long-term fallowing whatever the practice in north India. The failure of Marx's conception is that he suggested only one way (and for India the wrong one way) to achieve adequate water for agriculture, one that accorded with then prevailing Orientalist ideas. Are we not entitled—indeed do we not have the responsibility—to attempt to transform Marx's grossly erroneous formulation of what was a profound insight into a useful concept?

If that be granted, this discussion can conclude with several observations on some possibly general characteristics of a medieval Indian social formation based upon this discussion of south India.

First, cultural forms may be seen to extend the reach of even quite primitive forms of economic organization. The pervasive lineage organizations of south Indian peasants (that is, endogamous and cooperating sections of peasant subcastes) have persisted into recent times in south India and elsewhere; Brenda Beck's (1972) work on Kongu and Arvind Shah's (1964) and David Hardiman's (1981) on Gujarat attest to this. Lineage in south India provided the idiom not merely for associating ideas of property, kinship and locale, but, more significantly, for amalgamating these ideas into a potent, hegemonic ideology. Through marriage and commensal relations among peasant families, new entrants into positions of privilege could be recruited and older, weaker families dropped. Such groups defined by blood-ties, common residence, and power could also be amalgamated into subcastes which should be seen as political and territorial organizations, not as conventional social categories. Religious ideology and sectarian organizations are other ways in which local lineages of peasants extended their scope and maintained their locale-centredness while also being parts of larger formations. Bhakti ideology and temple worship involving the linking of local tutelary shrines with regional temples are important here. So are the activities of itinerant agents of sectarian orders in incorporating local, dominant groups and thereby representing them and their interests in the most important temple centres of south India. All of these cultural means contribute to the viability and the durability of very local lineages by allying them with other like bodies in ever more extensive organizations.

Second, Indian peasants had coercive power and they maintained martial traditions. In considering peasant and non-peasant relationships in medieval India (*pace* T. Shanin) not all peasants were underdogs. Medieval Indian peasants were not only 'free' in Mukhia's terms, but they were, taken as a whole, able within themselves to protect their mastery of the means of production. But it is wrong to take peasants as a whole, since in every peasant locality there were divisions—at times very sharp—between dominant peasant groups and other peasants. Peasant stratification was real and ancient in south India and probably elsewhere in India. To obfuscate this by denominating certain families among dominant peasants as 'gentry', or some such, is ahistorical. In pre-capitalist, or at least pre-colonial, India there was scarcely ever the ultimate coercive ability of a central state to give a 'gentry' its capacity, as a separate rural stratum, to exploit peasants. The dominance of ruling peasant lineages sprang from their own force, their ability to command that of other, subordinate, peasants and their systematic exploitation of the lowest rural groups. All of this was supported by cultural forms of appropriate rule as an entailed ideology. It was the achievement of colonial India to create the rich peasant-'gentry' category in the above sense and thereby to create the condition of rural class conflict we witness in more recent times. Several important consequences stem from the coercive power and ruling ideology of dominant peasant lineages. These include: the relative instability of states in many parts of the sub-continent, the relative small scale of such states, and the vulnerability of most to predation and conquest. South India was spared the most violent predations of the medieval age; this may account for its longer-lived states (Chola and Vijayanagara). But there were perhaps other factors involved in that, among which the nature of peasant chieftainship was important.

Accordingly, a third observation is that substantial power and authority vested with peasant chieftains in south India. The nature of chieftainship in much of north India appears to have been different, and upon this difference much can be seen to depend. The tradition of a separated ruling stratum of kshatriyas may have diminished the capacity for political massing attained in south India where little evidence exists of fixed, intermediate levels of authority between those with local dominance and annointed kings.

Chieftainship in medieval south India knows nothing of fixed positions in some supposed political hierarchy. Great chiefs and small based their local authority upon descent from early settlers and cultivators of their chiefdoms, and based their power upon kinsmen of their lineages and dependent cultivators. Authority and power so founded were fortified by relations with kings, for from these annointed figures of transcendent authority were obtained royal emblems (for example, fly whisk, umbrella, the royal tutelary for worship, and even the king's name) in return for homage and service of the chief. These transactions, involving rituals and symbolic exchanges, illustrate the way in which cultural forms extended the range of kinship linkages, the prime local connection among dominant peasant groups, and made possible a construction like the segmentary state. It was the quite legitimate control and use of force maintained by all great landed castes in south India, as well as others like Maratha Kunbis and Jats elsewhere, that made peasant chieftainships not only possible, but impressive. No intermediate statuses of offices stood between powerful peasant chieftains and kings; none ceased to identify themselves with the peasant lineages from which they came and through which they exercised their local authority. Extensive and enduring states were constructed in medieval south India from the tenth to the seventeenth centuries through such relations of peasant chiefs and kings.

A final observation is that Marx's hydraulic mover (but not its imputed consequences) must be given standing. In most parts of south India, at least, 'mastery of the means and processes of production' was vested in local peasant communities under whose chiefs there was sustained and successful development of irrigation potentials in the southern peninsula. It is notable that until the major river projects of the late nineteenth century, there was nothing that the British found to do to create irrigation facilities; both major and minor works and the provision for their maintenance were set up long before, and not by centralized states, but by local communities of peasants.

Water management means labour management. Even in the paleotechnic conditions of south Indian peasant agriculture, the division of labour and reward could be extremely complex, requiring from those in commanding positions—dominant peasant lineages—continuous and skilful orchestration. The conventional idea of peasant agriculture as a family affair has accordingly to be modified so as to apprehend this complexity of Indian agrarian systems. Account must be taken of relations among various peasant groups in any locality, some dominant (who might better be called 'the chief instruments of exploitation') and other subordinate; account must also be taken of the relations of both kinds of peasants with landless workers, with commodity producers (especially of textiles and metal products), and with mercantile groups (local, itinerant and urban). Finally, attention must be given to the relations between peasant chieftains and the larger political, economic and cultural contexts of their being.

Seizing all of this complexity is the central problem of constructing social formations, precisely what Mukhia has called for. To accomplish this means deconstructing, as he has, the concept of feudalism; it could also mean reformulating Marx's Asiatic mode of production conception. It must certainly involve systematic explanations of the totality of relations of production, of politics and of culture and ideology which is, after all, the promise and task of materialist analysis.

NOTES

1. Pages in brackets refer to Harbans Mukhia (1981) in the present volume. I thank Harbans Mukhia for his comments on an earlier version of this paper. Others to whom I am also grateful for comments are: N.B. Dirks, M.G.S. Narayanan, F. Perlin, Y. Subbarayalu, D.K. Stein and D. Washbrook.
2. The work of both D. Singh and M. Alam is contained in their Ph.D. theses submitted to Jawaharlal Nehru University, later published, see below. In addition to these works, I have benefited from seminar presentations of and conversations with both scholars. See also Siddiqi (1970).

REFERENCES

Alaev, L.B., 1982, in *Cambridge Economic History of India* (ed. Tapan Raychaudhuri and Irfan Habib), Vol. 1, Cambridge: Cambridge University Press, pp. 315-24.

Alam, M., 1986, *The Crisis of Empire in Mughal North India: Awadh and the Punjab, 1707-1748*, Delhi: Oxford University Press.

Beck, Brenda E.F., 1972, *Peasant Society in Konku*, Vancouver: University of British Columbia.

Dirks, Nicholas B., 1982, 'The Pasts of Palaiyakarar: The Ethnohistory of a South Indian Little King', *Journal of Asian Studies*, Vol. 41, No. 4, pp. 655-83. Papers by Arjun Appadurai, Carol A. Breckenridge, David Ludden and Pamela Price are also important.

Habib, Irfan, 1963, *Agrarian System of Mughal India, 1556-1707*, Bombay: Asia Publishing House.

———, 1967, 'The Social Distribution of Landed Wealth in Medieval India', *Mitt. d. Inst. f. Orientforsch*, Bd. 13, London: India Office Records and Library, P/T 5441, pp. 126-7.

Hardiman, David, 1981, *Peasant Nationalists of Gujarat: Kheda District*, Delhi: Oxford University Press.

Kumar, Ravinder, 1968, *Western India in the Nineteenth Century: A Study in the Social History of Maharashtra*, London: Routledge & Kegan Paul.

Mukhia, Harbans, 1981, 'Was There Feudalism in Indian History?', *Journal of Peasant Studies*, Vol. 8, No. 3.

Shah, A.M., 1964, 'Political Systems in Eighteenth Century Gujarat', *Enquiry*, No. 1, pp. 83-95.

Siddiqi, Noman Ahmad, 1970, *Land Revenue Administration under the Mughals 1700-1750*, Bombay: Asia Publishing House.

Singh, Dilbagh, 1990, *The State, Landlords and Peasants: Rajasthan in the 18th Century*, Delhi: Manohar.

Stein, Burton, 1980, *Peasant State and Society in Medieval South India (PSSMSI)*, Delhi: Oxford University Press.

Peasant Production and Medieval Indian Society

Harbans Mukhia

I feel truly overwhelmed by the generosity of response to my paper, 'Was There Feudalism in Indian History?' published in *The Journal of Peasant Studies* in 1981, and I greatly value the privilege of entering the challenging world of academic dispute, a world aesthetically far more satisfying than one of unanimity or forced consensus.

Since both agreement and disagreement of contributions to this volume extend to specific points as well as the general approach of that earlier paper, I visualize two options before me: to take up each point, especially if it is in dispute, and abandon, modify or reiterate it; or else, to keep the discussion to the main theme or themes of all our debates and going into detail only when indispensable for the argument. Without overlooking the fact that the detail and the main theme cannot always be counterposed, I yet choose the latter option, largely because I have not the competence to cover the wide range of issues and evidence that the six contributions have marshalled, and in part because interest in these issues is unlikely to be confined to a small group of specialists familiar with, or eager to pick up every little detail.

I

It had been stated earlier almost as an axiom scarcely capable of generating much controversy that, since capitalism was the *first* world system, feudalism could only be treated as a system that was specific to a region and a period. Anticipating comparison between the 'universal' aspects of feudalism and the universality of stone age, bronze age, etc., the comparability of these utterly dissimilar phenomena itself had been called into question (Mukhia, 34 and n. 2).

I was clearly a little too optimistic about the innocuous nature of the statement, much as Frank Perlin is today, for 'no one seems (to him) to claim for feudalism the status of a world system' (Perlin, 1985: 94). R.S.

Sharma does indeed make such a claim with the argument that, certain variations notwithstanding, feudalism in different medieval regions did possess some essentially similar characteristics and that, much like tribalism, stone age and so on with all the internal variations within each, it cannot be denied the status of a world system (Sharma, 83-4).

Arif Dirlik has in turn perceptively argued that universalization of the concept of feudalism has actually followed in the footsteps of the historical universalization of capitalism (Dirlik, 151), and that it is the 'essentialist' rather than the structuralist view of feudalism that earns for it the status of a world system; in the process the 'essence' of feudalism becomes so loose as 'to accommodate disparate economic and social structures' (167-70). He also makes a distinction between the 'universal' and the 'global' aspects of a phenomenon, though unfortunately he does not elaborate it fully (150).

Clearly then the argument about the universality of feudalism has followed two different notions of what constitutes a world system and I should like to elaborate my own notion. The classic Marxian formulation that capitalism is the first world system follows the logic that, with the spread of capitalist production and distribution on a world scale, the economies of all the different regions of the world, irrespective of their own stages of development, were integrated under the hegemony of the capitalist mode of production, and this integration was not a contingent but a structural phenomenon that inhered in the specificity of the capitalist mode of production. It is the ever expanding scale of production and distribution resulting from *generalized* commodity production and based on wage labour that gave capitalism the necessary dynamism to bring the world under its hegemony. While commodity production and wage labour were either separately or together not unknown to several civilizations since antiquity, *generalized* commodity production through wage labour was characteristic of capitalism alone.[1] Clearly then, pre-capitalist systems, though by no means static, did not possess the internal dynamism that would give them the hegemony we have been speaking of; in this sense they were incapable of becoming world systems.

It then remains to speak of a pre-capitalist system as a world system only by way of noting similarity of some or the other features amongst regional economies: the 'essentialist' approach. Usually similarity is observed in the fact that these were agrarian economies and that surplus, irrespective of its form, was appropriated from the primary producer through non-economic coercion. All this is true enough of all post-slave and pre-capitalist societies. But then for the very same reason focusing on these general features and treating them as the hallmark of feudalism reduces feudalism to a catch-all category; such a category can hardly serve as a rigorous definition capable of distinguishing one medieval society from another. We can speak of any precapitalist system as a world system only by reducing both the categories (of the world system and the pre-capitalist system) to considerable flabbiness. Is it not curious that even those of us who insist on rigour and precision in defining capitalism are willing to lower our guards when dealing with post-slave and pre-capitalist systems, and deposit all of them under the residual category of feudalism?

R.S. Sharma has buttressed his notion of 'Indian feudalism' by restating the argument of regional variants within the broad framework of feudalism (Sharma, 84-5).[2] If at the starting point this broad framework covers under its umbrella nothing more than general features such as agrarian economy and surplus appropriation through non-economic coercion, it can hardly take into account distinctive, and perhaps critical considerations such as production processes, social organization of labour and concrete forms of non-economic coercion, for it treats all forms of non-economic coercion as equivalent and interchangeable. And loose as the category of the broad framework of feudalism is, its heuristic utility is further compromised as we qualify it in regional contexts. We thus face the problem of either to dilute the already vague category of feudalism, or to dump under its banner such diverse social and economic structures that even this vague category can encompass only with discomfort. Besides, can we really terminate the category with the notion of regional variants? Logically, sub-regional variants are bound to follow in the footsteps of regional variants of this world system *ad infinitum*, further compromising it at every stretch. What then remains of the concept of feudalism as a social structure capable of illuminating all, or most, of the medieval world's variant regional and sub-regional economies? Indeed, the very search for such a universal pre-capitalist category appears to be anachronistic, for it follows in the aftermath of the universalization of capitalism in both history and historiography (Mukhia, n. 225; Dirlik, 151).

It is not my intention to question the very notion of regional variations in a pre-capitalist society, for surely scarcely any region would be a replica of another ecologically, economically or in terms of social organization. Variation could be a feature of the chronology of development of regions, or of its pace or even of its direction. But then it is useful to distinguish between the notions of regional variation imbedded in the structuralist and the 'essentialist' conceptions of feudalism (an insight I owe to Dirlik).

Marxists have usually understood feudalism in terms of politico-juridical specifics of non-economic coercion or surplus-appropriation, the divergence of their views on the universality of feudalism notwithstanding. Thus Anderson (1977: 404), Gottlieb (1984), Sharma (84) and Perlin (1985: 105, 110) have so defined their approach to feudalism. Valuable as this insight is, it nevertheless creates some further problems, for it implies that:

(a) underneath variations in the politico-juridical specifics lay a uniform production system over time and space;
(b) variations in the forms of non-economic coercion (rent in labour, kind or cash or collection of revenue) notwithstanding, these were equivalent and interchangeable; it thus treats feudalism as a static system;
(c) the historians' attention be focused on the relation of exploitation as the explanatory category for social change even at the expense of the totality of the production system; and
(d) the state (or ruling class) was the prime mover of pre-modern historical change; to the extent that the peasantry showed signs of dynamism this was in response to state action.

I should like to suggest that these problems could perhaps be resolved if we altered our perspective somewhat.

In the paper 'Was There Feudalism in Indian History?' and in a companion paper, 'Maurice Dobb's Explanation of the Decline of Feudalism in Western Europe—A Critique' (Mukhia, 1979-80: 154-84) I tried to view things in an alternative perspective without making any explicit statement to that effect. I should now like to elaborate its implications, since each one's perspective after all determines the structure of one's argument.

This alternative perspective focuses on interaction amongst the following three factors:

(a) the ecology of a region;
(b) the given level of technology at a point of time in the region; and
(c) the social organization of labour utilization.

The ecology of course is given to us by nature and it differs to a greater or lesser extent from one region to another. The nature of the soil and its suitability for the cultivation of some rather than other crops, the availability and types of sources of water supply, the topography and the duration of the sunshine are the starting points of peasants' labour, although they might to an extent alter the nature of some of these (e.g soil and water sources) over a pretty long stretch of time. Technology oı the other hand is a largely socially conditioned factor and the level o technological development in the society would depend, on the on(hand, on the social perception of ecology and on technological expertis((in other words, on knowledge) and, on the other hand on the forms o labour utilization in that society. Thus even between regions of similaı ecology, the level of technology might vary, given different socia. conditions; or, for that matter, even within the same region knowledge and utilization of techniques would differ from one stratum of society tc another.

A more decisive social intervention, however, occurs in the organization of labour utilization, even though in pre-capitalist societies non-economic coercion would characterise all forms of labour utilization. To an extent, the form of labour utilization would depend on ecology, technical level of a society and the demand and supply of labour in a region, but above all it would depend on the balance of power in that society, a balance that is not determined by the state or the ruling class alone. Slavery, serfdom or wage labour surely did not come into existence at the will of the ruling class; the silent and at times overt resistance of those who too possessed an enormous reserve of power, through being producers of society's wealth, also determined the form of social organization of labour; their rôle would be particularly important in the process of transition from one such form to another. On the other hand, the social organization of labour utilization would give us significant clues to the nature of the state presiding over that society.

This perspective, I believe, comprises a totality although it would be hard to locate the three factors in a permanent hierarchy, for none of them is privileged to determine the others in every circumstance.

In this perspective the economic infrastructures underlying medieval polities, far from exhibiting any degree of uniformity, would bring into high relief their deep-seated variation. Even within the same region changes in production processes over time could be detected with greater certainty and their implications for the other factors could perhaps be established. The succession of different forms of non-economic coercion (rent in labour, cash or kind or straight-forward collection of revenue) would rather suggest considerable changes in production processes, techniques, the demand and supply of labour and not least the influence of the market. To treat all these forms as equivalent and interchangeable, in isolation from the production system, would be tantamount to ignoring all these changes and treating the whole span of feudal economy as much the same from the beginning to the end. It is thus that historical change is better understood in the context of the entire system of production rather than merely as a process of stimulus-response relationship between the state and, in the case of medieval societies, the peasantry. Treating the state as the prime mover of social change attributes far too much of motive force to it. No society functions at the diktat of the ruling class, but rather through a balance between the power exercised at many levels—political, military, juridical and administrative power, the power of leadership of communities and not least the power that peasants (in medieval societies) commanded by virtue of carrying out the production processes. The dynamism for social change thus originates in friction at all the multifarious joints in society, and each social stratum participates in it, however differential its contribution.

Above all, this perspective by insisting on placing the precise form of non-economic coercion in the context of the production system and by distinguishing each form from the others—irrespective of the order of their succession, or even in the case of their co-existence in different regions—is able to focus on the form of peasants' resistance to their exploitation. The peasant who has to render labour rent would resist the lord in the very process of cultivating the demesne through lethargy, stealing of the lord's time, and by being careless. But a peasant who has to pay rent in cash can hardly adopt the same technique of resistance; he will have to haggle with the lord over the payment of money after the crop has been harvested and sold in the market. Or when he pays rent in kind, he takes resort to attempt at concealing part of the produce from the lord's or his agent's eye or bribing the agent.

The case of the revenue-paying peasant of medieval India is even further apart. The revenue was collected from the village as a unit after the crop had been harvested and each peasant had to contribute his share to it according to the size of his holding, though the rate per unit of land was the same for all. This implied that the Indian peasants' resistance took place outside the production process over the quantum of revenue demand and that of necessity this resistance had to be collective in nature, involving a major or at least a considerable part of the village society. This would be unlike the early medieval European peasant's resistance in the very process of production which therefore made his resistance more individual in nature, though of course on certain issues, such as the community's rights to pastures, there would be collective pressure.

Thus, whether peasants' resistance takes place in the very process of production or outside it, or whether there is a succession from one form of resistance to another, makes a vital difference to the history of that production system. Therefore when R.S. Sharma asks, 'If parts of the products are placed at the disposal of the grantee, what is the difference between enjoying the means of production, that is land, and the fruits of production?' and adds, 'Land does not mean anything without its products' (Sharma, 96), he is overlooking the critical difference, namely, the form of peasants' resistance which must correspond to the concrete form of non-economic coercion.

It was this totality that the definition of feudalism as 'the structured dependence of the entire peasantry on the lords' had sought to capture; the hiatus between the labour potential of each peasant family and its resources was, as Dirlik so rightly observes, a condition of feudalism (Dirlik, n. 2), and the 'structured dependence' its distinctive characteristic. The notion of 'the structured dependence' was posited in the context of the production system which in turn was visualized as transitional, though the transition was ascribed to class struggle, at times silent, imperceptible, inherent in the daily toil on the field, and at others in the form of violent outbursts. It is difficult to agree more with Wickham's perception that 'it is over the control of production that the dynamic of class struggle in feudalism is most acute' (Wickham, 136). It was in contrast with this feature that the medieval Indian peasantry was characterized as a 'free peasantry' whose process of production was free of extraneous control and whose class struggle therefore was of a different order from that of feudal lords and peasants in Europe. We shall return to this point later.

The role of ideology in class struggle, irrespective of its form, remains to be examined, though Marxist historians in general have largely ignored this vital question. However, my own neglect of it was not in any way an indication of its secondary importance; nor was it due to any implicit conception that 'the material base' must first be sorted out before attention is turned to the ideological superstructure. It was in fact born of my greatly limited familiarity with the them.[3] Nor is there much secondary literature on this theme, Marxist or non-Marxist, on which one could draw in the Indian context. References to the role of ideology in early and medieval Indian society or brief discussion of it (Chattopadhyaya, 1977: 276-86; 1980-81: 15-23; and mimeo: 29; Sharma, 103), however, tend to treat it as a kind of conspiratorial creation of the ruling class implanting its own ideology on to the peasants' (or artisans') mind and thereby impeding the growth of peasants' class consciousness and consequent class struggle. Thus R.S. Sharma observes: 'Classes with conflicting interests were kept together through the performance of *puja, japa, vratas, tirthas, samskaras, prayaschitas*[4] and through prospects of heaven and hell. The all-pervasive influence of astrology (*jyotisa*) and that of the doctrine of Vedanta kept the people reconciled to their lot. All factors brought people of opposite interests together' (Sharma, 103).

This is rather a partial vision, for it does not explain why the peasants came to accept an ideology so alien to their interests. It tacitly assumes that since the ruling class has at its disposal considerable intellectual, among other, resources, it develops a sophisticated ideology to defend its own interest which it then imparts to the peasantry. Since the peasantry can hardly be expected to command similar intellectual resources, it is in no position to resist the alien ideology. Support for this view could perhaps be drawn from Marx and Engels' observation: the ideas of the ruling class are in every epoch the ruling ideas: i.e. the class which is the ruling *material* force of society is at the same time its ruling *intellectual* force (Marx and Engels, 1972: 44) (emphasis in original).

I believe it amounts to considerable disrespect to the intelligence of peasants to treat them merely as victims of ruling class conspiracy. This is not to deny the influence of the ruling class ideology on peasants' minds, but to suggest that peasants accept that part of the ruling class ideology which corresponds to their daily experience; they do not accept all of alien ideology. Thus, for example, the medieval Indian peasant was renowned for his fatalistic attitude, an attitude which would reconcile him to considerable adversity. In that measure this mode of rationalization strongly buttressed the dominance of the ruling class. But the peasant would accept the notion of fatalism only when his crop had failed, for he had no one else to blame for it. Unlike the medieval European peasant whose process of production was under the control of the lord and who therefore had a visible target in case of crop failure, the Indian peasants' process of production being free from such extraneous control—a point I shall return to later in this article—he could hardly lay the responsibility for it at the door of any individual or institution; an invisible factor such as fate then came handy as an explanation. But the same peasant refused to blame his fate if the state or its agent demanded more revenue from him than was customary; he stood up for his rights, sometimes by submitting petitions, at other times by threatening to give up cultivation, at still others by actually migrating to other areas or into the forests and finally by taking up arms. This time his enemy stood before him, and one could hardly trace a sign of the fatalistic attitude in him.

But then the role of ideology can hardly be understood in terms of a one-to-one correspondence with the material interests of one or another class (Poulantzas, 1978: 28-46; Geertz, 1964: 47-75), much as R.S. Sharma and I have sought to do. At any rate the formation of ideology as part of culture is seldom a one-way process, originating at the top and flowing downwards; it usually evolves out of a complex interaction between rituals, beliefs and ideas of all the different strata of society.[5] Frank Perlin's contribution to this debate did set out to examine concretely the role of ideology in late precolonial Maharashtra society outside of this one-to-one correspondence (1985: 132-40). His insight does considerably deepen our understanding of that society, but it is doubtful whether historical explanation merely in terms of the notion of 'brotherhood' among the *vatandars* of Maharashtra is an adequate substitute for the Moreland/Habib/Mukhia orthodoxy.

II

Between 1965 when R.S. Sharma first published his *Indian Feudalism* and now ('How Feudal was Indian Feudalism?' in this volume) there has happily been a remarkable change in his notion of what constituted Indian feudalism. In the book Sharma conceived of Indian feudalism almost as a carbon copy of the Pirennean version of the rise and decline of feudal economy in Western Europe, and he made a point-by-point comparison with Europe, employing all the terms, categories and institutions in reference to which the Pirennean school had analysed feudalism in Europe: decline of trade, manor, serfdom, commutation of labour services into cash payment, revival of trade and urban centres, and so on. And if he did not find the Germanic invasions of Europe replicated in India, B.N.S. Yadav, another erudite proponent of the notion of Indian feudalism, drew attention to the Hun invasions of north India at about the same period of time (Mukhia, 48, n. 106, for references). Sharma's article in this volume, on the other hand, marks a search for a genuinely 'Indian' variant of feudalism, though in regard to the application to India of some of the important categories of European feudalism—such as serfdom—he takes somewhat ambivalent positions.[6] Nor has he revised his chronology, so that Indian feudalism in his view originated about the fourth or fifth century AD, as trade and urban centres declined and tapered off by the eleventh or twelfth century when trade and the process of urbanization once again revived. His argument is still focused on land assigned by the state to grantees. Along with land was assigned 'blanket authority' over peasants, which leads Sharma to conclude that this blanket authority 'may have' included the right to peasants' labour for purposes of agricultural production (92, 98). He speaks of a 'social crisis' and 'a crisis in production relations' created by the resistance of 'the lower orders' to performing the functions assigned to them which led to 'changes in the mode of production' whereby peasants were subjected to more arbitrary and greater exploitation in the period of Indian feudalism (100–1). Subject to numerous exactions, the Indian peasant was living at the bare level of subsistence by the twelfth century (Yadava, 1973: 301).

The early medieval period in India (*c.* fifth to twelfth century AD) was also the period of considerable technological and economic growth, especially in the sphere of agricultural production.[7] R.S. Sharma has graphically captured some of this progress in his contribution to this volume (103–4), and he observes that: 'This period was undoubtedly an age of larger yield and a great agrarian expansion.' Burton Stein has similarly located impressive expansion of agriculture in early medieval south India (Stein, 1980: 68–9). Technological and agricultural progress is also indicated by the three-stage evolution of the water-wheels which drew water from wells (Mukhia, 58, n. 214; Habib, in Raychaudhuri and Habib, eds., 1982, I: 49). Irrigation was (and still is) the chief bottleneck in agricultural expansion in India and the use of well-irrigation, through water-wheels and several other devices, brought this vital element within reach even of small peasants. The construction of wells should have induced both an extension and an intensification of cultivation; the amount of water required for irrigating each crop could also be regulated and overdosing of crops with water thus prevented; this would imply a more organized method of agricultural production. The brick-lined wells were particularly capital intensive;[8] this fact itself should lead the cultivator towards the production of high-value crops (Williamson, 1931: 621). There was, besides, considerable effort undertaken by the imperial and provincial states to provide irrigation by digging canals and huge lakes (Kumar, 1979: 211–14).

Agricultural progress in this period is also indicated by the growing number of new crops and an increasing number of varieties of old crops. There is evidence of the cultivation of rice (in Kathiawad region), wheat, barley, sesamum, peas and cotton in the Harappa culture. The *Rg Veda* refers to five crops: barley, sesamum (of the black and the white-seeded varieties), cucumber, bottlegourd and sugarcane; it makes no reference to wheat, rice or cotton, though the term for barley (*yava*) was possibly used as a generic term for corn and might have included wheat. The later Vedic texts such as the *Atharva Veda* and the *Taittiriya Samhita* do however mention rice; barley and wheat are mentioned in the *Atharva Veda* and beans and sesamum in the *Taittiriya Samhita.* Pearl-millet was perhaps a gift of Africa to India in the PGW phase. The *Arthasastra* mentions seventeen kinds of crops of which some ten were foodgrains, and rice was of two varieties. By the twelfth century AD twenty-four to twenty-five kinds of food crops, including vegetables and fruits, were being cultivated. In addition, new varieties of some crops were being produced. A medieval text, the *Sunya Purana*, tells us that more than fifty varieties of rice were being grown in Bengal. If we extend our survey to the end of the sixteenth century, the number of crops had risen to more than forty, though of course there was regional variation in both the number and types of crops. This number was not exceeded even in the 1920s.[9]

All this constitutes an impressive record of progress. However, if the very scale of state effort in encouraging agricultural expansion has ensured its transmission to historical record, the contribution of individual peasants, small and big, has largely, and unreasonably, remained unsung. However humble the individual contribution, the totality of it all would be no less substantial than that of the states' contribution. Of the 528 wells in a group of 18 villages that we have noted above, only 41 or 7.76 per cent were after all brick-lined; the rest were just shafts dug into the soil until the water table was reached. They would serve for a couple of years and then collapse, to be replaced by other such shafts—clearly the work of very small peasants who could not afford the cost of brick-lined wells. Yet, must we scoff at their effort? Or, for that matter, must we scoff at the effort of the better-off strata of peasants who provided leadership in this agricultural progress by experimenting with waterwheels, tanks and, not least, new and often capital-intensive crops? Down to the early twentieth century, by which time the scale of state intervention in agricultural production had grown much larger, the *Report of the Royal Commission on Agriculture* was appreciative of the great significance of the smaller irrigation works and urged the government to pay more attention to them (1928: 338-9). The early medieval and medieval Indian peasantry clearly possessed a much greater degree of dynamism than has usually been granted by historians until very recently (Mukhia, 1985).

But then how does one square the growing subjection of peasants to the blanket authority of the grantees and their ever increasing exploitation in all conceivable forms in the period of Indian feudalism (for such is the picture that R.S. Sharma has given us) with this record of considerable agricultural progress in which the same down-and-out peasants played such a significant role? One could perhaps ascribe the peasants' efforts to the pressure of the grantees. But then in so doing one must also assume peasants' utter helplessness in the face of this pressure—rather a doubtful assumption in view of the power they commanded by virtue of their control over the production process. It is also doubtful if peasants would make all the extra investment of capital and labour merely to meet the increasing demand of revenue or rent with little or no benefit accruing to them, and that not for a year of two but over centuries.

The picture of extensive land grants and the ensuing subjection of peasants to almost unrestrained exploitation by grantees creates some other problems as well. This picture really hinges on the assumption of the kings' unreserved right of ownership in land. This assumption, which R.S. Sharma makes (86-7), can be sustained only by ignoring an enormous amount of evidence to the contrary.[10] Besides, since the Delhi Sultanate, successor to the era of 'Indian feudalism', bears no evidence of such grants of land, along with the assignments of 'blanket authority' over peasants, are we to hail the Sultanate as the liberator of the oppressed peasants whose obligation was now more or less limited to the payment of specified taxes? This is a scenario that is unlikely to make a strong appeal to Irfan Habib, among others, for he has argued over the years that the establishment of the Delhi Sultanate in the beginning of the thirteenth century marked a new stage in the history of India by stretching the level of peasants' exploitation to its highest pitch, a feature that was to characterize the history of all the subsequent centuries down to India's independence (Habib, 1978: 297-8).

Above all, since in R.S. Sharma's perception Indian feudalism had declined by the eleventh or twelfth century AD with the revival of trade and urban centres, how are we to characterize the six centuries falling between its decline and India's colonization? Surely not as an era of capitalist development! Sharma of course has always restricted his researches to the terminal date of the twelfth century AD at one end, though at the other he has extended his study to pre-historic civilization; he might thus claim immunity from having to characterize the post-twelfth-century Indian social formation. But then all of us must reckon with the logic of our argument.

One might perhaps get around this problem by extending the period of Indian feudalism to the end of the seventeenth or early eighteenth century, the eve of colonization, and some historians have indeed done so, even though their problematic was different (thus Kosambi, 1975: 391-2; and Jha, 1979: 16).

In a way, the breathtaking simplicity with which a period of five or six centuries is just added on to the life of Indian feudalism is by itself a sad comment on the lack of rigour in the concept of Indian feudalism. But even if one were to concede these centuries, it still remains for us to explain the transition of a society characterized by a highly disintegrated administrative organization, decline of trade and virtual disappearance of currency, decline of urban centres and the almost unrestrained subjection of peasants to exploitation at will by the land grantees (all in the early medieval period), to a highly centralized administrative system covering a vast empire, with a strong base of commodity production in agriculture and handicrafts and a vibrant currency system, an almost extravagant number of towns and a peasantry whose primary obligation was to pay a fixed number of taxes, even if these taxes deprived it of the bulk of its surplus produce (characteristics of the late sixteenth and the whole of the seventeenth century)[11]—all of it within the framework of Indian feudalism.

It is of course true that European feudalism too was not the same from one end of its duration to the other and the memorable division Marc Bloch made between the First and the Second Feudal Ages has lost none of its validity, even though a great many parts of the picture he drew of feudal society have been substantially modified. But then it is also true that the processes which have transformed the first into the second feudal age have more or less clearly been identified in the historiography of European feudalism so that it is easy to visualize the changes in the later medieval Europe as the cumulative effect of the tensions which had characterized early medieval society. It is also easy enough to see that all these changes from the fifth to the fifteenth century had occurred within the structure of feudalism, although those very changes subverted the structure in the later Middle Ages.

If the historiography of Indian feudalism could establish such or similar order of linkages which would explain the transition of early medieval Indian society to the society of the seventeenth century, it could command a strong case in its favour. However, as we have already seen, even the story of the transition of (north) India from the eleventh or twelfth to the thirteenth century runs into awkward moments; the long-term transition is an item that has not yet even been placed on the historians' agenda. In such a situation the addition of five or six centuries to Indian feudalism would hardly amount to more than an intellectual sleight of hand.

If the concept of Indian feudalism is riddled with potholes, 'the Indian medieval economy' or 'the medieval Indian system' suggested by Irfan Habib (1978: 298; 1985: 49) also is not without problems. In putting this notion forward Habib has not discussed its characteristics; as such it remains a descriptive, empiricist rather than an analytical category. But it is possible to put together in outline certain of the characteristics of the medieval Indian economy as visualized by Habib over the past two decades. These are as follows.

(a) The predominance of peasant production in the context of a stratified agrarian economy. The peasants, however, were 'no better than semiserfs' for they 'were not masters of their domicile'. They were therefore to be brought back to their village by officials if they deserted it for whatever reason (Habib, 1982: 11, 20, 25; Raychaudhuri and Habib, eds., 1982, I: 54).

(b) Increasing pressure being exerted by the state, ever since the establishment of the Delhi Sultanate, on peasants in that the bulk of peasants' surplus was now collected as revenue increasingly in cash. This was a point of departure in Indian history and continued to be its characteristic feature down to India's Independence in 1947.

(c) The growing impoverishment of the peasantry owing to increasing demand of the ruling class for revenue. This in turn inhibited major technological and economic breaks, by denying to possible new technological devices a receptive market and ensuring abundance of artisan labour supply at low cost (Habib, 1963: 317-51; 1971).

In 1963 when Irfan Habib published his *Agrarian System of Mughal India* a major change in historians' perception of medieval Indian rural society was introduced. Until then that society had usually been perceived in terms of an egalitarian structure by virtue of the absence of property in land; Habib on the other hand portrayed a highly stratified society, a picture that has come to stay. His emphasis on the primacy of peasant production is also a valuable contribution to our understanding. Problems, however, arise in considering his notion of semi-serfs. Legal restriction on the free mobility of peasants is a feature first encountered in the *Arthasastra*. But the restriction was motivated entirely by the anxiety of the state to ensure continuity of cultivation and avert the loss of revenue. It was for this reason that the *Arthasastra* did not permit tax-paying peasants to settle 'in a village not inhabited by tax-payers' (*Kautilya's Arthasastra*, 1967: 197). Indeed, it even advised the state to compel cultivators to grow an additional crop on their fields if its financial needs so required (1967: 273).

Manu, the great law-giver of the second century AD, prescribed the imposition of a fine on a cultivator who did not cultivate his field in good time or protect the crop against animals (Mazumdar, 1960: 171). But the most graphic evidence of this comes from a document of the second half of the fourteenth century, when the peasants of one village, part of whose revenue had been assigned to a trooper, migrated to another and the trooper insisted on their return on the ground that the claim was not on the 'ownership of their persons' but the right to collect the assigned taxes from them (Raychaudhuri and Habib, eds., I: 54). Clearly then as long as taxes were paid—which the peasants must pay whether or not they had cultivated their fields—they could not be subjected to any other restrictions. We shall have to loosen the meaning of serfdom or even semi-serfdom considerably to equate it merely with legal restriction on free mobility of peasants, irrespective of its context.

At any rate, a little caution is in order in treating legal restriction on peasant mobility as evidence for the actual absence of such mobility. Indeed, after characterizing peasants as semi-serfs owing to the lack of mastery over their domicile, Irfan Habib observes, 'An interesting feature of agriculture during Mughal times was the mobility of the peasantry' (Raychaudhuri and Habib, eds., 1982, I: 218), and in support cites the oft-quoted statement of Babur, 'In Hindustan hamlets and villages—even towns—are depopulated and set up in a moment!' Habib reasonably explains this as being possible 'because of the large areas of virgin land available in most regions during the sixteenth and seventeenth centuries'. Surely, by that logic even larger areas or virgin land should have been available as we go back in time and therefore the possibility of peasant migration was likely to have been greater in the preceding centuries.

Irfan Habib has pioneered research in the production technology of medieval Indian agriculture, as in several other areas, which has immensely enriched our understanding of India's medieval past. Yet the great significance he attaches to the maximization of land revenue collection with the establishment of the Delhi Sultanate bears little relationship to the system of agricultural production. If the state's revenue demand under the Sultanate had risen, it could have done so either in a greater or lesser measure of correspondence with a rise in production levels, or as a result of an exercise of sheer will on the part of the ruling class, whether or not peasants obtained their subsistence. If indeed production levels had not registered any marked growth and peasants were compelled to pay much higher amounts in revenue to the Sultans (as Habib strongly implies in treating the establishment of the Delhi Sultanate as a major break in the history of the appropriation of peasants' surplus), surely they must have remained considerably under-exploited in the preceding centuries. And yet the picture of peasantry drawn by R.S. Sharma, B.N.S. Yadava and others, as seen earlier, is hardly one of a cheerful, prosperous peasantry in those centuries. It was, we are told, making do with a bare margin of subsistence in the twelfth century, just prior to the establishment of the Sultanate. It is of course true that the pre-Sultanate states collected the bulk of peasants' surplus under numerous heads and the Sultanate did so under a single head; but is that an important enough difference to demarcate a new stage in the country's history commencing with this change?[12]

The growing state pressure for a rising revenue demand also resulted, in Irfan Habib's view, in a kind of levelling effect over the various strata of peasantry. Habib has rightly pointed out the regressive nature of Mughal land revenue demand which appropriated the surplus at uniform rates irrespective of peasants' individual resources. Indeed, at times this demand was made even more regressive by differential revenue rates in inverse relation to peasants' resources and caste status (Singh, 1976: 301-2). Given a stratified peasantry and regressive taxation, the increasing pressure itself should have promoted relative differentiation. It is therefore not easy to reconcile the notions of stratification and levelling effect except by positing a highly progressive taxation—hardly a viable proposition.

If the peasantry remained highly stratified, that should by itself be a strong argument for the existence of a responsive market for new, even capital-intensive, technological devices if they were otherwise useful. Indeed, as I have noted already, in promoting agricultural progress in particular individual peasants at all levels played a significant role. However, technological and economic progress can seldom be judged with reference to the last peasant or artisan. The leadership is usually provided by their upper strata and it tends to percolate downwards; and medieval India was not devoid of such strata. If, therefore, medieval Indian economy did not undergo a basic transformation and did not move on to the stage of capitalism, it is hardly owing to a uniform absence of purchasing power by the Indian peasants. Nor need it be held that the abundance of cheap artisan labour was responsible for the absence of major labour-saving technological breaks. According to Joseph Needham several purely labour-saving devices were developed in China in the context of labour abundance (Needham, 1979: 33-4). Later in this article I shall try to explain the absence of the basic transformation of medieval Indian society in terms of the nature of social conflict embedded in that society.

Several of the problems we have discussed originate in the fact that these concepts have as their focus the relationship between the state and the peasantry, in which the state always commands the initiative.[13] This almost amounts to looking at peasants from the foot of the throne, as it were. The historian's sympathy rests quite obviously with the peasants, but their role in historical change is recognized only when eruption of their anger comes to notice in dramatic uprisings in reaction to excesses of the state. In the process, the peasantry's role in silently, almost imperceptibly changing production technology, its role in silently, equally imperceptibly resisting exploitation in the very process of production through daily toil or outside it, in various forms, which really create the setting for violent outbursts—these features of historical change are relegated to secondary significance.

It was this historical change that the notion of 'free peasant economy' in medieval India had sought to capture. 'Free peasantry' is a category open to different interpretations. For Irfan Habib such free peasantry existed only in the era immediately preceding the development of capitalism in Europe (193). Long and Richardson (1978), on the other hand, have postulated the existence of free peasantry engaged in subsistence agriculture in several pre-capitalist societies. Wickham in his article in this volume has drawn attention to the useful category of tied but free peasantry in Ottoman Turkey (129-30). Indian historians have usually understood the freedom of peasants in terms of their legal right to unrestricted mobility, a view which had come in for some questioning, following which the term had been defined with reference to the presence or absence of extraneous control over the peasants' process of production.[14] The free peasant neither rendered his nor his family's labour to any one in any form for purposes of production, nor employed outside labour; he cultivated his family farm with his own family's labour and resources, within of course the universal constraints of the regional ecology.

There is however the utilization of the labour of menial castes in the fields by the entire community of cultivators irrespective of its own stratification. Their labour was made available by denying them access to land, even in the context of land abundance, through the working of the caste system (Habib, 1963: 121-2; 1982: 14, 18). It is tempting to attribute the growth of this class of 'an ostracized rural proletariat', as Irfan Habib calls it, to the proliferation of untouchable castes in ancient and early medieval India. It is curious however that growth in the number of untouchable castes in ancient and early medieval India notwithstanding—a theme on which Vivekanand Jha has done such impressive research (1975: 14-31)—no contemporary evidence has yet been cited to the effect that the caste system (or the state) denied them the right to hold land.[15]

The history of this, one of the most significant developments in India's past, which is also a feature specific to Indian society, is therefore far from clear even in outline. One could perhaps draw some inferences to this end from the available evidence; but surely for studying such a major development, which is unlikely to leave any aspect of society untouched, one must have something more substantial than inferences to depend upon.

In view of the sharp criticism made by R.S. Sharma and Burton Stein of the degree of freedom the medieval Indian peasant enjoyed over his process of production, I realize the need for some qualifications. No freedom in any society is absolute, surely not one that concerns the production system, so critical to the existence of the entire society. Several restraints would influence a peasant's decision to go on cultivating a particular crop or changing over to another: his familiarity with the technique of producing one or another crop, the capital and labour needs of a new crop, the pattern of demand in the neighbouring market, the availability of the requisite amount of water and so forth, and it is always worthwhile keeping these in mind while speaking of peasants' freedom. But then several, if not all, of these would restrain agricultural production in all societies at the hands of all strata of agriculturists, even if differentially. The fact that the Indian peasant today continually faces the uncertainty of power or diesel supply to run his tubewell should hardly lead us to describe him as an unfree peasant. The question of freedom or unfreedom of a particular class of stratum of society must surely be distinguished from universal restraints.

In this qualified sense production at the hands of the 'free peasant' that we have been speaking of, or 'the independent producer' as Irfan Habib calls him, came to be consolidated by the seventh century AD, according to R.S. Sharma's testimony.[16] Clearly this could only be the culmination of a long-drawn-out process with considerable regional variation; indeed, through the whole of the early medieval and medieval periods the system of agricultural production based on free peasant labour was confined at best to north India. South India, especially its most fertile region, the Kaveri delta, retained a distinct form of agricultural production and labour organization, a form that was subverted only in the twentieth century, as Burton Stein has shown in his article for this volume (220, 222-3, 234). It might of course be added that along with communal control over land expressed in the periodic redistribution of fields there had also emerged individual landownership in the region (Karashima, 1984: 16-17).

Uma Chakravarti has, in an excellent article (*Chains of Servitude:*

Bondage and Slavery in India, 1985), graphically traced the changes in the forms of labour used for agricultural production in ancient India. The early Buddhist literature introduces us to a differentiated agrarian society where individual landholdings had become quite familiar. In the Buddhist texts we also come across large farms at times requiring 500 ploughs for tilling, for which the labour of *dasas*, *kammakarras* and *porisas* (usually translated as slaves, labourers and servants) was employed. Understandably, these texts also record the first appearance of the word *dalidda* (extremely poor people). Large state farms are also mentioned in the *Arthasastra* and these were worked by 'slaves, labourers and prisoners' (*Kautilya's Arthasastra*, 1967: 129). At the same time the *Arthasastra* sought to regulate the relationship between master and slave (Chakravarti, 1985); masters were clearly encountering considerable resistance from slaves, enough to require state intervention. From the Mauryan period onwards, debt-bondage, wage-labour and share-cropping appear to have grown in importance (Chakravarti, 1985). In the Gupta and post-Gupta periods our evidence does not speak of large farms, either state-owned or private; on the other hand the *sudras* were being transformed into petty peasants, a process completed by the first half of the seventh century AD, as we have seen earlier.

The consolidation of petty peasant production, however, occurred in the context of *a growing complexity of social stratification*, and this becomes increasingly evident from the inscriptions of this period. To a degree, the grants in revenue and land made by the state created the strong class of intermediaries who gradually acquired hereditary titles to these grants—the class which was itself highly stratified and which was to be known by the generic term of 'zamindars' from the thirteenth century onwards. On the other hand stratification would proceed at the other end too, with the upper strata of the class of landowners interposing themselves between the state and the rest of the peasantry, a process described by D.D. Kosambi as 'feudalism from below' (1975: 295-6). In incorporating them into the class of intermediaries, the state would perhaps give merely formal sanction to a *fait accompli*. This was particularly true of tribal chiefs whose tribes would merge with organized agrarian society, through either the use of force or by more peaceful 'persuasion' (Sharma, 1969: 16). In a number of cases spread over different regions of early medieval India the growing pace of stratification led to the establishment of new ruling lineages arising from the agrarian base.[17]

In speaking of the consolidation of petty peasant production, therefore, we can hardly view it as a substitution for stratified agrarian society. The emphasis on petty peasantry is an emphasis on the significant element of change which, starting earlier, had become crystallized by the seventh century AD.

This scenario seems to provide the social context in which the agricultural progress of early medieval centuries becomes intelligible. The absence of extraneous control over the peasants' process of production at all levels of stratified rural society (with all the qualifications that have been suggested) led them to participate in the 'great agrarian expansion' that R.S. Sharma speaks of. However, starting with unequal resources, different strata of agriculturalists would benefit differentially from this expansion, so that the very process of agricultural progress would further promote stratification and generate new forms of rural tensions. In a regional study, though of a much later period, the whole spectrum of such tensions has been brought alive and it has been shown that disputes were not only economic in nature (Bajekal, 1980); quite possibly the nature of tensions would vary over time and space but, equally possibly, with growing stratification and widespread agricultural progress, tensions would arise at a number of joints in that society.

Yet if I highlight the freedom of peasants' control over their process of production as the chief element of change that had occurred by the seventh century which was to characterize the social history of most parts of India down to the colonial era, it is to bring into relief the specific form of exploitation. In my earlier article it had been suggested that medieval Indian economy was characterized by high fertility of land, low subsistence needs of the peasants (and consequent high level of exploitation of peasantry yielding a very large amount of surplus to the ruling class), and peasants' freedom of control over their process of production. It was on the basis of this last feature that the medieval Indian peasant had been defined as a free peasant. R.S. Sharma's argument that the early medieval peasants' process of production, among other things, was subjected to the control of the grantees is merely an inference derived from his picture of the general subjection of peasantry to the authority of the grantees [which 'might even enable the beneficiary to force the peasant to work in his field' or the grantees 'may develop a natural tendency to control the process itself on which the nature and amount of yield depend' (Sharma, 93)]. Surely the very absence of definitive evidence to substantiate such a vital feature of our social history should justify some doubt about the viability of this argument.

The free peasant system of production decisively laid down the chief form of exploitation: from now on, peasants were to part with their surplus produce in payment of revenue to the state, in kind or cash. With the relation of exploitation firmly based on the appropriation of revenue, conflicts between peasants and the state arose on the question of revenue so appropriated. It is significant that most evidence of peasant protest in any form from the early medieval period onwards relates to the amount of revenue demand.

Burton Stein has made an extremely important and valid criticism of an element that the description 'free peasant economy' seems to ignore. Having posited a crucial binary relation of exploitation between the revenue-paying free peasant and the revenue-appropriating state ('the chief instrument of exploitation'), it remains for us to characterize the nature of the state as well. Besides, Stein rightly asks, can one really speak of the state in India over all its different region and long stretches of time in the singular? This really is a profound problem; it is also perhaps least researched in Indian historiography. If therefore what follows is rather elementary, to a small extent it is due to the hitherto general neglect of the problem by historians.

In a sense in defining free peasant economy as one in which the peasant paid revenue to the state but did not have to contend with extraneous control over his process of production, a definition of the state was also implied. The state exercised non-economic coercion to collect revenue from peasants and distributed it among different strata of the ruling class according to a *hierarchy of their rights in the produce of land.* The state's occasional grant of loans to peasants and digging of some canals notwithstanding, it remained by and large uninvolved with the processes of production. Its coercive power was therefore never rooted in the production system.

This, along with maintenance of law and order, seems to be the basic characteristic of the state's relationship with the peasant for nearly a thousand years preceding India's colonization. Given this characteristic there was considerable variation in the extent of territorial or administrative control of the succession of imperial and regional states in India over this period, the complexion and composition of the higher echelons of the ruling class, the degree of cohesion or conflict amongst the ruling strata, and so forth. Besides, even a grand state of imperial dimensions was able to establish its overarching system in the regions only with considerable degree of variation, often compromising with and incorporating in its interstices regional and local customs and institutions. Thus an imperial state system such as the Mughal system would not be exactly the same in one region as in another. With all these qualifications, however, the early medieval and medieval state existed primarily to collect revenue for maintaining a ruling class which remained alien to the actual processes of production.

Clearly this is a description of the functions rather than a characterization of the nature of the medieval Indian state. The notion of the tribute gathering state is also a mere description with the added disadvantage that the tributary mode of production,[18] in which it operates, covers not one but several systems of production over different regions and periods. On the other hand Burton Stein's characterization of the medieval state in south India as the 'peasant state' is original enough to have led to considerable discussion in India. Yet, in depositing all the different strata of landowners in the homogeneous category of 'peasant' as far as their control over state power is concerned, and in sidestepping the problem of the nature of state's coercive power with reference to surplus appropriation, Stein's conception of the state itself becomes severely handicapped.

We are thus back to the problem of characterizing the Indian state (or states) in our period. I should confess that describing the state comes easier than giving a name to it, and we all might perhaps begin our search for a name by trying to explicate what we understand by the state in early medieval and medieval India. The search is going to be long indeed.

The notion of the free peasant system of production where the state appropriates revenue allows us to visualize a continuum from early medieval India into the early colonial era; it also allows us to study the nature of changes taking place within the continuum. The free peasant production ensured a degree of gradual, steady development of the productive forces. Impressive as this development was, we could hardly speak of it at any stage in this period as a fundamental transformation of the production system. Its pace was evened out by the long time span so that we would be hard put to point to a cluster of changes in a relatively brief period that would lead the economy and society to a new stage, comparable to stages of development in European history.[19]

The explanation for this perhaps lies primarily in the nature of social conflict characteristic of that system of production. The medieval Indian peasant was, to be sure, heavily exploited. Indeed, it is possible to argue that, given the high fertility of the Indian soils and low subsistence level which nature in most parts of the Indian subcontinent permitted, the state collected from the peasants much greater amounts of surplus than the feudal lords were able to do from their peasants in Europe. Yet, once exploitation of the peasantry had come to be pivoted on revenue collection, conflict between peasants and the state came to the fore only after the production process had been completed, for the conflict related to the quantum of revenue demand. In other words the nature of social conflict remained extraneous to the production system. In early medieval Western Europe social conflict inhered in the very process of production, in which all the different strata of rural society had a degree of involvement; consequently a resolution of it was possible only in the transformation of the production system and redistribution of the means of production, giving rise to new classes. In medieval India on the other hand social conflict was limited to the distribution and redistribution of the surplus; the means of production did not get redistributed. Even a grave political crisis, such as the collapse of the mighty Mughal Empire in the early eighteenth century, was neither the effect nor the cause of social upheavals rooted in redistribution of the means of production or the emergence of new property forms.[20] Social tensions arising from upheavals in the class of zamindars (subordinate revenue appropriators) as often corroded the strength of the Mughal Empire as peasant uprisings did and these upheavals frequently occurred in the relatively prosperous regions of the Empire. The model of peasant rebellions led by the zamindars against the Mughal state's ever rising level of exploitation, which Irfan Habib had posited in 1963, when tested against village level evidence in a small region of north India, did not yield positive results. Except for the alliance between the Jat zamindars and Jat peasants, where caste clearly cemented their bond, in other subregions either such a bond was absent or else zamindars and peasants were at loggerheads with each other even when both of them are rebelling against the state.[21] At any rate, what did emerge from the debris of the Empire was the resurgent class of zamindars everywhere, a class that was older than the Mughal Empire and the Delhi Sultanate.

It is therefore arguable that, given these features of the system of agricultural production and of the nature of social conflict, medieval Indian society, far from being static or stagnant, was yet unlikely to have undergone a transformation whether or not colonialism had intervened.[22]

NOTES

Apart from the stimulus of the contributions to the special issue of the *Journal of Peasant Studies* on 'Feudalim and Non-European Societies', this article owes much to discussion and arguement with successive generations of my students at JNU and to long conversations with Krishna Bhardwaj, S. Bhattacharya, B.D. Chattopadhyay, Suvira Jaiswal, Majid Siddiqi, C.N. Subramaniam and Romila Thapar. The substance of its argument was also presented at a delightfully informal gathering of historians, economists and sociologists at the Nehru Memorial Museum and Library, New Delhi. To all these friends I repeat those simple and therefore beautiful words in gratitude: 'thank you'.

1. 'Generalized commodity production where labour is a commodity' is merely the abstraction of the capitalist mode of production. Prior to arriving at this point of abstraction a society might pass through various combinations of production and market relations so that commodity production could be combined with slavery, bonded labour, sharecropping, etc. It is of course useful to distinguish between 'purely' capitalist relations of wage labour and generalized commodity production and combinations of pre-capitalist production relations with generalized commodity production. It is equally useful to keep in mind the direction of the drift of these combinations. If the drift is towards the abstraction of capitalism, one could perhaps speak of a decisive tendency towards the development of capitalism even prior to its reaching the point of abstraction.
2. Sharma gets the impression from n. 225 of 'Was There Feudalism in Indian History?' that I had supported the notion of regional variants of feudalism. I regret having given him this impression, for I had in that longish note actually questioned even the methodology of positing regional variants of feudalism outside Europe.
3. I made an attempt to understand the nature of popular ideology in medieval Hindi literature in Mukhia (1978). Its success was rather moderate and at any rate I was unable to pursue it further.
4. Respectively: worship, repeated uttering of a sacred name or verse, fasts or domestic rituals, pilgrimages, rituals connected with life-cycle, and penances.
5. Duby (1968: 3-10), in the Western European context, and Chattopadhyaya (1983: 8), for India. Indeed, the Hindu religious system incorporates a large number of tribal gods, goddesses and rituals.
6. Thus, on p. 89 in this volume Sharma treats the early medieval Indian peasant as almost a serf; on pp. 96-7, the peasant is no longer treated as a serf; but on p. 98 serfdom is described as an important feature of early medieval society in India.
7. Curiously, the editors of *The Cambridge Economic History of India* (Raychaudhuri and Habib, 1982, I: xiii) insist on characterizing this period as 'a long period of economic decline' even in the face of considerable research supporting agricultural progress.
8. As late as the second half of the seventeenth century only 41 out of 528 wells in 18 villages of a *pargana* (revenue and administrative unit) in eastern Rajasthan were brick-lined. Information kindly given by my colleague Dilbagh Singh.
9. For evidence see Mukhia (1993).
10. Some of the evidence has been cited in Mukhia (55, n. 189); a far more impressive amount of evidence has been collected by Lallanji Gopal in his 'Ownership of Agricultural Land' (1980: 42-89). An important source giving

rise to the controversy is the refusal of most historians of ancient India to distinguish between a land- and a revenue-grant and treating all as land grants along with which all the king's sovereign rights over peasants were alienated. L. Gopal has made this distinction and has therefore reached an altogether different set of conclusions. It is of course essential to make the distinction in order to delineate the form of peasants' resistance.

11. For the summary discussion of these characteristics, see Raychaudhuri and Habib, eds. (1982, I). See also the review of this book in *The Indian Economic and Social History Review*, Vol. XXI, No. 1 (1984), pp. 111-27.
12. Irfan Habib does indeed seem to think so in Habib (1982: 27, n. 187).
13. R.S. Sharma indeed makes explicit in his article for this volume what had earlier been merely implicit in his argument, namely, that the state could call into existence a social structure. In support he mentions the examples of the Norman Conquest of England which had led to the imposition of feudalism from above, and colonial conquest in India (84: 100). Irfan Habib similarly refers to the 'influence' of the barbarian invasions of Europe and the Norman Conquest of England on the development of feudalism for drawing a parallel with the Turkish conquest of India and the consequent inauguration of a 'separate formation' (195).

    The old view that English feudalism was the creation of the Norman state had been upheld by Marc Bloch in *Feudal Society* (1964: 187-9, 244, 248), and Guy Fourquin in *Lordship and Feudalism in the Middle Ages* (1976: 76), though Fourquin's concern was with the lord-vassal relationship. This view has however been subjected to questioning lately and it has been argued that feudal land tenures as also feudal institutions and military obligations had preceded the Conquest of England and continued thereafter. See for a critical assessment of this literature J.O. Prestwich (1963: 39-57). Barbarian invasions and the evolution of feudal system in Western Europe were similarly preceded by the growing disintegration of the society in antiquity and the beginning of its transition to feudal society, a theme discussed so well by Perry Anderson in *Passages From Antiquity to Feudalism* (1974: 15-172). The view that colonial society in India was the creation of the colonial state is also being slowly questioned; see S. Bhattacharya (1979: 103 and 1984).

    The point, however, is not to deny the *influence* of the state on societal developments but to express doubt whether such *influence* can be equated with the state's *creation* of a social formation. The evolution and maturation of a social formation is after all a very complex phenomenon in which almost every conceivable element would play its part, however differentially; to attribute it entirely to the will of the state might perhaps amount to an unjust degree of simplification.

14. Mukhia (35-6, 55-6). Irfan Habib also suggests that the medieval Indian peasant 'was an independent producer' in 'Forms of Class Struggle in Mughal India' (1995: 235).
15. Since my familiarity with ancient Indian history is based on secondary

sources I requested three of my colleagues, B.D. Chattopadhyaya, Suvira Jaiswal and Romila Thapar, each a distinguished historian of ancient India, to help me out with primary evidence on this point; each has reported failure.

16. Sharma, in *Indian Feudalism* (1965: 61-3). The second edition of this book is a marginally revised version of the first.
17. Thus the Gurjara-Pratihara lineage arising in Rajasthan and extending at one stage to Bengal (Chattopadhyaya, 1983: 14); in south India the Vellalas, primarily peasants, had given rise to warriors from amongst their ranks (Stein, 1980: 187-8); the Chandellas too are said to have belonged to Gond or Bhar tribes and risen to become a substantial ruling lineage in central India (Thapar, 1984: 794); the Reddys of Andhra were a low-caste landowning community who rose to form the ruling stratum (Jaiswal, 1979-80: 35).
18. Currie (1980). Ms Currie was kind enough to send me a copy of her paper.
19. It has been suggested by Suvira Jaiswal that such an argument might amount to treating European developments as 'exceptional and unique' which in turn would be a Eurocentric vision of history (Jaiswal, 1979-80: 19, n. 3). I believe the 'rule' for Marxists is that all societies change and progress through social contradictions to which no society would be an exception; and neither Europe nor India was such an exception, certainly not the one in my vision. However, this 'rule' does not extend to a uniform pattern of development laid down by Europe even prior to the rise of capitalism; in the pre-capitalist world there was no 'rule' and no 'exception' as far as the patterns or stages of development were concerned in that different societies followed different paths into the world of capitalism/colonialism.
20. In a refreshing and original article, 'The Middle Classes and the Mughal Empire', Iqtidar Alam Khan has indeed argued for the existence of the 'middle classes' (or 'the middle stratum') in medieval India (1975: 113-41). However the 'middle classes' he has described were, despite some tensions, perfectly compatible with the agrarian economy of which they were a part; there was little possibility of their being 'the harbingers of a truly industrial bourgeoisie'.
21. See for a more elaborate argument and evidence Rana (1981: 287-326).
22. This was basically also the argument of my earlier article (especially 58-9), where an attempt was made to define the nature of social tensions in medieval India rather than to deny their existence or their intensity. Somehow Irfan Habib in his paper for this volume has seen in that argument an 'idyllic picture of pre-colonial India' for which he finds little justification in historical evidence and directs us to his own variant reading of the evidence set out in his *Agrarian System*. His own conclusion is that: '. . . there were just as intense contradictions as anywhere else; but that these were different in nature and consequences from the contradictions leading to capitalism in Europe' (193). One is left wondering, then, doesn't his own conclusion come perilously close to the one he has sought to dismiss by nothing more, as it were, than a wave of his hand?

REFERENCES

Anderson, Perry, 1974, *Passages from Antiquity to Feudalism*, London.

———, 1977, *Lineages of the Absolutist State*, London.

Bajekal, Madhavi, 1980, 'Rural Disputes in Eastern Rajasthan in the Eighteenth Century', M. Phil. dissertation, Jawaharlal Nehru University.

Bhattacharya, S., 1979, 'Notes on the Role of the Intelligentsia in Colonial Society: India from Mid-Nineteenth Century', *Studies in History*, Vol. 1, No. 1.

Bhattacharya, S., 1984, S.G. Deushkar Lecture, Centre for Studies in Social Sciences, Calcutta.

Block, Marc, 1964, *Feudal Society*, tr. L.A. Manyon, Chicago.

Chakravarti, Uma, 1985, 'Slavery and Bondage in Ancient India', in Utsa Patnaik and Manjari Dingwaney, eds., *Chains of Servitude: Bondage and Slavery in India*, Madras.

Chattopadhyaya, B.D., 1983, 'Political Processes and Structure of Polity in Early India: Problems of Perspective', Presidential Address, Ancient India Section, Indian History Congress, 44th Session.

Chattopadhyaya, Debiprasad, 1977, *Science and Society in Ancient India*, Calcutta.

———, 1980-81, 'Science, Philosophy and Society in Ancient India', *The Indian Historical Review*, Vol. VII, Nos. 1-2 (July-Jan.).

———, mimeo, 'Technology and Society in Ancient India'.

Currie, Kate, 1980, 'Problematic Modes and the Mughal Social Formation', *The Insurgent Sociologist*, Vol. IX, No. 4.

Dirlik, Arif, 1985, 'The Universalisation of a Concept: From "feudalism" to "Feudalism" in Chinese Marxist Historiography', *The Journal of Peasant Studies*, Vol. 12, Nos. 2 and 3 (Jan./April).

Duby, Georges, 1968, 'The Diffusion of Cultural Patterns in Feudal Society', *Past and Present*, No. 39 (April).

Forquin, Guy, 1976, *Lordship and Feudalism in the Middle Ages*, London.

Geertz, Clifford, 1964, 'Ideology as a Cultural System', in D. Apter, ed., *Ideology of Discontent*, New York.

Gopal, Lallanji, 1980, 'Ownership of Agricultural Land', *Aspects of the History of Agriculture in Ancient India*, Varanasi.

Gottlieb, Roger S., 1984, 'Feudalism and Historical Materialism: A Critique and a Synthesis', *Science and Society*, Vol. XLVIII, No. 1, pp. 1-37.

Habib, Irfan, 1963, *The Agrarian System of Mughal India*, Bombay.

———, 1971, 'Potentialities of Capitalistic Development in the Economy of Mughal India', *Enquiry*, New Series, Vol. III, No. 3 (Winter).

———, 1978, 'Economic History of the Delhi Sultanate—An Essay in Interpretation', *The Indian Historical Review*, Vol. IV, No. 2 (January).

———, 1982, 'Presidental Address', *Proceedings of the Indian History Congress*, 43rd Session.

———, 1985, 'Classifying Pre-Colonial India', *The Journal of Peasant Studies*, Vol. 12, Nos. 2 and 3 (Jan./April).

———, 1995, 'Forms of Class Struggle in Mughal India', in his *Essays in Indian History*, New Delhi.

Jaiswal, Suvira, 1979-80, 'Studies in Early Indian Social History: Trends and Possibilities', *The Indian Historical Review*, Vol. VI, Nos. 1-2 (July/Jan.).

Jha, D.N., 1979, 'Early Indian Feudalism: A Historiographical Critique', Presidential Address, Ancient India Section, Indian Historical Congress, 40th Session.

Jha, Vivekanand, 1975, 'Stages in the History of Untouchables', *The Indian Historical Review*, Vol. II, No. 1 (July).

Karashima, N., 1984, *South Indian History and Society: Studies from Inscriptions* AD *850-1800*, New Delhi.

Kautilya's Arthasastra, 1967 (tr. R. Shamasastry).

Khan, Iqtidar Alam, 1975, 'Presidential Address', Medieval India Section, *Proceedings of the Indian History Congress*, 36th Session.

Kosambi, D.D., 1975, *An Introduction to the Study of Indian History*, Bombay.

Kumar, Nand Kishore, 1979, 'Hydraulic Agriculture in Peninsular India (*c.* 300 BC to 1300 AD)', *Proceedings of the Indian History Congress*, 40th Session.

Long and Richardson, 1978, 'Informal Sector, Petty Commodity Production and the Social Relations of Small Scale Enterprise', in John Clammer, ed., *The New Economic Anthropology*, New York.

Marx, Karl, and Friedrich Engels, 1972, *On Historical Materialism*, Moscow.

Mazumdar, B.P., 1960, *Socio-Economic History of Northern India (1030-1194* AD*)*, Calcutta.

Mukhia, Harbans, 1978, 'The Ideology of the Bhakti Movement—The Case of Dadu Dayal', in D.P. Chattopadhyaya, ed., *History and Society: Essays in Honour of Professor Nihar Ranjan Ray*, Calcutta.

———, 1979-80, 'Maurice Dobb's Explanation of the Decline of Feudalism in Western Europe—A Critique', *The Indian Historical Review*, Vol. VI, Nos. 1-2 (July-Jan.).

———, 1981, 'Was There Feudalism in Indian History?', *The Journal of Peasant Studies*, Vol. 8, No. 3 (April).

———, 1985, 'Marx on Pre-Colonial India: An Evaluation', in Diptendra Banerjee, ed., *Marxian Theory and the Third World*, New Delhi.

———, 1993, 'Agricultural Technology in Medieval North India', in *Perspectives in Medieval History*, New Delhi.

Needham, Joseph, 1979, *The Great Titration: Science and Society in East and West*, London.

Perlin, Frank, 1985, 'Concepts of Order and Comparison with a Diversion on Counter Ideologies and Corporate Institutions in Late Pre-Colonial India', *The Journal of Peasant Studies*, Vol. 12, Nos. 2 and 3 (Jan./April).

Poulantzas, Nicos, 1978, *State, Power, Socialism* (tr. Patrick Camiller), London.

Prestwich, J.O., 1963, 'Anglo-Norman Feudalism and the Problem of Continuity', *Past and Present*, No. 26 (November).

Rana, R.P., 1981, 'Agrarian Revolts in Northern India during the late 17th and early 18th Century', *The Indian Economic and Social History Review*, Vol. XVIII, Nos. 3-4.

Raychaudhuri, Tapan and Irfan Habib, eds., 1982, *The Cambridge Economic History of India*, Vol. I, Cambridge.

Report of the Royal Commission on Agriculture, 1928, London.

Sharma, R.S. 1965, *Indian 'Feudalism*, Calcutta.

———, 1969, *Social Changes in Early Medieval India*, Delhi.

———, 1985, 'How Feudal was Indian Feudalism?', *The Journal of Peasant Studies*, Vol. 12, Nos. 2 and 3 (Jan./April).

Singh, Dilbagh, 1976, 'Caste and the Structure of Village Society in Eastern Rajasthan during the Eighteenth Century', *The Indian Historical Review*, Vol. II, No. 2 (January).

Stein, Burton, 1980, *Peasant State and Society in Early Medieval South India*, New Delhi.

———, 1985, 'Politics, Peasants and the Deconstruction of Feudalism in India', *The Journal of Peasant Studies*, Vol. 12, Nos. 2 and 3 (Jan./April).

Thapar, Romila, 1984, 'Legitimation politique et filiation: *le varna kshatriya en Inde du nord*', *Annales: Economies, Sociétés, Civilizations*, Vol. 39, No. 4 (July-August).

Wickham, C.J., 1985, 'The Uniqueness of the East', *The Journal of Peasant Studies*, Vol. 12, Nos. 2 and 3 (Jan./April).

Williamson, A.V., 1931, 'Indigenous Irrigation Works in Peninsular India', *The Geographical Review*, New York, Vol. XXI, No. 4 (October).

Yadava, B.N.S., 1973, *Society and Culture in Northern India in the Twelfth Century*, Allahabad.

The Feudalism Debate: The Turkish End—Is 'Tax-*vs.*-Rent' Necessarily the Product and Sign of a Modal Difference?

Halil Berktay

NOT ONE BUT TWO INTERCONNECTED CRITERIA FOR DISTINGUISHING MODES OF PRODUCTION

> Whatever the social form of production, labourers and means of production always remain factors of it. But in a state of separation from each other either of these factors can be such only potentially. For production to go on at all they must unite. The specific manner in which this union is accomplished distinguishes the different economic epochs of the structure of society from one another.
>
> Marx (1885/1967), 34 (*Capital* II, Part I, Chap. I, 'Second Stage: Function of Productive Capital')

> The specific economic form, in which unpaid surplus-labour is pumped out of direct producers, determines the relationship of rulers and ruled, as it grows directly out of production itself and, in turn, reacts upon it as a determining element. . . . It is always the direct relationship of the owners of the conditions of production to the direct producers—a relation always naturally corresponding to a definite stage in the development of the methods of labour and thereby its social productivity—which reveals the innermost secret, the hidden basis of the entire social structure, and with it the political form of the relation of sovereignty and dependence, in short, the corresponding specific form of the state. This does not prevent the same economic basis—the same from the standpoint of its main conditions—due to innumerable different empirical circumstances, natural environment, racial relations, external historical influences, etc., from showing infinite variations and gradations in appearance, which can be ascertained only by analysis of the empirically given circumstances.
>
> Marx (1894/1967), 791-2 (*Capital* III, Part VI, Chap. XLVII; 'Labour Rent')

One of my purposes in this article will be to pinpoint just what is useful and illuminating in Wickham's 'The Uniqueness of the East', and to strip away from that kernel other aspects that I think will hinder its full application in comparative history. Another will be to relate the issue to the Turkish debate over the nature of Ottoman society—a debate of which I am a part, and which echoes quite a few of the themes on which Indian historians play.

Some final notes will deal with the ultimate philosophical questions surrounding such discussions: given two alternatives of either (a) ascribing a different *modal dynamic* to each observed slice of concrete historical movement, or (b) handling such concrete historicities in terms of a more classical *base/superstructure dialectic*; can it be simply a matter of individual preference which we choose? So long as we define our terms clearly and remain internally consistent thereafter, will everything be all right? Or are there higher criteria, concerning the overall structure of Marxist theory and its value in practice, to which the problem of selecting a definitional, terminological framework should be referred?

POINTS OF AGREEMENT: TOWARDS A THEORY OF GLOBAL FEUDALISM

To that end, I shall first try to bring out the theoretical and methodological ambiguity of Wickham's article. With a lot of his premises, I am generally in agreement; with others, I believe I can show that he wanders from his initial, sounder perspective.

In terms of mostly explicit statements but also some extrapolations, our common ground covers five areas. These we may take in turn.

(1) Wickham criticizes and rightly dismisses 'the definition of feudalism . . . as . . . the existence of fiefs, vassals and military service based on contract' (Wickham, 116), as well as what he somewhat scornfully calls 'the private-justice-and-serfdom-and-labour-service version of the feudal mode' (Wickham, 118). Mukhia, says Wickham, sees feudalism as almost wholly specific to Europe 'because he defines it as constituted above all by labour service'. However 'very little of medieval Europe would be feudal if it were so' (Wickham, 115).

In Turkey, orthodox academic historians of a purely empiricist variety—like Omer Lütfü Barkan (1902-79) and Halil Inalcik—as well as proponents of the theory of the Asiatic mode of production (AMP)—Akat, Gürsel, Keyder, Divitçioglu—are united in holding the Ottoman Empire to have been non-feudal precisely because:

— *timars* (military fiefs) were non-hereditary;
— all fiefs whether large or small were handed out by the sultan (i.e. subinfeudation did not exist);
— timariot *sipahis* (small knights) did not exercise private judicial rights over the *reaya* (dependent tenants);
— and demesne production through compulsory labour services was exceptional within a generalized system of taxes and/or rents in kind.

The model of West European feudalism that is implicit in that argument is, of course, just what Wickham is rejecting, and is rather obsolete today.[1] Here, the chain of reception runs from Barkan to the others: it was the former who, trained in the narrowly legalistic formalism[2] of Western historiography in its 1850-1925 pre-Bloch phase, summarized that tradition in his authoritative articles of the late 1930s and the 1940s. During the Thermidor of the Kemalist Revolution, Barkan's particularism became the ruling orthodoxy in Turkish medieval studies.[3] After 1960, AMP-theorists, though searching for a Marxist interpretation, drank too deeply from that source of official ideology to be able to evade assimilating his peculiar theoretical assertions together with his empirical findings on Ottoman society.[4] With their inherited and outworn adherence to the yardstick of labour rent,[5] they would therefore do well to pay special attention when a professional Westernist of the present generation further notes that the three different forms of *feudal* rent did *not* correspond to three different economic systems (Wickham, 116); that demesne farming was not really predominant in the Western Middle Ages; and that even on the domesne, 'supervision tends to be counterbalanced by peasant customary practice' (Wickham, 136): 'Indeed, when they (the lords) do try to influence production, they do not always succeed; it is the peasant, after all, who actually does the producing under feudalism.'

More importantly, Wickham's observation that labour service did *not* constitute 'a landlordly control over the work-process different in *type* from that involved in the specification, say, of precise types of produce required as rent in kind' (Wickham, 115-16), directly cuts the ground from under the argument presented by Islâmoğlu and Keyder[6]—whose 1977 article Wickham unfortunately considers to be 'the analysis closest to mine' (Wickham, n. 36). On yet another aspect—state overlordship of the land—of alleged non-feudalism, which only too often is taken to be completely specific to the East, Wickham hints that it should be situated in the realm of superstructure: 'It is a theoretical possibility, of course, in any state society', therefore its mere existence 'certainly does not mean that such societies are "Asiatic" . . . ; William the Conqueror claimed no less full ultimate ownership' (Wickham, 129)—this last reminder nicely suggesting that as an example of relative centralization arising through orderly transplantation of already existing social stratification by conquest, the Ottoman case is not that original.[7]

(2) Empiricism is not simply a failure to use some magic words and phrases that are believed to be theoretical in themselves; nor is any professed allegiance to Marxism necessarily its antidote. Marc Bloch did not share the special jargon of historical materialism, but his *système sociale* was the functional equivalent of mode of production, and it was his careful application of this analytical tool that enabled him to achieve his goal of history as a science.[8] Completely overlooked by AMP-theorists, on the other hand, is Barkan's methodological point of departure—the Rankean assertion that 'the general resemblances which might result from a series of repeated abstractions' should concern only the sociologist; as for the historian, his interest must lie with 'the particularities of a given time and place', with accentuating 'particular forms' (Barkan, 1939: 675; also Berktay, 1983a: 84; Berktay, 1983b: 235; Berktay, 1985: 2470). Armed with this eclectic, agnostic affirmation of the existence of separate truths for History and Sociology, Barkan *would*, of course reduce the notion of feudalism to certain external features of the primitive physiognomy of the *early* Middle Ages in Europe, namely, large demesnes and extremely decentralized feodo-vassalitic relations. Mukhia shares the same premisses.

By contrast, Wickham (116) correctly rejects the idea that since 'in all other respects these latter societies (*ancien régime* France, Russia, Sung China, Qajar Iran, the late Roman Empire, etc.) are rather unlike Capetian France; . . . their modes of production cannot be the same, that is, cannot be feudal'. This indicates a methodological refusal to see each particular, concrete slice of historical reality (including its superstructural features) as a (different) mode of production in itself. Wickham would agree that any modal category can only be arrived at through theoretical abstraction moving upward/inward from a base of historical facts collected from *all* observed particularities corresponding roughly to the same main threshold in the development of productive forces. In other words, the general, abstract category of feudalism, whether by this or any other name, cannot be obtained simply by observing West European feudalism at this or that stage (even if the observations themselves are correct), and then transferring each and every one of its concrete characteristics on to the mode of production plane.

(3) Consistently with this, Wickham (113) insists that any 'Marxist' reversion—such as Perry Anderson's—to 'claims in traditional historical fashion for the historical uniqueness of specific areas' would necessarily go hand in hand with obliterating, in practice, the distinction between mode of production (theoretical abstraction), and society or socio-economic formation (historical concreteness) (see Wickham, 1984: 8, n. 9), by imploding into the modal level characteristics that properly belong to the superstructure, such as the form of the state, the legal formulae of surplus extraction, etc. This is justified, for Anderson does begin his crucial chapter with the announcement that 'the feudal *mode of production* that emerged in Western Europe was characterized by a complex unity' (shades of Blochian 'totality'), and ends that first paragraph with the following claim: 'This parcellization of sovereignty was constitutive of the whole feudal *mode of production*' (Anderson, 1974: 147-8; emphases added). Since 'complex unity' and 'parcellization (or any other from) of sovereignty' characterize not the mode but the actual society with all its superstructure, both opening and closing statements are misleading; between them, moreover, Anderson has indeed translated just about every detail of the West European historical landscape as a modal element. No analysis, no abstraction, no scale mapping; only description, even photography, a one-to-one reproduction of the original. 'Anderson . . . resolves the problem by *defining* a mode of production in terms of its superstructure—for feudalism, therefore, the political-military systems of vassalage and the rest', complains Wickham (116-17). In Hirst's words, 'this means that there can be as many modes of production as there are distinct legal-political constitutions and forms of extra-economic sanction which follow from them' (Wickham, 117; quoting Hirst, 1975: 462). For concrete historiography, this inevitably means that 'historical development *lies* in the history of the state, as Anderson would sometimes imply' (Wickham, 132). Therefore, 'Anderson is here abandoning Marxism—indeed, abandoning systematic economic analysis', Wickham (117) concludes.

I have dwelt on Wickham's criticism of Perry Anderson at such length because the latter's focus on 'parcellization of sovereignty' has, after all, exercised a great deal of influence; by now, it is woven into the very fabric of Turkish AMP–literature (for example, Keyder, 1976; Islâmoglu and Keyder, 1977; Akat, 1977). And it is not only Anderson that is at stake, for Wickham's entire approach amounts to a simultaneous refutation of Balibar as well. According to Balibar, a mode of production does not exist only at the economic level, but is an articulated combination of the economic, political and ideological levels (Balibar, 1967; Althusser and

Balibar, 1972). This automatically produces a different 'mode' fitted to every historical concreteness precisely because in reality, each historical concreteness is nothing but a different, specific articulation of these three levels. In other words, many 'modes of production' *revolving around the same basic relation(s) of production* (that is, the same economic level) *in the classical sense*, thereby become conceptually obtainable. Balibar actually melts basis and superstructure in one pot to call the resulting soup 'mode of production'; hence, if we accept Balibar's definition, there is no more room left within historical materialism for the relative autonomy of superstructure or its reciprocal effect on the economy—levers which in my view are the best safeguards against mechanical, unilinear economic determinism, and the proper tool for 'analysis of the empirically given circumstances', for 'concrete analysis' of 'a concrete situation', of 'precise and definite historical situations'.[9]

It is important to realise that for all Andersonian proliferations of pre-capitalist modes of production in the context of a seemingly 'Marxist' discourse, Balibar's definitional tampering is the requisite theoretical preparation. In Turkey, it is exactly this manipulation which makes it possible for some authors to *appear* to be undertaking 'economic analysis' on the way to asserting that the medieval West and the Ottoman Empire rested on different ('feudal' *vs.* 'Asiatic') modes of production, while actually using a version redefined to include the superstructure—a version, therefore, that is not really (only) the mode of production, but society in all its entirety, specificity and concreteness.

I refer to those AMP-theorists who, while tactically unwilling to let go totally of the idea of demesne production as somehow integral to feudalism,[10] have nevertheless recently moved towards a greater awareness of the essentially peasant character of occidental serfs, which tends to merge these with the Ottoman *reaya*.[11] How is it, then, that in the face of their own admissions concerning the 'strong tendency towards uniformity at the level of relations of production despite infinite superstructural variety' (Akat, 1977:48), such commentators persist in drawing a *modal* line of demarcation between East and West? Akat (1977: 36-7, 47) gives a clue when, after defining 'relations of production' purely at the economic level, on the pretext of overcoming 'economism', he (a) constructs 'property relations' through the articulation of the economic, political and ideological levels, and (b) grounds his own notion of 'mode of production' not on the 'relations of production' but on these 'property relations'. Since weak royal centre and hereditary fiefs for Capetian France versus strong imperial authority and state overlordship for the Ottomans are cast as different 'property relations', the desired modal distinction results. Idris Küçükömer (1977: 7, 10) has more openly declared that 'in sum . . . the relationship of political domination is included in the economic base', that political and ideological structures are not excluded from the basic structure but constitute its elements; hence they cannot be seen as apart from the economic base'. Finally, very significantly for my argument, Islâmoğlu and Keyder (1977: 56, n. 16) are conscious that 'the Asiatic mode of production exists as a mode of production, *provided that we accept the definition given in Althusser and Balibar* (1970)' (emphases added; also see Bailey and Lloberra, 1981: 316-17). They know, in other words, that the so-called AMP does not exist if mode of production in its usual sense of the economic basis of society is not merged with the superstructure in a new concept which bears the old name but is not that anymore.

This, Wickham is not aware of; and although he (114) lets drop a remark about 'the philosophers who have set out the complicated patterns in which mythic modes might behave', and goes on to counterpose that 'economic systems with their own procedures and logics of development cannot be unlimited', he refutes this tack directly only in Perry Anderson's case. Despite this failure to note the subtleties of Islâmoglu and Keyder—with 'the analysis closest to' his—Wickham himself concentrates on the (real) 'methods of surplus-appropriation', which must be reduced to a few basic types, as the proper means of classifying modes of production.

(4) As to the other leg of the argument for dividing the historical geography of pre-capitalism between 'feudalism' and 'the Asiatic mode of production', Wickham presents a critique of at least Marx's own original AMP concept on mostly empirical but also some theoretical grounds. At the factual level, he remarks that 'one or other or both of autarkic village communes, and a tax-raising state owning all landed property and carrying out large-scale necessary public works, are actually rather rare' (Wickham, 118). The so-called 'hydraulic state' is 'semi-mythical' (Wickham, 134); 'the absence of classes, another traditional feature, is nonsensical' (Wickham, 118); 'the very word (despotism) represents an abstention from sociological analysis' (Wickham, 132). Moreover, 'the Asiatic mode as it has always been formulated'—or: 'the traditionally defined Asiatic mode of production'—'cannot be regarded as having any analytical validity' (Wickham, 118). In words which are compatible with the anti-Balibar position set out above, 'the real problem about the Asiatic mode is that it is too politically and legally specific. Like the private-justice-and-serfdom-and-labour-service version of the feudal mode, it has

too many institutions arbitrarily attached to it for it to be of much help as an economic category' (Wickham, 118). Furthermore, Marx's AMP is singularly unfit to handle the Ottoman case. 'Indeed, the absolute predominance of state landed property . . . is a feature of societies so developed that village autarky and communality are effectively excluded' (Wickham, 118). Again, however primitive the *origins* of the absence of private property in land might be,

> it should be clear that only an unusually *developed* economic and political system was actually capable of maintaining it. Only the 'Islamic state' at its most centralized and sophisticated, at its most uncompromising, was able even to try to stop landed property from being *de facto* privatised. . . . The Ottomans could do it; the Qajar state, far less politically and economically developed, could not. . . . The extreme social forms of the Ottoman world that underlay what Marx sometimes called the 'Asiatic' mode were in fact at the opposite end of the run of human history from where he supposed. 'Static' is the least adequate adjective for the development towards the Ottoman state. (Wickham, 132)

On this basis, and almost for the benefit of some Turkish authors who are unaware of it, Wickham (118) talks of the 'loss of credibility' of the 'Asiatic mode' as an accomplished fact. Byres (26) adds in the same vein: ' . . . as far as the Asiatic mode is concerned, we must, of course, pay serious attention when a group of historians such as those represented in this volume, with mastery of modern knowledge of the societies in question, find no support for it'.

(5) Finally, Wickham (115) bases his own definition of feudalism on Hindess and Hirst's 'demonstration that the core of the feudal mode of production lies less in the political-juridical aspects of serfdom than in the rent extraction relationships *intrinsic to all pre-capitalist landlordship*'. The words I have italicized imply that rent here stands for the Political Economy concept of Rent as the general form of exploitation of pre-capitalist tenant-based production (comparable to Surplus Value for capitalism). Indeed, such a rent extractive relationship 'is not dependent on peasant unfreedom, for tenants can perfectly easily be legally free; it is their rent-paying . . . that defines their economic world as feudal, not their political subjection' (Wickham, 115). In contrast to those Turkish conservative academics and AMP-theorists who make much of the 'freedom' of the *reaya* as opposed to the 'unfreedom' of European serfs, this must by all rights include the Ottoman Empire.[12] Cleared, then, is the way, both empirically and analytically, for the re-establishment of a much broader, universal category *vis-à-vis* pre-capitalist history than those

involved in the derivation of 'multi-linearity' through a split between a Europe-specific 'feudalism' and one or more 'non-feudalisms' (including the AMP) covering the rest of the globe. Wickham (113), in fact, defines the basic outlook of his article as 'a critical response' to Mukhia's and Anderson's limitation of feudalism to Europe. Seen as a mode of production revolving around rent extraction, and without the requirement for dependent tenancy to take the form of servile tenancy, feudalism, he says, 'was a world system' (Wickham, 116).

POINTS OF DISAGREEMENT: WICKHAM'S EUROCENTRIST REVERSAL

After all this, why and how is it that Wickham persists in seeing most of Chinese, Iranian, Arab and Ottoman history as predominantly non-feudal?

The logic leading to that is composed of two main propositions. First, we are reminded that each concrete (historically existing, observable) society is probably a combination of several modes of production, among which, however, one must dominate the others (Wickham, 117). In other words, in the mental jump from the modal to the societal plane, Wickham *at this point* only proceeds from one mode to many, failing to mention explicitly that this move must also encompass he superstructure in all its relative autonomy and specific configuration.

Second, Wickham distances himself from the Political Economy concept of Rent implicit in his initial definition of feudalism, and comes to take rent and tax *as legally defined at a given time and place*, as two qualitatively different forms of surplus-appropriation, which he therefore considers to belong/correspond to two different modes of production. This involves drawing a sharp line between private landowning (or the 'patrimonial' form of domain, in Eric Wolf's (1966: 50ff.) Weberian terminology, of individual and hereditary lords over the land and the peasants, on the one hand, and the state's overriding rights (Wolf's 'prebendal domain'), on the other. 'Direct personal control of the land' is 'the feudal mode' (Wickham, 130); and rent extraction is no longer 'intrinsic to all pre-capitalist landlordship' (Wickham, 115) or the general form of drawing surplus from a peasantry (Wickham, 133), but something that only the private landowner does. Tax, on the other hand, while not equal to the 'traditionally defined Asiatic mode of production' (Wickham, 118), is the form of surplus extraction practised by 'a "state class" . . . with political rights' from 'a peasantry that it does not tenurially control'

(Wickham, 118). This 'simpler relationship represented by a state bureaucracy (whose bureaucracy? supra-class?) taxing a peasantry' (Wickham, 118) is all that Wickham retains of Marx's version of the AMP, and it is enough; for while he draws away from the other elements of that original model as well as its geographic name, what he holds on to is in a sense irreducible and crucial. In effect, it enables him to take Samir Amin's 'tributary mode' (which was invented to comprise both 'feudal' and 'Asiatic', 'patrimonial' and 'prebendal' variants), split it back into the two forms it was intended to unite, and arrive at 'tax (the state) and rent (private feudal landowning)' (Wickham, 132) as two separate modes of production.

Putting his two propositions together, then, Wickham argues that the 'feudal' and the 'tax' modes, equi-level in the sense that they are based on more or less the same productive forces, coexist in conflict throughout pre-capitalist history, which is therefore marked by an oscillation between these two poles. The medieval West is feudal because there and only there did the 'feudal mode' achieve predominance over the 'tax mode', while in the East the 'tax mode' never lost its ascendancy, never fully allowed the 'feudal mode' to break out from under its aegis, although there were periods in which it seemed as if the 'feudal mode' might do so.

Wickham, in other words, has changed only the terms of the universalism-*vs.*-particularism problematic; it is not that the 'feudal mode' does not exist at all in the East (and the 'tax mode' in the West), but that while both are globally present, the 'feudal mode' dominates Europe and the 'tax mode' rules over Asia. This perpetuates, therefore, the *essentialist consequences* of the more usual classification of pre-capitalist history. Others who see feudalism *explicitly* as having to do with private, hereditary fiefs and therefore as specific to Europe have also spoken of a *repressed* feudal potential existing elsewhere; thus, Guy Bois (1980: 62-3) claims that

> in all these broad areas—Western Europe, the Byzantine Empire, the Moslem world, India—we can probably observe the same *tendency towards the development of feudalism*: an unequal development, *victorious in Western Europe* and perhaps in Byzantium, helped on there by Westerners from the end of the eleventh century onwards.... But some of its elements, at least, are always present: *tendency* towards the establishment of great domains, the power of the military class, etc. (italics mine)

So much would be admissible by any Turkish empiricist academic;[13] among AMP-theorists, a picture of Ottoman society as incorporating a certain unaccomplished, immature movement towards feudalism has been put forth by Taner Timur (1979). Can Wickham say that his conception of the transition to feudalism is ultimately any different from theirs; that is, any different from a process of further and further privatization? As for the nature of the East, as Byres (28) notes,

> despite Wickham's assertions to the contrary, and despite his robust dismissal of the Asiatic mode, this tributary mode (Wickham's, not Amin's) bears more than a passing resemblance to that much-maligned notion. . . . What he seems to have done . . . is to re-formulate it—without village autarky and communality, and with class—and present it as a watered-down version. Are we not witnessing the Asiatic mode being sneaked in through the back door?

In Turkey, too, AMP-theory in the 1960s went through an early phase of trying to fit Marx's original sketch, inspired not by the medieval Near East but by the real East in Antiquity, and embodying a moment of societal evolution more backward than even the 'Ancient' or the 'Germanic' paths of dissolution of tribalism, to the Ottoman Empire. Efforts to discover large-scale irrigation works or internally undifferentiated village communes or lack of division of labour and commodity exchange between town and country in the Turkish Middle Ages proved unfruitful, however; the more so as the model of Ottoman society that AMP-theorists were sizing up against Marx's version was one that they had taken over from the conservative Ottomanists—an idealization, in other words, that had been stretched in the *opposite* direction to make it seem even more advanced than it really was, in fact to make it seem post-feudal. 'The economic and social structure of the (Ottoman) Empire', which after all had 'dominated the Near East for many centuries', could not be explained as 'a simple and primitive organism which had not even realised the stages of "slavery" and "feudalism" in the Marxian scheme of human development', grumbled Barkan (1973: 1).

Then in the second half of the 1970s, a younger generation of AMP-theorists, best represented by Akat (1977) and Islâmoğlu and Keyder (1977), retreated to more or less the same position as Wickham's in order to ensure that Ottoman society fitted *some* variant of *some* non-feudal mode of production. As indicated in sub-section 3 (of part one: 'Points of Agreement'), they half-accepted that West European feudalism was basically a peasant society, as the Ottoman Empire very obviously was;[14] to keep pre-conceived boundaries intact, they then equated feudalism with small producers plus individual lordship, and AMP with small producers plus strong state, and went on maintaining that the Ottoman regime was based not on the feudal but on the Asiatic mode of production. But as I have shown in that same sub-section 3, to do this, *they had explicitly to re-define the concept of mode of production itself, following Balibar, to include superstructures.* Wickham, however, *rejects this inclusion in principle.*

Thus, the dilemma of Wickham's article insofar as modal taxonomy is concerned becomes this. It presents a move towards universalism which, however, is still heavily burdened by an Asiatist particularism that derives from entanglement in superstructures without wishing to be so—a particularism reduced to its most crucial element, beyond which it is not possible to go without abandoning modal distinctions between East and West altogether. In other words, apparently from within the camp of single-mode universalism, Wickham's position acquires the character of a logical last defence for particularism, because he has granted so much to universalism already. That is why I am tackling his contribution rather than any other to the *JPS* Special Issue on *Feudalism and Non-European Societies.* If this trench, too, falls, it seems to me that there is none other left for AMP-theory or derivative standpoints.

INTERNAL CRITICISM: REPETITION OF MUKHIA'S, ANDERSON'S, BALIBAR'S ERRORS

Has Wickham really shown that privatization of landholding-*vs.*-the state's overlordship, rent-*vs.*-tax, is not simply a legal/formal distinction but a modal difference? Has he stuck to his promise 'to exclude political and legal definitions from . . . (his) counterpositions' (Wickham, 133), already foreshadowed by his open critique of Anderson's procedure? My initial, internal criticism will be addressed to this question; but I shall also, under the next heading, supplement this with an external critique by attempting to demonstrate that an alternative, non-modal explanation is perfectly possible for the phenomena which Wickham observes, which, therefore, invalidates his insistence that these phenomena *must* be the result and sign of a modal difference.

First, then, the internal, de-constructive critique. In his Section II, which makes up fully half of 'The Uniqueness of the East', Wickham only *assumes* that tax-*v.*-rent is a modal difference; he says he will prove this 'presupposition for my whole argument' (Wickham, 133) in Section III, and on the force of that assertion leads the reader through a rich historical account of the inner tension of Oriental history between centralization and decentralization. Being entirely cast in terms of the feudalism-*vs.*-non-feudalism dichotomy,[15] however, this elegant portrayal may easily leave one with the impression that the terminological choice for expressing it is inevitably the only one. This, of course, is not so: the story of that ebb and flow is at least as valid if cast in terms of the central state-

vs.-the local hereditary aristocracies, or in terms of state feudalism-*vs.*-private feudalism, etc.

The point is that when we do get to Section III of Wickham's article, we are not given the promised proof. It is worth noting, in this connection, that Marx provides not one but two criteria for distinguishing modes of production, which on closer examination can be seen to be linked logically. These are the two quotes, from *Capital*, Vols. II and III respectively, that I have placed at the head of this article.

For me, therefore, adequate proof would have to consist of the following:

(a) A demonstration that in the case of the 'feudal' or 'rent mode' on the one hand, and the 'tax mode' on the other, we are faced with two different ways in which the direct producers and the means of production are combined;

(b) A further demonstration that *out of these* two different 'ways of combining', there *necessarily flow* two different economic types of surplus extraction;

(c) A final demonstration that a + b together determine two different essential class structures. All this may also be expressed by saying that we have to be shown two different social forms of existence of labour-power; two different basic relations of production between a (different) principal producing class and a (different) principal exploiting class.[16] The criterion of forms of surplus extraction is acceptable only insofar as it is a shorthand for the whole of this; wherever it is divorced from an understanding of the relationship of the direct producers to the primary and secondary means of production, however, the danger of confusing economic types with legal forms (with 'forms' formally understood) will immediately arise.

I think this is precisely the trap into which Wickham falls in his supposition that tax and rent are automatically different forms of surplus extraction. As already indicated, he is taking the subjective, legal perception of these levies in isolation from a specific type of producer, a social form of existence of labour-power, a certain basic exploited class. Thus in Section III, he in fact admits that he knows both the 'tax mode' and the 'rent mode' to be based on the *same* combination of direct producers with the means of production, namely, peasants in effective possession of their own small economies: 'the two (tax and rent) are sometimes difficult to tell apart, and sometimes, as in the Ottoman state, even fused . . . the latent reason for this (is) that both are modes of surplus extraction based on peasant production, individual or collective' (Wickham, 133). Therefore,

> there is a strong if varied body of experts who do not distinguish between tax and rent at all, or, to be more exact, who see them as centralized (public and private) variants of the same economic system, which most of them call feudal. A good percentage of Soviet scholars would say this, for example; so would Amin, though he calls the whole mode tributary; so, from different positions, would the French Byzantinist Éveline Patlagean. This is certainly a better stance than that of those who have a much-more Western-based definition of feudalism, and try and fit Asia to it. . . . ' (Wickham, 133)

To this, Wickham's first objection is that 'almost all of world history would thus come under the same heading'—of this, more in the final part below. 'But the major problem about this formulation is that its presupposition is that all extra-economic surplus extraction from a peasantry has to have the same economic form; has to be the same mode of production. Is this really true?' (Wickham, 133). Since he has already closed to himself the alternative path of trying to show that tax-*vs.*-rent *grows out of* more deeply underlying economic differences—a path which would necessitate going back to demesne production and *corvées* as an essential feature of 'feudalism' and 'feudal rent', for only there do we have a really different, non-peasant combination of producers and means of production[17]—Wickham's attempt to demonstrate that tax and rent are qualitatively distinct forms of surplus extraction has to revolve around the idea, at the other end of the causality chain, that they are different because they might *make* an economic difference.

Difference for whom—for the peasants? Wickham cannot say that this is directly so: it is doubtful 'whether peasants themselves ever saw tax and rent as separable' (Wickham, 128); more strongly,

> seen existentially from the peasant standpoint, there might seem not to be a lot of difference between them in that they are both unnecessary outgoings enforced, ultimately, by extra-economic coercion of various kinds. The peasant's perception of this equivalence is most evident when he is also the tenant of a landlord, for in most tax-raising societies (through not all), tax under these circumstances is passed on by the landowner, who has extracted it in the rent-taking process. (Wickham, 133)

Wickham therefore has to take the roundabout way of first proving that tax-*vs.*-rent extraction patterns cause the ruling classes to adopt different behaviour patterns; and second, that these in the end have different impacts on the economy as a whole.

Even here, however, his sense of historical realism will not allow him to exaggerate. Orthodox Turkish Ottomanists and AMP-theorists alike hold the European feudal lord to have been *directly* engaged in production as the manager of one large, integrated agricultural enterprise, in contrast to the Ottoman timariot who in his capacity as pure 'tax collector' is supposed to have had *absolutely nothing* to do with production.[18] Wickham, after a lot of qualifications,[19] confines himself to this more careful formulation: 'One can say that the difference between the ruling classes of the feudal and the tributary modes is between the *relative separation* of the former and the *near-total separation* of the latter from the processes of production . . . ' (Wickham, 137). Furthermore, it is not true that 'the tributary mode involves no economic relationship at all between ruler and ruled; the link is not just arbitrary, based on the motiveless extraction of surplus;[20] instead,

> there is a *positive* contrast in the methods and aims of economic interventions inside the two modes. And it is for this reason, too, that state tax-raising and coercive rent-taking by landlords cannot be conflated. . . . Their differences, their antagonisms, lie in their divergent interventions in the peasant economy. (Wickham, 137)

What the eventual outcome of these 'divergent interventions' might be, Wickham does not specify. Most AMP-theorists would have put it this way: the predominance of the central state inhibits development; by contrast, 'feudal' decentralization provides better opportunities for the emergence of the pre-conditions of capitalism because individual lords cannot control peasants and/or towns and merchants as effectively. This is why captialism came out of feudalism in the West, and therefore, why only the West should be called feudal, they claim: different dynamics, different historical outcomes; hence, different modes of production.[21] Anderson's position that with a universal category of feudalism, 'the unique western development towards capitalism becomes inexplicable' (Wickham, 116), is obviously similar.

I bring this last example up intentionally, for despite Wickham's critique of the methodology of *Passages from Antiquity to Feudalism*, his approach is at this point moving visibly closer not only to AMP-theory but also to Anderson's. To hypotheses concerning adverse consequences of relative centralization *after a point*, I have no *a priori* objection. Once past its initial ascendancy in which state-building played a progressive role in the deepening of feudal relations of production (in the Hilton sense and in the Hindess and Hirst sense; not in Wickham's sense of privatization of rent extraction), it is quite possible:

(a) That the Ottoman Empire possessed greater ability than Western representatives of a fragmented sovereignty to bring back runaway peasants and re-attach them to the land;

(b) That as compared with the degree of urban autonomy in the West, the full integration of towns into the political fabric of the Turkish state as the very seats of power meant that here, '*stadtluft macht nicht frei*';

(c) That the existence of one uniform authority covering both town and country, plus the close relationships of mutual support and supervision between Ottoman guilds and the state, implied fewer chances of success for breakaway attempts at developing extra-guild production: whereas in Western Europe, merchant capital, stifled by craft guild-dominated urban communes, could, when the need arose, take to the countryside and seize control of scattered peasant production there, the Ottoman state always heeded the complaints of guildmasters in this regard to stamp out much more efficiently similar undertakings everywhere;

(d) That especially from the sixteenth century onwards, when Imperial expansion reached its limits and the profits of war ceased to cancel out its outlays, the vast Ottoman administrative and military machine weighed too heavily on the backs of the *reaya*, giving rise to a fiscal super-exploitation which hindered expanded reproduction of the peasant economy and hence reduced the amount of agricultural surplus that could enter town-country trade networks and there undergo commodization;

(e) That for all these reasons taken together, internal polarization of petty commodity production and proto-industrialization in Ottoman society was at least delayed until a point where Western capitalism, which had arisen independently in the meantime, overtook this area of relative retardation, decisively asserted its hegemony, and created Turkish underdevelopment.

From work done so far, there seems to be some evidence for much of such provisional assertion,[22] and in any case they can only constitute so many topics for careful empirical investigation—together with, of course, climate and soil conditions, cultivation techniques and land: labour ratios, which also impinge heavily on peasant productivity and on the possibilities for developing commodity production under feudalism.[23] The questions I would pose are: In what way is all the above any different from saying that the relative centralization of the Ottoman Empire *provided a stronger, more rigid superstructural barrier* to the dissolution of pre-capitalist relations of production than the legal-political constitution of feudalism in Western

Europe? Supposing every such statement concerning the ultimate effects of centralization-*vs.*-decentralization[24] to be empirically verifiable; what is here that cannot and should not be handled—if we are to stick to rejecting Balibar-type manipulations—within the theoretical category of *different impacts on the same economic base of different, specific superstructural configurations?* Observe that in the Wickham quotes given above, the 'economy' subjected to 'divergent interventions' is the *same* 'peasant economy'; it is *only* 'the methods and aims of economic interventions' emanating from the ruling class(es) that are different: from there, Wickham can get to '*two* modes' only if he aggregates both the same 'peasant economy' and the 'divergent interventions' of the polity *inside* the concept of mode of production. That, however, would be equivalent to Anderson's and Balibar's inclusion of superstructure at the modal level, and thus inconsistent with Wickham's earlier theoretical choices.

This is why I wish Wickham had realised that the move from the modal to the societal level implies not only the possible juxtaposition of several relations of production, but also the juxtaposition of these with superstructures. Note also that the definition of 'tax' as the distinct form of surplus extraction by a 'state class', through certain 'political rights', from 'a peasantry that it does not tenurially control' (Wickham, 118)—apart from the fact that its implicit imputation of the absence of tenurial control to the Ottoman system is empirically wrong[25]—reverts to the criterion of tenurial (private)-*vs.*-non-tenurial (public) control as a distinguishing feature of feudalism. Is not this specific, narrowed-down concept of tenurial control that allegedly characterises only the 'rent mode', something that is very close to the old 'private justice' formulation, and therefore also definitely superstructural? Alternatively put, why should we consider the capacity of some states to control peasantries without the intermediary of fief-holders (although that is not the Ottoman case), or to keep those fief-holders in check (which is what the Ottoman case is all about), as a non-superstructural element?

This brings me to a curiously original aspect of Wickham's argument: his peculiar distinction between 'legality' and 'power'. Wickham admits that 'public-*vs.*-private . . . cannot define an *economic* opposition. . . . The formal constitution of the state, and the legal characterisation of landed property, are equally superstructural.' However, 'what matters for the constitution of states . . . is not so much law as power' (Wickham, 133-4). For example, 'the Saljuqs in Turkey, and, still more, the Ottomans, went beyond this: (in contrast to William the Conqueror) they did not merely have eminent rights; they owned. This difference does not turn on legal prerogatives; it turns on power' (Wickham, 129). Again, the ability of the Ottoman state repeatedly to stop 'feudalization' (Wickham, 131-2). Wickham seems to be saying that whereas 'legal form' is superstructural, 'power' is not only product but even part of the mode of production.

This is awkward and artificial. It is one thing to argue that legal forms (or appearance) and reality are not the same thing in history; that you have to have the legal form of royal eminent rights really backed up by a certain degree of power (say, in the form of a salaried central army and bureaucracy), in order to be able, for example, centrally to control fief allocation. It is another thing to say that 'legal form' and 'power' do not operate at the same (superstructural) level.

In actuality, legal form and political-military power are both distinct and interrelated. Legal forms derive their existence from, and crystallize, real power relations between the ruled and the ruling classes, or between different sections of the ruling classes, or between different states, at a given point in time. But of course their existence may be prolonged, and often is, beyond that point, with the result that they turn into hollow shells. A new balance of power between the ruling class as a whole and the peasantry, or between the king/emperor and his primary vassals/functionaries, or between barons and knights, etc., may initially erode the old forms and then create new forms in their place. This will mean a change of superstructural configuration; it may involve the assumption of a more 'aristocratic' or a more 'bureaucratic' appearance by the basic exploiting class. *Given* the fundamental substratum of 'peasant economy', the specific power relations (the power of the centre *vs.* local power or *vs.* the power of fief-holders or *vs.* the power of the hereditary founding aristocracy) within the ruling class, that in turn stamp the superstructure with this or that legal form, will generally be the product of 'historical circumstance' in the broadest sense; more rigorously, they will be the product of the specific genesis process of the specific medieval polity in question. Feudal land-rights are usually a combination and interlocking of (a) the king's/emperor's highest overlordship; (b) the rights of the aristocratic/bureaucratic fief-holders and/or the landowners; (c) the rights of the village community; (d) the rights of the peasant household. These various strata exist in practically every case; it is their internal balance or mix that varies, and that is very much a matter of degree-of-power-expressed-as-legal-form. By virtue of one ducally/royally led eleventh century act of conquest, the centre of developed Norman feudalism, taken out of France and superimposed on Anglo-Saxon feudalism, achieved a greater concentration of 'eminent rights', a more orderly fief system, and greater leverage for royal courts and taxation than was possible in the country of its incubation, but not enough, for example, to prevent subinfeudation. By virtue of another, much later act of conquest in the Eastern Mediterranean and in an epoch when firearms prevailed (hence the appellation by McNeill (1967) and Hodgson (1974) of 'gunpowder empires'), the Ottoman centre concentrated enough extra power—and gave it legal form—to also prevent subinfeudation and hereditary privatization of fiefs granted out of state land. This state of affairs, moreover, lasted not indefinitely but until the end of the sixteenth century, after which local dynasties of *eşraf* and *âyân* began to make themselves more and more felt. Hence the Ottoman degree of royal power was indeed greater but not by so much as to eliminate all potential social sources of centrifugal tendencies.

Wickham does not even think of calling William the Conqueror's state 'non-feudal' in contrast to 'feudal' Capetian France. What, then, is the logic of calling the Ottoman state 'non-feudal' in contrast to William's 'feudal' one? Why is William's degree of power a non-modal quality but that of the Ottomans supposedly enough to prove a modal distinction?

The point I am trying to make is that difference of degree of power does not necessarily mean difference of type of power involved. Treating a certain manifestation of state power as indicative of the dominance of a non-feudal mode of production is justified if and only if it can be *separately* shown that such a non-feudal mode actually exists at the economic level, and that the state power in question derives from and rests on—is the superstructure of—that non-feudal mode.

We need to be convinced, in other words, that the unfamiliar-looking state power before us is not actually exhibiting the secondary characteristics imparted by quantitative accretions within the same, feudal mode of production—such as three more centuries (from 1066 to the Ottomans) for the maturation of the relations of production; a higher (but still pre-capitalist) degree of trade and money economy permitting the maintenance of a standing army as a counterweight to the more traditional territorial cavalry; the additional presence of firearms. The basic way of doing this would be to demonstrate that the state whose centre manages to curb its fief-holders and/or landowners, and to maintain its own tax-rights represents *not* just a sub-section, a superior faction of the same ruling class that also includes these fief-holders, etc., *but* a different ruling class which obtains the surplus it lives on in an entirely different economic way.

Since *all* states, in East or West, whether slave, feudal, capitalist or socialist, tax, the bare fact of taxation tells us nothing about what mode and what class it arises from, what basic form of surplus it feeds on. Now the question of who the state represents is best answerable by looking at the fundamental class-content of its codes, at the system of exploitation they legitimize, at the class interests they write into 'justice'. Thus, for the capitalist mode of production, we have bourgeois law, which overall embodies not just the specific interests of this or that section of the bourgeoisie, but first and foremost its general interests by absolutizing private property and sanctifying the 'freedom' of the market process. Its counterpart for the feudal mode of production is a set of laws, whether 'private' or 'public', customary or formal in origin and dressing, which materially and morally, in theory and in practice, disarm the peasantry while arming the whole host of landlords and warlords, palatial functionaries and fief-holders, so as to ensure the transfer of agricultural surplus from the former to the latter class. The *re*distribution of this surplus within the ruling class and the provision of legal forms for this purpose may also be settled by these codes, but is decidedly secondary. At the end of this third part, I shall show that Wickham observes correct procedure in handling the class *continuity* between the decentralized phase of Western feudalism and its epoch of absolutism. But for claims of *disparity* in state power: can he show that the Ottoman centre with its tax-powers represented a different ruling class (based on a different mode of production) from the mass of its fief-holders *it delegated most of its tax-rights to*? It is impossible to show any such thing: Ottoman law did regulate the special interests of the Crown—by giving to the sultan sole authority for all fief grants, holding the small *sipahis* to relatively low revenues, making rapid rotation the rule in larger fiefs, and creating an 'independent' judiciary—but *before* all this, it created a typical medieval estate-system of 'the military' and 'the peasantry', each hereditary in itself; it tied the peasantry to the land and forced them to pay their taxes to the *sipahis*, their fief-holders; therefore it set up a regular transfer whereby the military class (the *askerîs*) composed of the sultan and the large-medium-small fief-holders absorbed the surplus produced by the peasantry in predetermined proportions among themselves. What was specific to the Ottoman 'legal form' was the formulation of this surplus extraction as 'taxation', by which stroke fief-holders also acquired the visage of 'a state class'.

This is purely superstructural, however, not 'economic analysis'; moreover, it is more concerned with the sphere of *redistribution* than with the sphere of *production*, with intra-ruling class contradictions than with the principal class structure itself. And Wickham comes close to admitting as much when he says that 'the problematic of the tributary mode concentrates on the state', or when he describes what he has done as characterizing the opposition 'between tax (the state) and rent (private feudal landowning) *principally at the political level of my various social formations*' (Wickham, 132; emphases added). The affinity with that second generation of Turkish AMP-theorists who, retreating before orthodox Ottomanists' empirical criticisms *vis-à-vis* attempts to ascribe Marx's own pre-slave model to the Ottoman Empire, have undertaken the same step as Wickham while continuing to call *their* version 'the Asiatic mode of production' (instead of 'the tax mode') is here too strong to miss. As with Akat (1977), Küçükömer (1977), and Islâmoğlu and Keyder (1977), Wickham's 'tax mode' *has to* rest on including 'the political level' in the mode of production.

Long-term applications of these concepts, furthermore, lead to problems which again and again reflect the kinship between Wickham, Turkish AMP-theorists, and more traditional historians. I have already indicated (see note 13) that Halil Inalcik, the empiricist Ottomanist *per se*, operating with a crude definition of feudalism as decentralization, is in the habit of treating relatively centralized stages (b) . . . (d) . . . (f) . . . of Seljukid-Ottoman history as 'non-feudal' while being inclined to admit that other, relatively decentralized stages (a) . . . (c) . . . (e) . . . were perhaps 'feudal'. This is strange enough; but since Inalcik, instead of conceiving of feudalism as an economic system, uses it to denote only a particular form of the state, and is not interested in questions of comparative history, it may not bother him to have hypothesized a periodic alternation of 'feudalism' with 'non-feudalism' through some four or five centuries when we know and he knows the economy not to have changed greatly. However, if anyone insists on not giving up the mode of production category and at the same time implodes superstructures like political forms back into the level of mode of production, that cycle of centralization and decentralization will now be portrayed as an oscillation between the 'feudal *mode of production*' and the 'Asiatic *mode of production*'. So much has actually been asserted by Akat through his theory that the 'feudal mode' and the 'Asiatic mode' are equi-level and mutually transformable into each other.[26] In Wickcham's formulation, the same oscillation would be between the predominance of the 'tax mode' and the weakening of that predominance. But it would still be an oscillation expressed in systemic or modal terms.

How correct and scientific is it to maintain that from Manzikert to Lepanto, Anatolian Turkish society changed its mode of production three or four times? In what way does it enhance our understanding of the eleventh-sixteenth centuries to say so? For me, the patent impossibility of that position is a teacher by negative example. Clearly, any conceptualization that loses sight of the basic socio-economic unity of this period must be kept away from; by contrast, failure to break fully with Inalcik-type notions raises the danger of falling back to the idea that 'historical development *lies* in the history of the state, as Anderson would sometimes imply'. As the Ottoman state developed through successive conquests, it first consolidated and codified locally existing 'rents' as 'taxes', and then allocated the tax-collection rights of specific localities as fiefs to timariots. Traditional Turkish Ottomanists like Barkan and Inalcik claim that this meant a 'liberation' *en masse* of the Balkan peasantries from 'serfdom', therefore from 'feudalism'.[27] But does it make sense for Wickham as a Marxist to see this as a switch from the 'rent' to the 'tax' mode of production? As royal power grew in the medieval West, state taxation gradually superimposed itself upon private lords' rent extraction.[28] Should we consider this as the emergence of the 'tributary mode', and by the same token ascribe to it the earlier centralization of England, while the 'rent mode' still prevailed on the continent? No, says Wickham at this point, because 'such taxation is generally regarded as a concentrated version of feudal rent'.[29] Therefore the absolutism of the Later Middle Ages in Europe remains: feudal absolutism; the class which taxed was not a different, non-feudal ruling class. Why, then, when *sipahis* cannot be shown to have been very different from European lords in their relationship to peasant production, Ottoman taxation and Ottoman absolutism are called 'non-feudal', I cannot understand.

EXTERNAL CRITICISM: AN ALTERNATIVE EXPLANATION

My de-constructive critique of Wickham ended with a note on what happens to the dialectice between tax and rent as feudalism develops and enters its later stages; I will now focus on the specific genesis of each feudalism, or better, of each feudal state and its fief system, as a *non-modal* explanation of this tension and alternation. For the biggest weakness of Wickham's position is that the distinctions between 'private' and 'public', 'rent' and 'tax' are explicable simply by tracing out the twin processes of class formation and state formation. Wickham ascribes all phenomena that he has not thought back to their historical origins, to a modal difference. This develops within the lacuna in his treatment where he dwells on the *effects* of state survival and state action, but does not pose the question of *how* and *at what point* this or that state came into being in the first place.

It is a basic principle of historical materialism that while states have a class content, they also have a life of their own in relative autonomy from the ruling class whose overall interests they systematically represent. Thus there will always be a certain underlying tension between the daily, spontaneous socio-economic existence of the ruling class (or sections or individual members thereof), and its own state; they may move more apart and then come closer, but rarely will they exactly overlap. The American bourgeoisie lives directly off surplus value; the American state taxes everyone, and it also taxes part of this surplus value which would otherwise be added to the fund of distributed profits; the bourgeoisie resents this and different ruling class parties or factions have policy debates over the tax rate, but all keep on paying taxes just the same; somewhat different tax structures exist in, say, Germany, Spain, Brazil, England and Sweden, each of which represents not just the capitalist mode of production but also a given sum of historical circumstances, including this or that degree of class conflict/compromise and this or that degree of tension between the state and the bourgeoisie; all this does not mean that the state rests on a 'tax mode' distinct from capitalism, nor that the bourgeoisie is a class separate and different from the 'state class'.

In parallel fashion, my claim for pre-capitalism is that the various interpenetrations of *feudal tax* and *feudal rent* are nothing but so many reflections of the various ways in which the feudal state's 'eminent rights' and the more particular land-rights of the feudal ruling class may meet in conflict and submerge one another within one specific synthesis, which then gives way to another specific synthesis as the balance of power changes. More concretely, each such conjunction of the feudal state and the feudal ruling class will be a product of:

(a) when and how the rise of a rent extracting class ('aristocracy') overtakes the peasant substratum;
(b) when and how the development of the state overtakes a stratified society composed of peasants and aristocrats;
(c) the extent to which this state will then be able to send its own apparatus, its fief system as the carrier of its own 'eminent rights', downward and outward into the society surrounding it, be able thereby to reorganize the old or independent or previous aristocracy around itself, and then be able to limit the inevitable centrifugal tendencies of the stratum of fief-holders, which may be drawn from old or new origins, and which may further continue to coexist, clash and mingle with hereditary proprietors, local gentry, entrenched families.

Throughout, the state is always essentially the state of the entire feudal ruling class endowed with—various sorts of—legal and political rights to subject and exploit the peasantry; most importantly, endowed with a *class monopoly*—whatever the degree of privatization this monopoly might undergo—of that principal and irreproducible means of production, the land.

As perceived concretenesses, all feudal state societies are the products of both a common material basis *and* of specific genesis processes woven out of many 'accidental' factors such as climate, geography, ethnicity, culture, fate in war, conquest.[30] I define the essence of feudalism, or *feudalism as a mode of production*, in similar fashion to Hilton, to Hindess and Hirst, to Amin's 'tributary mode', and to Wickham himself as summarized in point of agreement 5 above (provided we do not legalistically narrow the concept of rent). Feudalism is the juxtaposition of a rent-collecting aristocracy (including effective aristocracies disguised bureaucracies or 'state classes' by the convolutions of relatively strong state apparatuses), in an exploitative and contradictory relationship, with a class of peasant direct producers in possession of their own small economies, who for that reason have to be tied to the land and otherwise coerced extra-economically to make possible the appropriation of all or part of their surplus labour. This fundamental class structure corresponds to and is determined by that level of productive forces which roughly speaking emerged with the Neolithic Revolution, and comprises field-cultivation based on organic energy plus hand implements, capable of sustained surplus production as well as reproduction of the peasant family. That common material threshold which makes a society feudal by causing it to rest on the feudal mode of production, I would call the *primary determinant* of every feudal society. However, each such society is not just the feudal mode but also its entire superstructure, which, moreover, comes into being as a concrete historical reality through a specific genesis process woven by innumerable hazards, and each such society thereby also incorporates elements of the past of the soil on which it arises. It may, then, usefully be considered as the simultaneous product of a *secondary determination* which imparts its secondary, distinguishing characteristics to that given feudal society.

At the modal level, *the* transition to feudalism comprises the *simultaneous formation* of a dependent peasantry as the basic productive class on the one hand, and, opposing it, a rent-collecting aristocracy that subjects this peasantry as it rises on its shoulders by gradually concentrating the overlordship of the land in its hands. But each specific transition to feudalism is somehow different.

As the most basic types, there are cases in which (as in most parts of the world) the dissolution of tribal society leads directly into feudalism, and other (rare) cases in which slavery has intervened, so to speak, between primitive communalism and feudalism, so that, as in the Mediterranean, feudalism supersedes not tribalism but a collapsing slave civilization. Then again, this last 'passage from Antiquity to feudalism' may combine within itself the jump of one ethnicity (the Romans) from the slave mode to the feudal mode and the jump of another ethnicity (the Germans) from the tribal mode to the feudal mode. Around these main paths may revolve sub-cases of the essentially internal origin of the ruling class and/or the state (the original Indian *rajas*, whenever that was), and sub-cases which mix internal with external derivation (confluences of: German warriors, Roman estate owners and Gallo-Roman village chieftains; Mongol overlords and Chinese bureaucrats; Anglo-Saxon thegns and Norman barons; Arab or Persian or Turkish *iktâ/timar* holders and Persian or Turkish village *dihkân*). These in turn may be the result of waves of feudalization arising through great conquests in which ethnically homogeneous, semi-nomadic proto-feudal victors *take over* the defeated feudal state whose fabric nevertheless survives (the Oghuz irruption into eleventh-century Iran; in a sense Ottoman expansion in Thrace and Anatolia), or of waves of feudalization arising after ethnically heterogeneous, agriculturalist proto-feudal victors accelerate the complete dissolution of the dying post-slave state, creating a relatively empty space for their own diverse, disparate polities (the birth of the Western barbarian kingdoms). And of course all these may take place in very many different centuries and regions, each with its own degree of development of communications technology, money economy and weaponry—sub-variants within the limits of the main threshold which forms the *primary determinant.*

These considerations have some bearing on the eventual configuration of that striking feature of feudal societies that is called a fief system. What is its primary determinant?

Medieval statehood calls for the solution, within the context of primitive levels of transport and monetization, of the double problem of maintaining the basic producing class, spread out over the face of the earth, in subject and tax-paying status (in other words, preventing any evasion of surplus transfer), and of sustaining, with a part of these revenues, the army and the bureaucracy. Whatever the starting point may be, the typical method adopted sooner or later is to distribute the land, together with the peasant families attached, in the form of at least initially conditional allocations of *pronoia* (Byzantium), *beneficium* or *feodum* (Western Europe), *kat'ia* (classical Islam before the Turks), *iktâ* (the Seljukides of Iran and of Anatolia), *timar* (the Ottomans), etc., to commanders and soldiers; it must be added that in a society divided into estates, where the exploited are entirely disarmed, there is a close correspondence between the army and the greater part of the ruling class. That is to say, the aristocracy, by means of a fief system, positions itself to appropriate landed income at the source; at the same time, it spreads itself out over the land in order to make sure that the peasantry is effectively supervised and exploited on the spot, that law and order is maintained, that local defence is promptly organized against external attack. The primary and secondary distributions of the social product (the flow of surplus from the producers to the ruling class, and its subsequent sharing out among members of that ruling class) is there simultaneously achieved according to the hierarchy of these fiefs or *timars*. In all medieval societies, furthermore, those who receive fiefs assume the same sorts of obligations towards the donor—the royal centre itself and/or lords who have themselves received their fiefs from the royal centre or from others. It is a secondary matter whether such a relationship is the outcome of reciprocal initiative, of the adherence of a weak warlord to a more powerful one, or of rules established by a locus of superior power stronger than either.

Even though, as in the case of the Later Roman Empire, one may have a society in which feudal relations of production are evolving between landowners and peasants but the machinery of direct administration that is the heritage of a 'slave-commercial' past (Cameron, 1977: 434) has not yet broken down into a fief system; and also societies where, as in Merovingian and Carolingian times, the ideological pressure of an admiration for the Roman tradition leads to attempts to repair that outworn machinery, the impossibility of that task is inevitably realised and all feudal states turn to fief allocation *in the long run*. That is why Marc Bloch (1940/1966: 446) was justified in citing 'widespread use of the service tenement (that is, the fief) instead of a salary, which was out of the question' in second place in his definition of feudalism. But this necessity is also the beginning point of a permanent tension within the ruling class between the centre of fief distribution and its beneficiaries; between king and baron, suzerain and vassal, emperor and *pronoiaire*, sultan and *iktâdar* or *muktaî*, padishah and timariot. Reasons which render fief allocation inevitable are also reasons which create all kinds of difficulties for the centre in its efforts to keep control of fiefs in any fairly large country. All systems of enfeoffment therefore engender the *potential* of autonomization of the title-holders and of the privatization of fiefs in the distant provinces. What will happen after that point, where the balance of forces between the distributing centre and the beneficiaries will come to rest in the future, whether the superior donor will be able to conserve its original authority or not, will depend on the historical specificities of each feudal society, therefore on what I have called its secondary determinants.

'Tributary states . . . normally co-existed with feudal ownership' notes Wickham (132). This is an insight, but the contrived use of the two adjectives 'tributary' and 'feudal' clouds it; that states and landowners coexist would have better gone to the heart of the matter. Take, for example, a hypothetical path of purely internal feudalization in an ancient and geographically isolated tribal society. Along this path, between

(1) a totally collectivistic village community that is as yet subject to no exploitative hierarchy,

and

(3) mature feudal society, based on a *village* that still exists as a certain communal bond, but which has travelled quite a bit along the road of internal differentiation to turn into an agglomeration of *individual family holdings*, and with a chieftaincy stratum becoming a *rent-collecting aristocracy* now resting on top of the first two levels,

there stretches a very long process whose intermediate stations are constituted by

(2) *different combinations* of village communities in various stages of dissolution and subjection, with rent-collecting aristocracies and/or bureaucracies also at various stages of crystallization, either within the villages and/or in inter-village space.

This chain of forms will already give us local, village-level rent in various guises depending on the degree of individualization of the peasant economy. Thus, at a relatively backward point along the chain, it might give us not rent paid by peasant households, but collective rent paid by the village as a whole, representing the moment of which Marx took a mental still-shot as the 'Asiatic mode of production', not recognizing its transitory nature.

Now let us begin to bring the state into the same picture. As Wolf (1966: 11) observes, 'the processes of state-building are multiple and complex. Different areas were integrated into states in markedly different ways and at different times'. Suppose that at first it is the 'early state', in a borrowing from rather descriptivist anthropological work (see, for example, Claessen and Skalnik, 1978)—the initial and original repressive mechanism of the indigenous incipient aristocracy in this particular locality. Even this primitive form will probably impose its own levies on all the villages and their lords that it encompasses; therefore 'rent' and 'tax' will come to exist side by side. Denote these first-generation 'rents' and 'taxes' by r_1 and t_1 respectively.

Let it rest at that for some centuries, so that things really get formalized and ossified, and the origins of all these customary practices are forgotten. Then have this small-scale state invade or be invaded by another, nearby small-scale valley state. New 'taxes' (t_2) will thereby be imposed on old 'taxes' and 'rents' as a manifestation of this takeover; hence, t_1 and r_1 might now assume reduced forms t'_1 and r'_1, which would now be encountered alongside t_2 at the same point in chronological time. Moreover, the functionaries whom the victorious state sends into the loser's territory to supervise the collection of t_2 may in time sink local roots there, forcibly extracting new 'rents' for themselves (r_2), or appropriating as new 'rents' part of the new 'taxes' of the same generation ($t_2 \rightarrow r_2 + t'_2$). On the backs of the peasantry of the loser's territory, therefore, we would get a mixture of r_2, t_2, r'_2, t'_2.

Again, give everything time to settle, and let the above set of 'rents' and 'taxes' come to represent a stable 'law of the land'. Then suddenly bring into, say, the Indian subcontinent a wave of Mongols, or the Arabs into Egypt, or the Turks into Anatolia, or the Franks into Gaul, each led by its own conquering military aristocracy and carrying its own 'law of the people', its *yasag* or *sharia* or *örf* or *bannum*—a new level of customary law expressing and justifying the victors' eminent rights over the land, its inhabitants, and its previous traditions. From this, derive a third generation or crust of 'taxes' (t_3). But also turn the tribal rank-and-file of the Turks or Franks into a new dependent peasantry so that at least in places, they are initially exempt from the first and second generation 'rents' in reduced forms which the older peasantry continues to pay alongside the newest 'taxes'. Vary a little by allowing that Egypt and Gaul are not evacuated while the Byzantine ruling class withdraws from Anatolia (that is, pre-conquest private landowners, representatives of Wickham's 'rent mode', disappear from the scene *as an outcome of political, military, religious conflict*); vary a little more by introducing different sub-stages of proto-feudal social and political evolution for the conquering peoples, with somewhat different resulting capacities for creating efficient administration. On top of all the already existing levels of 'taxes' and 'rents', in the larger states, make the kings resort to fresh fief-distribution because they cannot rule all that area directly; then introduce different rates of conversion of fief-holders into new landowners, of 'taxes' into privately retained 'rents', simply because *secondary conditions* in the ninth-century Carolingian Empire are not as advanced as those in fifteenth-century Ottoman Serbia.

Allow more time to cool; then, with everything in the way of royal 'tax' rights and seigneurial 'rent' rights that they have distilled from all previous incrustations, have the Norman aristocracy—of Viking origin, prepared in France—descend on a nearby island that had been undergoing its own successively internalized Roman-Celtic—Anglo-Saxon incrustations of 'tax' and 'rent' for some time. Add varying degrees of peasant resistance and revolt. Add varying degrees of commercial development and urbanization (leading to a greater consensus within the aristocracy in favour of a more centralized state, and/or to the greater power of kings to curb their respective aristocracies).

Finally, try arresting these various strands of a non-Eurocentric medieval history at different point. You will indeed get a different centralization/decentralization, public/private, tax/rent mix in each cross-sectional slide you put under the microscope.[31] Yes, you will get periodic oscillations between the two poles; and very possibly the varying outcomes will have something to do with when and where capitalism first arises.

But in their origins, all these different tax/rent mixes will have had *nothing* to do with a so-called 'tax *mode*' or a 'rent *mode of production*'. To see nothing but a frozen slide hinges on forgetting the *whole*, the *total process*. The ultimate fallacy, against which Wickham's theorization provides no brakes, would be to equate statelessness (no 'tax', pure 'rent') to feudalism. The tension, the flux and wane, between the fief-distributing centre and the fief-holders out in the countryside, between the king/emperor with his weaker or stronger palatial apparatus and the other elements, large or small, of the ruling class, is a contradiction *internal* to feudalism; not a contradiction between 'feudalism' on one hand and some 'non-feudalism' on the other, as the terminology Wickham reserves for describing the way it concretely unfolds in different places would imply. In essence, it is an intra-ruling class contradiction over the redistribution of peasant surplus; its historical solutions will reflect concrete power relations within the same ruling class, which in turn will be mediated by 'historical circumstance'. Each specific feudal tax/rent mix (r_n, t_n), in other words, *within the limits set by the feudal mode of production*, will be the product and sign of *a specific social, political and military history*, which without reverting to Anderson and Balibar cannot be reduced to a modal difference.

IN QUEST OF METHODOLOGICAL CONSISTENCY

Let me now put my entire argument in reverse, not as a critique but as an appreciation of what Wickham has done.

In the context of the conventional, Barkan-type distinction between Sociological Theory and History as such, it seems to me that 'The

Uniqueness of the East' is historian's history more than anything else. The main intention of that article is not to attempt yet another modal classification of pre-capitalist class society. It is, as Wickham repeatedly anounces,[32] to bring out an actual contrast between East and West that occurs in the concrete flow of history: that revolving around the survival or non-survival of a state with a relatively large area of effective control as each new wave of feudalization (in my sense) takes off, leading into another comparison revolving around the capacity or non-capacity of the state centre to keep a tight rein on its fief-holders and the other peripheral elements of the ruling class as each such wave of feudalism deepens. In this perspective, 'The Uniqueness of the East' must be seen as a sequel to 'The other Transition: From the Ancient World to Feudalism' (where Wickham dealt specifically with the 'failure' of the Roman Empire to maintain its tax base by checking the encroachments of the rising private aristocracy), rather than as a response to Mukhia.

This is truly a very important subject of inquiry. Comparing the Roman-German synthesis that produced the West European variety of feudalism with, for example, the Arab conquest of the Byzantine-Persian Near East, or the Oghuz seizure intact of the lands of 'classical Islam', or the Seljukid-Ottoman expansion in Anatolia, in Thrace, then again in Anatolia, one cannot fail to be struck by the relative vacuum that the total destruction of Rome left that is so different from the continuity of state structures throughout the production of the Turkish-Islamic synthesis.[33] Wickham (139) rightly concludes that 'it is survival (of the state) that is the norm, failure that is the deviation'.

Working with a theory of feudalism as the basic and most universal pre-capitalist mode of exploitation, I have written elsewhere that it is the specific Western transition to 'private' feudalism over the ruins of an Ancient state once based on slavery that is the exception; the various Oriental transitions of 'state' feudalism out of tribal society *or* as the offshoots of previous feudal states that are the rule (Berktay, 1983b). Concerning the comparison between West European feudalism and Ottoman feudalism in particular, I have hypothesized as follows: that the relatively decentralized character of the former might have been shaped initially by a process of feudalization that broke loose from previous constraints when semi-tribal agriculturalists making up the autonomous units of a heterogeneous mass advanced into the more or less empty and loose historical space left by the nearly complete dismantling of the state structures of the invaded society to create their numerous, separate barbaric kingdoms. On the other hand, the relatively centralized character of Turkish-Islamic feudalism might have received its initial push from a process of feudalization that advanced in a rather full and firm historical space, where the nomadic-pastoralist invaders who moved in proto-politically confederated masses with unified leaderships (as in the Arab, Oghuz and Mongol tides) came into and took over the non-shattered political, ideological, legal, cultural superstructures of the states they had defeated but not erased. One step further back, the resilience of the overlapping Iranian-Abbasid-Seljukid-Ottoman polities *vs.* the infirmity of late Roman-Merovingian-Carolingian central apparatuses might have had something to do with the degree to which trade and money economy were quantitatively more developed in the Eastern Mediterranean in the tenth-fourteenth centuries than in the Dark Ages of Western Europe. As already mentioned, the Ottomans had gunpowder from a very early point of their state history. One should keep in mind, in this regard, that the product of the Turkish-Islamic synthesis was *a chronologically delayed feudalism* by Roman-German standards—a tardiness the causes of which might go as far back as the original climate, geography and demography of the Eurasian land mass, which must be taken as pre-historically *given* conditions for the persistence of the Central Asian reservoir of nomadic pastoralism right down to the fourteenth century, whose proximity can be seen to have repeatedly halted the stabilization of settled agricultural relations of production in the Near East until, ultimately, the rise of the Ottoman Empire.[34] But comparisons of these dimensions cannot even be posed unless we broaden our perspective to include all of world history instead of placing a single slide under the microscope. And finally, one *would* expect a feudalism which succeeded slavery to display demesnes and labour services to a much greater extent than that involved in the tribalism-to-feudalism succession.[35] Once more: not modal questions, but questions of specific genesis and secondary determination, each and every one. . . .

Perhaps this is a roundabout way of saying that in the last analysis, I find Wickham's historical account most useful as a prop for *my* kind of theoretical approach. Obviously, I come within that category of people 'who do not distinguish between tax and rent at all, or . . . who see them as centralized and decentralized (public and private) variants of the same economic system, which most of them would call feudal' (Wickham, 133). *If* we can consider the claim of real economic (modal) difference between 'tax' and 'rent' to have been eliminated by the remarks above, Wickham's remaining objection would be that 'almost all of world history would thus come under the same heading'.

I would reply, first, that this by itself is not a valid argument if the existence of another mode of production (AMP, 'tax mode', etc.) equi-level with feudalism cannot independently be shown.

Second, that objecting on these grounds to the extension of the category of feudalism to cover China, 'classical Islam' and the Ottoman Empire, is not very different from objecting in the first place to its extension to cover *ancien régime* France, Russia and Qajar Iran.

Third, that there is nothing wrong with positing a very broad coverage for feudalism in history as long as we can properly handle, and not obliterate, specificities within such generality.[36] In some parts of this article, I have tried to indicate how this can be done by reference to primary and secondary determinations, to specific genesis, to the reciprocal effect of superstructures on the mode of production. The *only* alternative has always been to throw such concepts out of the historian's tool-box altogether, either by directly adopting a purely empiricist position, or, like Perry Anderson and Etienne Balibar, indirectly by blurring the distinction between the abstract and the concrete, between mode of production and social formation, between pure contradiction and overdetermination.

Which to opt for? I think Wickham (114), with his correct emphasis on 'understanding the world better . . . so that we can change it' rather than 'the devotional elements' involved, would agree that this is ultimately a question of the integrity, utility, simplicity and applicability of the theory within and for which we work. I cannot see my way to either writing good history or transforming society with a 'Marxism' which has no more place for the superstructure/mode of production dialectic, therefore for the relative autonomy of superstructure, therefore for accident, hazard, conscious human action and overdetermination. What I am suggesting is that classical Marxism is actually less dogmatic, less schematic, more simple but less simplistic in this regard than some varieties of Western Marxism, 1960s-style. Trying artificially to fit different modes of production to historical specificities, or to explain such specificities by various 'mythic modes', does not enrich but only impoverishes; it injects laziness into our historiographical and historical efforts.

To understand this better, it is worth taking a closer look at the logical structure of recent attempts to proliferate pre-capitalist modes of production. These started with the reaction within Western Marxism to economism, economistic determinism, models of unilinear and mechanistic evolution. It was observed that pre-capitalism did not everywhere give way to capitalism; neither did the development of capitalism automatically result in socialist revolution. The search for solutions took, and can only take, two roads. Very sketchily, the first is to account for uneven development by keeping in mind the gist of Engels's letter to J. Bloch about 'last instance' and applying it to 'the concrete analysis of concrete situations', which are never singular but multiple determinations. The second is to believe every different perceived historical dynamic to have been the consequence of a separate economic basis. 'Capitalism did not arise in the East; therefore, wherever it did not arise, feudalism must not have been the pre-capitalist mode of production.'

This is as fallacious as asserting that if at any given point in time a woman is observed not (yet) to have borne a child, then she must not be a woman. Many secondary factors (other than sex) can interfere with pregnancy and childbirth; many secondary factors (other than mode of production) can interfere with the actual rhythm of societal development. Failure to recognize this perpetuates a Hegelian Eurocentrist essentialism—which with his 'tax mode' Wickham cannot entirely evade—concerning Oriental retardation. The potential line of evolution that could flow out of the innermost contradiction of the principal mode of production in a given social formation, manifests itself in the concrete only as a perceived, actual historical movement that has been overdetermined both by the specific forms of its own superstructures and by elements from other modes that can be present in the same social formation. That is why the movement of concrete historicities can never be reduced to the theoretical movement of any one mode of production.

Now, the dogmatic, unilinear view of history goes wrong, because it does not allow for this overdetermination; its vulgar economic determinism consists in holding that the actual movement of any given society will reflect the potential dynamic of its (dominant) mode of production fully and completely—that that potential dynamic, in other words, will be realized 100 per cent in practice. This vulgarization that *reduces concrete societies to abstract modes of production* cannot be overcome, however, by mentally multiplying the modes of production that correspond to a given threshold of the productive forces; for this second vulgarization then *reduces modes of production to the external-features of observed historicities* either through accepting each society as a mode in itself, or through defining mode of production to include superstructures. As anti-economism and anti-dogmatism swing into empiricism, therefore, the main methodological assumption remains the mirror image of the first vulgarization: the idea that to any given mode of production, the same trajectory of societal movement must always correspond, becomes replaced by the idea that to any given trajectory of societal movement, there fits a mode of production that must generate that trajectory only. By contrast, I take the view that the mental reproduction and full theoretical appropriation of the rich multilinearity of human history can and should be achieved only through giving full play to the relative autonomy of the political and ideological levels and their differential effects on the economy, and really integrating this principle into a perspective of overdetermined movement of society, thus eliminating the soil of essentialist particularism and opening up a broad avenue for 'the concrete analysis of concrete situations'.

This is where research articles like Wickham's come in to supply precisely the extended, refined sort of historical analysis that my theoretical framework is in need of. There is no mental laziness in Section II of 'The Uniqueness of the East'; it does not explain away the detailed profile of Asian events and processes by ascribing them to the so-called 'tax mode'; in fact, it does not presuppose the 'rent mode'/'tax mode' distinction, as Wickham thinks it does—it would work even better without it. Dare I say, hence, that there is a misfit between Wickham's history and his theory; that the approach I have suggested is more suitable for handling historical specificities of state survival *vs.* non-survival, ancient and medieval? A pity if Wickham's work should continue to be read in the future as mere taxonomic theory; all the more so because it is in that direction that its weaknesses, not its strengths, lie.

NOTES

This article is the direct outcome of extended discussions with Chris Wickham himself, who generously helped improve an argument critical of his own position. Rodney Hilton, too, went far beyond reading and commenting on the original manuscript to provide material reinforcing the interpretation of late-medieval royal taxation as generalized feudal rent. The actual writing took place during two trips to England financed by a Mediterranean Studies Fellowship for 1985-6 from the Aylwin Cotton Foundation.

1. In his *Feudal Society*, Marc Bloch explicitly raised 'a subject peasantry' to first rank in his definition of feudalism. In other major works, he pointed out with respect to this peasantry that its small holdings (and not the demesne) were probably the major part of most manors even in the ninth century; that of its two possible sources, the earlier, unsubjected peasantry of Frankish tribal society (and not Roman slavery) was the more important; that this was generally reflected in the preponderance of the free manse over the servile manse; that therefore the term *servus* did not correspond to social reality. With respect to the origins of the aristocracy, he added that the Gallo-Roman ruling class of Caesar's time was a caste of village chieftains deriving most of its income from dues owed by the peasants; that it was a simple matter for

heads of tribes or clans to be transformed into manorial lords; that as the case of Wales proved, any kind of demesne, let alone a demesne of vast dimensions, need not arise along this path of social evolution; but that wherever large masses of slaves existed ready-to-hand as part of the Roman façade put on tribal institutions, demesne farming would receive a relative push. Hence, it is possible to say that Bloch had the *elements* of a theory of direct transition from (Germanic) tribalism to feudalism in which the historical specificities of the resulting West European variety were imparted by the conditioning effect of the previous existence of a developed slave society. These special features—demenses and *corvées*—were moreover a part of the concrete visage of only the *early* medieval *seigneurie*; and the line of development from great proprietor to rentier landlord was carefully traced by Bloch in an account in which he stated flatly that peasant revolt was as typical of medieval feudalism as the industrial strike of capitalism in modern time. This is a strong insight if we consider that ultimately, any social formation is best classified according to the basic kind of class struggle it generates. All these aspects of Bloch's work may be woven into a good case for the essentially peasant nature of the West European Middle Ages revolving around the fundamental contradiction of the lord-peasant relationship. See Bloch (1931/1966), (1940/1966), (1941/1971).

There is, of course, another aspect to the Bloch tradition: a certain eclecticism; the inability to stop enumerating a full list of 'characteristics'—a practice which replaces definitions with descriptions; the idea of an 'ambiance sociale totale' which conditions one to look for the same 'totality' elsewhere as *the* (impossibly strong) requirement for a non-European feudalism. Thus Bloch himself cannot let go of graduated ties of dependence as indispensable to his 'totality', and it is because he rediscovers them in the internal articulation of the Japanese aristocracy and its particular form of sharing out its class monopoly of the land, that he feels relatively safe in talking of Japanese feudalism. In Turkey, Kiliçbay (1982) makes much of this second aspect to obliterate the first; this is not proper procedure. More generally, this dichotomy can be seen as roughly corresponding to the two sides of the debate over non-European feudalism, with, for example, Rodney Hilton's work over the years accentuating the first, and Perry Anderson and Harbans Mukhia following up the second. But there can be no doubt that Bloch renders the demesnes-and-labour-services version of feudalism untenable.

2. See Postan (1961) for a non-Marxist evaluation of Bloch's contribution to overcoming the Anglo-German emphasis on 'the story of baronial and knightly contracts of military service' and the legalism it entails. In Bloch, this will make itself felt as the secondary aspect discussed in note 1 above.
3. This requires some explanation. The central (but never openly acknowledged) proposition in contemporary Turkish nationalist historiography is that 'we' are not like the others, 'we' resemble only ourselves, 'ours' is a *sui generis* path of development; whatever classifications and periodizations might be devised for world history, the history of the Turks must remain original and exceptional.

Upon closer examination, this takes the form of: 'We' resemble only ourselves because of the absence of classes and class struggle, and this is because 'our' Middle Ages were not feudal. To this, an important corollary would be that 'we' had a universal empire, 'we' were imperial. The idea here is that feudalism equals political decentralization; decentralization leads to the arbitrary, unbounded power of local lords over peasants; and exploitation and oppression consist only of such arbitrariness. But an empire—that is different, that means political centralization, that is, uniform public law, that is, justice, that is, legitimate and fair taxation (as the opposite of arbitrary exploitation).

I have argued elsewhere (Berktay, 1986) that in its inception, this was nothing but the subjective consciousness of the Ottoman establishment. Great empires like Egypt, China, Persia and Byzantium, through ruling vast areas for centuries, even millennia, tend to erect ideological structures that are far more rigid, far more resistant to change than other, more peripheral polities (compare, for example, Japan with China). Such mentalities weave greatly detailed, immutable cosmogonies around a faith-imbedded belief in their own absolute *superiority* and *uniqueness*. In the case of the Ottomans, such imperial self-glorification was cut to a minimum—but not eliminated completely—by the Kemalist Revolution: the wave of radical Jacobinism surrounding its peak was reflected in content of historiography by sharp hostility to the Ottoman system, state, and ruling class. In the methodological field, this anti-Ottoman attitude went hand in hand with the ascendancy of notions of material causality. It even became briefly fashionable to at least allude to classes and their conflicts of interest, as, for example, in Fuat Köprülü's treatment of the social origins of various religious sects, or of the primordial freedom of nomadic tribes and their resistance to incorporation, as a subject peasantry, in any political order. Significantly, all this was manifested in the rise of a universalist outlook; thus, schoolbooks of the very early 1930s spoke of a 'Turkish-Islamic feudalism' comprising both 'Seljukid feudalism' and 'Ottoman feudalism', and only then went on to speak of their secondary differences from the West European species. On Köprülü's bourgeois materialism, see Berktay (1983a) and (1985); on Kemalist textbooks, see Perinçek (1985).

But in the late 1930s and the 1940s, as the Turkish Revolution stopped halfway in the completion of its bourgeois-democratic tasks, as the new state that had arisen in opposition to the feudal past began to ally itself more and more with that past in its hardening opposition to demands from below, that residue of imperial ideology that had not been fully eradicated started to grow and expand. The refusal of the Republican transformation to move any further meant the restoration of pro-Ottoman thought and sentiment. When the Turkish ruling classes felt the practical need to slow down the dissolution of medieval relations and superstructures once institutionalized by the Ottoman regime, they also felt the theoretical need to erase class concepts from that section of Turkish history. As Turkish nationalism moved further and further away from its Kemalist variant politically, it also abandoned notions of material causality and universality in the realm of historiography, and came to re-glorify the Ottoman order in an approach quite at odds with the perspectives of the Kemalist Enlightenment, but strikingly reminiscent of the romantic restorationism of Metternich's time in Germany. This was done through the double theory of (a) the supra-class, extra-historical character of the Ottoman state, and (b) the *sui generis* character of the Ottoman system in its lost golden age of organic unity and harmony.

All this implies that the work of the professional Turkish Ottomanists is property approached not simply as archival digging, but only if placed in the context of the history of ideas, of a materialist critique of the development of Turkish thought against the background of the ebb and flow of Turkey's bourgeois-democratic revolution. In the absence of such a continuous critique, the proposition that in its classical period of the fifteenth-sixteenth centuries Ottoman society was not feudal maintains its dominant position in academic literature.

4. When Barkan died in 1979, he was much praised as the man who had allegedly shed more light than any other on Ottoman history. Such estimates must be taken with more than a grain of salt. In the complex personality of Barkan were united empirical researcher and—despite his professions of impartial empiricism—theoretician; in his works, important factual discoveries and peculiar opinions are to be found side by side. Thus in many passages, Barkan notes: that Ottoman society was composed of two principal classes called *askeriye* (the military) and *reaya* (literally: the ruled flock, that is, the tax-paying subjects, more specifically the peasantry); that these two classes formed separate, hereditary estates; that the most important of the permanent privileges of the *askerîs*, the right to receive and hold *timars* (in other words, the existence of a fief system), was the consequence of a material necessity common to all medieval societies; that the *reaya* was attached to the soil as 'hereditary and eternal tenants'; and that it might not have mattered much whether peasants owed their obligations to individual lords or to the state. Here and there, he comes even closer to viewing Ottoman institutions as part of a general problematic of the Middle Ages; and there is one extraordinary moment when he lets fall a single remark on the *timar* system as 'a typically medieval feudal organization' (Barkan, 1964). All this, however, does not constitute his main interpretative thrust. Barkan's initial study on 'The Legal Status (*nota bene*) of Agrarian Classes in the Ottoman Empire' appeared in 1937-8. From that until Barkan (1973) and Barkan (1974), he consecrated an entire career of 35 years to a veritable crusade against the thesis of Ottoman feudalism, going against his own empirical evidence. His line of attack will be discussed in note 12.
5. An extreme example is Kiliçbay (1982), who in order to support his position, quotes Hilton (1953/1976) and (1976) as speaking of 'the struggle between lords and peasants for *labour* rent' as the prime mover of feudalism. In Turkey, this textual distortion was initially exposed by Oyan (1983).

6. Typically, Islâmoglu and Keyder (1977) insist that the work-process in their AMP—which as we shall see is equivalent to Wickham's 'tax mode'—is different from the work-process which characterizes the feudal mode:

> It was mentioned above that the production process in the Asiatic mode of production does not create conflict or a confrontation between the producers and the appropriators of surplus. The individual peasant comes into contact only with the tax-collector, who acts in the name of the central authority, only after the production process, which he carried out as a free peasant. In this way the Asiatic mode of production is distinguished from the slave, feudal, or capitalist modes of production; class conflict is not graspable in the production experience. For this reason its principal dynamic is to be found in intra-class and not inter-class conflict. (Bailey and Llobera, 1981: 307)

Note, first, that since the authors have earlier defined 'the Asiatic mode of production' as 'characterized by independent peasant production' (ibid.: 301), this amounts to a statement that the essence of the 'feudal mode' is *not* peasant production but work on the demesne, therefore the predominance of labour rent. Most AMP-theorists are similarly unable to fully relinquish the idea of a demesne-centred feudalism in order to be more easily able to differentiate it from their version of the AMP. In this regard, Wickham stands alone.

Second, note that 'class conflict . . . in . . . production' is thereby supposed to be contingent on demesne and *corvées*, and therefore absent from 'Asiatic' societies. This is a repetition of conservative Ottomanists' arguments concerning exploitation and oppression as having to do only with slaves or quasi-slaves; the *reaya* as being 'free peasants'; class struggle as being absent from Turkish history—initially touched upon in note 3 and extended in note 12.

Third, note that classes nevertheless exist. We have in the AMP-dominated social formations, in other words, class societies in which classes enter the football pitch and perhaps line up at opposing ends, but do not further advance upon each other to begin struggling. For a critique of such misconceptions, see Ste. Croix (1981).

Fourth, note the connection between the supposed absence of *basic* class antagonism and the idea, common in AMP-theory, of the stagnancy of such societies. Keyder (1976), in fact, maintains that the 'Asiatic mode of production' (read: Ottoman society) could not get moving without some sort of external impact, which therefore becomes *generally* progressive. This is a pure statement of Hegelian Eurocentrist essentialism concerning Oriental retardation.

Finally, note how very similar Mukhia ('Peasant Production and Medieval Indian Society': 242) is: 'the medieval Indian peasantry. . . as a "free peasantry" whose process of production was free of extraneous control' does not have any behaviour pattern like 'the *early* medieval European peasant's resistance in the very process of production'! The word 'early' that I have italicized shows Mukhia to be fully aware of the extent to which his definition of feudalism as 'the structured dependence of the entire peasantry on the lords' is contingent on demesne production, *and* of the extent to which this feature is limited in time. It is interesting that Mukhia does not confront *at all* Wickham's criticisms in this regard, but on the contrary cites the latter as agreeing with his own standpoint. Reject taking empiricist still-shots of this or that feature only of early medieval Europe; admit that Western feudalism was also based on small production—and the entire position of both Islâmoglu and Keyder and Mukhia collapses.

7. This point is especially valuable for me because elsewhere, I noted the following: 'Maturing on French soil, Norman feudalism was through this invasion transplanted on English soil, where . . . Anglo-Saxon feudalism had . . . developed to the point of being capable of tolerating this superimposition; through the sudden victory of a centralized act of conquest, this transplantation resulted in the most orderly, least anarchical, hierarchy of fief-distribution in Western Europe' (Berktay, 1983b: 267). In a footnote on the same page, I added that the relative centralism of the Norman feudal state with its royal courts and royal council shed partial light on the specificities of the Ottoman political system.
8. I would like to thank Guy Bois for recently bringing this point to my attention. Functional equivalence, however, is not conceptual identity. Although essentially rooted in the sphere of production, Bloch's '*système sociale*' nevertheless fails to distinguish rigorously between that and the realm of superstructures; it therefore leaves the door open to incorporating much superstructural specificity into distinctions between 'social systems'. The search for an 'ambiance sociale totale' as the hallmark of each 'social system'—criticized in note 1 above—is based on precisely this implicit definition. Keeping that contrast in mind is part of the main theme of this article.
9. The last two expressions are quoted by Byres (23; also notes 7-8) from Lenin. The first is Marx's; see the second quote at the beginning of this article. By juxtaposing all, I wished to underscore the continuity of thought involved.
10. See the summary of Islâmoglu and Keyder's position in note 6 above. Similarly, Akat (1977: 42), when he gets down to actually describing the 'feudal mode of production', cannot refrain from suggesting that 'the extraction of surplus from the producers (serfs) in the form of surplus labour' and 'the separation of the feudal lord's own land and the fields on which the serfs reproduce themselves' were constituent elements thereof—*alongside* his main argument, summarized in the text, that small producers plus strong state gives a mode of production different from small producers plus individual lords.
11. Akat (1977: 37-8, 39-40, 42-4, 48), who admits that small peasant production is the common basis of his general category of 'mature agricultural modes of production' comprising both the 'feudal' and the 'Asiatic' varieties, is the clearest on this point.
12. Did the Ottoman military caste, comprising both large and small fief-holders, not possess a class monopoly of the right to bear arms and of eminent rights

over the land? And were not both European serfs and Ottoman *reaya* thereby attached to the land and compelled to surrender all or part of their surplus in the form of taxes and/or rents to their overlords? Were they not, therefore, basically the same type of producers—a 'subject peasantry'—enmeshed in the same type of exploitative subordination and dependence? Despite the supposition, widespread among Turkish academics but not based on close readings, that Barkin emphasized *economic and social* history, it it in his way of handling this question or objection that his thinking stands revealed as formalism of a very narrowly *legalistic* sort. In brief, he informs us that only the subject status of European serfs is really 'unfreedom' because it is the result of 'arbitrary' constraints imposed by individual lords within the context of private law; by contrast, the limitations on the freedom of movement of the *reaya* do not constitute 'unfreedom' because they are imposed by the Ottoman state as 'reasonable' measures of public law for the purpose of ensuring that its 'fiscal needs' are covered. See Barkan (1937-8) and Barkan (1939-40). Hence, instead of getting an ordering of the basic qualitative levels of subjection like:

(1) ancient slavery,
(2) all medieval gradations of semi-freedom in a single category, and
(3) contemporary freedom (of the wage-earner under capitalism);

we are given the following implicit scale:

(1a) the unfreedom of the slave or the prisoner of war;
(1b) the unfreedom of the European serf, which is alleged to be derived from and not too different from that of the slave;
(2a) the freedom of *reaya*;
(2b) contemporary freedom.

Included in this tortuous logic is an erroneous identification of exploitation and oppression with slavery or quasi-slavery, a whimsical manipulation of the concept of freedom, and a flagrant application of double standards, of two different criteria of causality, to the respective status of serfs and *reaya*. The idea that imperial taxation stipulated by public law does not incorporate any (feudal) exploitation is here clearly seen to rest on a mystification of the Ottoman state as a supra-historical Being that acts out of its own *raisons d'état*, behind which lurk no class-determined material requirements. Compared with Fuat Köprülü's observation less than a decade earlier that the Empire was founded by a military aristocracy that transformed itself into a landed aristocracy in the process (Köprülü, 1934: 48, 180, 182; Berktay, 1983a: 78-9), this involves an entire theoretical retrogression.

Adherence to the Barkanian dogma about the *reaya's* 'freedom' lands AMP-theorists in a dilemma. Thus, Islamoglu and Keyder (1977), immediately after talking about the Ottoman 'free peasant' in the paragraph quoted in note 6, have to add that 'the peasant was "free" in the sense that he was not a serf. He was, however, restricted in movement. He had to pay a tax if he wanted to leave his village permanently, and his land could be confiscated if left uncultivated for three years in succession.' *Nowhere* do the authors tell us what the lack of freedom of the serf consisted in that was supposedly so different.

What makes all this so interesting is that Barkan's ratiocination concerning *reaya* 'freedom' is repeated word for word by Mukhia! Irfan Habib has observed that Indian peasants were 'no better than semi-serfs' because they could not desert their villages. This is embarrassing for Mukhia, who realises that it cuts the ground out from under his position; he does not want 'to loosen the meaning of serfdom or even semi-serfdom ... to equate it merely with legal restriction on free mobility of peasants'. He therefore argues that the state had good reasons for imposing such legal restrictions in the Indian case: it 'was motivated entirely by the anxiety of the state to ensure continuity of cultivation and avert the loss of revenue' (Mukhia, 250). But was not this precisely the economic logic *everywhere*, including Western Europe, behind the restrictions imposed on subject peasantries? Or does Mukhia believe, like Barkan, that European lords acted completely arbitrarily out of no economic logic at all?

This apart, it is clear that the *only* aspect of European serfs' unfreedom that could be considered 'in excess' of the subjection of Indian or Ottoman peasants is the serfs' liability to compulsory labour. The whole line about Oriental peasants being 'free, unlike serfs, but restricted in movement' therefore turns into the argument already examined on the alleged importance of demesne production.

13. In contrast to Barkan, who concentrated his efforts on a cross-sectional analysis of fifteenth-sixteenth century Ottoman society, Halil Inalcik, another leading Turkish historian, has provided, in addition to similar reflections on its *sui generis* nature, detailed accounts of its origins and rise, its maturity, and finally its decline. Equating feudalism to decentralization leads Inalcik to define the second of these three stages as non-feudal, whereas for the first phase of incomplete elimination of local dynasties and for the third phase of their post-1600 resurgence as *esraf* and *âyân*, he is not averse to 'semi-feudal' or 'quasi-feudal' designations. On that point, he is close to Claude Cahen (1968) as well as to the late Osman Turan (1950), (1965), (1971), who used to attach the 'feudal' label to the semi-tribal autonomies of the formative period of the Seljukid state in Iran—structures which, using the criterion of relations of production, would at best be classifiable as proto-feudal, since they involve only an incipient chieftaincy and the extraction of lump-sum tributes from subjugated tribal masses whose internal cohesion has not yet been broken down, and who still have to be transformed into a substratum of dependent peasant households. Besides this inversion of the correct relation of tribalism to feudalism, unfamiliarity with the analytical tool of mode of production causes Inalcik (*vis-à-vis* the Ottomans) as well as Cahen

and Turan (*vis-à-vis* the Seljukides) to postulate oscillations of one and the same society between 'feudalism' and 'non-feudalism' although no qualitative change has taken place one way or the other in the economic basis. With Inalcik, too, therefore, 'non-feudalism' has a tendency to be transformed into 'feudalism' if and as fiefs are privatized and local landowning dynasties arise. See Inalcik (1955, 1964, 1972, 1973, 1977, 1980a, 1980b) on this question.

14. Because of the absence of a distinct lords' economy consisting of demesne fields and meadows.
15. Some examples: 'more *feudal* South (China)'; 'the (Arab) tributary state was tending towards *feudalism*'; 'In Turkey . . . all relationships that can be called *feudal* . . . withered'; 'the *feudalising* dangers of the timar system'; 'to stop landed property from being *de facto* privatized, from *falling back into* feudalism'—all in Wickham (123, 126, 129, 130, 132), italics mine.
16. This procedure is strictly observed by Hilton (1976: 14): 'Given the effective possession of the subsistence-producing holding by the peasant family, the transfer of surplus must be forced, since the peasant, as contrasted with the wage labourer, does not need to alienate his labour power in order to live.' In the same vein, also see Hilton (1984: 85):

> It (the feudal mode of production) is differentiated from the 'slave' or 'ancient' mode in that the exploited class from which surplus is exacted is, though servile, in possession of its own means of subsistence. The serfs are an unfree peasantry. The ruling class consists of landowners/landlords who take the surplus of peasant production. . . . It is, of course, differentiated from the capitalist mode of production where the owners of capital exploit a free but powerless class of wage workers by the extraction of surplus value in the manufacturing process, by paying wages less than the full value of their labour.

It should be evident that Hilton's focus on the inner connection between 'ways of combining' and forms of exploitation goes hand in hand with the same *general* distinction between freedom and unfreedom that I have suggested in note 12. Specifically concerning that last point, he adds that 'the term "serfdom" in Marxist discussion is often unnecessarily ambiguous, an ambiguity which seems to be derived from non-Marxist historical research. Surely Takahashi is right to insist that 'serfdom is the existence-form of labour in the feudal mode of production'. Having accepted this broad definition, 'many different juridical and institutional forms of serfdom can exist which in many—perhaps most—cases are not necessarily considered to be "servile" in the eyes of the law. This has given rise to much confusion among historians' (Hilton, 1976: 14). The last lines would seem to have been written almost for the benefit of Barkan, Turkish AMP-theorists, and Mukhia.

17. The first draft of 'The Uniqueness of the East', which Chris Wickham allowed me to read before it was published, contained a statement, later deleted for other reasons, to the effect that if landlords did closely direct the work-process on their demesnes, 'the mode might even be better seen as the

slave mode'. This is very much to the point; in Berktay (1983b: 237-45, 268-71, 317-22, 339-41, 345-9), I have argued that if the demesne on any manor swallowed up all the peasant holdings and the work-week of the serfs thereby came to consist entirely of labour services, this would imply a reversion to the slave mode of production. It is, of course, implicit in Bloch and also Duby (1974: 40). What it means is that demesne production based on *corvées* should *theoretically* be seen not as an element of the feudal mode, but as a vestige of the slave mode within the medieval European social formation dominated by the feudal mode of production. This, indeed, would be the correct application of the idea that social formations are always combinations of elements from more than one mode. Note, however, that this does not empirically imply any direct line of descent to medieval *corvées* from gang labour in Roman times. On this, see note 35.

18. Apart from the ideas of Islâmoglu and Keyder quoted in note 6 above; for the orthodox Ottomanists, see Barkan (1939-40). For AMP-theorists, here is first Berkes (1969: 51, 52, 56): 'These (timariots) are not, as in Western Europe, feudal lords who own and manage great lands. In the West, . . . lords . . . themselves are the producers, i.e. farmers in charge of an enterprise. . . .' 'The lord of the *timar* is not concerned with productive technology. The feudal lord, on the contrary, is a man directly concerned with both the work of production and the technology of the means of production. The feudal lord is situated within an economic process, whereas the lord of the *timar* is situated within a statist and fiscal one.' And now Küçükömer (1977: 21-2):

> The slave-owners of the classical age and the feudal lords of Europe were inside production as productive factors (agents). . . . Although the new land- and slave-owner of Rome might have become a master, he was basically a farmer all the same; he closely controlled and supervised slave-labour as a means of production just like the land. . . . The European feudal lord is also after all a farmer, although serfs, on condition of producing a greater surplus than the slaves, were subjected to lighter control and supervision (the serf is slightly freer).

Observe that among AMP-theorists as well as conservative historians, the alleged continuity from slaves to serfs is complementary to the alleged continuity from slave-masters to feudal lords, both adding up to a theory of direct descent of the manor from the latifundium. Elements of this exaggerated continuity, moreover, are handled at the level of mode of production, not, as I have indicated in note 17, at the level of social formation, so that the feudal mode becomes little more than a 'slightly' reformed version of slave civilization.

19. State taxation is 'mediated and formalised', says Wickham (134-6); the state needs surplus in an abstract way and is not so interested in controlling production, whereas 'landlords relate to peasants more closely', and this 'extends to involvement in production itself'. Hence, 'the state under pressure will attempt to increase the intensity of exploitation'; 'the landlord

is as, or more, likely to attempt to increase his influence over the productive process'. Therefore 'landlords are more likely to respond to opportunities'. But are all these probabilities and adverbs of comparison enough to distinguish two modes of production?

20. Note that, as Barkan talks of the arbitrariness of European lords, there are Western scholars who see arbitrariness to have been a trait of the state in Asia—a view that Wickham rightly criticizes. But does not this symmetry provide food for thought, more generally, on just how much of this debate is the creature of respective ethnocentrisms; of the readiness to mystify, to dismiss, to attribute to any *dues ex machina* what is not immediately familiar over a distance from this or that national standpoint?

21. Note that *this* is now opposed to the viewpoint of orthodox Ottomanists: while it considers, with them, relative centralization to be indicative of 'non-feudalism', it also holds it to have had *adverse* consequences for the future development of Ottoman society (toward capitalism). Most Turkish academic historians, caught up in a romantic nostalgia for the glorious days of the Empire, would attach no such negativity to (any excess of) state power. This is a significant, though secondary, disagreement between Turkish AMP-theorists and conservative professionals. I have indicated in (Berktay, 1985) that in this regard there is common ground between myself and AMP-theorists—provided, of course, that such specificity is handled at the superstructural level, and provided that we make allowance for the *positive* role state-formation played in the Ottoman 'feudal mutation' in the thirteenth-fifteenth centuries (quite comparable to the role state-building played in the 'feudal revolution' of Western Europe).

22. This is one instance where the empirical work of Barkan and Inalcik becomes so important, although they do not know how to draw the proper conclusions from it. On Ottoman land-codes, see Barkan (1943), where text after text attests to the authority of the Ottoman state to bring runaway *reaya* back as late as *15* years after the event; the points about the political autonomy of towns as centres of attraction for serfs in Sweezy's and Dobb's contributions to the 'Transition' debate of the 1950s provide good material for contrast. On how guildmasters' complaints motivated Ottoman state action, see Inalcik (1969). On the non-existence of an Ottoman proto-industrialization, see Keyder (1981). The deepening of crises of under-production is further attested by the occasional attempts of the state in the seventeenth century to allow certain regions to go tax-free for a few years, and to even distribute seed to them, in order to facilitate the resumption of at least simple reproduction. This proves not the 'benevolence' of the state, but the extent to which the peasantry was beginning to be crushed by wars, civil wars, military confiscations, prestations, taxation.

23. In a country with a high land: labour ratio, the state could not be sure of preventing tax leaks without *watching* the process of production. On the importance of this ratio, see Hilton (1984). Curiously, however, very little

attention has been paid to these questions in Turkey; it seems easier to talk philosophically about modal explanations of Turkish underdevelopment than to look closer into the material conditions and evolution of peasant reproduction.

24. Once more, I say 'ultimate' advisedly, for I think this is a case of something turning into its opposite; of relative centralization, beneficial at the outset for new, feudal relations of production and therefore for the prosperity of the Ottoman state, becoming the fetters of further development from the sixteenth century onward.

25. Wickham (134–5 in particular) occasionally has a way of talking about the Ottoman state *as if* it did not basically rule through an intermediate stratum of fief-holders; *as if* real, direct 'state ownership' of the land leading to *direct taxation* was achieved in practice, etc. But after all, what did the Ottomans do with this category of 'owning'—supposedly so different from 'eminent rights'—that arose through conquest? They distributed it as fiefs, of course; and the state's superior 'ownership' had only so much power behind it as to prevent hereditary privatization of these fiefs, but not enough to rule without fiefs and fief-holders. In the end, the Ottoman state did control the peasantry tenurially: it positioned and empowered its fief-holders to watch agricultural production quite closely, so that a peasant could not change his main crops, could not freely change arable to meadow or *vice versa*, could not let his land go uncultivated for three years in a row without paying a fine or risking confiscation of his holding, could not even cut down certain trees on his land without the timariot's permission—Ottoman land-codes give hundreds of examples of regulation of this kind. As for the even stricter supervision of urban crafts, see main text above note 22. It is misleading, therefore, when Wickham (135) says that in the 'tax mode', 'the state does not need to control the economic and social lives of its subjects'.

26. This is what Akat (1977: 42–3) actually says: 'When we look into its internal dynamics, we see that the feudal mode of production, through the rivalry between feudal lords to grow in strength, carries within it a tendency for a central state to be created. . . . When we look into its internal dynamics, we see that in the Asiatic mode of production, the rise of powerful families of warlords and bureaucrats leads to a tendency for central authority to be shattered.' Given that the author has by that time defined small producers plus strong state as the AMP, and small producers plus individual lordship as the feudal mode, that means that the relative loosening or tightening of the political ties between the centre and the fief-holders is interpreted as a modal change. Note, however, that the author is saying *absolutely nothing* here about economics, about production.

27. Barkan (1937–38: 336) is quite lyrical—for descendants of the conquered Balkan peoples, insultingly so—on this subject:

> Thus we can say that the peasants of the countries annexed into the Ottoman Empire were, as a natural consequence of this conquest and annexation, liberated from serfdom

at one stroke and in wholesale fashion; from being the *slaves* of innumerable individual petty lords whose bodies were left lying on the battlefields, they moved to the status of being only the tax-paying *reaya* . . . of a great *Empire*. Since this involved immense improvements in their *legal*, social status . . . and perhaps implied immediate obtainment of their freedom, which they could otherwise have only bought individually for money, the arrival of the *Imperial* order must have meant for them the solution of a social problem, the achievement of a great Land Reform on an international scale which by expropriating the *feudal lords who were great landed capitalists*, turned their lands over to the state. Such factors are worth paying attention to for explaining the miraculously rapid and irresistible rise of the Ottoman Empire.

Note the key words 'slave', 'Empire', legal', 'capitalists' which I have italicized. Barkan (1939–40) repeats the same theme several times as follows: 'In the countries where it was constituted, the Empire abolished those obligations which were *arbitrary* and *reminiscent of the powers of the slave-owner* over his *slaves*; replacing them with tax-systems which set out their obligations in regular and precise form and made them into clauses of law. Hence, we can say that the peasants of the countries annexed by the Ottoman Empire were as a consequence . . . liberated from serfdom'; once more, italics added.

Inalcik, by contrast, is a bit more hesitant. He takes up the theme of the articulation of the Ottoman regime with the pre-conquest land regimes of the Balkans while exploring the existence of Christian timariots in Roumelia (Inalcik, 1954), and then again in connection with the conversion of Serbian *corvées* into the Ottoman monetary tax called *raiyyet rüsumu* (Inalcik, 1959); in each case, the very ease of this articulation presses on him a certain sense of the essential identity and continuity of the two regimes, but he is ultimately forced by the weight of the entire particularist edifice to turn to the Barkanian conception of the commutation of labour services as an anti-feudal social revolution.

28. A recent CNRS colloquium on 'Genèse de l'Etat Moderne', held in Fontervraud (France) on 16–17 November 1984, seems to have produced a fresh pile of evidence concerning this development; see especially the papers by Bonney, Bottin, Hilton, Lindkvist, Prestwich, Quesada. I thank Rodney Hilton for providing me with this material.
29. (Wickham, n. 41). In his very recent review of the work of M. Barg, Christopher Hill (1986) says once more that in France after the fifteenth century, 'centralized feudal rent' in the form of royal taxes became more important than collections by individual lords; he cites Fortescue via Barg on how the French peasant came to owe five *écus* to the king for every *écu* he owed to his lord. In the medieval English 'Song of the Husbandman', too, 'always every fourth penny must go to the King', complains the farmer. This last text was, again, brought to my attention by Rodney Hilton.
30. The account below is from Berktay (1983b: 37–43, 46–50, 233–6, 279–376).
31. Wickham (1981: 27) himself discusses one such case of settling down and simplification of power relations, sets of landrights, and ownership hierarchies

in early medieval Italy: with the collapse of various local social ladders into the Byzantine army and thence their moulding into the new landowning aristocracy, that country, he says, became 'a very much simpler world than late Roman Italy, even if . . . not wholly different'. The same process of simplification is evidenced by the existence of a mixed tax/rent form in the early period of Turkish statehood in Anatolia: the so-called *malikâne-divani* system described in Barkan (1939), in which certain dues owed by the peasant were appropriated by his private landowner and other dues were appropriated by his timariot. Later, all dues passed into the hands of the latter. The existence of this intermediate form in the primitive stages of the development of Ottoman feudalism indicates that at least in places, the Ottoman military class was superimposed on a middle stratum of landowners, only part of whose incomes it at first channeled to itself, before coming to assimilate it all eventually. This splitting up of pre-conquest rents into taxes and rents, and finally into all taxes, is here clearly seen not as a modal combination but as a political-military process reflected in legal definitions of tax and rent.

32. See Wickham (113, 118, 132-3, 139). Byres, however, reads and criticizes Wickham only as formal, modal taxonomy, while Mukhia does not confront him much; see note 6.
33. In Turkey, this last term denotes a conservative adherence to the traditional values of 'Turkish nationality, Islamic faith'. I have used it on purpose to demystify its real historical content as the origin of Turkish-Ottoman feudalism.
34. It was Marc Bloch (1940/1966) who first observed that the relative immunity of Western Europe from any new invasions from the tenth century onwards might have played an important role in its later historical, economic, dynamism. Was this not in large part a consequence of the relative distance of this region to the heartland of nomadic explosions—the plains of Central Asia? And can it, therefore, have any explanation other than as a geographical 'accident'?
35. I am aware that Verhulst (1966) has demonstrated the lack of continuity, given the present state of the documentation, between Roman gang labour on private estates and medieval *corvées*; I do not mean to imply that the work-process on the demesne was directly descended from the work-process on the *villa*. Nevertheless, it must be true, as Bloch observed (see note 1), that the presence of large masses of slaves in early medieval Western Europe had something to do with the ease with which compulsory labour services were 'reinvented', if that was the case, as lordship arose; and that this presence of large masses of slaves itself, if not any continuity in demesnes, was a heritage of the developed slave civilization that went before. At the very least, it is correct to say that West European feudalism developed in an environment inhabited by lots of slaves and quasi-slaves, and that Turkish-Ottoman feudalism developed in an environment where there were few slaves and they were not employed in production.

36. Hobsbawm (1964: 62-3) has noted both the problem and the eventual direction of its possible solution:

> Since very early post-Marxist times there have been attempts to see a sort of primitive or proto-feudalism as the first general—though not necessarily universally occurring—form of class society growing out of the disintegration of primitive communalism. Out of this proto-feudalism, it is suggested, the various other formations developed, including the developed feudalism of the European (and Japanese) type. On the other hand a reversion to feudalism from formations which, while *potentially* less progressive, are in actual fact more highly developed—as from the Roman Empire to the tribal Teutonic kingdoms—has always been allowed for. Owen Lattimore goes so far as 'to suggest that we think, experimentally, in terms of evolutionary and relapse (or devolutionary) feudalism, and also asks us to bear in mind the possibility of the temporary feudalization of tribal societies interacting with more developed ones'.

Hobsbawm goes on as follows:

> The net result of all these various tendencies has been to bring into currency a vast category of 'feudalism' which spans the continents and the millennia . . . It is indeed likely that all these can be brought under one such general classification, and that this has analytical value. At the same time it is clear that without a good deal of sub-classification and the analysis of sub-types and individual historical phases, the general concept risks becoming much too unwidely.

In this context, what I am doing can be seen partially as an attempt to set out the theoretical terms and building-blocks of such a sub-classification.

Another support for my entire argument comes from Hilton (1978: 18), who in his definition of feudalism centred around the Political Economy concept of Rent and serfdom, has allowed for the 'transfer of surplus . . . to the landed aristocracy *and its states*' (italics mine). On this understanding, Hilton (1984: 85) proceeds to note that 'the exploitation of servile peasants by a landowning class is widespread in world history, from Asia to the Americas, from ancient to modern times. If this is the feudal mode of production then feudalism has been almost everywhere, at some time or another.' To be fair and not to put any words into Hilton's mouth, he then does make something of a Eurocentrist move by considering local, private jurisdiction as part of the relations of production. But overall, Hilton's work with its tight focus on the small production carried out by a peasantry in possession of its own economy provides solid support for universalist views.

REFERENCES

Akat, A.S., 1977, 'Tarihî Maddecilik ve Kapitalizm-Öcesi Toplumlar: Asya Toplumu-Feodalite Tartismasina Yeni Bir Yaklasim' (Historical Materialism and Pre-Capitalist Societies: A New Approach to the Asian Society-*vs.*-Feudalism Debate), *Toplum ve Bilim* (Society and Science), No. 1, pp. 34-48.

Althusser, L., and E. Balibar, 1972, *Reading Capital*, London: New Left Books.

Anderson, P., 1974, *Passages from Antiquity to Feudalism*, London: New Left Books.

Bailey, A.M., and J. Llobera, eds., 1981, *The Asiatic Mode of Production*, London.

Balibar, E., 1967, 'The Basic Concepts of Historical Materialism', in Althusser and Balibar (1972).

Barkan, Ö.L., 1937-8, 'Osmanli Imparatorlugunda Çifçi Siniflarin Hukukî Statüsü (The Legal Status of Agrarian Classes in the Ottoman Empire), *Ülkü Mecmuasi*, Vols. IX-X, Nos. 49-59.

Barkan, Ö.L., 1939, 'Malikâne-Divani Sistemi' (The Half-Estate, Half-State System), *Türk Hukuk ve Iktisat Tarihi Mecmuasi* (The Journal of Turkish Legal and Economic History), Vol. II.

———, 1939-40, 'XV ve XVI nci Asirlarda Osmanli Imparatorlugunda Toprak Isçliginin Organizasyonu Şekilleri' (Forms of Organization of Agricultural Labour in the Ottoman Empire in the Fifteenth and Sixteenth Centuries), *Iktisat Fakültesi Mecmuasi* (Journal of the Faculty of Economics), Vol. I, Nos. 1, 2, 4.

———, 1943, *XV ve XVI' nci Asirlarda Osmanli Imparatorlugunda Ziraî Ekonominin Hukukî ve Malî Esaslari* (Legal and Financial Principles of the Agricultural Economy in the Ottoman Empire in the Fifteenth and Sixteenth Centuries), Istanbul.

———, 1964, '16.Asrin IkinciYarisindaTürkiye'nin Geçirdigi Iktisadî Buhranlarin Sosyal Yapi Üzerindeki Tesirleri' (The Effects of the Economic Crises Experienced by Turkey in The Second Half of the Sixteenth Century on the Social Structure), in *Iktisadî Kalkinmanin Sosyal Meseleleri* (*Social Aspects of Economic Development*), Istanbul.

———, 1973, '"Feodal" Düzen ve Osmanli Timari' (The 'Feudal' System and the Ottoman Timar), in *Türkiye Iktisat Tarihi Semineri* (Proceedings of the Seminar on Turkish Economic History), Ankara: Hacettepe Üniversitesi (published in 1975).

———, 1974, 'Timar', *Islâm Ansiklopedisi* (Encyclopaedia of Islam, Turkish version), Vol. XII/1.

Berkes, N., 1969, 100 *Soruda Türkiye Iktisat Tarihi* (Turkish Economic History in 100 Questions), Vol. I, Istanbul: Gerçek Yayinevi.

Berktay, H., 1983a, *Cumhuriyet Ideolojisi ve Fuat Köprülü* (Republican Ideology and Fuat Köprülü), Istanbul: Kaynak Yayinlari.

———, 1983b, *Kabileden Feodalizme* (From Tribe to Feudalism) Istanbul: Kaynak Yayinlari.

———, 1985, 'Tarih Calismalari' (Historiography), in *Cumhuriyet Dönemi Türkiye Ansiklopedisi* (Encyclopaedia of Republican Turkey), Vol. 9, Fasc. 78, Istanbul: Iletisim Yayinlari.

———, 1986, 'Osmanli Devletinin Yükşelisine Kadar Türklerin Iktisadi ve Toplumsal Tarihi' (Economic and Social History of the Turks up to the Rise of the Ottoman Empire), in Sina Aksin, ed., *Türkiye Tarihi*, Vol. 1, Istanbul: Cem Yayinlari.

Bloch, M., 1931/1966, *French Rural History: An Essay on Its Basic Characteristics* (tr. Janet Sondheimer), Berkeley: University of California Press (original printing in 1931).

———, 1940/1966, *Feudal Society* (tr. L.A. Manyon), 2 vols. Chicago: University of Chicago Press (original printing in 1940).

———, 1941/1971, 'The Rise of Dependent Cultivation and Seigniorial Institutions', in M.M. Postan, ed., *The Cambridge Economic History of Europe*, Vol. I, Cambridge: Cambridge University Press (1st edn., 1941).

Bois, G., 1980, (Remarks during the discussion following Harbans Mukhia's paper titled 'Peut-on appliquer le concept de féodalisme au cas indien?'), *Compte rendu des séances de la Société d étude du féodalisme*, 1979-80, III-IV, pp. 54-63.

Byres, T.J., 1985, 'Modes of Production and Non-European, Pre-Colonial Societies: The Nature and Significance of the Debate', in Byres and Mukhia, eds. (1985), pp. 1-18.

Byres, T.J., and H. Mukhia, eds., 1985, *Feudalism and Non-European Societies*, London: Frank Cass; also see *The Journal of Peasant Studies* Special Issue (Vol. 12, Nos. 2 and 3, Jan./April) under the same title.

Cahen, C., 1968, *Pre-Ottoman Turkey* (tr. J. Jones Williams), New York: Taplinger.

Cameron, K.N., 1977, *Humanity and Society: A World History*, New York: Monthly Review Press.

Claessen, H.J.M., and P. Skalnik, eds., 1977, *The Early State*, The Hague: Mouton.

Duby, G., 1974, *The Early Growth of the European Economy: Warriors and Peasant from the Seventh to the Twelfth Century* (tr. Howard B. Clarke), Ithaca: Cornell University Press.

Hill, C., 1986, 'The Bourgeois Revolutions in Soviet Scholarship', *New Left Review*, No. 155 (Jan.-Feb.), pp. 107-13.

Hilton, R.H., 1953/1976, 'A Comment', in R.H. Hilton, ed., *The Transition from Feudalism to Capitalism*, London: New Left Books (article originally appeared in 1953).

———, 1976, 'Introduction', in R.H. Hilton, ed., *The Transition from Feudalism to Capitalism*, London: New Left Books.

———, 1978, 'A Crisis of Feudalism', *Past and Present*, No. 80, pp. 3-19.

———, 1984, 'Feudalism in Europe: Problems for Historical Materialists', *New Left Review*, No. 147, Sept.-Oct., pp. 84-93.

Hirst, P.Q., 1975, 'The Uniqueness of the West', *Economy and Society*, Vol. 4, pp. 446-75.

Hobsbawm, E.J., 1964, 'Introduction', in Karl Marx, *Pre-Capitalist Economic Formations*, London: Lawrence & Wishart.

Hodgson, M.G.S., 1974, *The Venture of Islam*, Vol. 3, *The Gunpowder Empires and Modern Times*, Chicago: University of Chicago Press.

Inalcik, H., 1954, 'Stefan Dusan'dan Osmanli Imparatorluguna' (From Stefan Dushan to the Ottoman Empire), in his *Fatih Devri Üzerinde Tetkikler ve Vesikalar* (Researches and Documents on the Period of Mehmet the

Conqueror), Ankara: Türk Tarih Kurumu Yayinlari, pp. 136-84.
———, 1955, 'Land Problems in Turkish History', *The Muslim World*, No. 45, July, pp. 221-8.
———, 1959, 'Osmanlilar'da Raiyyet Rüsumu' (The So-Called Tenancy Tax of the Ottomans), *Belleten* (Bulletin of the Turkish Historical Association), Vol. XXIII, No. 92 (Oct.), pp. 576-610.
———, 1964, 'The Nature of Traditional Society: Turkey' in Ward and Rustow (eds.), *Political Modernization in Japan and Turkey*, Princeton, NJ: Princeton University Press.
———, 1969, 'Capital Formation in the Ottoman Empire', *The Journal of Economic History*, Vol. XXIX, No. 1, pp. 97-140.
———, 1972, 'The Ottoman Decline and its Effects upon the Reaya', in H. Birnbaum and Speros Vryonis, Jr., eds., *Aspects of the Balkans: Continuity and Change*, The Hague: Mouton, pp. 338-54.
———, 1973, *The Ottoman Empire: The Classical Age* 1300-1600, London: Weidenffeld & Nicolson.
———, 1977, 'Centralisation and Decentralisation in Ottoman Administration', in T. Naff and R. Owen, eds., *Studies in Eighteenth Century Islamic History*, Carbondale, pp. 27-52.
———, 1980a, 'Ottoman Social and Economic History: A Review', in *Türkiye'nin Sosyal ve Ekonomik Tarihi* (1071-1920) (Social and Economic History of Turkey, 1071-1920), Ankara: Hacettepe Üniversitesi Yayinlari, pp. 1-8.
———, 1980b, 'Military and Fiscal Transformation in the Ottoman Empire, 1600-1700', *Archivum Ottomanicum*, VI, pp. 283-337.
Islâmoğlu, H. and C. Keyder, 1977, 'Agenda for Ottoman History', *Review*, Vol. I, No. 1, pp. 31-55. Largely excerpted in Bailey and Llobera (1981).
Keyder, Ç., 1976, 'The Dissolution of the Asiatic Mode of Production', *Economy and Society*, Vol. 2 (May).
———, 1981, 'Proto-Endustri Kayrami ve Çevre Ulkelerde Emperyalizmin Yol Açtigi Tahribat' (The Concept of Proto-Industrialisation and the Destruction caused by Imperialism in Peripheral Countries), *Toplum ve Bilim* (Society and Science), No. 13 (Spring), pp. 93-106.
Kiliçbay, M.A., 1982, *Feodalite ve Klasik Dönem Osmanli Üretim Tarzi* (Feudalism and the Classical Ottoman Mode of Production), Ankara: Gazi Üniversitesi Yayinlari.
Köprülü, F., 1934, *Osmanli Imparatorlugunum Kurulusu* (1981 rpt.) Istanbul: Otüken Nestriyat (originally presented as lectures at the Sorbonne, Paris, in 1934).
Küçükömer, I., 1977, 'Asyagil Üretim Biçimi, Yeniden Üretim ve Sivil Toplum' (The Asiatic Mode of Production, Re-production, and Civil Society), *Toplum ve bilim* (Society and Science), No. 2 (Summer), pp. 3-30.
Marx, K., 1885/1967, *Capital*, Vol. II, New York: International Publishers.
———, 1894/1967, *Capital*, Vol. III, New York: International Publishers.

McNeill, W., 1967, *A World History,* New York: Oxford University Press.

Mukhia, H., 1981, 'Was There Feudalism in Indian History?', *The Journal of Peasant Studies,* Vol. 8, No. 3, pp. 273-310.

Mukhia, H., 1985, 'Peasant Production and Medieval Indian Society', in Byres and Mukhia, eds. (1985), pp. 228-51.

Oyan, O., 1983, '1980'ler Türkiyesi'nde Feodalizm Tartismalari ve Bir Feodalizm Anlayisi' (Feudalism Debates in Turkey of the 1980s and One Notion of Feudalism), *Yarin (Tomorrow),* Nos. 27-8.

Postan, M.M., 1961, 'Foreword', in Bloch (1940/1966), pp. xi-xv.

Perinçek, D., 1985, 'Kemalizm ve Devlet' (Kemalism and the State), *Saçak,* No. 23, Dec.

Ste. Croix, G.E.M. de, 1981, *The Class Struggle in the Ancient Greek World,* London; Duckworth.

Timur, T., 1979, *Kurulus ve Yükselis Döneminde Osmanli Toplumsal Düzeni* (The Ottoman Social System in the Periods of its Foundation and Ascendancy), Ankara: Siyasal Bilgiler Fakultesi Yayinlari.

Turan, O., 1950, 'Iktâ', *Islâm Ansiklopedist* (Encyclopaedia of Islam, Turkish version), Vol. V/2, pp. 949-59.

———, 1965, *Selçuklular Tarihi ve Türk-Islâm Medeniyeti* (Seljukid History and Turkish-Islamic Civilisation), Istanbul.

———, 1971, *Selçuklular Zamaninda Türkiye* (Turkey in the Time of the Seljukids), Istanbul: Turan Nésriyat Yurdu.

Verhulst, A., 1966, 'La genese du régime dominial classique en France au haut moyen âge', *Settimane di studio,* XIII, pp. 135-60.

Wickham, C.J., 1981, *Early Medieval Italy: Government and Local Society,* 400-1000, London: Macmillan.

———, 1984, 'The Other Transition: From the Ancient World to Feudalism', *Past and Present,* No. 103, pp. 3-36.

———, 1985, 'The Uniqueness of the East', in Byres and Mukhia, eds. (1985), pp. 166-96.

Wolf, E.R., 1966, *Peasants,* New Jersey: Prentice-Hall.

Pre-Capitalist Modes of Production in Non-European Societies

Ashok Rudra

I propose to structure this intervention in the debate on feudalism in non-European societies by making critical comments on some of the theoretical concepts that are considered essential for arguments in the area of discourse and some of the different theoretical issues that arise out of their use. I shall not start by taking any position in the debate. I shall do so at the end, though my position will gradually become apparent as I proceed.

Before plunging into substantive discussion, it is worth noting the lamentable state of non-communication among scholars concerned with this question. The Special Issue of the *JPS* on 'Feudalism and non-European Societies' appeared in the first quarter of 1985. During that same year another collection appeared with the title 'Feudalism: Comparative Studies' (Leach et al., 1985), containing a number of papers on exactly the same subject as those of the *JPS* debate. It is a remarkable fact that none of the authors writing in either of the volumes makes any reference to the authors writing in the other volumes. The volumes were not available to any of the authors. But, surely, they had long been working on the problem. Yet they were apparently not aware of the work and thought of other scholars on the same issue. Even more unfortunate is the fact that none of the two volumes makes a single reference to a collection in French that preceded them by many years, namely, *Sur le Féodalisme* (*CERM*, 1974), or to Godelier who has been concentrating all his energy on working with a team of researchers on the problem. One ceases to be surprised after this to notice that the debate on Transition that is taking place once again in the pages of *Science and Society* makes hardly any reference to the works just mentioned.

Situated as the present author is in the Third World, he is used to Western scholars knowing very little about debates and discussions taking place in Third World countries. In intellectual matters, too, the exchange between the Centre and the Periphery is an unequal one, though in this case it is to the advantage of the Periphery. But it is amusing to notice that the insularity of scholars in the Western world is so much as to constrict exchange even between neighbouring countries like England and France. Bennet (1985: 124) writing in the Leach volume expresses Anglo-Saxon self-satisfaction about French historians being given to 'grandiose visions of feudalism', whereas British Marxist historians are so much more down to earth. He fails to notice that French Marxists (with the exception of Guy Bois) and historians have largely kept away from the Transition Debate or the quest for the Laws of Motion of the so-called Feudal Mode of Production. Not that I myself underestimate the importance of the transition question or the problematic of the motive force of feudalism. My observation is on the deplorable state of scholarly isolation: a reading which is in sharp contrast with that of those who express satisfaction at the fruitful exchange across national frontiers.[1]

IMPORTANCE OF THE MODE OF PRODUCTION CONCEPT

Byres in his excellent introductory essay in the *JPS* volume makes it amply clear that the theoretical framework within which the debate has to be carried out has to be one of mode of production and social formation. He sets the terms of reference of the debate in the following words:

> . . . when we consider the relevance or irrelevance of the category feudalism we are examining the nature of the *dominant mode of production* in a particular society, or, to use the Marxist notion, in a particular *social formation*. I would insist upon the central importance of the mode of production concept. . . . (Byres, 16-17)

Then again, 'The Marxist historians' central working concept, mode of production, is indeed pivotal'. Later on, he records that, 'Our contributors are all sensitive to the importance of a mode of production analysis'. Byres is, of course, in very good company. But for the exception of Cohen, everybody seems to be agreed that 'it would be impossible to understand a specific society in history without understanding the nature of the pre-dominant mode of production within it . . .' (Hilton, 1984: 84) and that

> the mode of production constitutes the structure which determines what form the growth of the productive forces and the distribution of the surplus will take, how society can or cannot change the structures and how, at suitable moments, the transition to another mode of production can or will take place. It also establishes the range of superstructural possibilities. In short the mode of production is the base of our understanding of the variety of human societies and their interaction, as well as of their historical dynamics. (Hobsbawm, 1984: 46)

It is not only the concept that attracts agreement. There is also accord on the sacrosanctity of the word 'mode'. In the 1950s, Dobb frowned upon Sweezy for using other words: 'But in referring to a "*system* of production" he seems to be saying something other than this, and to be contrasting a *system* of production with a mode of production in Marx's use of the term. What precisely a system of production is intended to cover, I am not clear' (Dobb, 1978: 57). But Stalin, too, talks of system. He, of course, is spared.

Dobb was thus treating the word 'mode' as a technical term with a precise meaning which cannot be substituted by such a word as 'system'. In this attitude of terminological purity, Marxists have remained faithfully steadfast. However, exceptions are not at all uncommon. When Irfan Habib writes of his 'medieval Indian system' he seems to be knowingly and deliberately avoiding the term mode of production. But when Sharma uses the phrase 'mode of socio-economic formation' (100) and again just 'socio-economic formation' one does not understand what exactly he means, but one is clear that he is not using the Hindess and Hirst vocabulary. Similarly, Stein (1985) uses the phrases 'socio-economic formation', 'social formation', and simply 'formation' with meanings which are entirely his own. Lest one is too harsh towards Sharma and Stein, let us remember that Marx himself was not very particular about this terminological purism. As Wickham observes, 'he . . . himself was less bothered by such intricacies; he used "social formation" and "mode of production" more or less as synonyms, and so do many people writing today' (1984: 7). Thus, consider the following all too well-known passages from Marx:

> In all forms of society there is one specific kind of production which predominates over the rest whose relations thus assign rank and inference to the others. (1973: 106-7)
>
> Whatever the social form of production, labourers and means of production always remain factors of it. (1885/1961: 34)
>
> The specific economic form, in which unpaid surplus labour is pumped out of direct producers, determines the relationship of rulers and ruled. . . . It is always the direct relationship of the owners of the conditions of production to the direct producers which reveals the innermost secret, the hidden basis of the entire social structure. . . . (1894/1967: 772)

We would draw the attention of the reader to the phrases, 'forms of society', 'kind of production', 'social forms of production', 'social structure', etc. Many other permutations of words can be easily located in Marx. They are not obviously technical terms with rigorous, definite meanings. That, of course, is no reason to find fault with those latter-day Marxists who might wish to develop terms like mode of production and social formation into technical terms. After all, if Marxism is a science and if it has to develop further as a science, there has to be an ongoing process of sharpening and chiselling of concepts by introducing rigour and precision where there is looseness and vagueness: explicanda have continuously to be rendered into explicata. I now turn to some of the meanings that have been attached to the terms mode of production and social formation.

SOCIAL FORMATION: MEANING

Burton Stein (205) uses the following definition of socio-economic formation in relation to south India:

> . . . as a society, a major portion of South India can be apprehended as arising from a particular material structure—economic and social relations manifesting particular property and productive relations—together with contingent political and ideological features and . . . this set of elements comprised a structure (that is, that it was a self-regulating unity capable of transformation).

Surely this will not be recognized as the Marxian concept of social formation by those Marxists—and they are in the majority now—who define it as a 'concrete combination of different modes of production, organized under the dominance of one of them' (Anderson, 1974a: 22). But what exactly is achieved by those who use this apparently sophisticated, theoretical-sounding definition? Byres, who cites this definition approvingly, significantly points out the possible difficulties with the notion in the following words:

> Precisely what 'articulation' might entail, either in strict theoretical terms or in the treatment of concrete situations is not immediately self-evident. Those who have operated with the idea . . . have failed, for the most part, to rise above simple assertion: the assertion that articulation is of central significance. (20)

He proceeds further: 'Similarly the criterion whereby one might identify dominance remains unspecified.' As to the latter, I would add that this is not just a problem of difficulty, but one of possibility. I doubt that it may be possible at all to establish scientifically which mode is dominant over what other mode in a particular context. The problem would not arise if one were comparing forces of production or relations of production. One can measure, and therefore, compare each element in the set of forces of production. Similarly, one can count the number of persons entering into a particular production relation (say, tenancy) and find out whether that is more or less than the number of persons entering into another production relation (say, wage labour) and settle which is more important. But there is no means of comparing one 'articulated combination' of forces and relation of production with another.

These theoretical difficulties apart, the way the term social formation is used seems to justify Perlin's observation that 'often "social formation" is simply a national or regional unit given to the writer rather than defined by him, thus no unit at all' (1985: 99) and Wallerstein's stricture that in 'the last 25 years, Western Marxists have substituted the term "social formation" for "society". This is just flim-flam. It changes nothing. Everything one can say about the ontological vacuity of "society" applies equally to the concept of "social formation"' (1977: 2). It cannot be said that there is any overdoing in these criticisms, given the way many authors use the term. Thus, Byres himself, while emphasizing the importance of theoretical concepts, writes in the passage quoted before '. . . in a particular society or to use the Marxist notion in a particular *social formation*' (17); and, again refers to '. . . pre-colonial, non-European societies (or social formation, 15)'. Berktay, too, used such formulations, in striking contrast to his emphasis on rigour (270). Wickham, without being critical, says, 'Modes of production are ideal constructs; social formations are real societies in all their complexity, and thus in practice virtually irreducible to formal categories' (114). One may, therefore, well ask the question: if society and social formation mean the same thing, why use the second term, giving the impression of there being yet another theoretical concept? Have we not got enough problems with the theoretical concepts that we already have and which are not superfluous?

MODE OF PRODUCTION: MEANING

While everybody seems to be agreed about the crucial, central, fundamental importance of the concept of mode of production, most authors use it without stopping to define it, as if the term were self-explanatory or all too well known to everybody.[2] Byres (17), however, takes care to state clearly what the terms means for him: 'By mode of production, we mean, following Hindess and Hirst . . . "an articulated combination of relations and forces of production" ' (1975: 9).

He points out that from the definition of Hindess and Hirst, he has omitted the part 'structured by the dominance of the relations of production', for the very good reason of refusing to accord primacy either to the relations of production or to the forces of production: 'There seems to be no binding reason, in theory, why one should posit relations of production or forces of production as dominant', a position that seems to me eminently supportable.

Byres, however, does not seem to face any problems with the idea of 'articulated combination of forces and relations of production'. It is easy to understand combination as such. Let F(t) represent the set of elements which constitute the forces of production at a time point t, and let R(t) be the set of elements which characterize the relations of production at the same time t. Let M be the set of modes of production which contains a very small number of elements like slavery, feudalism, capitalism, AMP (probably), etc. Now, if the elements of this last set are defined as combinations of the first two sets then obviously there has to be some set-theoretic rules of mapping or projecting from the sets F(t) and R(t) to the set M, which is probably what is meant here by 'articulation'. Obviously, every different combination of F(t) and R(t) does not define a new mode.[3] As time passes and t changes, F(t) and R(t) both change, but that does not mean that the mode changes. The mode changes only with certain critical changes in the sets of F(t) and R(t). What these critical changes are is not made clear by stating that a mode is an 'articulated combination of the forces and relations of production'. Berktay among the contributors to the *JPS* debate makes the most of what he terms 'modal differences', but he does not use the 'articulated combination' definition to distinguish between two modes.

In fact, this general definition of a mode is hardly ever used to derive the particular definition of any particular mode like, say, the 'feudal mode'.[4] As is well known, and as the debate brings out ever more clearly, there is no agreed definition of either feudalism or the feudal mode. There are definitions galore. At one extreme there are definitions which include not only production relations, not only 'the soical form of labour', but also various superstructural features; at the other extreme are the definitions, favoured by those Marxists who treat feudalism as a universal category, a 'world-system' involving only coerced labour or only rent paying peasants.[5] Right through the spectrum there is one common element and that is the absence of any reference to the forces of production. Byres (17) utters the caution: 'It is essential to note than no treatment within a general mode of production analysis . . . can be deemed adequate without careful treatment of both relations and forces of production' and that 'the proposition that these two primary elements in a mode of production must be seen to be articulated is important'. But he fails to notice that it is not just Stein and Perlin but nobody writing in the *JPS* volume, for that matter nobody writing anywhere on the feudal mode or any other mode, has ever seriously treated the forces of production.

Thus, take the generalized commodity production or the wage labour definitions of capitalism. Where in it is any reference to forces of production?[6] Take the serfdom definition of feudalism advanced by Dobb and accepted by most Marxists belonging to the feudalism-as-a-universal-mode school. This definition does not even spell out the relations of production. Serf is understood here as any unfree direct producer in agriculture. There seems to be some vagueness around the concept of free and unfree labour. Some think of freedom from attachment to land. Some think of freedom from attachment to persons. In either case, freedom seems to be connected with the idea of mobility. Some others think of freedom from any kind of domination: extra-economic coercion does not necessarily imply attachment either to land or to person. It need not even imply any juridico-political control. Thus labour subject to caste restrictions in India is also unfree labour according to some.[7] This last position understands free labour as being free in the sense of being a commodity. Anyway, whatever one may understand by free labour, a definition of the feudal mode based on labour being unfree is one which has nothing to do with the concept of the forces of production.

All these universalist definitions[8] would seem to treat as a *differentia specifica* of a mode 'the specific economic form, in which unpaid surplus labour is pumped out of direct producers' (Marx, 1894/1962: 772) and not any particular combination of forces and relations of production, articulated or otherwise.

This omission of the forces of production is clear and explicit in Berktay's submission as to what constitutes for him modal differences. He argues that the following constitute the criteria for deciding that one is faced with two and not just one mode:

> (a) . . . two different ways in which the direct producers and the means of production are combined;
> (b) a further demonstration that out of these two different 'ways of combining' there *necessarily flow* two different economic types of surplus extraction;
> (c) A final demonstration that a+b together determine two different essential class structures (305).

Immediately after this Berktay proceeds to elaborate:

> All these may also be expressed by saying that we have to be shown two different social forms of existence of labour power; two different basic relations of

production between a (different) principal producing class and a (different) principal exploiting class. The criterion of forms of surplus extraction is acceptable only insofar as it is a short-hand for the whole of this.

Surely, there cannot be any doubt left that the 'whole of this' excludes the forces of production? We observe in passing that while Berktay makes an impressive show of theoretical rigour he is not much worried about the vagueness with which he uses the concepts of 'ways of combining' direct producers and the means of production, 'economic types of surplus extraction' and 'class structure'. He does not think it necessary to specify how to differentiate between these 'different ways', 'different types' and 'different class structures'.

FEUDAL SOCIETIES: STATIC COMPARISON

The mode of production framework of analysis presents the problem being debated as one of the possible applicability of the feudal mode of production as a universal category applicable to all societies. But before we take that up it is necessary to take a view of a related problematic which does not involve the concept of mode. It has to be acknowledged that feudalism is a term that is not an invention of Marxists and that they have no monopoly over it nor are even the dominant among those who are concerned over its usefulness. The term has been in use (and has been an object of controversy) for a very long time as an analytical category with which to comprehend certain features of society prevailing in certain parts of West Europe during well-defined periods. It has also to be acknowledged that most standard historical works on feudalism do not place the study in any mode of production framework. This is as much true of Marc Bloch as of Ganshoff and almost all French medievalists. Marc Bloch's summary characterization, which enjoys wide acceptance as capturing the essence of West European feudalism as prevailing in its heartland during its period of pre-eminence, is as follows:

> Subject peasantry, widespread use of the service tenement (that is, the fief) instead of a salary, which was out of the question, the supremacy of a class of specialized warriors, ties of obedience and protection, which bind man to man and, within the warrior class assume the distinctive form called vassalage, fragmentation of authority leading inevitably to disorder.

This masterly summarization cannot be reproached for including super-structural features, as Marc Bloch did not write of any feudal mode of production in his vast work. His object of study, as his title indicates, was Feudal Society. Other authors in their treatment of feudalism have chosen to emphasize different features which occur as parts in the comprehensive characterization of Marc Bloch. Ward (1985) has done a good job of distinguishing as many as ten foci in the scholarly understanding of feudalism. Thus, Focus I emphasizes 'ties of dependence or vassalage'. Focus II is on the institution of the 'fief', defined as land held in conditional rather than absolute tenure, that is upon the condition of provision of service. Focus IV makes specialized military service the touchstone of feudalism, the authors cited being Cronne (1939-40) and Stephenson (1941). Focus V is on the tendencies of parcellization and centralization of political power. Only Focus IX refers to

> seigneurialism or lordship over land as a productive unit (manorialism), an economic system in which whatever its variation in detail, the peasants who occupied and tilled the land were not its owners. Agrarian property was privately controlled by a class of feudal lords, who extracted surplus from the peasants by politico-legal relations of compulsion.

Likewise, Guerreau (1980), even though writing in a Marxian framework, presents an excellent account of the dynamic perspectives of the different conceptions of feudalism found among historians, mainly French and not all Marxists. Incidentally, he rightly discounts the importance of Marc Bloch's classical work lacking a dynamic dimension. The collection edited by Leach and others (1985) is largely non-Marxist in orientation but cannot for that reason be ignored. The fact is that the debate about feudalism being a universal or a particular category is not confined to Marxists. Coulborn (1956) took up the question long before many Marxists did. The debate carried out in non-Marxian terms therefore cannot but hold interest for Marxists. This is all the more so as many Marxists themselves use the concept of feudalism not as a mode of production but as a social structure bearing certain important resemblances with society in certain parts of West Europe during the period called feudal. Sharma, for example, in his first essay on Indian feudalism (1965)

> made a point by point comparison with Europe employing all the terms, categories and institutions in reference to which the Pirennean school had analysed feudalism in Europe: decline of trade, manor, serfdom, commutation of labour services into cash payment, revival of trade and urban centres, and so on. And if he did not find the Germanic invasion of Europe replicated in India, B.N.S. Yadav, another erudite proponent of the notion of Indian feudalism, drew attention to the Hun invasions of India at about the same period of time. (Mukhia, 245)

I have myself criticized Sharma for this caricature [see Rudra (1981)] but would all the same hold that if feudalism is to be used at all as a universal category, attempts like that of Sharma, to compare feature by feature in a static framework, need not be dismissed out of hand with sarcasm. That is because, going by results obtained, such static comparisons, which do not make any distinction between infrastructure and superstructure, have yielded better results than comparisons within the mode of production framework which we shall take up in the next section. The most one can obtain from such a non-modal, static comparison, is, of course, 'a cluster of family resemblances, associated together in groupings derived from the specific history of Europe and its regions' (Jeffcott, 1985: 158), the usefulness of which lies as much in directing attention to 'contrasts as well as resemblances'. One may well agree with Perlin that in the case of India, 'comparison on this level, such as those by Tod and Wills, have proved highly useful as have also those of a later generation of Indianists . . .' (1985: 107). Perlin gives many other examples of such acceptable comparisons. However limited the gains, they are probably more than those obtained from comparisons on a mode of production basis as we shall see in the following section.

The most serious reservation I have on this approach of comparative study of societies lies in its Eurocentricism. Why should Europe be accorded the privilege of providing yardsticks with which to compare non-European societies? Why should one use such terms as 'seigniorial rights', 'serfdom', 'sub-infeudation', 'manorial', etc., as Sharma, for example, does, in a way begging the question of similarities? Why should one not try to understand European society in terms of, say, the caste system, zamindari, etc? Surely, one will find family resemblances in European institutions of these purely Indian types?

THE FEUDAL DYNAMIC

Mode of production is a dynamic concept. Its importance lies in its being the crucial element in the view of history as a sequence of modes, logically connected with each other. This view of history, regarded as a basic plank of Historical Materialism, derives its authority from the following important proposition in the celebrated passage in Marx's 'Preface to the Critique of Political Economy': '. . . in broad outline, the Asiatic, ancient, feudal and modern bourgeois modes of production may be designated as epochs marking progress in the economic development of the society'. It attained orthodoxy in terms of the somewhat different formulation, proclaimed in Procrustean terms by Stalin as follows: '. . . the primitive communal system was succeeded precisely by the slave system, the slave system by the feudal system and the feudal system by the bourgeois system and not by some other' (Stalin, 1938: 26). The view has been echoed more elaborately by various scholars who have extensively researched the problem during the last few decades. For instance,

> Before 1964 Historical Materialism was generally interpreted to mean that history displayed a single sequence of universally occurring stages of social development, each of them corresponding to a different stage in the development of productive forces. The immanent logic of the development of material production was taken to be such that each stage of the succession would appear, unveil its inner contradictions and give rise to the next, higher phase of economic production and social development. (Sawer, 1977: 188)

Since 1964 there has been a big change, in that many Marxists do not subscribe anymore to the unilinear view of an identical succession of stages applicable to all societies. They advance a pluralistic view which retains the concept of history as a succession of stages, but with different sequences for different parts of the world. There is a vast literature on the subject among which Sawer (1977) and Melotti (1977) are particularly informative. The essential point to retain for us here is that each of these stages corresponds to a particular mode of production. As is well known, one concedes that at no stage is there only one mode of production: there is more than one and one of them is dominant and characterizes the stage.

What is essential for us is the idea, clearly stated in the extract from Sawer, and which would be accepted by all Marxists as being essential to the concept of mode of production, that there is some kind of inner dynamism in each mode which makes it '. . . appear, unveil its inner contradictions and give rise to the next' mode of production. It is to this dynamic that one refers when one talks of the Laws of Motion of a mode.[9] It is of this that one talks when one uses such terms as the 'motive force' or the 'prime mover' of history. It is, however, important to recognize that while everybody is convinced about the existence of laws in each mode, nobody has really been able to unravel them. Marx himself devoted all his life to discovering the laws of motion of the capitalist mode. He, however, did not leave behind anything that might be called laws of motion of the feudal mode of production or the slave mode of production. Very little work has been done since his time on the laws of motion of the 'slave' mode.[10] There have, however, been quite a few attempts at discovering the dynamic of the feudal mode.

The terms 'motor' or 'Prime Mover' invoke the image of an engine generating movement in history—they obviously draw inspiration from the laws of physical dynamics and may be expected to be of the nature of such laws as that of the Falling Rate of Profit for capitalism. There has been at least one attempt to formulate such a law, that of Guy Bois (1984). Guy Bois's law of 'The Diminishing Rate of Feudal Levy' is extracted from his meticulous study of the movements in prices and production in Normandy in the first few centuries of the second millennium. Likewise, Witold Kula (1976) has offered what he calls an 'An Economic Theory of Feudalism'. He studies separately the 'short term dynamic' and the 'long term dynamic' in terms of movements in employment, output, prices, etc. Hilton (1978) responded to Sweezy's query as to what constituted the prime mover of feudalism by blandly stating that it was the class struggle between lords and serfs.[11] Dobb endorsed the view and Brenner (1976 and 1982) later on took up the cue and extensively analysed the decline of feudalism in terms of the struggle between lords, serfs and the monarch.

The purpose of this rapid review of literature is not to inform, for all these are well known. Our purpose is to proclaim the King to be naked. Somebody has to break the silence over the fact that while everybody seems to be agreed that here is a feudal dynamism which leads to decline and the subsequent genesis of capitalism, nobody has been able to put his finger on that mechanism. If indeed there has been some kind of a clockwork ticking away within the feudal mode, history has hidden it very well indeed and it has eluded the efforts of all explorers.

As to Guy Bois's model, Brenner (1982) concedes that it seems to fit the Norman evidence extremely well but is 'contradicted by the radically different English data of the same period'. Maurice Aymard (1981) on his part shows how Bois' model does not fit at all the history of Italian feudalism. We may, for our part, add that Bois's model can at the most explain a pattern of cyclical changes during the period when feudal class relations and institutions were dominant. It does not in any way explain either the genesis of feudalism or its dissolution, not to speak of the emergence of capitalism out of its ruins. Similarly, Kula's work is highly enlightening about the short-term and long-term movements of the Polish economy of the period studied by him, but as Postan observes, after showering well-deserved praises on the author, Kula's 'Polish feudalism appears to display characteristics uniquely its own' and 'there is little in his analysis to demonstrate how and why Polish feudalism prepared its own decline and its replacement by a different economic order' (Postan, 1977: 75). Also his model, if it can be called a model, explains neither the emergence nor the decline of feudalism.

Brenner himself advances what he calls a 'class struggle model' of West European feudalism. He concentrates his attention mainly on the contrasting courses of feudal history in England and France and he explains the differences in terms of the divergence in the balance of class forces and state structures in the two countries, and the consequent differences in the class struggles in the two cases. Brenner's arguments are, of course, highly persuasive, but their limits are not to be overlooked. His is a story of the decline of feudalism.[12] Like Guy Bois, he fails to account for the ascending phase of the feudal period which witnessed considerable expansion of the forces of production, now termed by some as the first Industrial Revolution of the twelfth century. Nor is his success any the more in explaining the second Industrial Revolution, the familiar one of the eighteenth century. His class struggle model, including only the lords and the serfs and excluding the bourgeoisie, does not even attempt to explain the appearance of entrepreneurs, merchants, bankers, manufacturers, etc., who played such important parts in the emergence of capitalism.

It is, however, not my intention in the least to underrate the importance, from the point of view of the Marxian theory of history, of the contributions of Guy Bois, Kula or Brenner. On the contrary, it will be my argument, which I shall develop more fully in the next section, that the Marxian tools of analysis, properly applied, will necessarily result in the uncovering of dynamics which are regionally specific. The various authorities that I have quoted previously suggest, wrongly in my judgement, that there are identifiable universal laws of feudalism comparable to the universal laws of capitalism. It is understandable that in this climate of thinking both Guy Bois and Kula should claim for their regional models validity of a universal nature.[13] On this last point they are wrong, but that does not diminish the value of their work. Feudal dynamics in that clockwork sense, to which alone such graphic terms as the prime mover or the motive force may be justifiably applied, is a chimera that seems to have seduced a whole generation of Marxist scholars. The sooner it is recognized as unattainable, the better.[14]

FEUDAL MODE: DYNAMIC COMPARISONS

If societies are grouped together on the basis of the predominant mode, the procedure of so analysing them would be justified only if there were some dynamic similarities within each group. If not, there would be no point in resorting to such grouping. This view is held by many historians who have reservations about extending the coverage of the feudal mode to encompass practically all pre-industrial pre-capitalist societies. Irfan Habib (188) speaks for many when he writes: 'We are interested in feudalism (as in Western Europe) chiefly for elucidating the development of capitalism. For such purpose its "laws of motion" are most important for us.'

Likewise, Perry Anderson (1974b: 402) writes:

> if, in effect the feudal mode of production can be defined independently of the variant juridical and political super-structures which accompany it, such that its presence can be registered throughout the globe wherever primitive and tribal social formations were superceded, the problem then arises: how is the unique dynamism of the European theatre of international feudalism to be explained?

Anderson is referring to the uniqueness of European feudalism having a dynamic which led to the genesis of capitalism.[15] Both Habib and Anderson are emphasizing the incapability of the infrastructure alone to explain the dynamic exhibited by European feudalism. Anderson says categorically: 'No structural analysis of feudalism considered simply as an "economic system"—that is as a mode of surplus extraction—can explain the dynamics of feudalism. . . .' Habib elaborates:

> Dobb (1946: 35) holds that feudalism is to be treated as 'virtually identical' with serfdom but it was surely much more than that: its distribution system rested on the fief . . . and the entire fabric of vassalage. It is impossible to analyse its development and dissolution (in Western Europe) without considering these institutions.

Habib states his general approach in the following words:

> . . . if each economic formation is distinguished by its own specific laws of motion—and even a specific prime mover—it cannot simply stem from the conditions of labour alone, but must arise out of an interaction of these with other elements of the property system, an interaction which cannot also remain unaffected by factors external to both (187).

Habib invites trouble by writing loosely in terms of economic formation and vaguely in terms of 'laws of motion' and the 'prime mover'. It has been seen in the last section that such mechanical imageries as 'prime mover' and the idea of laws comparable to those of the natural sciences are best done without while dealing with history. Similarly, Anderson when he invokes the sacred cow of the feudal mode of production. What they have to say can be said without using these vague ambiguous terms. (If the avoidance of these terms invites the charge that Marxism is being abandoned, so much the worse for that kind of Marxism. Marxism, in my judgement, has acquired sufficient maturity as a science not to depend on a few vague phrases.)

It is only natural that what Habib and Anderson have to say would be echoed by many of those who have sat down actually to study or write the history of particular societies, rather than only talk about how history has to be written.[16] The point at issue is the importance to be accorded to superstructure. It is this that provokes the violent and contemptuous reaction of self-appointed defenders of the purity of Marxism like Berktay. We shall consider the latter's position in due course. Before that, we note the ensemble of historians who declare their incapacity to write history without taking superstructure into account. Thus Brenner: '. . . it is indeed central to my viewpoint that "fusion" (to put it imprecisely) between "the economic" and "the political" was a distinguishing and constitutive feature of the feudal class structure and system of production' (1982: 28). He adds, ignoring the scorn that he might provoke among orthodox defenders of Marxian purity: 'It seems to me, therefore, that those historians who have insisted upon a narrowly "political" definition of feudalism as a "form of government" have grasped an essential driving force of the system' (1982: 40). Brenner, of course, does not only assert: he has actually demonstrated the working of this driving force. Strong support to this position is lent by Hilton in the following words:

> . . . the specific features distinguishing medieval European feudalism are often supposed to be of a superstructural character. In fact the 'feudal' tenures of post Carolingian Northern Europe were not universal over Europe, but the hierarchy of kings, dukes, counts and knights was fairly general as was the ethos of feudal loyalty. . . . An aspect of European feudalism which is normally regarded as superstructural was the fragmentation of political authority, particularly in its jurisdictional aspect. (1984: 85-6)

The upshot of the above seems to be the following. Practising historians are agreed that movement in history is generated not by the spring-like working of some 'motor', representing the method of surplus extraction, but by the interaction of the relations of production and—we shall commit the heresy of adding, relations of distribution—with not only the forces of production but also the different parts of the superstructure.

Is it possible for anybody to contest this position? It might appear on a first reading that Berktay is vehemently opposed to this view. That, however, is not a correct reading. All of Berktay's powerful onslaught is directed at the intrusion of any element of the superstructure into the sacred confines of the mode of production, in which he would accommodate only the method of surplus extraction. His opposition to '. . . ascribing a different modal dynamic to each observed slice of concrete historical movement' is well taken and everybody will agree that the only sensible alternative is that of 'handling such concrete historicities in terms of a more classical base-superstructure dialectic'. Is Berktay not crashing through an open door? Are Anderson or Habib or Hilton suggesting anything other than proceeding in terms of such a base-superstructure interaction?

It is an altogether different matter when one talks of a 'fusion' of the 'economic' and the 'political'. Such fusion, of course, is quite different from interaction between the 'economic' and the 'political'. We would, on our part, point out a way in which such 'fusion' takes place which is different from the sense in which Brenner talks of it. We would point out that the base cannot move by itself. Forces of production like machinery, energy, skills of labour, technological knowledge, etc., do not grow by themselves; they are made to grow by human agents in the form of workers, entrepreneurs, inventors, etc. Similarly, relations of production do not change by themselves. They are the results of class struggle between the owners of the means of production and the actual producers. In either case, these activities are stimulated or thwarted by the values and attitudes of human agents. In certain times and places (as in post-Renaissance Europe) human agents worked intensively for the improvement of the forces of production, whereas in certain other times and places (like Mughal India, as demonstrated by Irfan Habib) human agents were not oriented towards making technological improvements. Likewise, class struggle also varies in intensity, depending on the time and the place. It is the ideology of the society that has such effects on the forces and relations of production.

Where there is substantive difference is that Berktay, along with all others who subscribe to the view of universal feudalism, chooses to ascribe to all pre-capitalist societies a common modal designation. Those who object to this are worried about the pointlessness of the exercise of grouping all these diverse societies under the umbrella of a common mode. The problem does not lie in the logic of the operation. Any kind of grouping is always feasible. If the feudal mode is to be defined in terms of coerced labour alone then there can be no logical objection to the grouping of all societies '. . . from the France of 1788 to the Nigerian emirates, from Tsarist Russia to nineteenth century India or China' (Melotti, 1977: 10) and call them feudal. Berktay does not even insist upon peasants being unfree. For him it is feudalism as long as they are obliged to pay rent or tax. The entire burden of his long essay is an effort to show the modal equivalence of rent and revenue. Once this definition is accepted it is logically foolproof that even though 'Ancien Regime France, Russia, Sung China, Qajar Iran, the late Roman empire are societies very different from Capetian France', all of them can be treated as being dominated by the feudal mode of production. There is no scope for any logical fallacy here—just as a tautology is always true. The point is, what does one gain by this modal characterization?

WHY CLASSIFY?

While we have held the view that a modal classification of societies can be meaningful only if one can group together certain dynamic similarities, Berktay seems to think fit to subject such an approach to ridicule. Thus, he caricatures Anderson's and and Habib's concern about European feudalism possessing the essential and crucial property of having led to the birth of capitalism with such words as the following '. . . different dynamics, different historical outcomes; hence different modes of production' and 'capitalism did not arise in the East; therefore, wherever it did not arise, feudalism must not have been the pre-capitalist mode of production'. Ridicule reflecting one's 'individual preference' is no substitute for serious arguments and surely does not constitute any 'higher criteria concerning the overall structure of Marxist theory'.

Berktay devotes considerable energy to obliterating what he calls 'modal differences' between the East and the West and establishing modal uniformity even across the barrier of rent and tax. His many times repeated strong reservations about there being 'as many modes of production as there are distinct legal-political constitution and forms of extra-economic sanction which follow from them' [Hirst (1975: 462) criticizing Anderson] is quite well taken, for '. . . there is no doubt that the inclusion of the superstructure in the mode . . . automatically produces a different "mode" fitted to every historical concreteness precisely because in reality, each historical concreteness is nothing but a different, specific articulation of these three levels' (Berktay, 298).

Berktay is obviously right that it is useless to have a system of modal classification of societies if every concrete historical society has to be ascribed a distinct dominant mode. One resorts to taxonomy in order to reduce the number of types to be distinguished. If there are, say, N elements, to group them into K types, as one does in the Life Sciences, achieves the purpose of helping comprehension: it is easier to comprehend K distinctions rather than N distinctions, when N is very large and K relatively small. Surely, if one resorts to a system of classification whereby every one of the N elements to be classified is regarded as a class by itself, each class containing a single member, then, of course, there is no point in such a classification. This is the problem given rise to by the fusion of the superstructure and infrastructure to which Berktay draws our attention, and he is of course quite right. However, is there any greater justification in a scheme of classification which results in just a single class including all the N members? That is exactly what results from the application of the concept of a universal feudalism. If one takes the coerced labour definition of feudalism then all pre-industrial and pre-capitalist class societies become feudal.[16] If, on the other hand, one takes Berktay's definition of surplus extraction through rent or tax, such feudalism would cover all societies other than those based on slave labour. Berktay is well aware that such a definition would group together societies with very different forces of production, very different superstructures and therefore very different dynamics. He categorically refuses to be bothered by this heterogeneity. Given that the different societies thus grouped together would have different dynamics, he is obviously giving up the idea of history being a sequence of modes, there being only a few alternative sequences to choose from.[17] What then is the common element in the group? Of course, the defining characteristic, namely, the method of surplus extraction, is common. But what else? If nothing else, then what is the analytical advantage of doing the grouping at all?

It would be unfair to Berktay to suggest that he does not answer the question. He does. To judge by the criteria he presents for recognizing modal differences and therefore modal uniformity (which we have referred to in our first section), he seems to be suggesting that all societies which have the common characteristic of surplus extraction through rent or tax have identical or at least very similar class structures. This is such a proposterous claim that we can do no more than record our stunned disbelief that anybody in his senses could make it. Leaving aside tax, even when surplus is extracted only through rent, Mukhia (1985) has shown persuasively how even differences between labour rent, produce rent and cash rent would have different impacts on class struggle and therefore on class structure.

MARXIAN METHOD WITHOUT MODE OF PRODUCTION

Anyway, Berktay's concern to prove that rent and revenue cannot by themselves give rise to modal differences is not my main interest here. My concern is with the uselessness of a scheme of classification which results in a single class. If the choice is between N classes for N elements and a single class for all N elements it seems to me that both are equally unsatifactory and one should not be forced to choose either of them. The obvious option is to drop the idea of classification altogether. In this particular case, it means dropping the concept of mode of production.

Surely, this would provoke reactions amongst many that we are abandoning Marxism.[18] I do not, however, take that view. Marx himself did not attach that central importance to the concept of mode, as his various uses of the term with different meanings indicate. For me the essence of the Marxian method consists in analysing movements in history in terms of interactions between the forces of production and the relations of production, and not just that but also interaction between these two with the superstructure. We would suggest that whenever history has been properly written, use has been made explicitly or implicitly of this methodology. This is as much true of Marx's own historical writings as of Marxist historians who have written history rather than talked about how to write history. This is true of Dobb, Hilton, Hobsbawm, Perry Anderson, Brenner and others writing about Europe, Kosambi's masterly work on ancient India and Irfan Habib's standard work on Mughal society. In none of the above cases did the historians work with mode of production as an instrument of analysis, not even Dobb.

They have made passing references to the concept but that is not the same thing as making use of its as a central instrument. I therefore venture to suggest that these works would retain all their value if the phrase 'mode of production' were not to be mentioned in them at all.

Am I then suggesting that the usual way of thinking of European history as a succession of slavery, feudalism and capitalism is to be forgone because it is not helpful? Not quite that. It is indeed helpful to think of European history as a succession of epochs during which slave relations, feudal relations and capitalist relations of production were dominant. As I have argued in the first section, dominance of relations of production is a much more tractable concept than mode of production dominance. It is also permissible to hazard the guess that if one studies in detail the history of, say, India, one should be able to identify the dominant class relations during any period and divide its history into epochs corresponding to such different class dominance. This approach has the virtue of making a non-problem of the question of how to characterize mode-wise pre-colonial India or different parts of that long historical period. In this connection, it may be recalled that even those who subscribe to the theory of an Indian feudalism like, say, R.S. Sharma, leave the entire stretch of several centuries from 1300 onwards without any modal characterization. Looking for dominant class relations in different periods is a serious research problem. Trying to fill gaps with modes of production is a game in nomenclature.

That history is the history of class struggle, struggle between a class that wants to take the forces of production forward and a class or classes that want to retain them unchanged, that historical movement is generated by the resultant interaction between the forces of production and the relations of production, that these struggles and interactions are conditioned by political, juridical and ideological factors—all these are accepted by all Marxists and I am not saying anything new. What is new in what I am saying is that the idea that this process of struggle and interaction results in the emergence, the ascendancy and the decline of certain modes of production is a seductive, grandiose vision but with no particular analytical advantage. History studied in terms of the dialectic of the forces and relations of production, of the infrastructure and the superstructure might reveal a succession of dominant relations of production. If there are as many sequences as there are societies we do not see any harm in that. We do see much harm in trying to force all these different trajectories observed in different societies into the straitjacket of a single or at most a few sequences.

NOTES

1. I here refer to the enthusiastic survey of the resurgence of Marxian intellectual output in the Western world in the course of which Perry Anderson (1983: 27) writes; 'the new exchanges between history and theory and across national frontiers—have been among the most fruitful changes in the past decade'.
2. Perlin (1985) seems to be more aware than other contributors to the debate about the problem given rise to by all the different meanings associated with the term 'mode of production'. His distinction between the micro and macro concepts of mode of production is, indeed, extremely important. It is, of course, clear that in the debate one is concerned with the macro, holistic definition which alone occurs in the notion of history as a sequence of modes.
3. I have made some uses of set-theoretic language since this is essential if one is to understand the relations between forces of production, relations of production and mode of production. It is not at all clear what one is to make of such expressions as 'simple juxtaposition of a set of relations and a set of forces' (Hindess and Hirst, 1975: 11); or what 'juxtaposition' means in analytical terms.
4. An exception is Hilton (1984) who attempts to present a definition of the feudal mode explicitly including a characterization of the forces of production. One may, however, have doubts about how far his references to forces of production are satisfactory. He talks mostly about organization of peasant production and makes no references to such things as technology, means of

production, skills, etc. Also, it may be kept in mind that Hilton belongs to the school which would include super-structural features in the feudal mode of production. He cannot, therefore, be grouped together with those who defend a universalist definition of feudalism.

5. One protests against the use of the term 'world-system' to describe the universality of the feudal mode. There are enough problems with terms that are used with different meanings and terms that are used interchangeably. Mukhia ('Peasant Production and Medieval Indian Society') has done a good job of clarifying the meaning with which the term 'world-system' is used by Wallerstein and Braudel.
6. Think of the changes that have taken place in the forces of production since Marx's time till today's nuclear and electronic technology. This fantastically wide spectrum has not brought about any change in the capitalist mode of production, even though it is consistent also with whatever be the mode of production dominant in the Soviet Union. One wonders how one may go about defining a capitalist mode of production giving an important part to the forces of production for purposes of modal identification.
7. In our view Marx meant by 'unfree labour' nothing other than a negation of the concept of labour being free in the sense of being a commodity. From this understanding there could not be any question of peasants in medieval India being free labourers. Peasants in medieval India might or might not have been free from different kinds of attachment to land or persons, but surely there was no labour market with sellers of labour power. Mukhia deliberates a lot about forces outside the village not having much control over the peasants. The inside-outside distinction seems to be irrelevant here. Given the caste system and the Jajmani system (of customary allocation of remuneration in kind) there could not possibly be peasants selling their labour power freely. Even in present-day India poor peasants are mostly subject to various restrictions which prevent them from being free sellers of labour power.
8. Here is a sample of various universalist definitions of feudalism:

   Sedov: 'Given that cultivators work on their own land with the aid of their own implements and they alienate their surplus labour in the interest of the third person or third persons, they are therefore subject to feudal exploitation' (1968: 71-84).

   Hilton: 'The essence of the feudal mode of production in the Marxist sense is the exploitative relationship between landowners and subordinated peasants, in which the surplus beyond subsistence of the latter, whether in direct labour or in rent in kind or in money, is transferred under coercive sanction to the former' (1978: 30).

   Dobb: '. . . an obligation laid on the producer by force and independently of his own volition to fulfil certain economic demands of an overlord, whether these demands take the form of services to be performed or of dues to be paid in kind . . .' (1983: 36).

Dobb: '. . . the mode of production under feudalism was the petty mode of production—production by small producers attached to the land and to their instruments of production. The basic social relation rested on the extraction of the surplus product of this petty mode of production by the feudal ruling class—an exploitation relationship that was buttressed by various methods of "extra economic compulsion" ' (1978: 165).

Wickham: 'Coercive rent-raking is the fuedal mode of production . . .' (118).

Perlin: 'Any system of production may be described as feudal when "surplus" is generated through non-economic forces (say, through political and military power backed up by jural institutions—the permanent institutionality of the forces of repression)' (1985: 90). (Perlin is referring to what he calls Type 2 definition used by many others.)

Bois: 'feudalism is the hegemony of small-scale individual production (hence the level of productive forces that this hegemony presupposes), plus the seigneurial levy secured by a constraint of political (or extra-economic) origin' (1984: 398).

Takahashi is explicit that not even all aspects of the productive relations but only labour relations are sufficient: 'When we consider the ancient, the feudal and the modern bourgeois modes of production as the chief stages in economic history, the first thing to be taken into account must always be the social existence form of labour power, which is the basic, the decisive factor in the various modes of production' (1978: 70).

9. Most Marxists seem to be given to the idea that there are such laws. Thus:

Hilton: 'There is a law of feudal (as of other) societies which eventually generate the conditions for the transition from feudalism to capitalism' (1978: 12).

Hobsbawm: 'the mechanism which *necessarily* leads feudalism to be replaced by capitalism, as the historic tendency of capital accumulation, in Marx's analysis, leads capitalism to its doom' (1978: 159).

Godelier: 'the laws of appearance, development and disappearance of different types of socio-economic relations . . .' (*Godelier*, 1981: 162).

10. We agree with the following assessment of Pryor: 'Marxist scholars interested in pre-capitalist modes of production writing during the last hundred years or so have attempted to elucidate the characteristics of the feudal mode of production as sketchily outlined by Marx, but in most cases, at least in the European context, the result has been a barren exercise in philosophy. . . .The same is true, I believe, of all other pre-capitalist or non-capitalist modes of production' (1985: 168).

11. Hilton wrote in his intervention in the Transition Debate: 'A struggle for rent was the "prime mover" in feudal society' (1978: 115); and Dobb wrote: 'The basic conflict must have been between the direct producers and their feudal overlords. This was the crucial class struggle under feudalism and not any

direct clash of urban bourgeois elements (traders) with feudal lord.' This does raise the question: was it the bourgeoisie that developed capitalism or was it the serfs?

12. Brenner writes in his long essay: 'the system-wide consequences of this structure of reproduction . . . was a built-in secular trend towards declining productivity of labour and ultimately to large scale socio-economic crisis' (1982: 17). Is not Brenner's entire study, begun in 1977 and completed in 1982, devoted to showing the working of this dialectic resulting in declining productivity and finally to crisis? What of the ascending phase? Has he anything to say about how that is to be explained? Hilton has suggested that 'the necessary if fluctuating pressure by the ruling class for the transfer to itself of peasant surplus labour or surplus product was a root cause of the technical progress and improved feudal organization which made for the enlargement of the disposable surplus' (1978: 27). But then he does not follow up his own suggestion to show how this expansion of productive forces took place as a result of the lords' increasing demand for rent.
13. Bois writes in his introduction: '. . . the economic system before capitalism remains a question mark. Its actual functioning—its specific mechanism and internal logic—is still essentially unknown.' And then he expresses his 'conviction that the solution to this problem probably in the next ten years, will be a fundamental turning-point in medieval economic historiography' (1984: 4). Likewise, Kula writes: '. . . this book is not so much a study of the Polish economy in the modern age but rather an attempt to develop methods which enable us to study the history of economic life in a country in which the market economy is weakly developed . . .' (1976: 10).
14. Sweezy alone has had the courage of his conviction and categorically rejected the concept of a feudal mode of production in the following words: 'The whole notion of feudalism as a mode of production with an independent existence and its own internal laws of motion seemed to me such a violent abstraction from—and hence distortion of—reality as to be quite useless as an aid to historical interpretation' (1986: 83).
15. It is not clear why Berktay attacks Perry Anderson alone for ascribing to feudalism a dynamism that leads to the development of capitalism. Hobsbawm has also worried about this to quite an extent. For instance, writing about the universalist definition of feudalism with which he says he does not necessarily agree, he observes 'it is very doubtful whether we can speak of a *universal* tendency of such a feudalism to develop into capitalism' (1978: 160). He adds, à propos of European feudalism, 'it is certainly probable that there exists a fundamental contradiction in this particular form of feudal society which drives it ever forward towards the victory of capitalism. The nature of this contradiction has not yet been satisfactorily clarified' (1978: 163). Hobsbawm thus sees a distinction in European feudalism from other feudalisms.
16. Scholars who object to the concept of universal feudalism offer reasons that are similar. Thus, for example:

Hilton: 'The exploitation of servile peasants by a landowning class is widespread in the world history, from Asia to the Americas, from ancient to modern times. If this is the feudal mode of production, then feudalism has been almost everywhere, at sometime or other' (1984: 85).

Leach: 'There have been hundreds, perhaps thousands, of quite different social and political structures which deserve the title "pre-industrial society". If this diversity is squeezed into a single category "Feudalism", the category becomes redundant' (1985: 8).

Hobsbawm: 'In practice this means that "feudalism", having become a sort of residuary legatee, now stretches over a vast expanse—from primitive societies up to the triumph of capitalism, which in some countries is in this century, and from China to West Africa, perhaps even to Mexico' (1978: 160).

But this very generality enthuses Berktay and Wickham. Wickham writes: 'It seems to me that feudalism was a world-system . . . because empirically there have been few if any class societies that have not experienced some form of landowning and coercive rent-taking. This experience unifies Capetian France and Ancient Regime France and Russia and Sung China and Qajar Iran and the late Roman Empire and modern Guatemela' (Wickham, 116).

17. If a mode of production does not necessarily emerge from another given mode nor is necessarily succeeded by another given mode, if the same mode can be preceded and followed by many different modes, then surely the number of sequences that one would observe in history would be much larger than one has talked about in the literature on sequences of mode. If there are as many different sequences as there have been societies in history one fails to understand what is the advantage of thinking of history in this particular fashion.

18. Wickham writes: 'Anderson is here abandoning Marxism' (117). It is high time that Marxists rose above the adolescent habit of calling each other names for not being sufficiently Marxist. There are canons in a religion but never in a science. If one rejected the Theory of Relativity or Quantum Mechanics by saying that that was abandoning Newton one can imagine the state modern physics would be in today. We have learnt how to understand history, economics, politics, etc., from Karl Mark and that is why we are Marxists. Need there be binding constraints on our thinking because we are Marxists?

REFERENCES

Anderson, Perry, 1974a, *Passages from Antiquity to Feudalism*, London: New Left Books.

———, 1974b, *Lineages of the Absolutist State*, London: New Left Books.

———, 1983, *In The Tracks of Historical Materialism*, London: Verso.

Aymard, Maurice, 1981, 'L'Europe Moderne: Féodalite Ou Féodalités?', *Annales*, No. 3 (Mai-Juin).

Bennet, J. Michael, 1985, 'The English Experience of Feudalism', in Edmund Leach, S.N. Mukherjee and John Ward, eds., *Feudalism: Comparative Studies*, Sydney: Sydney Association for Studies in Society and Culture.

Berktay, Halil, 1987, 'The Feudalism Debate: The Turkish End—Is 'Tax-vs-Rent' Necessarily the Product and Sign of a Modal Difference?', *Journal of Peasant Studies*, Vol. 14, No. 3 (April).

Bois, Guy, 1984, *The Crisis of Feudalism: Economy and Society in Eastern Normandy c. 1300-1550*, Cambridge and Paris: Cambridge University Press and Editions de la Maison des Sciences de l'Homme.

Brenner, Robert, 1976, 'Agrarian Class Structure and Economic Development in Pre-Industrial Europe', *Past and Present*, No. 70 (Feb.).

———, 1982, 'The Agrarian Roots of European Capitalism', *Past and Present*, No. 97 (Nov.).

Byres, T.J., 1985, 'Modes of Production and Non-European Pre-Colonial Societies: The Nature and Significance of the Debate', *Journal of Peasant Studies*, Vol. 12, Nos. 2 and 3 (Jan. and April).

CERM (Centre d'Études et de Recherches Marxistes), 1974, *Sur le Féodalisme*, Paris.

Coulborn, Rushton, ed., 1956, *Feudalism in History*, Princeton, NJ: Princeton University Press.

Cronne, H.A., 1939-40, 'Historical Revisions, XCI. The Origins of Feudalism', *History*, Vol. XXIV.

Dobb, Maurice, 1963, revd. edn., *Studies in the Development of Capitalism*, London: Routledge & Kegan Paul.

———, 1978, 'A Further Comment', in Rodney Hilton, ed., *The Transition from Feudalism to Capitalism*, London: Verso.

Godelier, Maurice, 1981, 'D'Un Mode de Production a L'Autre: Théorie de La Transition', *Recherche Sociologique*, Vol. XII, No. 2.

Guerreau, Alain, 1980, *Le Féodalisme: Un Horizon Theorique*, Paris: Le Sycamore.

Habib, Irfan, 1969, 'Potentialities of Capitalistic Development in Mughal India', *Journal of Economic History*, Vol. 29, No. 1.

———, 1985, 'Classifying Pre-Colonial India', *Journal of Peasant Studies*, Vol. 12, Nos. 2 and 3 (Jan. and April).

Hilton, Rodney, 1978, 'Introduction', in Rodney Hilton, ed., *The Transition from Feudalism to Capitalism*, London: Verso.

Hilton, Rodney, 1984, 'Feudalism in Europe: Problems for Historical Materialists', *New Left Review*, No. 147 (Sept./Oct.).

Hindess, B. and P.Q. Hirst, 1975, *Pre-Capitalist Modes of Production*, London: Routledge & Kegan Paul.

Hirst, P.Q., 1975, 'The Uniqueness of the West', *Economy and Society*, Vol. 4.

Hobsbawm, Eric, 1978, 'From Feudalism to Capitalism', in Rodney Hilton, ed., *The Transition from Feudalism to Capitalism*, London: Verso.

———, 1984, 'Marx and History', *New Left Review,* No. 143 (Jan./Feb.).

Jeffcott, Colin, 1985, 'The Idea of Feudalism in China and its Applicability to Song Society', in Edmund Leach, S.N. Mukherjee and John Ward, eds., *Feudalism: Comparative Studies,* Sydney: Sydney Association for Studies in Society and Culture.

Kula, Witold, 1976, *An Economic Theory of the Feudal System,* London: New Left Books.

Leach Edmund, 1985, 'Talking about Talking about Feudalism', in Edmund Leach, S.N. Mukherjee and John Ward, eds., *Feudalism: Comparative Studies,* Sydney: Sydney Association for Studies in Society and Culture.

Leach, Edmund, S.N. Mukherjee and John Ward, eds., 1985, *Feudalism: Comparative Studies,* Sydney: Association for Studies in Society and Culture.

Marx, Karl, 1885/1961, *Capital, Volume II,* Moscow: Foreign Languages Publishing House.

———, 1894/1962, *Capital, Volume III,* Moscow; Foreign Languages Publishing House.

———, 1973, *Grundrisse,* Harmondsworth, Middlesex: Penguin Books.

Melotti, Umberto, 1977, *Marx and the Third World,* London: Macmillan.

Mukhia, Harbans, 1985, 'Peasant Production and Medieval Indian Society', *Journal of Peasant Studies,* Vol. 12, Nos. 2 and 3 (Jan. and April).

Perlin, Frank, 1985, 'Concepts of Order and Comparison, with a Diversion on Counter Ideologies and Corporate Institutions in Late Pre-Colonial India', *Journal of Peasant Studies,* Vol. 12, Nos. 2 and 3 (Jan. and April).

Postan, Michael, 1977, 'The Feudal Economy', *New Left Review,* No. 103 (May/June).

Pryor, John, 1985, 'The Historical Foundations of a Feudal Mode of Production' in Edmund Leach, S.N. Mukherjee and John Ward, eds., *Feudalism: Comparative Studies,* Sydney: Sydney Association for Studies in Society and Culture.

Rudra, Ashok, 1981, 'Against Feudalism', *Economic and Political Weekly,* Vol. XVI, No. 52 (26 Dec.).

Sawer, Marian, 1977, *Marxism and the Question of the Asiatic Mode of Production,* The Hague: Martinus Nijhoff.

Sedov, L.A., 1968, 'La Societe Angkorienne et Le Probleme du Mode de Production Asiatique', *La Pensée,* No. 138.

Sharma, R.S., 1985, 'How Feudal Was Indian Feudalism?', *Journal of Peasant Studies,* Vol. 12, Nos. 2 and 3 (Jan. and April).

Stalin, Joseph, 1938, *Dialectidal and Historical Materialism,* New York: International Publishers.

Stein, Burton, 1985, 'Politics, Peasants and the Deconstruction of Feudalism in Medieval India', *Journal of Peasant Studies,* Vol. 12, Nos. 2 and 3 (Jan. and April).

Stephenson, C., 1941, 'The Origin and Significance of Feudalism', *American Historical Review,* Vol. 46.

Sweezy, Paul, 1986, 'Feudalism to Capitalism Revisited', *Science and Society*, Vol. 2, No. 1 (Spring).

Takahashi, Kohachiro, 1978, 'A Contribution to the Discussion', in Rodney Hilton, ed., *The Transition from Feudalism to Capitalism*, London: Verso.

Wallerstein, Immanuel, 1977, *The Politics of the World Economy*, Cambridge: Cambridge University Press.

Ward, John, 1985, 'Feudalism: Interpretative Category or Framework of Life in the Medieval West', in Edmund Leach, S.N. Mukherjee and John Ward, eds., *Feudalism: Comparative Studies*, Sydney: Sydney Association for Studies in Society and Culture.

Wickham, Chris, 1984, 'The Other Transition: From the Ancient World to Feudalism', *Past and Present*, No. 103 (May).

———, 1985, 'The Uniqueness of the East', *Journal of Peasant Studies*, Vol. 12, Nos. 2 and 3 (Jan. and April).